THE COMING
OF THE CELTS,
AD 1860

Celtic Nationalism
in
Ireland and Wales

CAOIMHÍN DE BARRA

University of Notre Dame Press
Notre Dame, Indiana

University of Notre Dame Press
Notre Dame, Indiana 46556
undpress.nd.edu

Library of Congress Cataloging-in-Publication Data

Names: De Barra, Caoimhín, 1984– author.
Title: The coming of the Celts, AD 1860 :
Celtic nationalism in Ireland and Wales / Caoimhín De Barra.
Other titles: Celtic nationalism in Ireland and Wales
Description: Notre Dame, Indiana : University of Notre Dame Press, [2018] |
Includes bibliographical references and index. |
Identifiers: LCCN 2017055845 (print) | LCCN 2018007086 (ebook) |
ISBN 9780268103392 (pdf) | ISBN 9780268103408 (epub) |
ISBN 9780268103378 (hardcover : alk. paper) |
ISBN 0268103372 (hardcover : alk. paper)
Subjects: LCSH: Celts—Politics and government. | Celts—Ethnic identity. |
Nationalism—Ireland. | Nationalism—Wales. | Civilization, Celtic.
Classification: LCC DA42 (ebook) | LCC DA42.D47   2018 (print) |
DDC 320.540941509/034—dc23

Le Kathy agus Aisling, mo mhná maoiní

CONTENTS

ACKNOWLEDGMENTS

In the process of researching and writing this book, I have relied on the assistance of many wonderful people in a variety of different ways. I would like to take the opportunity to acknowledge those people here.

This project began as part of my doctoral research while I was studying at the University of Delaware. My adviser, John Montaño, was instrumental in first helping me secure a place in the program at UD and then helping me craft and write my dissertation. Two other faculty members at UD, Owen White and Jim Brophy, very kindly agreed to serve on my doctoral committee, and through their rigorous critiques this book took shape. Paul O'Leary of Aberystwyth University also gave very generously of his time in serving as an outside reader on my committee. All four have continued to offer advice and mentorship since I completed my doctoral studies, and I owe them all a deep debt of gratitude.

Attempting to write a book about the history of Ireland and Wales while living in the United States means that undertaking research can be a daunting financial proposition, especially for a junior scholar. I am very grateful to both the History Department and the Office of Graduate and Professional Development at UD for providing me with fellowships that enabled me to travel, research, and write during my final two years of graduate school. I also wish to acknowledge the generosity of Dean Bob Ready and Assistant Dean Bill Rogers of the Caspersen School of Graduate Studies at Drew University. As my employers, they provided the funds to allow me to spend several weeks in Wales in the summer of 2015, engaging in research that was essential for the completion of this book.

In order to access relevant material in the National Library of Ireland, I was required to spend weeks and months at a time in Dublin in recent years, and I was very lucky to have several friends who were willing to host me in their homes. Pat Crowley and Lisa Halpin found a space for me in their apartment in January 2011. Ken O'Conner and Nadine Rödel allowed me to stay with them for most of the summer in 2011. More recently the O'Rorke family, Ciarán, Marian, Shane, Barry, and Oisín, have very kindly made a bedroom available to me on several occasions, and unfortunately their generosity has been rewarded only by my inclination to keep showing up at their doorstep. I would like to thank Shane O'Rorke in particular, as he has also been willing to go to the National Library to check files on my behalf. To all of my friends who have helped me out over the years, thank you very much.

I would like to thank the staff of both the National Library of Ireland in Dublin and the National Library of Wales in Aberystwyth. The employees of both institutions were always very helpful, considerate, and patient in dealing with my extensive file requests over several weeks at a time.

Two of the chapters that appear in this book are based on material I have already published. The chapter "Protestants Playing Pagans" is an expanded version of a chapter that appeared in *Authority and Wisdom in the New Ireland,* edited by Billy Gray and Carmen Zamorana Llena. The book was published by Peter Lang Ltd., who have very kindly given me permission to republish that material. The chapter "A Celtic Paradise" is largely based on my article "A Gallant Little Tírín: The Welsh Influence on Irish Nationalism, 1870–1918." This material was published in *Irish Historical Studies,* no. 153 (May 2014), and editor Robert Armstrong has kindly given me permission to publish it once more.

I would like to thank my editor, Eli Bortz of the University of Notre Dame Press, for all of his assistance in bringing this book to term. As someone who has never engaged in this process before, I was very unsure at times how to go about it, but Eli was incredibly helpful and supportive from the beginning, and his suggestions and recommendations have greatly improved this book.

My father, Kevin, must also be thanked. Not only did he instill within me a love and passion for history from an early age, but he also played an invaluable role in helping me with the many administrative tasks that arose over the course of putting this book together.

Finally, I would like to thank my wife, Kathy. She has always been my strongest supporter in my academic endeavors. Kathy has had to make many sacrifices to help make this book a reality, including being press-ganged into the role of research assistant from time to time, taking vacations in locations conveniently near archives, and having to spend several weeks alone at home carrying our first child while I traveled overseas for research. For all that and more, I thank her from the bottom of my heart.

INTRODUCTION

On April 24, 1916, Patrick Pearse entered the General Post Office in Dublin and read a proclamation announcing Ireland's independence from British rule as the first step of a plan to forge an Irish republic through armed rebellion. Part of Pearse's justification for this bold action came from his belief that the Irish nation, as an expression of Irish culture, was in decline. A distinct Irish identity could be preserved only through the establishment of an independent government that would foster and cherish the Irish language. Pearse had spent much of his adult life championing the cause of the native language of Ireland. Although he was not an Irish speaker from birth, Pearse developed a passion for the language from spending time with his Irish-speaking relatives. He had joined the Gaelic League as a teenager, and he quickly became one of its most active members. Pearse received a BA in modern languages, including Irish, from the Royal University of Ireland before becoming editor of *An Claidheamh Soluis*, the Gaelic League newspaper, in 1903. He wrote stories and poetry in the Irish language, and in 1908 he established St. Enda's, a bilingual school in which students were encouraged to develop a deep love of the Irish language and culture. Pearse's perception of Irish identity, therefore, was inextricably bound up with the Irish language, and his belief that it needed to be saved ultimately led him to take up arms against Britain.

1

On December 7, 1916, David Lloyd George became the prime minister of Britain at a time of monumental importance, with the country embroiled in war against Germany. Among many other things, Lloyd George is remembered as the only British prime minister whose first language was not English. Lloyd George was born in Manchester but raised in a Welsh-speaking household. Having trained as a solicitor, he became active in politics and was elected to Parliament as the representative of Caernarfon in 1890. He became quite interested in Welsh issues and helped coordinate an unsuccessful effort to organize a Welsh home rule party in the 1890s. Despite this failure, Lloyd George retained his distinct Welsh identity throughout his career, regularly addressing political rallies across the Principality in the Welsh language. Welsh was also the language of his home when he lived in Downing Street during his premiership. But for Lloyd George, nothing about his identity as a Welsh man or Welsh speaker precluded his involvement in British politics. As a member of the Liberal Party, he championed causes for the benefit of Britain as a whole, not just Wales. In short, he saw no contradiction in taking pride in both his Welshness and his Britishness.

The year 1916, then, was important in both Irish and Welsh history.[1] On one level, it is possible to interpret the events of this year as evidence of significant differences between the two nations. Certainly nationalists in both countries celebrated their national distinctiveness from England, based on their separate culture and language, but this had resulted in very different political expressions of nationhood. Pearse, a man who had learned Irish, believed that Ireland could be a nation only through rebellion and independence, while Lloyd George, the native Welsh speaker, was the embodiment of how Welsh identity was accommodated within a wider sense of Britishness. But comparing the careers of Pearse and Lloyd George also reveals the connections between Ireland and Wales. Pearse had spent time in Wales, examining how the Welsh language had been introduced as a school subject in English-speaking schools in Cardiff. He was impressed by what he found, and wrote in *An Claidheamh Soluis* that the approach to teaching Welsh in Welsh schools could and should be adopted in relation to the teaching of Irish in Ireland. Lloyd George, for his part, had come to political prominence in Wales through his promotion of Welsh home rule in the 1890s. Although Lloyd George himself was always somewhat hesitant to link the cause of Welsh home rule to that of Ireland, it is undeniable that the push for Welsh self-government was heavily influenced by the success of the Irish Parliamentary Party in winning political concessions for Ireland. Furthermore, both Lloyd George and Pearse identified themselves, and their respective nations, as Celtic. Indeed, Pearse had taken part in the first Pan-Celtic conference in Cardiff in 1899, and he tried to encourage the Gaelic League to take a more active part in the Pan-Celtic movement. Lloyd George was not as interested in fostering connections between the respective Celtic countries, but he did deliver a speech at the Pan-Celtic congress held in Caernarfon in 1904. Pearse and Lloyd George then, were Celts, and Wales and Ireland were Celtic countries, but as 1916 had demonstrated, Celtic nationalism meant different things on the two sides of the Irish Sea.

The relationship between Ireland and Wales stretches back into the mists of time, before entities known as "Ireland" or "Wales" even existed. Anyone who studies the two languages that are indigenous to these countries is struck by their similarities, despite the fact that speakers of both are mutually unintelligible to each other. Linguists disagree as to when Irish and Welsh became different languages and whether this separation occurred before or after the languages traveled from Europe to Britain and Ireland. Regardless, the linguistic relationship suggests that the roots of the Irish and Welsh nations can be traced back to a common point of origin in the remote past. Prionsias Mac Cana has observed that the major factor "in shaping the historical relations between Ireland and Wales is the geographical one, the fact that they face each other across the Irish Sea . . . and by now it is something of a cliché to say that in ancient times the sea served to join lands rather than to separate them."[2] In early modern Wales, there was a tradition that the original inhabitants of that nation were Irish speakers, who were driven out of the territory by invading Welshmen.[3] While few scholars support this viewpoint today, it is widely acknowledged that Irish settlements had developed in Wales by the fifth century CE. This is demonstrated by the presence of approximately forty stones inscribed with ogham, an early Irish alphabet, across parts of Wales. The stones are mostly found clustered in two areas, namely in Pembrokeshire in the southwest, where the ancient kingdom of Dyfed stood, and in Gwynedd, in the northwest of Wales. That Irish settlers should arrive in these particular areas is not surprising, as these are the parts of Wales that are physically closest to Ireland.

Little is known about the nature of these settlements or what became of them, although Iwan Wmffre has suggested that the Dyfed region may have been home to Irish-speaking aristocrats ruling over a Welsh-speaking population from the fourth to the sixth century.[4] The Welsh poet Thomas Gwynn Jones reported that even in the twentieth century there were old people living in Carmarthenshire who counted sheep up to twenty in Irish.[5] Jones appeared to be implying that this was the legacy of Irish settlement in the area dating back to the fifth century, but this seems highly unlikely.

There is also a great deal of evidence for ecclesiastical exchanges across the Irish Sea prior to the arrival of the Vikings. The legend of St. Patrick is the most famous example of a Christian missionary traveling from one country to another, although there is no certainty that Patrick lived in, and was kidnapped from, the area known as Wales today. The most obvious influence of British Christians traveling to Ireland was the orthography adopted for the Irish language, based on the Latin alphabet that the missionaries brought with them and how they pronounced it.[6] According to the hagiographies of various Irish and Welsh saints, several of them crossed the Irish Sea to further their religious education, and "Irish and Welsh monks and clerics lived and worked side by side in the same communities." St. Finnian of Clonard studied at the monastery of Saint David in modern Pembrokeshire, and St. Cadoc of Wales sailed to Ireland to study under St. Mochuda at Lismore.[7] Scholars who have compared the annals of medieval Ireland and Wales see evidence of "an interesting intellectual commerce" taking place between monastic centers in Ireland and Wales.[8] The interest among Welsh and Irish clerics regarding their counterparts appears to have continued up until the eleventh century.

Traveling across the Irish Sea was not limited to clerics, however. Records from the early medieval period show that Irish and Welsh princes and military leaders often fled across the water when political circumstances at home took a turn for the worse. For example, Fogartach ua Cearnaigh was a king of Brega who, when his forces were defeated in 714, fled to Britain for two years then returned to claim the high kingship of Ireland. Rhodri the Great, king of Gwynedd, was forced to flee to Ireland in 877 following a defeat at the hands of marauding Danes. The Irish annals also record the presence of Welsh mercenaries at several battles fought in Ireland in the seventh and eighth centuries, demonstrating that political ties did exist between Welsh and Irish kingdoms.[9] The arrival of Viking raiders and settlers changed the political, social, and economic dynamic around the Irish Sea. The establishment of Dublin by Norsemen as well as the development of Viking settlements in Gwynedd joined parts of Ireland and Wales in what Colmán Etchingham has called an "Insular Viking zone."[10] The evidence suggests the Norse rulers of Dublin considered parts of northern Wales to be within their suzerainty, and this is likely the reason that, having captured Dublin himself, Brian Bómhara (Boru) was recorded as "high king of the Gaels of Ireland, and the foreigners [Norse] and the Welsh" at the time of his death in 1014. Similarly, one scribe referred to Díarmait mac Máil-na-mBó, king of Leinster up until his death in 1072, as "king of the Welsh and the Hebrides and Dublin and the southern half of Ireland."[11]

Perhaps the most famous example of the existence of political and military ties between medieval Welsh and Irish kingdoms comes from the biography of Gruffydd ap Cynan. Gruffydd was the grandson of Iago ap Idawl Foel, who had been king of Gwynedd before his assassination in 1039. Iago's young son, Cynan, fled to Ireland, eventually marrying Ragnhildr, daughter of the king of Dublin, who gave birth to Gruffydd. As a result, Gruffydd was raised in Ireland among the Hiberno-Norse, and it is reasonable to assume he adopted many Irish customs and spoke the Irish language. Beginning in 1075, Gruffydd made several efforts to capture the throne of Gwynedd, using Irish and Norse mercenaries to help him in his bid. Three times Gruffydd was defeated and forced to return to Ireland before he was able to consolidate his rule of Gwynedd, beginning in 1099.[12] According to legend, Gruffydd was so impressed by the high quality of Irish poetry and music that he insisted that these standards be replicated in Wales. Gruffydd supposedly called for Irish bards to travel to Wales and meet their Welsh equivalents in the year 1100. Gruffydd insisted that the Welsh bards adopt the regulations used by Irish poets and musicians in composing their work. Mac Cana has observed that the medieval Welsh and Irish poetic orders "are indeed remarkably similar in their repertoire and professional structures" but maintains that "there is as yet no clear and convincing evidence that the Irish poetic system exerted any substantive influence on that of Wales, through the agency of Gruffudd ap Cynan."[13]

The Anglo-Norman invasion of Ireland in 1169 marked a significant turning point in the historic relationship between Ireland and Wales. Many of the Norman knights who came to Ireland had previously won lands in Wales, married there, and brought their experience of fighting the Welsh to bear in conflict with the Irish. Indeed, they brought Welsh mercenaries with them to Ireland, as well as tenants to people their new estates from their territories in Wales, many of whom would have been Welsh natives.[14] In one sense, the Norman invasion created new networks across the Irish Sea, with marcher lords holding estates in both countries, using profits from one to improve the other, fleeing political trouble in one part of their domain by escaping to the other, and bringing Irish armies to Wales and vice versa. However, many of the old links between Ireland and Wales were severed after 1169. As Seán Duffy notes, "Because the east coast of Ireland was the area most densely colonized, it formed a wedge securely driven between native Wales and Ireland."[15] Where once defeated Irish and Welsh leaders had crossed the Irish Sea for respite, now this option was no longer on the table, as the likely authors of their declining fortunes, vassals of the English state, exerted considerable power in both countries. Furthermore, church reform in Ireland in the wake of the Norman Conquest appears to have changed the relationship between Irish and Welsh clerics, and the free intercourse that once had existed between them seemingly ceased. Mac Cana writes that one could "argue that the beginning of this final period before the disintegration of the old social order—1200–1600 in very broad terms—marks out the practical separation of Ireland and Wales as nations sharing the same comprehensive cultural heritage."[16]

Nevertheless, the cultural memory of these Irish and Welsh interactions lived long after 1169. The name Walsh or Welsh is the fourth most common surname in Ireland, and this reflects the extensive Welsh influence in the Norman invasion.[17] Cecile O'Rahilly has noted that the name *Breathnach* (Briton, or Welshman) referred not just to native Welsh speakers but also to Norman and Flemish settlers who came to Ireland via Wales. Furthermore, several towns across Ireland contain *brannagh* or *brennock* in their names, essentially anglicizations of *Breathnach*.[18] The Welsh language, for its part, also reveals the intertwined history of Ireland and Wales. The Welsh word for an Irishman is *Gwyddel*, which comes from *gwŷdd*, meaning "wild, barbaric, uncultivated." Mac Cana observes that one could compile a rich thesaurus from Welsh literature of casual and unflattering references to the Irish, such as "an Irish trick," "an Irishman of a problem," "farting like an

Irishman," and the word *Gwyddel* generally being a term of abuse.[19] Despite such familiarity between the two populations, Irish and Welsh interactions after the Norman invasion appear sparse when compared to the centuries preceding it. In the sixteenth century, thousands of Irish men and women seeking to escape the constant warfare that plagued their native land settled in Pembrokeshire. This caused some concern among local officials, who sent letters to London asking that the situation be remedied.[20] Welsh troops participated in the suppression of the 1798 rebellion, when Sir Watkin Williams-Wynn led a cavalry regiment raised in Wales and known as the "Ancient British Fencibles." The Great Famine in Ireland brought a surge of refugees to Wales. Those who crossed the Irish Sea found little sympathy among the Welsh population, suspicious of the immigrants because of their poverty, their perceived lack of hygiene, and, most importantly, their Catholicism.[21]

However, the large-scale migration of the Irish to Wales heralded a period of renewed interactions across the Irish Sea. The late nineteenth and early twentieth centuries were an era in which intellectuals, writers, and politicians in Ireland and Wales were greatly interested in each other's affairs. The central argument of this book is that between approximately 1860 and 1925 the people of Ireland and Wales became more sympathetic toward each other than ever before or since, leading to an exchange of ideas across the Irish Sea that reshaped the political and social landscape in both countries. A number of factors explain why Irish and Welsh affairs became more relevant to the respective populations of the two nations. First, the middle of the nineteenth century marked the point at which the people of Ireland and Wales, as well as Scotland, Brittany, the Isle of Man, and Cornwall, came to regard themselves as ethnically and racially "Celtic." Although the use of *Celtic* implied an ancient lineage and shared heritage, its adoption by the Irish and Welsh populations was quite modern and had itself been created by a combination of linguistic and archaeological studies, the advent of modern science, the rise of ethnic nationalism, and the development of mass literacy. In short, Irish and Welsh peoples did not identify each other as "Celtic cousins" in 1800, but by 1860 they did. Meanwhile, changing circumstances in Ireland and Wales pushed nationalists in both countries to study their fellow Celts for ideas on how to improve the affairs of their own people. The dramatic decline of the Irish language in the late nineteenth century, at a time when the number of Welsh speakers was growing, naturally led those interested in saving Irish to look to Wales for lessons on how to preserve a Celtic tongue in the face of increasing Anglicization. Meanwhile the disestablishment of the Anglican Church in Ireland in 1869 was of enormous interest to the largely Nonconformist population of Wales, which resented the supremacy given to the Anglican faith in their country. Up until the middle of the nineteenth century, Wales had largely been considered a culturally distinct part of England, as opposed to a separate political unit within the United Kingdom. But Welsh observers noticed that the Irish population gained disestablishment, land reform, and increasing government attention and funding, all through the efforts of the Irish Parliamentary Party. Inspired by the Irish example, Welsh nationalists for the first time insisted that Wales was a distinct political entity, entitled to separate legislation to address its unique needs. Amid this growing rapprochement between Ireland and Wales, several attempts were made to promote more formal ties through the Pan-Celtic movement, but a sense of "Celticness" was never able to trump national allegiances among the masses, or at times even among those dedicated to Pan-Celticism. This heightened awareness among Irish and Welsh nationalists regarding each other lasted up until around 1925, when the Irish War of Independence and Irish separation from the United Kingdom meant that the experiences of the Irish and the Welsh were no longer as relevant to each other. Ultimately, I argue that although nationalists in each nation regularly used the other as an example of what they wanted their own country to be, Celtic identity usually operated as a superficial mask to be taken up or laid down depending on convenience and circumstances.

Of course, in a discussion of Celtic nationality within Britain and Ireland, one would expect Scotland to figure prominently, but I have decided to largely exclude Scotland from this study for a number of reasons. First, a number of works have already explored the relationship between nationalism in Ireland and Scotland,[22] and Welsh and Scottish forms of nationalism during the twentieth century have also been compared,[23] but there is little literature probing the connection between Ireland and Wales. Second, to a degree different from both Ireland and Wales, the notion of Scotland as a "Celtic" nation was more contested, owing to the fact that many people living outside the Scottish Highlands rejected their alleged "Celtic" ancestry and instead saw themselves as descended from Anglo-Saxon stock. Scottish nationality also differed from that of Wales or Ireland in that it was based in part on Scotland's history as a state, whereas Irish and Welsh nationalists focused on their cultural differences from England to accentuate their own identity. For the most part the Scottish middle class could (and did) see themselves as partners (albeit junior ones) within the British Empire, whereas many Irish and Welsh subjects did not always believe they were full participants within the imperial project.

There are a couple of other reasons why I decided to focus exclusively on Ireland and Wales. In terms of their "Celtic" background, the connection between Ireland and Wales is more tenuous than either country's connection to Scotland. Irish nationalists viewed the Scottish Highlands as an overflow of Gaelic Ireland and acknowledged the linguistic and cultural bond between the two countries. Welsh nationalists believed that a similar bond existed between themselves and the Bretons in France, owing to the similarity of their languages. Meanwhile, the fact that Wales and Scotland were identified as peripheral regions on the same island helped form a sense of common cause between them. It is precisely because the supposed bond of common Celtic identity was weakest between Ireland and Wales that I believe their relationship merits further study. Scholars such as Eric Hobsbawm and Benedict Anderson have commented on how communities are created through "invention" or "imagination." It seemed to me that the relationship between Ireland and Wales would be flexible; a bond of Celtic brotherhood could be imagined when suitable, but the differences between the countries could also be stressed when necessary. Therefore, in terms of exploring how nationalist (or pan-nationalist) communities were created in the public imagination, I believe that the connection between Ireland and Wales is a particularly fertile area for research.

A number of scholars have highlighted how nationalists construct a national identity by emphasizing the nation's distinctness from the national "other"—a country that is shown to embody different values and characteristics from those of the people who are members of their own nation.[24] For both Welsh and Irish nationalists, England filled this role. In *Inventing Ireland*, Declan Kiberd writes that England served as a political and psychological double for Ireland, a foil against which Irish identity could be created.[25] Similarly Gwyn A. Williams, in his essay "When Was Wales," argues that Wales cannot be defined without England.[26] Without disputing the fact that national identity in Ireland and Wales was partially formed through juxtaposition with England, it seems inevitable that Irish and Welsh nationalists would also have made comparisons with their fellow Celts. After all, the Irish and Welsh lived in the same state and shared linguistic ties and (supposedly) a biological and historical connection. I argue that, for Irish and Welsh nationalists, their brethren across the Irish Sea served as something of a mirror in helping them form their own identity. Through comparison, nationalists in both countries could measure the achievements of their own nation and draw inspiration from their Celtic cousins while at the same time stressing their distinctness as individual nations.

I would like to say a quick word about some of the terminology used in this book. I employ the word *Celticness* throughout; this is to be understood as a broad term referring to anything that could be defined as Celtic. It does not imply a narrow or rigid ideology because, as will be demonstrated, many people had multiple, at times contradictory, ideas regarding what made a person, item, or region "Celtic." Although a few individuals emerge as important figures in the context of this book, for the most part I have attempted to analyze the ideas and concepts of "Celticness" held by a wide section of the populations of Ireland and Wales. The convenient shorthand I use to describe these often-diverse people is *nationalists*, broken down further into *cultural nationalists* and *political nationalists*. Again, these terms are to be understood in the broadest sense. By *political nationalists* I mean people who have expressed an interest in some form of political autonomy for their nation, and by *cultural nationalists* I mean people who wish to promote or preserve a particular aspect of what they believe to be their native culture. By this definition, there were people in both Ireland and Wales who could be labeled cultural nationalists but not political nationalists, and, perhaps less frequently, vice versa. In discussing those who made organized efforts toward preserving the Irish language, I regularly describe these people as *activists*. Although it is not a term that these people would have used themselves, I think it is an appropriate description for them. Furthermore, *activist* appears to be a better choice than *enthusiast*, a word that has come under increasing suspicion within Irish-speaking circles because it implies that those who wish to promote the Irish language are mere "hobbyists." I do occasionally use *enthusiast* in place of *activist* in this book, but only to avoid monotony in my writing. Also, to avoid excessive repetition of the words *Wales* and *Ireland*, I occasionally employ *the Principality* and *the Emerald Isle* respectively as synonyms. These terms are slightly problematic, because some Welsh people feel that *Principality* contains an implication that Wales is not a "real" nation, while some Irish people find *Emerald Isle* to be grating. Having considered all the alternatives, I decided to use these terms because they are the least likely to confuse readers. No derogatory insinuations or romantic sentimentalizations are intended by their inclusion.

A final word on translation. A considerable amount of the source material for this book was written in Irish or Welsh. Unfortunately, constraints of space meant that the original material, which I translated into English, could not be included. All translations in this book, including any errors or mistakes, are mine alone.

CHAPTER 1

THE COMING OF THE CELTS

In March 2015, an article entitled "The Fine-Scale Genetic Structure of the British Population" appeared in the journal *Nature*, reporting on the recent conclusions of a genetic study on the population of the United Kingdom.[1] The findings showed that there was a great deal of genetic difference between various regions of the country. One conclusion that appeared to baffle researchers and the general public alike was that there was no common genetic link between the supposedly Celtic peoples of Britain and Ireland. Professor Mark Robinson, an archaeologist at Oxford University who was a member of the research team, was quoted as saying, "I had assumed at the very early stages of the project that there was going to be this uniform Celtic fringe extending from Cornwall through to Wales into Scotland. And this has very definitely not been the case." Peter Donnelly, a geneticist and colleague of Robinson's at Oxford, stated, "One might have expected those groups to be quite similar genetically because they were Celtic. But while we see distinct groups in those regions, they are amongst the most different." Robinson said that these findings had left him "very surprised."[2]

It says something powerful about how widely accepted the idea of a Celtic identity is that highly educated people could be surprised by the fact that the people of Northern Ireland, Scotland, Wales, and Cornwall do not share the same genetic makeup. Yet this revelation was shocking because it challenged, indeed completely undermined, the popularly held assumption that the Welsh, Irish, and Scottish populations were the descendants of the ancient Celts who once dominated Britain, Ireland, and continental Europe. While overt celebrations of a common Celtic bond are rare between the people of Ireland, Wales, and Scotland, the belief that some kind of affinity exists between them is widely accepted in all three countries. During their campaign of violence, the Provisional IRA never attacked targets or detonated bombs in Wales or Scotland because they accepted the idea that they shared an ethnic connection with the Welsh and Scottish. IRA statements included rhetoric claiming that they stood "with our Celtic brothers and other subject nations of Europe." Such sentiment is still common today. Journalists and online commenters regularly use terms like *our Celtic neighbors* or *our Celtic cousins* when referring to the people from one of the other Celtic nations.[3]

The use of the term *Celtic cousins* is particularly telling. Aside from the obvious attraction of alliteration, the word *cousin* reinforces the idea that a relationship based on family ties and blood exists between the three populations. Indeed, one could go as far to argue that in the twenty-first century the only clear basis for the existence of a Celtic connection is an assumed shared genetic heritage.[4] The Celtic people live in Ireland, and various corners of Britain and France, so geography does not offer any clear basis for unity. Linguistically, the Celtic languages are related, but they are not all mutually intelligible, nor are they spoken by a majority in any of the Celtic countries, so this isn't the foundation for the bond either. The modern Celts do not have a common culture, or rather (and leaving aside Brittany for the moment) it is more accurate to say that they have an extensive common culture, but since they share much of this with the rest of the Anglophone world, it cannot be called uniquely Celtic. Furthermore, the fact that the English language and English-based customs are viewed as having being imposed on the Celtic nations by way of conquest makes any emphasis on the actual shared cultural traits of the contemporary Celts all the less appealing. All that remains, then, is an assumed ancient biological connection. Of course, in a post-Nazi world, most people are quite wary about championing any identity based on shared bloodlines. In the case of the Celts, the idea of a racial bond among them is rarely openly spoken of. It is merely implied, existing subtly in terms like *Celtic cousins* or *Celtic brothers*. Furthermore, as the populations of the Celtic countries are relatively small, and as no Pan-Celtic state exists in which a government might abuse any biological sense of Celticness, there seems to be no political danger in believing that the Welsh, Irish, and Scottish share much of their DNA. In terms of its minimal, almost subconscious, acknowledgment and nonthreatening implications, Celticness has been a most benign form of racial identity.

But now the possibility of any scientific foundation for this ethnic Celtic identity has been removed. Mark Robinson may have been surprised by this development, but others were not. When we think of the Celts, we envision marauding warriors terrorizing the civilized people of Europe in antiquity. We remember figures like Brennus, the Celtic leader who invaded Greece and later sacked Rome itself in 390 BCE. The populations of Ireland, Wales, and Scotland naturally assume that these Iron Age Continental Celts were their ancestors, who migrated to the islands on the northwestern fringe of Europe sometime in the distant past. Why wouldn't they? The use of the term *Celtic* to identify an ancient people and a modern people clearly suggests that they are, on some level, the same. This is shown by the presence of a replica of the sculpture *The Dying Galatian* in Leinster House, seat of the Irish government in Dublin. This sculpture, dating back to the Roman Empire, depicts a naked Celtic warrior who has been wounded in battle and is struggling to get back to his feet. By placing this sculpture in the home of the Dáil, the government is celebrating the link between the Irish of today and the Celts who lived on the Continent over two millennia ago. These ideas are not just assumed: they are actively taught. I remember being a student at University College Cork taking courses in Celtic civilization in 2002. Lectures about the archaeological findings at the Celtic sites of Halstatt (in modern Austria) and La Tène (Switzerland) were given alongside discussions of the early medieval literature of Ireland and Wales. The message was unambiguous. Those people who lived in the middle of Europe before the birth of Christ were essentially the same as the individuals who, living in Britain and Ireland centuries later, wrote down the tales of the *Táin Bó Cúailnge* and the *Mabinogion*.

In recent decades, however, the belief that the ancient people who inhabited Ireland and Britain were Celts has come under increasing attack. In 1992, Malcolm Chapman published *The Celts: The Construction of a Myth*. A social anthropologist, Chapman first questioned whether any group had ever self-identified as Celts in antiquity, noting that the name was used by

Greek and Roman writers to label the barbarous hordes beyond their northern borders. As he was skeptical about the existence of the "original" Celts, it is not surprising that Chapman also believed that the modern conception of Celtic identity was essentially based on a falsehood. Chapman was adamant that the only thing that bound the ancient Celts and the modern Celts together was the "continuity of symbolic opposition between a central defining power and its own fringes."[5] In other words, the concept of the Celt was something that had primarily been projected onto Celts by other people, rather than a strong sense of identity they claimed for themselves. This process was, according to Chapman, reversed by the coming of Romanticism, when some Irish, Welsh, and Scottish writers embraced a Celtic identity as a way of rejecting materialistic, urban, industrial England. These poets and writers believed they were reclaiming an almost extinct sense of spiritualism and heroism from the Celtic past, seemingly unaware that the link between contemporary Celts and the Celts of antiquity was somewhat tenuous.

Archaeologists have also challenged the idea that Celts from the Continent migrated to Britain and Ireland and settled them as Celtic colonies. In *The Atlantic Celts: Ancient People or Modern Invention*, Simon James notes that for much of the twentieth century archaeologists believed that Britain and Ireland had been overrun by a series of Celtic invasions. Yet James argues that much of the evidence to support this hypothesis has been undermined. He observes that, unlike in the Po Valley, where archaeology clearly supports the idea that an invasion from beyond the Alps took place in the fifth century BCE, the evidence for a similar event in either Britain or Ireland is lacking. Simply put, if the Celts came to either Ireland or Britain, we would expect to find evidence of the sudden arrival of a new culture through changes in art, burial customs, farming systems, and house construction. Instead, archaeological evidence suggests considerable continuity between Bronze Age Britain and Ireland and the Iron Age that followed. Meanwhile, artifacts that point toward some kind of shared cultural connection between the Continental Celts and what James refers to as the "Atlantic Celts" are rare.[6] Serious doubts have been raised, then, regarding the legitimacy of the claim that the modern Welsh, Scottish, and Irish people are the direct descendants of the ancient Celts. This is, to borrow a term from Patrick Sim-Williams, "the problem of Celticity."[7] A sense of Celtic identity clearly exists today, but what exactly is meant by *Celtic*, and what things should and should not be categorized under this label, remain ambiguous.

So how did the Celts become Celts? The story begins with George Buchanan, a Scottish scholar. In 1582, the last year of his life, Buchanan published *The History of Scotland*, claiming, on the basis of his study of the Gaelic and Welsh languages, that the ancient Irish, Scottish, and Welsh peoples "appear . . . to have sprung from the Gauls."[8] To support this idea, Buchanan quoted the Roman historian Tacitus, who observed that the language of Gaul did not "differ widely" from that of ancient Britain. From this, Buchanan inferred that the two languages were "formerly the same" and he compared ancient place-names from Britain and France as proof of the linguistic relationship.[9] At around the same time, the English historian William Camden had largely come to the same conclusion as Buchanan regarding the relationship between the people of Gaul and the Welsh. Both Buchanan and Camden had also noted that the Gauls were Celts, with Buchanan referring to the Irish as Celts who came to Ireland via Spain.[10] While neither wrote that the aboriginal people of Ireland and Britain were collectively Celts, readers could clearly come to that conclusion on their own. These ideas were taken up again over a century later by Paul-Yves Pezron, an abbot from Brittany. In 1703, Pezron published *Antiquité de la nation, et de langue des Celtes, autrement appellez Gaulois*. Pezron began his project by trying to trace the ancestry of the Breton people back to the book of Genesis. In doing so, he claimed that the Breton people were the descendants of the Gauls who had once occupied modern France. Pezron, like Buchanan and Camden before him, asserted that these Gauls were really the Celts who had inhabited much of continental Europe. At the same time, Pezron also commented on the similarity of the Welsh language to Breton. This was not new; earlier antiquarians had already noted that Welsh and Breton had surely once been the same language.[11]

However, Pezron was frustratingly vague about why he was so sure that the Bretons and Welsh were descendants of the Gauls. He noted that "the Bretons of France and the Welsh in Great Britain, have still the same language, that in the time of Julius Caesar and Augustus was spoken through all Gaul." But evidence to support this claim, which became central to the idea that the people of Britain were Celts, was not forthcoming. Pezron simply wrote, "This is a matter that needs no proof; the learned own the truth of it."[12] Nor did Pezron explain why it was that the Welsh and Breton people spoke a similar language. According to medieval sources, Brittany had been settled by Welsh speakers from Britain beginning in the fourth century, a hypothesis that modern archaeologists support.[13] But this presents a complication for Pezron's claim that the Bretons and Welsh were essentially the same people as the Gauls and therefore Celts. If the Bretons were the last remnants in France of an ancient Gaulish culture, then the similarity of the Breton language to Welsh would be convincing proof that the Britons and Gauls were one and the same. But if the linguistic similarity between Breton and Welsh was due to a migration that took place centuries after the Roman conquest of Gaul, then the related nature of the two languages could not be evidence by itself that the ancient Britons were basically Gauls and, by extension, Celts. Pezron said nothing about any migration from Wales to Brittany. But in observing that contemporary Bretons took their culture "from the ancient Gauls, whose language and customs they still retain, as being descended from them," he certainly seemed to suggest that Brittany was the last redoubt of ancient Gaul, rather than a later Welsh colony.[14] Despite (or perhaps, because) of these ambiguities, Pezron had reintroduced the possibility that the prehistoric people of Britain were Celts. Like Buchanan and Camden before him, Pezron never called the Welsh a Celtic people, nor did he directly state that the Celts had invaded Britain, but both conclusions were very much implied in his work.[15] He also said nothing about a possible kinship between the Welsh and the Gaels of Ireland and Scotland, but the concept of British Celts was gaining traction.

The ideas of Pezron were expanded further by his contemporary, a linguist by the name of Edward Lhuyd. Born in England to Welsh parents, Lhuyd was fascinated with Pezron's book, in part because he was simultaneously studying the relationship between the various languages of Britain and Ireland. In 1707, Lhuyd published *Archaeologia Britannica: An Account of the Languages, Histories and Customs of Great Britain, from Travels through Wales, Cornwall, Bas-Bretagne, Ireland and Scotland*. In his book, Lhuyd concurred with Pezron that the Brythonic languages of Britain, namely Welsh and Cornish, had originated in Gaul. But, like Pezron, Lhuyd was a little unclear on the details. He suggested that "Gaulish" was actually a collective name for several nations, only some of whom spoke a Celtic language. At the same time, he stated that the Gaulish language, now extinct, could be "in great measure retrieved" by comparative study of the indigenous languages of Britain and Ireland.[16] In other words, the modern languages of Britain were descended directly from Gaulish. Like Buchanan, Lhuyd felt that the resemblance in the names of people and places in ancient Britain and Gaul offered proof that their languages were related. But Lhuyd went further than this. Through an empirical comparative study, he revealed that the Goidelic languages, Irish, Scottish Gaelic, and Manx Gaelic, were also related to Welsh, Cornish, and Breton. Although Buchanan had hinted at this, Lhuyd's work represented the first time that this group of tongues had been recognized collectively as forming a single language family. Lhuyd claimed that while the Brythonic languages had come to Britain through migration from Gaul, the Goidelic languages had similarly arrived in Ireland, Scotland, and Man via an invasion from Spain.

Lhuyd was hesitant to refer to the speakers of these languages as Celts, nor did he declare that these languages should be called Celtic. However, in his preface, he did call the comparative section of his book "a sort of Latin-Celtic dictionary." He also referred in passing to the languages of Wales, Brittany, and Cornwall as "Celtique."[17] These humble sentences eventually led to a complete reimagining of the ancient history of Britain and Ireland. Lhuyd's evidence had proved that the Brythonic and Goidelic languages were related. By referring to a "Latin-Celtic dictionary," Lhuyd implied that the indigenous languages of Britain and Ireland, as well as ancient Gaulish, could be collectively labeled Celtic. If these were Celtic languages, and they were brought to Britain and Ireland by a Celtic migration from Gaul and Spain, then the only conclusion one could draw was that the Irish, Welsh, and Scottish were Celts. No one called these people Celtic in 1700, but by 1900 a sense of Celticness was deeply entwined in the perception of national character in Wales and Ireland particularly.

So now we know where and when the idea of the British and Irish Celtic populations stemmed from, and the question becomes "When did the people of Ireland and Wales start regularly referring to themselves as Celts?" Simon James writes that once the Irish and Welsh languages were called Celtic "the label was quickly used also to describe cultural or national *identities*, past and present; and both ideas became accepted as established fact throughout Britain and Ireland with remarkable speed."[18] Certainly historians and antiquarians of the eighteenth century began to use the term *Celtic*. Charles O'Conor, in his *Dissertations on the ancient history of Ireland* (1753), referred to the Irish, Welsh, and Scottish nations as "Celtic Countries" or "Celtic Peoples," although for the most part he used the adjective *Celtic* only when referring to languages.

Yet it is interesting to note that these writers, as well as others, mostly tended to describe the ancient people of Britain and Ireland, rather than their more modern descendants, as Celtic. Furthermore, several books written in the eighteenth century that we might expect to refer to a Celtic past simply didn't. Focusing just on Ireland for the moment, Henry Brookes, in his *Essay on the Ancient and Modern State of Ireland* (1760) uses the word *Celtic* only once. Meanwhile in Thomas Comerford's *History of Ireland from the Earliest Account of Time, to the Invasion of the English under King Henry II* (1752), Charles Smith's *Ancient and present state of the county and city of Cork. Containing a natural, civil, ecclesiastical, historical, and topographical description thereof* (1750), and Thomas Leland's *History of Ireland from the Invasion of Henry II* (1773), among others, the word *Celtic* is never used at all. Clearly, then, Simon James's assertion that the practice of referring to the ancient and contemporary people of Britain and Ireland was quickly and widely adopted after 1707 needs to be qualified. It was used by some people, certainly, but not all and, at least in the eighteenth century, was far more likely to be used as a label for the distant past and indigenous languages of Britain and Ireland rather than describing the people we call the Celts today.

Despite this ambiguity about when the people of Ireland and Wales referred to themselves as Celts, scholars often fall into the trap of adopting the contemporary use of *Celtic* and applying it uncritically to the past. For example, in his essay on the impact of the Reformation on Ireland and Wales, Brendan Bradshaw refers to the two countries as "the English crown's two Celtic borderland dominions."[19] To call Ireland and Wales "Celtic borderlands" in the sixteenth century is anachronistic and seems particularly misplaced in an essay exploring "identity formation." Murray Pittock, in *Celtic Identity and the British Image*, writes that in the eighteenth century the Jacobite Risings had an "implicit threat of Celtic irredentism" and indeed that for most of British history a continuing tension existed between those loyal to the state and the Celtic "other."[20] To demonstrate this, Pittock describes some of the insulting caricatures penned about the Welsh, Irish, and Scottish, and his book shows several images depicting the Scots as uncivilized barbarians. The problem is that none of his examples from the eighteenth century refer to the Irish, Scottish, and Welsh people, either collectively or individually, as Celts. English writers in the 1700s certainly had many derogatory things to say about these people, but calling them Celts does not appear to be one of them. The example of these writers shows how a sense of an ancient Celtic heritage is fostered. By applying the contemporary use of the term *Celtic* to people who did not use it, these historical writers are unintentionally giving the concept of the Celt a historical validation it does not merit.

We have seen that the use of *Celtic* in the eighteenth century was sporadic and that it was primarily used to describe the ancient, rather than the modern, people of Ireland, Wales, and Scotland. But when did this change? A word search of Irish and Welsh newspaper digital archives offers some clues. By entering the word *Celtic* into a search engine, one can track the increased use of the term over the course of the nineteenth century. Such methodology naturally has limitations: we cannot tell what the concept of being Celtic meant to readers or how they understood it in terms of their day-to-day existence. But we can see in what decade readers were more likely to encounter the word *Celtic* in their newspaper and can assume that this reflected a more widespread use in society as a whole. Table 1 shows how often Irish newspapers in the nineteenth century used *Celtic* in their pages.

Table 1.   Irish Newspapers

Time Period	No. of newspapers	Total no. of times *Celtic* used	Average no. of times used per paper over period
Pre-1800	3	12	4
1800–1819	3	30	10
1820–39	9	143	16
1840–49	14	1046	75
1850–59	14	2170	155
1860–69	16	2482	155
1870–79	16	4651	291
1880–89	21	5342	254
1890–99	25	4702	188

While these bare numbers cannot fully explain the complex process involved in the Irish population's adoption of a sense of Celticness over the course of the nineteenth century, they certainly offer an indication of when this process took place. At the end of the eighteenth century, the small number of Irish newspapers rarely made use of the term *Celtic*, which would suggest, as has already been put forward, that the word was not widely used as a marker of Irish identity at that time. Indeed, we do not see a dramatic increase in usage of *Celtic* until after 1840; then after 1850 the regularity with which the word is used doubles again. While the growing number of newspapers partly explains the increased regularity, individual newspapers on average were far more likely to refer to something or someone as Celtic in 1865 than in 1835.

In Wales, similar trends existed, as can be seen in the analysis of Welsh newspapers in table 2. Broadly speaking, we observe the same increasing usage of *Celtic* over the course of the nineteenth century. In particular, 1870 or thereabouts appears to be the year when we see a dramatic growth. But there are a number of interesting differences as well. In Ireland, the regularity with which the word *Celtic* was used in newspapers increased markedly between 1840 and 1860, but in Wales the growth was much less pronounced. Meanwhile, in Ireland, the regularity with which *Celtic* appeared in print peaked in the 1870s, declining somewhat over the last two decades of the century, while in Wales the use of *Celtic* increased fourfold after 1870. In short, Wales seems to have lagged behind Ireland in terms of when its newspapers began using the word *Celtic*, and the Welsh organs seem to have been far less likely than their Irish equivalents to refer to something as Celtic. The latter is more easily explained. There are far more Welsh titles than Irish ones included in the digital archives. Many of the Welsh newspapers were local in their focus and therefore perhaps less likely to have columns or articles that explored questions of race and national identity, where we might expect the *Celtic* adjective to be used. Hence the statistic for average use may have been diluted by the inclusion of numerous, predominantly local, papers. The earlier enthusiasm for the *Celtic* label on the part of Irish newspapers is more of a mystery. It is possible that because a distinctly Welsh form of nationalist politics did not emerge until the 1870s Welsh writers were less likely to refer to their Celtic distinctiveness within the British state until this time, whereas Irish journalists had already been doing so for decades.

Table 2.   Welsh Newspapers

Time period	No. of newspapers	Total no. of times *Celtic* used	Average no. of times used per paper over period
1804–20	3	46	15
1821–39	8	188	24
1840–49	9	319	35
1850–59	18	358	20
1860–69	37	624	17
1870–79	45	3639	81
1880–89	56	4526	81
1890–99	71	9257	130

At any rate, after 1860 or so, more people in Ireland and Wales were reading, and presumably using, the word *Celtic* than ever before. But what was happening to explain this proliferation of Celticness? First, a newly defined concept of race was emerging in the middle of the nineteenth century. For centuries Western science, guided by the teachings of the Bible, had accepted the common origin of all humankind. But at the end of the eighteenth century, in the wake of growing contact between Europe and the rest of the world, some scientists, like Johann Friedrich Blumenbach, put forward a theory of polygenism, claiming that different human groups had evolved separately from one another and were different species. As a result, people in the nineteenth century increasingly believed that cultural differences between groups could be explained by their separate biological inheritance. The study of linguistics, meanwhile, seemed to offer an insight into the relationship between humans. Broadly speaking, each language was assumed to mark a subspecies of the various human races. Many of those interested in the biology of humankind were also interested in the evolution of languages, so it is not startling that knowledge from one field transferred to the other. James Cowles Prichard, for example, was an English physician who wrote about racial differences in humans as well as the relationship between the Celtic languages and Sanskrit. Perhaps not surprisingly, then, scientists began to suggest that the Celtic languages were spoken, or at least had been spoken, by a distinct Celtic race. George Gliddon and Josiah Nott, influenced by the polygenist ideas of Samuel George

Norton, published *Types of Mankind* in 1854. Like Hall, Nott and Gliddon argued that the Celts were a subgroup of Caucasians, claiming that "the Celts who, with the cognate Gauls, at one period, extended their tribes from Asia Minor to the British Islands, are now chiefly confined, as an unmixed people, to the west and southwest of Ireland."[21] Hence, from the 1850s onward, there was a growing acceptance of the Celts as a distinct race, separate from England not merely in terms of culture but in terms of biology also.

At the same time that scientists created the idea of a Celtic race, writers were discussing what specific characteristics the Celts possessed. In 1854, the French philosopher Ernest Renan published *La poésie des races celtiques* (The poetry of the Celtic races). While Renan's essay mostly focused on Welsh and Breton literature, it also offered an insight into the unique traits of the Celtic race. First, however, Renan had to clarify who exactly the Celts were. He wrote, "I ought to point out that by the word *Celtic* I designate here, not the whole of the great race which, at a remote epoch, formed the population of nearly the whole of Western Europe, but simply the four groups which, in our days, still merit this name, as opposed to the Teutons and to the Neo-Latin peoples." These four groups were "(1) The inhabitants of Wales or Cambria, and the peninsula of Cornwall, bearing even now the ancient name of *Cymry*; (2) the *Bretons bretonnants*, or dwellers in French Brittany speaking Bas-Breton, who represent an emigration of the Cymry from Wales; (3) the Gaels of the North of Scotland speaking Gaelic; (4) the Irish, although a very profound line of demarcation separates Ireland from the rest of the Celtic family."[22] The fact that Renan had to spell out who exactly he was talking about shows us that even in the 1850s the Celticness of the Irish, Welsh, Scots, and Bretons was not necessarily widely known or appreciated.

Renan began his essay by highlighting just how different the Celtic nations were from the rest of Europe in terms both of their physical appearance and the environment they inhabited:

> Every one who travels through the Armorican peninsula experiences a change of the most abrupt description. . . . A cold wind arises full of a vague sadness, and carries the soul to other thoughts; the tree-tops are bare and twisted; the heath with its monotony of tint stretches away into the distance; at every step the granite protrudes from a soil too

scanty to cover it; a sea that is almost always sombre girdles the horizon with eternal moaning. . . . A like change is apparent, I am told, in passing from England into Wales, from the Lowlands of Scotland, English by language and manners, into the Gaelic Highlands; and too, though with a perceptible difference, when one buries oneself in the districts of Ireland where the race has remained pure from all admixture of alien blood. It seems like entering on the subterranean strata of another world, and one experiences in some measure the impression given us by Dante, when he leads us from one circle of his Inferno to another.[23]

What is interesting to note is that Renan is not talking about the Celts of yore but rather the people still living in Ireland, Scotland, Wales, and Brittany. Antiquarians in the eighteenth century had mostly discussed the Celts in the past tense, referring to the ancient ancestors of the Welsh, Scottish, and Irish. But the new language of race was changing how people conceptualized the relationship between the past and present. If race was a scientific, objective category, then it stood to reason that the differences that had once marked the Celts apart from the other people of Europe would still exist in some regard in the contemporary world. Renan, then, was collapsing the distinction between the Celts of antiquity and the people living on the western seaboard of Europe. He wrote, "Sufficient attention is not given to the peculiarity of this fact of an ancient race living, until our days and almost under our eyes, its own life in some obscure islands and peninsulas in the West . . . still faithful to its own tongue, to its own memories, to its own customs."[24]

Renan's ideas came before the public at almost the exact same time as another important milestone in the development of the modern Celtic identity, namely, the publication of Johann Kaspar Zeuss's *Grammatica Celtica* in 1853. Zeuss, professor of history at the lyceum in Speier, undertook exhaustive research over thirteen years to produce his magnum opus. Written in Latin, Zeuss's *Grammatica Celtica* drew two major conclusions: (1) the Celtic languages were part of the Indo-European language family, and (2) the division in the Celtic languages lay between its Goedelic and Brittonic branches, and not between Continental and Insular (Britain and Ireland) Celtic languages. Far more than this, however, was the fact that

Zeuss's labors brought rigorous scientific methodologies and a sense of scholarly gravitas to the study of the indigenous languages of Britain and Ireland, something the field had lacked before *Grammatica Celtica*. Zeuss had created a new academic discipline in the study of Celtic linguistics, and in his wake universities in Britain and Europe devoted more resources to the study of Celtic matters.[25] Combined with naturalist studies that included the Celts as a distinct race, scholarly research on the Celtic languages gave a further scientific foundation to an emerging sense of Celticness. The average person in Ireland and Wales in the late nineteenth century might not have known much about the various debates in Celtic linguistics, but many were aware that Continental scholars were intensely interested in Celtic affairs, giving a greater legitimacy to their own emerging sense of Celtic identity.

At the same time that Zeuss's research was earning plaudits among Europe's linguists, archaeological discoveries in Switzerland brought more glamour to Celtic affairs. In 1857, an archaeologist named Hans Kopp collected forty iron swords near the village of La Tène, on the shores of Lake Neuchâtel. This discovery highlighted to scholars the importance this site must have had in the ancient world, and a flurry of further explorations followed. In 1863, another Swiss archaeologist, Ferdinand Keller, announced that the La Tène site was the remains of an ancient Celtic settlement, as the stilt houses that had been excavated at the lake appeared to be identical to those of the Helvetti, the Celtic tribe described by Julius Caesar in his *De bello Gallico*.[26] This idea was taken further by Hans Hildebrand, who, as general secretary to the Congrès Internationale d'Anthropologie et d'Archéologie Préhistorique held in Stockholm in 1874, told his audience that Iron Age Europe had been dominated by the Celts. Hildebrand noted that there had been two distinctive Celtic societies, an earlier, more primitive one (Halstatt) and a more advanced, later culture (La Tène).[27] As Lake Neuchâtel continued to yield more artifacts, it became clear that the people who had once lived there were not only skilled metalworkers but also artistic, as evident from the beautiful swirling patterns and spiral designs that appeared on their weapons and tools. This helped reshape the traditional image of the ancient Celts in Europe, from warrior barbarians to sophisticated craftsmen. Naturally, the idea that a Celtic civilization had once been widespread across continental Europe made this Celtic identity all the more attractive to Welsh and Irish nationalists, and the story of the ancient Celts was increasingly adopted into the nationalist histories of these respective countries.

Perhaps the most famous contribution to the Celtic discussion came from an English poet, Matthew Arnold. For the most part, Arnold portrayed the Celtic peoples as a sentimental race, full of poetry and romantic whims but ultimately doomed to fail in the modern world because of their lack of discipline. He wrote, "*Sentiment* is, however, the word which marks where the Celtic races really touch and are one; sentimental, if the Celtic nature is to be characterised by a single term, is the best term to take. . . . Sentimental,—*Always ready to react against the despotism of fact.*"[28] The Celts were dreamers, in other words, unable to negotiate the material and practical realities of industrialized society, in large part because they could not accept "fact." If any group of people were to thrive, Arnold argued, they required balance, measure, and patience. Unfortunately, "Balance, measure, and patience are just what the Celt has never had."[29] Arnold depicted the Celts as romantic losers. They might show a great talent for music, but "What has the Celt, so eager for emotion that he has not patience for science, effected in music, to be compared with what the less emotional German, steadily developing his musical feeling with the science of a Sebastian Bach or a Beethoven, has effected?" The Celtic people, Arnold claimed, had a deeply poetic nature, but their lack of reason prevented them from producing master poets: "The Celt has not produced great poetical works. . . . His want of sanity and steadfastness has kept the Celt back from the highest success."[30]

If Arnold believed that Celtic sentiment hindered the ability of the people of Ireland, Wales, and the other Celtic nations to compose music or poetry of the highest caliber, then he saw them as even less suited to the world of politics and business: "The skilful and resolute appliance of means to ends which is needed both to make progress in material civilisation, and also to form powerful states, is just what the Celt has least turn for."[31] The Celts might once have harassed and harried the civilized world, but they lacked the right temperament to form their own organized political entity. The Celt, being "undisciplinable, anarchical, and turbulent by nature, but out of affection and admiration giving himself body and soul to some leader," did not have "a promising political temperament." In fact, it was "just the opposite of the Anglo-Saxon temperament, disciplinable and steadily obedient within certain limits, but retaining an inalienable part of freedom and self-dependence."[32] To the modern reader, this might sound like an incredibly unflattering commentary to make about any group, but Arnold insisted that the same sentimentality and lack of discipline that hindered the Celts in the modern world was also worthy of admiration. Their romantic nature, he believed, was a positive counterbalance to the stoic but unimaginative Teutonic character of England. Within a short period of time, Arnold's characterization of the Celts could be found in newspaper editorials and books across the United Kingdom. Perhaps more than any other person, Arnold helped popularize the idea that the people of Ireland and Wales had distinctive character traits that pointed to a common racial identity among their populations and a different biological heritage from the people of England.

Thus the Celtic identity was born. Simon James has claimed, with some justification, that these developments mark one of the clearest examples of "ethnogenesis" in modern Europe.[33] An ethnic identity that simply didn't exist in 1700 was claimed by millions of people less than two hundred years later. At first, the concept of a Celtic identity had mostly (though not exclusively) been confined to discussions about distant history. This changed in the middle of the nineteenth century. Over a twenty-year period, linguistic scholars gave the Celts a sense of prestige, scientists gave them a racial categorization, archaeologists gave them a glorious past, and littérateurs gave them easily identifiable characteristics. Other factors contributed as well. In the face of growing anglicization in Wales and Ireland, Celticness offered a durable foundation upon which to construct a national identity, as well as a sense of common bond among the other groups in the United Kingdom in the face of England's growing political, industrial, and demographic might. Perhaps most importantly of all, rising literacy and an accelerating rate of growth in the number of newspapers brought regular reminders to Irish and Welsh readers of their Celtic heritage. As a result, politicians, writers, and journalists in both countries were more likely to look across the Irish Sea and compare their nation to its Celtic counterpart in a way that their predecessors would not have done. What followed was a sustained flow of commentary and ideas between Ireland and Wales that significantly shaped both countries' modern development.

CHAPTER 2

A CELTIC PARADISE

In July 1934, a Celtic congress was held in Dublin to allow representatives from the six Celtic countries to meet and discuss matters of common interest. The opening address was delivered by Éamon de Valera, the Irish taoiseach. De Valera stressed the necessity of preserving Irish as a community language in the Gaeltacht and extending it throughout the country. In attempting this, de Valera said that the Irish people "had before them the heroic and successful efforts of a neighbouring Celtic people."[1] De Valera believed that the Welsh had succeeded in reviving their native language and that therefore the Irish could do the same. Irish schools provided every opportunity for the youth of the country to learn the language, he declared, and "If they do not speak it, it is for want of a healthy spirit of nationalism such as the . . . Welsh have."[2] In praising the Welsh people, de Valera was following in the footsteps of the leading Irish cultural nationalists of the late nineteenth and early twentieth centuries who looked across the Irish Sea and saw a Celtic paradise, one they believed that the Irish nation could emulate, and surpass, in championing their distinctive culture.

There is a tendency to view nationalists as cultural xenophobes who loathe outside influences that corrupt their vision of an ideal nation. Yet one legacy of the spread of emigrants in the decades after the Great Famine was that people in Ireland were very aware of political and social developments elsewhere, because of regular correspondence with relatives overseas.[3] John

Hutchinson points out that cultural nationalists, far from trying to drag their country back toward an ancient Celtic past, instead sought to establish Ireland as a preeminent modern country, albeit one whose modernity bore distinctive Irish hallmarks. To do this, Hutchinson argues, cultural revivalists appealed "to the intelligentsia to borrow from other cultures in order to regenerate rather than to efface the national community."[4]

That Irish nationalists would look across the Irish Sea for inspiration in forging a nation is not surprising. As Seamus Deane has noted, British nationalism has been "a predominant political and cultural influence. In fact, Irish nationalism is, in its foundational moments, a derivative of its British counterpart."[5] Deane spoke primarily of how Irish nationalists copied their British counterparts in placing religion at the center of their national vision. Yet if we stop using the term *British* as a mere synonym for *English* and allow the fuller meaning to come to the fore then other British influences on Irish nationalism become more apparent. In particular, the example of the Welsh language helped shape the nature of the cultural nationalist revival in Ireland at the turn of the twentieth century, influencing the demands and policies of linguistic nationalists. Declan Kiberd wrote that the English helped invent Ireland through their fantastical depictions of the magical isle to the west, which demanded that the Irish create their own interpretation of their homeland.[6] This is indeed so, but as Irish nationalists came to understand their identity as offset by their English "other," so the land between Ireland and England offered insights into how the Irish could best express their Irishness.

The story of the Welsh language featured prominently in Irish nationalist cultural discourse from the 1860s up until the outbreak of the First World War. The Welsh example was important not only because it offered Irish nationalists a vision for what could be achieved in Ireland but because it inspired Irish-language activists to promote literacy, create cultural festivals, and demand legal rights for Irish speakers, all in the belief that this would allow the Irish language to attain the prosperity enjoyed by its Welsh equivalent. The latter half of the nineteenth century witnessed a surge of interest in Gaelic culture, coupled with the belief that Ireland could be "de-anglicized" through the restoration of the Irish language and "authentic" Irish cultural pastimes. Throughout this period, Irish nationalists held the Welsh up as an example for how a nation could revive its traditions and successfully resist anglicization while remaining economically prosperous.

Writers used the fact that the Welsh supposedly shared a Celtic heritage with the Irish to show language revivalists that their task was not impossible and that what the Welsh had done the Irish could also do. However, while nationalists celebrated the Welsh achievement, at times they also belittled the Irish people for failing the test of nationhood in comparison with their Celtic kin.

But it was the differing fortunes of two languages in seemingly similar positions that caught the attention of Irish commentators. In the wake of the Great Famine, the Irish language went into free fall. The association of the Irish language with poverty and ignorance encouraged parents to avoid passing the language on to their children; Irish speakers, in essence, committed "linguistic suicide."[7] As the number of people who spoke Irish declined dramatically, the Welsh language in contrast appeared to be in rude health. The number of Welsh speakers doubled during the nineteenth century as the Welsh population grew, with 910,289 Welsh speakers recorded in the census of 1891.[8] Naturally, those who were interested in preserving the Irish language looked to Wales in order to understand how the obstacles facing their language could be overcome. Indeed, for anyone who traveled to England, the example of Wales was difficult to avoid. One traveler noted that the Welsh language was not confined to Wales but was used on the Irish Sea right into Dublin. He wrote that as soon as someone boarded a ship to cross the Irish Sea, "One notices immediately that the sailors and staff on board speak a different language from that heard in Ireland. It is Welsh they are speaking. On Holy Island, where one lands, and thence through North Wales to Bangor, Welsh is used everywhere, in some places to the exclusion of English."[9] For any Irish observer interested in the language question, the example of Wales could not be ignored, and the story of the Welsh language helped shape the demands Irish Gaels made of their fellow countrymen.

By the 1860s, it was apparent to many commentators that Welsh was in vibrant health while the Irish language was dying. A writer to the *Nation* wrote, "Alas! A few years ago there was a greater number of Irish-speaking Irishmen in Ireland than Welsh-speaking Welshmen in Wales."[10] These commentators praised the manner in which Welsh was the language of every social class in Wales. One writer with the pseudonym "O'M" declared that "the people all through speak Welsh, *most of them nothing else.* And this is not confined to the poorer classes. The better farmers, those who live in excellent houses, all speak Welsh as their ordinary language."[11]

Another commented on how the "Cymric language" was "the ordinary and everyday language of the noble and of peasant, of merchant and of workman." Indeed, the Welsh had shown themselves to be more resilient than the Irish because "under difficulties and disadvantages a thousand fold greater than any we can point to, they have nobly adhered to the national customs of their forefathers."[12] In the eyes of these writers, the Welsh had resisted "Anglo-mania" while the Irish had succumbed to it. One commented that the Anglophilia that existed in Ireland, a "vile monster, full of gall and venom, venting its hatred and abuse upon everything national, ridiculing, disparaging, undervaluing," could not take root in Wales because the people had more dignity. He cheered "Bravo! Taffy. Stand Firm."[13] The Irish language could have been saved, another journalist noted, if efforts had been made "one-hundredth part as vigorous as the efforts of our Cymric neighbours." The Welsh example had shown the "bitter truth" to the *Nation's* readers, namely that the Irish "appear to lack the perseverance, concentration, and unity of effort in working out a national project."[14] In preserving their language, the Welsh "have set us Irish an example worthy of imitation."[15] After watching a Welshman thwart the efforts of an English tourist to make him speak English, "O'M" wrote, "Thought I to myself— 'Paddy, we have something much to learn—Neighbour Taffy stands firm: he's right.'"[16]

To stem the decay of Irish, the Society for the Preservation of the Irish Language (SPIL) and the Gaelic League were established in the late nineteenth century. Both societies looked to the example of Wales as proof that their own efforts could be successful. In the first annual report of the SPIL in 1876, the Welsh received hearty praise for maintaining their national language. The report stated that "notwithstanding their intimate social and geographical connection with England, the Welsh are assiduously cultivating their native language, which is one of the oldest offshoots of our more ancient Gaelic. They have several daily and weekly newspapers, and other periodicals, publishing in their own language."[17] The SPIL also exchanged annual reports with the Honorable Society of the Cymmrodorion, a Welsh literary society dedicated to preserving Welsh, in the hope of learning what could be done to save the Irish language. The SPIL wanted to create a bilingual Ireland that mirrored bilingual Wales, with people speaking their "native" language at home but also mastering English. The society's report for 1882 urged, "Surely Irishmen can do what Welshmen are doing, namely, preserving their own language, while studying English." The report noted that Wales had slightly more Welsh speakers than Ireland had Irish speakers, but hoped that this situation would soon be reversed. "With the spirit, which, we trust, has begun to animate our people, we are sanguine that the next census will see us in advance of Wales. We have a larger field to work upon, and, surely, in regard to our language, we ought not to be less patriotic."[18]

Similarly, the Gaelic League hoped to learn from the Welsh example while also using it as a patriotic spur for the Irish people. Within a couple of months of its founding in 1893, the Gaelic League announced that it desired friendship and cooperation with the Society for the Utilization of the Welsh Language in Education.[19] The League also invited a member from that organization, a Mr. Jones, to give a public speech on the Welsh language. In particular, the Gaelic League was interested in placing the Irish language in a more prominent position in the education system, similar to that enjoyed by the Welsh language. When the League published its list of objectives in 1896, it stated that one of its aims was "to endeavour to secure that, as in Wales, the national language shall be the medium of instruction in the National Schools in those districts where it is the home language of the people."[20] However, when the League was first formed, not everyone in Ireland was even aware that a Welsh language existed. Father John Hogan recalled attending one meeting in 1894 where "one budding orator remarked that 'Welsh' and 'Scotch' were English dialects and not very far removed from the written language. That was the type of man that Gaelic League representatives had to address and listen to."[21] As the Gaelic League expanded, members sought to educate the public about the strength of the Welsh language. Irish revivalists persistently urged the public to be as patriotic as their Welsh counterparts, while berating the government for not providing equal treatment for speakers of the Welsh and Irish languages.

Irish-language enthusiasts repeatedly pointed to how successful the Welsh people had been in maintaining Welsh as their community language. At a meeting of the Gaelic League in 1896, Eoin MacNeill, one of the founders of the society, declared that the League wanted to do for Irish "what has been done for the Welsh language. We wish to make it a leading element in our national life and in our national culture . . . to create and foster the spirit of self-respect and self-reliance. All this has been done in Wales, why not then in Ireland?"[22] At League meetings all across the country, the Welsh were placed on a pedestal as devoted patriots whom the Irish people should emulate. During a public meeting in Gougane Barra, Father Hurley told his parishioners that "they should take example by the gallant men of Wales, who looked upon the Welsh tongue with respect and reverence."[23] Another priest, Father James McNamee of Clones, told a crowd gathered for the opening of the Monaghan branch of the Gaelic League that a nation could survive only if it protected its language as the Welsh had done. The Welsh, Father McNamee said, "were not led astray by the foolish cry of those who said, "What is the use of learning our language: it is of no commercial value." Indeed, McNamee claimed, Wales thrived economically while preserving Welsh. He believed that "fifty years from hence Ireland would be like Wales—a distinct nationality, preserving its own language and having its own characteristics." Father McNamee foresaw such success because he knew "that the Irish people were determined in their hearts to follow the example Wales had set."[24]

Supporters of the Irish language wanted their native land to be similar to Wales in two important respects: they wanted it to be a bilingual nation where everyone had command of both tongues and a country where people were proud, rather than ashamed, to speak the indigenous language. Norma Borthwick, a member of the executive committee of the Gaelic League, asked, "Can people not learn English without giving up Irish? When we travel to London from Holyhead do we not hear guards and porters at the Welsh stations conversing among themselves in Welsh, and breaking off at a moment's notice to speak English to a passenger? What is to prevent the same bilingual state of affairs in Ireland?"[25] Praise for Welsh bilingualism was common. Father Thomas Kearney of Skibbereen told a Gaelic League gathering that the Welsh people "talk English, of course, but they prefer to speak their own language."[26] Another priest, Father Quirke from Cashel, stated, "I saw with great pleasure Welsh gentlemen from their carriages talking Welsh to the peasantry in Bangor and other places. I must say the pleasure had a feeling of jealousy mixed with it."[27] Thus Irish-language activists wanted the Irish people to be able to speak English when necessary but to speak Irish out of habit. They wanted, as the Reverend John Gunning told a public meeting in Mayo, "to make the Irish what the people of Wales had made the Welsh—a living, all-pervading language, the language of the fair and the market, the language of the school and the language of the home (long and prolonged cheers)."[28]

League members believed that the biggest impediment to attaining this bilingual state was not simply teaching the language to people but getting those who already knew it to speak it. According to the 1891 census, almost 20 percent of the Irish population could speak Irish, but many did not do so because of the stigma of being an Irish speaker. Gaelic Leaguers felt this in part explained the different linguistic environments in Ireland and Wales: the Welsh were proud to speak their language while the Irish were ashamed to do the same. Discussing this very issue at a meeting in Castlebar, Eoin MacNeill described traveling by ferry across the Irish Sea. As he recalled:

> I made some inquiry, in English, of a sailor, who replied very civilly in that language. At the same time another sailor was talking close by to a passenger. The two sailors, turning to each other afterwards, began conversing in Welsh—in a way which would lead a person to believe that they knew no English, which of course, was not a fact. They spoke English civilly and obligingly to anyone who required it; but when the occasion arose to speak among themselves, they turned away from the language—which then they never thought of using—and spoke in the language of their own country.[29]

This was a perfect example of Welsh bilingualism in operation. But MacNeill doubted whether such a scenario would have played out like this in Ireland. "I wonder how often such as that happens in the county of Mayo?" MacNeill asked his audience. "The people of Mayo, who know Irish, and when they have to talk English, do they, when they turn round, speak Irish to one another? Do they drop the English language . . . as a sense of duty to their nationality, and begin to speak in the language of their country?" He doubted this was so and told his listeners that unless "they had the spirit of the Welsh people, they would not gain the respect of other nations, or—what they wanted much more—the respect of themselves."[30]

In other words, the Irish language was in crisis because Irish speakers lacked the spirit of their Welsh peers. Douglas Hyde, president of the Gaelic League, observed that there were Welsh speakers who did not like to admit they could speak English. "That is not our circumstance in Ireland, alas, where many a man and woman were here at this time, and they had great Irish, the shame wouldn't let them admit that they had a mouthful of words, and I am afraid to say that one or two remain here."[31] Father Kearney recalled encountering Welsh speakers while holidaying across the Irish Sea: "I fell in with a party of Welsh people who were discussing the Irish question in some language unknown to me. Afterwards some friends came in, and they spoke English fluently. They told me they were Welsh people, and I was admiring the way in which they spoke their own language, and they told me that they in Wales would be ashamed if they were not able to speak the same language spoken by their fathers."[32] Kearney felt that this exact spirit needed to be duplicated in Ireland. He hoped to see a situation in which Irish people would be ashamed if they were "not be able to speak their own tongue, and the persons who will not speak it will be looked upon as ignorant and vulgar, and that the table will be turned upon those who, in the past, thought Irish too vulgar to speak." With its bilingual status and deep linguistic patriotism, Wales was the dream that Irish-language activists aspired to.

Richard Kelly, a journalist who was forced to stop in Cardiff because of bad weather, spoke of his amazement at how the Welsh language lived in the Principality. Kelly wrote, "What struck me, a Celt . . . was the vitality and popularity of the Welsh language. . . . Welsh is spoken and sung, read and written by practically all classes. I can only admire and envy such sturdy and creditable patriotism, and say with all my heart, *Esto perpetua*."[33] In Cork, Father Thomas Kearney encouraged the people of Skibbereen to believe that Irish could be saved by looking at "the gallant little language of Wales; see what has been done."[34] At a meeting of the Gaelic League in Dublin in 1899, the Welsh example was again used to boost morale among League members. One member, speaking in Irish, said that another nation had shown that a language could be revived. "I refer to Wales," the speaker said, "a little country near us. It is a part of England, as you would say, Wales, but if so, the English never succeeded in stripping their language from them."[35]

Members of the Gaelic League did not have to travel to Wales to see the strength of the Welsh language for themselves. A Welsh chapel on Talbot Street catered to the small Welsh community living in Dublin. Ernest

Blythe, who would be elected to the first Dáil and would serve as a government minister in the 1920s, was one Gaelic Leaguer who was impressed that the Welsh of Dublin maintained their language. Speaking in 1951, Blythe recalled, "When I joined the Gaelic League and began to learn Irish, one of my fellow members told me, almost with bated breath, that the Welsh community in Dublin had its own church in which services were conducted in Welsh." Blythe, who was from a Presbyterian background, went to visit the chapel "one Sunday morning to revel in the sound of a language closely related to Irish. That little Welsh-speaking congregation, maintaining its individuality in a foreign city, made quite an impression on me."[36]

It is evident that both the leadership and the rank and file of the Gaelic League greatly admired the tenacity of the Welsh language. However, the championing of Welsh was a double-edged sword. Although it offered hope for the restoration of Irish, it also highlighted how much the Irish language had declined, and many commentators could not resist charging the Irish population with shameful neglect. In comparison with Wales, it seemed that Ireland had betrayed its heritage. "While Wales is thus maintaining its individuality, what is Ireland doing in the same direction?" one writer asked.[37] "Very little . . . outside the domain of politics," was his conclusion. In Turlough, County Mayo, the local parish priest told a public meeting that in Wales "you will hear the Welshman speaking his native Welsh; but in Ireland what do you hear? Every scalthane speaking broken English."[38] Another scribe declared, "Our Cambrian neighbours jealously retain their ancestral Welsh. . . . The decline of the Irish language is discreditable to our nation."[39] The *Southern Star* newspaper pointed out that Welsh was not in danger of decline because "a very large section of the population use it exclusively, and . . . most of the remainder use it in preference to English. In Ireland . . . the vast majority who know both Irish and English prefer to use English—a fact not very creditable to our national self-respect."[40] Another writer, using the pen name "Eirionnact," compared the Welsh and Irish unfavorably when he stated, "The Welsh people have thus shown an honorable sentiment of self-respect widely different, I regret to say, from the slavish indifference of our Irish population to the preservation of their ancestral tongue."[41]

Anecdotes regularly appeared in the Irish nationalist press that sought to cast the Irish people in an unfavorable light compared to the Welsh population. One Irishman who lived in England spoke of visiting a Welsh-speaking town in North Wales and being amazed at the vitality of the local language. He told a story of an Englishman who visited the town and

> only heard Welsh spoken by the people of the house where he got lodgings, except when they would speak with him. He didn't like this, and after a day or two he said to the woman of the house that he was tired to be listening to their Welsh and he would prefer not to hear any, because to him it was only a barbarous language. He had more to say against Welsh but the woman put a stop to his talk. "I prefer," she said, "not to have someone like you as our company, and get out of my house this minute." And he was thrown out without thanks.[42]

The Welsh people, said the Irishman, would not allow this kind of insult on their language, and he added, "It is a pity that this is not the case with the Irish people." By way of comparison, he then told a story about some Irish laborers working in a field in England. "The farmer came upon them and they were speaking Irish together one time, and he started laughing at their speech. What do you suppose these Irishmen did? Shame came upon them speaking their native language, and they began speaking English without delay." The author concluded by saying, "I will leave it to the reader to decide which of these earned contempt, the Welsh woman or the Irish labourers?"[43]

The point was not subtle. The Irish people were being outshone by the Welsh in patriotism and should be ashamed as a consequence. Another man writing to *Fáinne an Lae*, a bilingual newspaper that supported efforts to revive Irish, recalled a conversation that had taken place between two miners, one Welsh and one Irish, in Butte, Montana:[44]

> "Sean O'Rodaigh," said the Welshman to the Irish man, "do you speak Irish?"
>
> "No," said Sean, "I don't speak any other language apart from English."
>
> "You are not Irish then, but English," said the Welshman.
>
> "You lie," said Sean, getting riled up with anger, "I am not an English man at all, but an Irishman, and as a sign of that, my father and mother spoke Irish."

"They were a funny father and mother you had," said the Welshman, "and they didn't teach Irish to you when they spoke the language."

This individual humiliation of an Irish miner in faraway Montana could be read as a wider condemnation of the Irish nation, at the hands of their fellow Celts no less. Indeed, while cultural nationalists believed the decline of Irish was a national shame, what made it worse was the reports of the unflattering opinions that the Welsh people had of the Irish for failing to maintain their language. A report in *An Claidheamh Soluis* marveled at how much Welsh was spoken at a political rally in the Principality. The writer noted that "the Welsh are not slow, too, in a friendly way, to point out how much Irishmen are lacking in this particular. Irishmen visiting Cardiff from time to time have been left under no doubt as regards Welsh opinion."[45] One particular incident that was reported widely in the Irish provincial press concerned an Irishman who was visiting Wales. Walking through a Welsh town, the Irishman noticed a rock specimen in the window of a shop. He entered the shop and asked, in English, about the rock. The store owner told the man that he knew he was Irish because of his accent. Curious, the Irishman asked what the store owner knew of the Irish people. "I know this," he replied scornfully, "I know that they are poor spirited cowards to let their language go. Here in Wales we can all talk English, as you see, but our own language is the language of our hearts and of our homes." The Irishman later told an audience in Dublin that "I could say nothing . . . for I myself did not know one word of Irish."[46] In this way, retelling the story of Wales served a dual purpose to Irish-language activists. It showed their audience that it was possible to preserve their distinct language even in the face of competition from omnipresent English. But in juxtaposing the respective positions of the Irish and Welsh languages, commentators hoped that a sense of shame would spur those who proclaimed themselves to be Irish patriots to be more proactive in their own efforts to learn and speak the language.

Many Irish nationalists were enthralled by the example of the Welsh language because they believed that the circumstances faced by the Irish language at the end of the nineteenth century were identical to those faced by Welsh a century earlier. In published letters and speeches, these commentators encouraged supporters of the Irish language to believe their efforts would not be in vain, as the Welsh language had once known similar dark days but had been revived. Logically, their argument went, what had been done for Welsh could be done for Irish. In reality, the story of the fall and rise of the Welsh language, as told in Ireland, was greatly exaggerated. Welsh had never sunk as low as Irish had by the turn of the twentieth century, but neither had it become as dominant over English as some Irish commentators proclaimed. Nationalists misconstrued the story of the Welsh revival in order to offer hope to Irish-language supporters that the language could be not only saved but restored to a position of supremacy in Ireland.

Whenever writers spoke in glowing terms about the healthy position of Welsh, they usually prefaced this by telling their readers that Welsh had almost died out a century ago, before being rescued from the abyss. In a letter to the editor of the *Nation*, a writer named "M" declared that "Welsh should have died the death a long time ago. . . . Welsh was far more heavily handicapped than Irish; and at one time seemed as perilously near extinction as even our language is at present. Yet we see it to-day flourishing as it never flourished before."[47] Similarly the SPIL tried to rally enthusiasm for the cause of the language by highlighting how Welsh had once flirted with extinction as Irish now did. Their report for 1892 noted that "the Welsh have rescued their language from a condition almost as bad as that of the Irish of present day."[48] Stephen Brown, a member of the Kildare County Council, told an assembly in Naas that everyone knew "that the Welsh language had almost disappeared nearly 100 years ago from Wales. It stood much in the same position as the Irish language stands in today in Ireland, but steps were taken by some earnest men in Wales, and . . . Welsh is again the National language of the Welsh people."[49] Father Michael O'Hickey, professor of Irish at Maynooth College, declared at a meeting in Belfast in 1899 that "in Wales, one hundred years ago, it was a matter of history that the Welsh language was in its death throes. However, a few patriots—and they were patriots (applause)—took up the work of reviving the Welsh speech, and to-day they found that practically every person within the confines of Wales was either an exclusively Welsh speaker, or, at all events, a bilingual speaker."[50]

Eoin MacNeill claimed at another Gaelic League meeting that "the Welsh people found their language two generations ago in as bad a condition as the Irish language is in many parts of Ireland (cries of 'Worse'). That did not prevent the movement for the resuscitation of the Welsh language from succeeding." Douglas Hyde drove home this message, telling the same audience that "a hundred years ago there was not a tombstone in Wales on which the name of the dead was not written in English; to-day there is not a tombstone in Wales that is not written in Welsh."[51] Another anonymous Gaelic League member pointed out that just as people in Ireland rejected the notion that Irish could be revived, so had some people in Wales when the future of that particular language looked bleak. He wrote, "The struggle for the national position of the Welsh language was an uphill fight. The defenders of the language were few, chiefly some clergymen. The people who shook their heads and cried 'No go' and 'What's the good' were numerous. In those days the prince of royal blood who attended a Welsh banquet would have been thought a madman. The sneer at 'Celtic ardour' held the field, and many were they that quailed before its potency." Of course, he added, "The movement for the preservation of the Welsh language has completely succeeded." Irish-language supporters were to take heart from this. Welsh had once almost died out, but it had been revived. Welsh revivalists had been subjected to scorn and derision, but they had overcome the challenge. There was consequently no reason why Gaelic Leaguers could not do the same.

The typical Irish nationalist's version of the story of the Welsh language emphasized not only the dire prospects the language had once faced but the wondrous position it presently occupied in Wales. Cardinal Logue told a League meeting in Louth that the "Irish language was never so far gone in Ireland as the Welsh was in Wales, and now it is universally spoken throughout the principality." He praised the perseverance of the Welsh by saying, "Welsh was nearly completely gone; but by throwing themselves into the struggle to preserve it, in the true spirit of nationality, and exercising a little zeal, and a great deal of labour, they brought the language to the splendid position it occupies today."[52] The idea that, having been saved, the Welsh tongue was now the dominant language throughout Wales was reinforced in various speeches and articles. One speaker at a Catholic Club in Ulster assured his audience that "in Wales, Welsh is now the universal language."[53] Delivering a lecture entitled "The Example of Wales," a Cavan priest told a Gaelic League gathering that "in Wales one hundred years ago there wasn't one word of the language spoken: today it was their universal dialect."[54] In Mullingar, a local magistrate spoke to an audience about the fantastic revival of Welsh, "until at the present time everyone in Wales speaks it, and not only that, but in Wales 40 years ago, certainly not 50, not more than 10 percent of the people spoke the language. What was possible in Wales was possible in Ireland."[55] Mr. D. Carolan Rushe, a solicitor in Fermanagh, speaking at a Gaelic League meeting in Rosslea, told those assembled that "in Wales 80 years ago a similar movement was started. There were then 100,000 people who spoke Welsh. To-day, there is not a man who cannot speak his native tongue. We have nearly 700,000 Irish speaking people, and if the Welsh succeeded with 100,000, why should not we succeed with 700,000?"[56]

Hence the Gaelic League and its supporters presented a consistent narrative on what Ireland could learn from Wales, namely that Welsh had once been far worse off than Irish was but that through ardor and hard work it had become the dominant language in Wales. In truth, the story of the decay of Welsh had been molded to mirror Irish circumstances, rather than to reflect reality, and its successes had been exaggerated to make the aspirations of Irish activists appear more achievable. Certainly there had been something of a Welsh literary revival, or "renaissance," in the eighteenth century.[57] A new wave of Welsh humanist writers gained popularity among an increasingly literate Welsh population. Griffith Jones of Llanddowror sought to bring literacy to Welsh monoglots when he established his first circulating school in 1734. Both adults and children alike were taught to read and write Welsh in these schools, and by the time of Jones's death in 1771, 3,325 schools had been established across Wales.[58] Religion also played a role, as Welsh Nonconformists used the Welsh language to win converts among the masses, thereby solidifying the position of Welsh as the language of the chapel.

While the position of the Welsh language within Welsh society improved in the eighteenth century, Irish talk of a dramatic Welsh revival was inaccurate. Welsh as a spoken community language had never witnessed a collapse as spectacular as Irish had in the latter half of the nineteenth century. Furthermore, though Welsh was in a relatively strong position when the Gaelic League was formed, the claim made by League members that it was the universal language of Wales was equally misguided. Certainly the number of Welsh speakers had grown throughout the nineteenth century. In 1800, there were an estimated 470,000 Welsh speakers; this number grew to 929,824 in 1891 and peaked at 977,366 in 1911. But the proportion of the population that spoke Welsh actually fell during this time, from about 80 percent in 1800 to 49 percent by 1891. While the number of Welsh speakers doubled during this time, the number of English speakers increased seventy-fold.[59] Although Welsh was in a far healthier condition than the Irish language at the moment the Gaelic League drew attention to it, the seeds of its own decline had already been sown.

Occasionally, some writers pointed out that the elevated status that had been bestowed upon Welsh in the Irish imagination might not be deserved. As early as 1875, one critic declared, "Welsh is more gradually disappearing, and, notwithstanding the tenacity with which the Welsh cling to their language, there is no doubt but that it is going down."[60] Others accepted that Welsh was in a flourishing state but felt that the description of how it had attained this position was too vague. A Cork student called for the Gaelic League to distribute a pamphlet to explain its aims and objectives. In this pamphlet, he believed, "the case of Wales—apparently so hopeless a hundred years ago—and now so flourishing, should be explained."[61] Some accurate descriptions of the Welsh "revival" could be found among Gaelic League publications. William Patrick Ryan, in his pamphlet *Lessons from Modern Language Movements*, gave a reasonably straightforward account of what had happened in Wales in the eighteenth century.[62] However, in describing the Welsh literary renaissance, he tended to use the term *revival* and never explained that the spoken language had not gone into decline. Apparently many Irish revivalists assumed that the "revival" must have referred to growing numbers of people speaking as well as reading in Welsh, spawning a series of inaccurate comparisons between the languages. The Welsh parable, however mistaken, was too alluring for Irish supporters to ignore. The somewhat similar position of each language in relation to English, coupled with the supposed kinship between the Welsh and Irish people, meant that it offered Irish nationalists an ideal means of channeling their Celtic spirit in defiance of encroaching "Anglo-Saxonism." Once the story of the Welsh language had been modified so that its former decline was overstated and its successes were embellished, it became a teaching tool par excellence for orators and writers across Ireland who sought to rally the people to the cause of the Irish language.

Yet while Irish observers misunderstood the history of Welsh, they were nevertheless very aware that the British government extended certain privileges to Welsh speakers that did not exist for Irish speakers. In particular, commentators noted that the Welsh language was tolerated in courts in a way that the Irish language was not. One Irishman traveling through Wales struck up a conversation with a Welshman about the court system and explained that in Ireland witnesses were forced to testify in whatever English they had. To his surprise, the Welshman informed him that in Wales "it is *the privilege of the witness* to choose the language in which he conceives he can best give his testimony." Reflecting on how matters were conducted in Ireland, the traveler declared the judicial system to be a "vulgar villainy" and wrote "Noble Wales! Where the native language is so respected that none could venture to slight it."[63] When a Welsh MP raised the question of whether judges who could not speak Welsh should be appointed to Welsh-speaking districts, the matter was keenly discussed in the Irish press. In 1872, George Osborne Morgan pointed out in the House of Commons that if a judge could not speak the language of the people miscarriages of justice were far more likely to occur. The home secretary, Henry Bruce, promised that in the future the government would seek barristers who were competent in Welsh.[64] One Irish observer, using the pseudonym Eadhmonn An Chnuic, stated that in Wales, "unless a person knows the language, he cannot get any post or office, from judge to school master, and the language is respected throughout the country. It is not so in Ireland."[65]

Of course, it was not true that Welsh was essential for all jobs in Wales. Nevertheless, the Welsh language was used in some official capacities in a way that Irish was not, and there was a clamor among Gaelic Leaguers for this to be rectified. One writer noted that "anybody who has seen the farcical entertainment enacted at the quarter sessions when an Irish case is being heard will at once admit that the ignorance of the judge is calculated to challenge distrust [sic], to make injustice possible, and to degrade the dignity of the law."[66] Michael Cusack, founder of the Gaelic Athletic Association, wondered why Irish judges did not have to speak the local language as Welsh judges did, writing that there appeared to be one law for Wales and another for Ireland. He asked, "Why insult me constantly by telling me that my countrymen are dealt with as impartially as those in other parts of the kingdom while I find two branches of the same race separated only by six hours' journey dealt with so differently?"[67] There was further outrage in 1899, when a district judge in Mayo threw out the case of a plaintiff named O'Connor because he could give his evidence only in Irish. The Ballinrobe

District Council condemned this action, declaring, "We maintain that the Irish-speaking peasant has as much right to give his evidence in the Irish language as the Welsh people have to give theirs in the Welsh language. . . . It should be compulsory for judges administering the law in Irish-speaking courts to have a knowledge of the Irish language."[68]

Some Irish cultural nationalists believed that the Welsh and Irish languages were not treated identically partly because Welsh MPs supported Welsh language rights in Westminster, while Irish MPs did not. One Irish activist, using the pen name "Tír Fhiacra," demanded that Irish MPs "take the matter up in real earnest . . . and . . . press upon Parliament the necessity of having Irish properly taught in the national schools in the Irish-speaking districts. Thanks to the efforts of Welsh members, Welsh is now fully taught in all the schools of Wales."[69] Bernard Doyle, editor of *Fáinne an Lae*, observed that Welsh MPs had pushed for a Welsh-speaking governor to be appointed in the prison at Carmarthen: "This is an instance of the vigilance of the Welsh M.P.'s in watching over the interests of their native tongue. When may we expect to hear of the Irish Members busying themselves about the appointment of Irish-speaking officials at such prisons as Galway, Tralee, and Castlebar?"[70] Doyle went further, calling for an alliance of Celtic MPs in Parliament who could rally together in support of the most Celtic marker of their identity, their respective native languages:

> Our Irish Members of Parliament should realize that in any measures tending to the preservation of the Irish language they are certain of the support of Welsh members if they ask for it. If our Irish members were as active in this matter as they ought to be, they, together with thirty-five Welsh members, could raise a pretty authoritative voice on the language question. Besides, the Highlanders have also to be reckoned with. Conversely, the Irish members should support the Welsh in all language grievances. . . . This is a matter of race, not religion or politics, and no insult to a Celtic language should be allowed to go unpunished.[71]

The Gaelic League, meanwhile, focused its attention on how the post office gave official recognition to Welsh but not to Irish. Visitors to Wales noticed that all signs in Welsh post offices were bilingual, and that postmasters in Welsh-speaking districts were required to have a knowledge of Welsh.

In 1905, the position of postmaster at Machynlleth became vacant, and the job advertisement stressed that "a knowledge of Welsh was necessary." The Gaelic League believed that "there is no more reason why 'a knowledge of Welsh is necessary' in Machynlleth than Irish is necessary in Galway or Westport."[72] Irish politicians asked Lord Stanley, the postmaster general, about this discrepancy. He replied that "the practice followed in certain districts of Wales is not followed in Ireland, because the circumstances are not similar."[73] In many ways, this reflects the attitude of various British administrations to the language situation on the Celtic fringe. Welsh was a permanent fixture in the Principality and could not be ignored, whereas Irish appeared to be dying out and therefore did not need to be catered to. Nevertheless, as the Gaelic League demanded more official recognition for the Irish language from the government, it frequently presented evidence from Wales to accuse Westminster of being inherently biased against Irish.

Those who compared the linguistic environments in Ireland and Wales noticed differing attitudes not only in bureaucratic circles but also among the respective clergy. The fact that Methodist ministers played a central role in upholding the prestige of the Welsh language did not go unnoticed among Gaelic League members. Dr. John St. Clair Boyd told a League assembly in Buncrana, "It was from practice of the Wesleyan Ministers preaching to their congregation in the language of their country that the Welsh language had obtained the position which it holds today."[74] The *Anglo-Celt* newspaper informed its readers that "the grit and the national pride of the Welsh people, and the whole hearted cooperation of their ministers of religion, who have always made a point of teaching and expounding the Scriptures in the National language, are the main factors in perpetuating the Welsh language and Welsh nationality."[75] Of course, this comparison painted the Catholic clergy of Ireland in an unflattering light. As early as 1864, the *Nation* had lamented that "the clergy and people of Wales proudly treasure and anxiously preserve their ancient customs and heritage. The clergy and people of Ireland allow theirs to disappear without an effort, as if they were relics of barbarism and ignorance."[76] William O'Brien, founder of the United Irish League, observed that "the very cause that keeps the Welsh language flourishing—the fact of its being intertwined with the religion of the people—has in this way acted to some extent in the reverse in those districts of Ireland where the Gaelic had its firmest hold."[77]

Bernard Doyle in particular regularly made critical comparisons be-tween the Welsh and the Irish clergy. When the St. Teilo Society produced a Welsh-language prayer book for Welsh-speaking Catholics, Doyle fumed that there was "almost certainly not one Welsh-speaking Catholic in Wales for every hundred Irish-speaking Catholics in Ireland. Nevertheless, the Welsh Catholic clergy do not look on the use of Welsh in religious affairs with the same callous indifference with which unfortunately too many of the Irish clergy look on the use of Irish." He added, "We hear a great deal about what the schools can do for Irish. In Wales the Sunday schools held out for the native tongue when it was banned from the day schools. How does Irish stand in the Sunday schools?"[78] The production of a Welsh-language hymnal by the St. Teilo Society prompted Doyle to ask, "Who will write and publish a hymnal in their own language for Irish Catholics?"[79] The announcement that the Passionist Fathers were to open a monastery in Carmarthen and to teach Welsh to clerical students also got Doyle's atten-tion. He wrote: "We are sure that the members of this Order in Ireland, who so frequently go on missions to towns in or near Irish-speaking dis-tricts, and many of whom come from Irish-speaking districts themselves, will not allow the lesson of this Welsh mission to be lost on them, but will recognize that charity begins at home, and that the Cork and Kerry and Connacht and Donegal Irish-speaking man has as much claim to be min-istered to by priests understanding his native language as any Welshman east or west of Offa's Dyke has."[80] So although Irish revivalists made compari-sons between Ireland and Wales primarily to encourage the populace to learn the Gaelic language, they also highlighted how governmental and clerical officials were not doing enough to promote Irish.

While the example of the Welsh served as a rallying cry for Irish cul-tural nationalists, it also offered a guide for what needed to be changed in Ireland to allow the indigenous language to prosper. Irish observers of Wales noted two key elements that they believed explained the vitality of Welsh in comparison to the declining status of the Irish language. First, the Welsh language had a strong print culture, with books, magazines, and newspapers selling well among a public with a high level of literacy. In comparison, lit-eracy and print in Irish were almost nonexistent. Irish writers also saw the Welsh eisteddfod (loosely translated from Welsh as "to be sitting," a cultural festival in which competitions were held in music and poetry) as being largely responsible for promoting literacy in Welsh; they hoped to re-create a similar festival in Ireland that they believed would go some way to restoring the language to a place of prominence in Ireland. In short, Irish activists tried not only to emulate Welsh determination but also to learn what strategies the Welsh had used to protect their language.

One difference observers seized upon to explain the relative strength of Welsh in comparison to Irish was the fact that most Welsh speakers could also read and write in Welsh. In particular, Irish commentators were amazed by the voracious appetite of the Welsh for reading material in their native language. One Irish traveler in Wales in the 1840s was incredulous upon discovering bookshops that sold only Welsh books. Quoting a book about Wales, he told readers of the *Nation* that "the Welsh press pours forth its publications in various forms. Independently of its works on history, music, and divinity, there are no less than *fifteen* monthly periodicals regularly issued from the press." In his conversation with one woman who owned a bookstore, he learned that her husband had taken many Welsh books and grammars to America, where there was a huge demand for them among Welsh emigrants.[81] The SPIL was similarly impressed with how successful Welsh publications were. It reported to its members that the Welsh were far in advance of the Irish because they "have several daily and weekly newspapers, and other periodicals, publishing in their own language."[82] William Patrick Ryan noted that the Welsh language thrived because "the native Press and literature have decisively advanced. Some 9,000 books were published in Welsh in the last century, the proportion increasing with the years, and the Principality has over fifty periodicals in the native language."[83] Councilor Edward Thomas of Cardiff boasted in 1899 that "there were 136 magazines and newspapers printed in Welsh in the Principality, and £200,000 had been spent on Welsh literature."[84] One writer for *An Claidheamh Soluis* told his readers how twenty thousand copies of one Welsh volume had been sold before it went to press. He wrote, "Of course Wales is a much richer country than Ireland, but, at the same time, it must be remembered that the population is less than one fourth that of Ireland. We have a lot to learn yet in the way of consistency of action and practical effort."[85]

The government had also noticed the literary gap between Irish and Welsh and used it to justify allowances made for Welsh speakers that were not extended to Irish speakers. In 1877, Sir Michael Hicks Beach, the chief secretary for Ireland, told the House of Commons:

In Wales the Welsh language is not only the spoken language, but also the written and the printed language. Newspapers are printed in it, books are written in it, placards and public notices are constantly seen in it. In Ireland there is nothing of the kind, with very rare exceptions, in reference to the Celtic language. There is no such thing as a Celtic newspaper; you never see a Celtic advertisement; and if any book is printed in the language now it is exceptional. I do not think it will be reasonable to treat the two countries in the same manner.[86]

For those who wanted to preserve Irish, the lesson from Wales appeared to be that a prominent print culture in the language would be essential. As in the case of the story of the Welsh-language revival pushed in Ireland, there were exaggerations of how much reading material was available in Welsh. Contrary to the claims that Wales supported several daily newspapers, a regular daily newspaper in Welsh never actually existed.[87] But certainly a large number of people read regularly in Welsh, a situation very different from that in Ireland. The renowned Irish writer Tadhg Ó Donnchadha estimated that as few as fifty people could read and write in Irish in 1882.[88] To give some perspective on how rare print material in the Irish language was, it is worth sharing an anecdote from Tomás Bán Ó Conceanainn. Ó Conceanainn became a hero within the Gaelic League in the early twentieth century for his work as a *timire* (organizer), which involved organizing Irish classes and helping found League branches across Ireland. He was born in 1870 in Inis Meáin, which was largely a monoglot Irish community at the time. He emigrated to the United States in 1887, but not until a decade later, when he was twenty-seven years old, did he discover that his mother tongue existed as a written language! Ó Conceanainn recalled receiving magazines and newspapers from Ireland that had some Gaelic articles in them: "I wasn't able to make heads or tails of the Irish that was in them, because I had never before set eyes on printed Irish, nor had I known that one could write in the language."[89] Clearly Irish, at the end of the nineteenth century, lagged far behind Welsh in terms of a vibrant print culture.

The lesson seemed to be that, if Irish were to survive, it would need readers as well as speakers. The first step in this direction was the creation of *Irishleabhar na Gaedhilge* (The Gaelic Journal) by the Gaelic Union in 1882. Published irregularly, it failed to attract a wide readership and soon encountered financial difficulties. It was eventually taken over by the Gaelic

League, and by 1899 it was running an annual deficit of £100. Eoin Mac-Neill urged the branches of the League to do more to support the journal, declaring, "Wales has fourteen magazines, why can we not support one in Ireland?"[90] Wales was the main source of inspiration for those trying to create a readership in the Irish language. One friend of MacNeill suggested trying to establish a weekly newspaper in Irish, noting that "Welsh is kept up by its papers and if the Irish people won't support a small weekly I for one will think . . . Irish were dead."[91] Within a couple of years, the Gaelic League had a weekly bilingual newspaper, *An Claidheamh Soluis*, and Irish printing presses began to produce some Irish-language literature. In 1901 the *Connaught Telegraph* reported that "Wales spent £200,000 a year on printed matter in Welsh. The G.L. [*sic*] bids fair to soon make Ireland rival Wales. A few months ago it was considered a wonderful thing that the Gaelic League had sold 7,000 Irish books in one month. In February the sale had increased to 16,000."[92] The Welsh example had convinced Irish revivalists that printing material in the language would help secure its survival. Of course, the language also needed readers, but in observing the success of the Welsh eisteddfod, members of the Gaelic League found a vehicle they hoped to copy in order to create a new generation of Irish men and women who were literate in the Irish language.

As for the Welsh example of the eisteddfodau, these festivals go as far back as the Middle Ages, but they were revived in the late eighteenth century by the Gwyneddigion Society. Their popularity increased in the mid-nineteenth century thanks to the work of Thomas Price, an Anglican clergyman who helped organize the Abergavenny eisteddfod from the 1830s on.[93] The popularity of the Abergavenny eisteddfod encouraged more communities to stage their own festivals, and a national eisteddfod was held for the first time in 1861. As the eisteddfodau grew in popularity, Irish commentators took note.[94] One article in the *Nation*, under the title "How the Welsh Love Fatherland," gave a long description of the events of an eisteddfod held in 1866. The writer declared that Ireland had much to learn from the eisteddfod: "If a mere handful of people scattered over the mountains and valleys of Wales can find sufficient patriotism to encourage such assemblages . . . surely Ireland, with its still millions of children, ought to be able to imitate an example so honourable and necessary."[95] Over the following decades, there were numerous calls for an Irish eisteddfod to be created. One writer, using the pseudonym "A Celt," spelled out why Ireland needed to imitate the Welsh in this regard:

Now, sir, don't you think something of this kind would do an incalculable amount of good in Ireland? Surely we are not behind the Welsh in patriotism, and I am sure such a festival held every year would be warmly supported by the warm hearted people of our land, for it would, I think, give a great impetus to the study of our dear old tongue, it would cause those who speak it but imperfectly to become proficient, and would cause it to be studied by those to whom it is now an unknown language. . . . Surely the affair is as practicable to Irishmen as to Welshmen, and the good done would be immeasurable.[96]

Others not only saw the benefit of creating an Irish eisteddfod but lamented that it was the Welsh in particular who outshone their Celtic brethren. An editorial in the *Freeman's Journal* asked, "Why is there never held an Irish Eisteddfod? Wales is not much bigger than an Irish province. The language of Wales is confessedly only an inferior Irish. The native literature of Wales is scantier and poorer. . . . Yet Wales . . . has its annual Eisteddfod . . . and Ireland never has anything of the kind."[97] A man named R. O'Donoghue wrote to the *Nation* declaring that Ireland could take a lesson from the eisteddfod and profit from it considerably. He added that if a people like the Welsh, who "have long since lost every spark of national sentiment, continue to celebrate customs revered by our ancestors, why should not we, whose proudest boast is our imperishable nationality, revive in our midst an institution that may be the means of popularizing and perpetuating the beautiful language and literature of Ireland?"[98] By the late 1880s, demands for an Irish cultural festival were increasing. In 1887 the Reverend Euseby D. Cleaver offered to donate fifty pounds to be used as prize money for a festival that celebrated Irish music and literature.[99] Within a decade, Ireland would have not one but two annual festivals based on the national eisteddfod of Wales.

In 1894 Thomas O'Neill Russell sparked a vigorous correspondence when he wrote a letter to the *Evening Telegraph* lamenting the neglect of Irish music by the chief representatives of musical activity in Ireland. Within a few months, a general committee had been formed by Dr. Annie Patterson with a view to creating an Irish music festival.[100] A circular announced, "It is proposed that the Festival shall last at least four days, and that it shall be known by the Gaelic word Féis. Its objects may be illustrated by reference to the Welsh Eisteddfod."[101] The Feis Ceoil Association was established by Patterson in 1896, and the first *feis ceoil* (music festival) was held in Dublin in 1897. Throughout the festival, the link between the *feis ceoil* and the national eisteddfod was celebrated, although the two events were not altogether similar in that the *feis ceoil* focused solely on musical competitions. The program notes for the first *feis ceoil* claimed that the idea of the *feis* had a connection to the eisteddfod dating back almost a thousand years:

> It is certain that the Irish bards of the sixth century of our era were the recognized leaders in musical art. Griffith ap Cynam, Prince of North Wales, who had been born in Ireland, brought over some Irish musicians in order that they might impart to their Welsh brethren their manner of playing the Harp. But while in Wales the musical genius of the people was for centuries sustained by the Annual Bardic Congress, known under the name of the Eisteddfod, an institution so brilliantly revived within the last centuries, the Irish meetings, so often associated with Tara, decayed with the fall of the bards and their privileges.[102]

The herald bard of Wales, T. H. Thomas, was an official guest of the *feis ceoil* and spoke at the opening of the festival. He told the audience, "Wales owed most of its musical knowledge to this country, and showed that the first pipers who performed in Wales came from Ireland." In a gesture of solidarity with the *feis ceoil*, he also announced that the national eisteddfod had decided to award a prize for the best piece of Irish music in its upcoming competitions.[103] The *Western Mail*, the largest Welsh daily newspaper, sent a special representative to report on the *feis ceoil*, and the *Irish Daily Independent* noted that the warm Welsh support for an Irish musical festival "further testifies to the spirit of friendly cooperation in which the Welsh people regard the Feis Ceoil, and their desire to draw together the Welsh and Irish festivals in bonds of national amity."[104]

Shortly afterwards, the national eisteddfod of Wales invited the general committee of the Feis Ceoil Association to attend the eisteddfod being held in Newport. A committee consisting of Edith Oldham, Joseph Seymour, and Edmund Fournier traveled to Wales and were initiated into the circle of the Gorsedd, a community of Welsh druids, as a gesture of friendship.[105] When Oldham returned to Ireland, she wrote an article for the *New Ireland Review* discussing the commonalities between the national eisteddfod and the *feis ceoil*. Oldham wrote that the happiness of a nation depended upon "the realization of its peculiar and individual ideals, as distinct from those of any other nation." She said that a fraternity "with such aims and aspirations has existed for some hundreds of years in Wales, and, by the holding of festivals, called Eisteddfodan, has endeavoured, and successfully endeavoured, to keep alive in the people of Wales the interest and enthusiasm in the higher things, such as poetry, music and art."[106] Oldham wrote that she hoped the *feis ceoil* would one day be as influential in Ireland as the eisteddfod was in Wales but observed that the program of events could not yet be as broad as the Welsh festival, as individual societies presided over the differing branches of the arts in Ireland. Indeed, the visit to Wales had shown Oldham just how much work would be required to put the *feis ceoil* in an equal footing with the eisteddfod: "We might as reasonably compare our small cathedral at Christ's Church with St. Peter's in Rome. . . . Compared to the Eisteddfod, [*the feis ceoil*] was as is the reed growing in the river bank to the steadfast oak."[107]

Although the scale of the eisteddfod dwarfed that of the *feis ceoil*, Oldham was confident that the quality of competition at the Irish festival was actually better. "This," she wrote, "I say unhesitatingly, with regard to all the instrumental solo competitions, but even in the choral competitions, in which lies, of course, the great strength of Welsh music." In concluding her article, Oldham declared that the purpose of the *feis ceoil* was to teach "a people to stand firmly on its own merits, not to imitate the fashions and ideas of another race, but to lift its head up among nations, as a self-respecting and self-reliant entity in the civilization of the world. . . . This is the true nationality."[108] Of course, there was a certain irony in Oldham highlighting the influence of the eisteddfod on the *feis ceoil* while urging her readers not to imitate other nations. But Oldham, like many Irish cultural enthusiasts, was worried about the anglicization of all aspects of Irish culture, and if preventing this required borrowing ideas from their fellow Celts, then that was acceptable as the lesser of two evils.

While the Feis Ceoil Association admired the musical delights of the national eisteddfod, the Gaelic League saw how this festival was used to promote Welsh literature and hoped to create their own literary fair to do something similar for the Irish language. A conference of Gaelic League branches held in Dublin in August 1896 passed a resolution "that an Oireachtas, or public assembly, on behalf of the Irish language, be held annually by the

Gaelic League, at which prizes would be offered for readings, recitation, songs, and dramatic sketches." There was no doubt that the resolution had been inspired by "the excellent results which our Welsh friends have attained in the cultivation of their literature by means of an annual Eisteddfod."[109] Father Eugene O'Growney, the renowned Irish-language scholar, was overjoyed that "at long last something is to be done towards having in Ireland an institution like the Welsh Eisteddfod." He wrote, "We know how much the Eisteddfod has done to promote the study of Welsh and the formation of a fine modern Welsh literature. With the present men in charge of the Gaelic League, the proposed *Oireachtas* will in three or four years produce wonderful results."[110] The Gaelic League made no secret of the fact that the *oireachtas* was modeled on the national eisteddfod. In inviting guests to the event, Douglas Hyde described it as "something on the lines of the Welsh Eistedfod [*sic*]."[111] One newspaper advertisement announced that the "Gaelic League will hold an Irish Literary Festival (On the lines of the Welsh Eisteddfod),"[112] while the Lee branch of the Gaelic League said the *oireachtas* was "a frank imitation of the Welsh Eisteddfod, even to the extent of combining a musical to a literary display."[113]

The first *oireachtas* in 1897 celebrated its connection with Wales by inviting delegates from the national eisteddfod to the opening ceremony. Among these delegates was Thomas, who was already in Dublin for the *feis ceoil*. In his opening speech, J. J. O'Meara, the chairman of the *oireachtas*, said, "It is encouraging to the members of the Gaelic League that they have the sympathy of those who have been foremost in the work in Wales." O'Meara urged the city of Dublin to give a hearty welcome to the Welsh, and said he trusted "that when they return they will be fortified with the opinion that they are not singular in their exertions, that here in Ireland the same old spirit exists amongst the Irish of the present day."[114]

The celebration of Ireland's Celtic connection with Wales was even more pronounced at the *oireachtas* in the years after the inaugural event. In 1899, the representatives of the national eisteddfod were welcomed onstage by the tune "March of the Men of Harlech," and several Welsh songs were sung throughout the program. One Welsh delegate, Edward Thomas, told those gathered that if Ireland "wanted any assistance from Welshmen in their organization they could rely on Wales to give them every possible help."[115] The English poet Lionel Johnson, who developed a deep interest in Ireland, offered the substantial prize of five pounds, five shillings, for the best Irish-language essay at the *oireachtas* on "What Wales Can Teach Ireland as to the Preservation of Celtic Speech."[116] The winning essay was written by Peter Toner MacGinley of Belfast. In many ways, MacGinley's essay echoed the ideas other Irish nationalists had about Wales. He wrote that "there is nothing connected with keeping a language alive that the Welsh can't teach the Irish, for they have kept their language alive, and we have nearly lost ours."[117] He highlighted the difficulties that faced the Welsh people in trying to preserve their language and praised their defiance in overcoming them and their refusal to abandon Welsh. As others before him had done, MacGinley urged the men and women of Ireland to be equally defiant: "Now that we see the amount that the Welsh did, we must ask what should we do to follow in their footsteps in relation to the language."[118] He maintained that it was important for the *oireachtas* and similar local festivals to continue in order to mirror the success of the Welsh eisteddfod. In particular, MacGinley hoped that Ireland would learn from the example of widespread Welsh literacy as a way of preserving its own national language. Commenting on the fact that over £200,000 was reportedly spent annually on Welsh reading material, MacGinley exclaimed, "Look how much money is spent on literature! When our people are willing to spend two hundred thousand pounds on Irish literature every year we will have won!"[119]

To Irish observers, the Welsh language thrived because the national eisteddfod promoted literacy in Welsh. In order to revive the Irish language, the Gaelic League wanted the *oireachtas* to similarly promote literacy in Irish. Hence a special emphasis was placed on literary competitions in the *oireachtas* as well as in the *feiseanna*, which were local cultural festivals modeled on the *oireachtas*. In an editorial in *Fáinne an Lae*, Bernard Doyle emphasized that the first step required to save Irish was to revive it as a literary language. He stated:

> In former times this was a matter of less consequence, for with fewer schools tradition had a greater influence over language than the written page. In our day that is all changed, for every civilized language is now written by the majority of the people and by all the children who speak it. The habit of writing is fatal to tradition, and the natural consequence of the change in our habits must be that the unwritten

language, if it should survive at all, must in a few short generations be degraded to the level of a mere gabble.[120]

These sentiments were widely held throughout the Gaelic League and explain why revivalists placed a strong emphasis on encouraging people to read and write in Irish. As one *oireachtas* advertisement declared, "Songs, pipes and harp music, recitations and speech-making will form part of the externals of the Festival, but its real work and purpose is to test the literary ability of Irish writers and to set the seal of its approval on the best works submitted."[121] This statement summed up the attitude of the executive committee of the Gaelic League toward its own events: music and singing helped make the festivals popular, but their purpose was to encourage literacy.

The Gaelic League had full control of the *oireachtas* and could mold it as it saw fit. Individual branches of the Gaelic League, however organized their own local cultural festivals, called *feiseanna*. Ensuring that the *feiseanna* were as dedicated to promoting Irish literacy as the *oireachtas* proved to be a challenge for the League's central body. Many of the League's branches were filled with members looking a social outlet rather than seeking to join a crusade to revive Irish. Hence local Gaelic League committees frequently organized *feiseanna* that were filled with the dancing and singing competitions that people took part in for entertainment, rather than offering a platform to cultivate new Gaelic literati. When Eoin MacNeill and other senior Gaelic League members attended a *feis* at Aghabullogue in Cork, they noted that "the proceedings at the Feis were not altogether satisfactory, the competitions were in dancing and singing only, without any trace of literary or written compositions." Worse again, as they saw it, many of the songs sung were ordinary English songs rather than traditional Irish airs. The visitors concluded that there was "much evidence of energy and enthusiasm, but little of an understanding of the movement."[122] A few months later, Patrick Pearse supported Eoin MacNeill's successful resolution that "it be a recommendation to branches, that in all future Feiseanna, held under the auspices of the Gaelic League, the highest prize be allotted to a written composition in Irish."[123]

For the most part, the local Gaelic League branches complied with this. The following decade saw the popularity of Irish cultural festivals increase around the country. A glance through the programs for the various *feise-anna* shows that while the top billing (and prize) were usually reserved for the literary competition, the programs tended to be dominated by dancing or musical events.[124] Thus efforts to use literature to promote the Irish language did little to stem the decline of Irish as a spoken language. Perhaps this is not surprising. The Welsh eisteddfod thrived because of the existence of a high rate of Welsh literacy—it did not, in and of itself, create literacy. Welsh children usually learned to read and write in Welsh at Sunday school.[125] Perhaps partly for this reason, to say nothing of the profound difference between learning a language at weekly meetings and using it in general society, efforts in Ireland to use cultural festivals to promote literacy in Irish met with only modest success.[126]

While the influence of Wales on many of the Gaelic League's initiatives is apparent, it seems that the very language employed by Irish cultural nationalists to distinguish those who were to be included and excluded from the nation also had some Welsh inspiration. A suggestion by a priest that Irish nationalists should mimic the Welsh distinction between "Welsh Wales" and "English Wales" led to the coining of the term *Irish Ireland*. The debate in the first decade of the twentieth century about the exact parameters of "Irish Ireland" marked a growing intolerance and militant spirit among Irish cultural nationalists. It is ironic that the term *Irish Ireland* was inspired by a Welsh influence, because as the *oireachtas* grew and as bilingual education was established in Ireland, Irish commentators, expressing a narrow-mindedness that was became increasingly evident in Irish nationalist circles, came to doubt whether Wales really had anything to offer Ireland and put forth the idea that it was rather the Welsh who should be learning from the Irish.

In 1899 Father Richard Henebry wrote to Eoin MacNeill to complain about the apathy of the Irish people toward the Irish language. He told MacNeill: "We must raise the cry of nationality therefore. Could they be persuaded of the truth? I think a good many of them, i.e. those who wish to be Irish or prefer to be Irish, would begin to study. The distinction like 'Welsh Wales and English Wales' has never been heard amongst us. I think it has done a vast deal of good for Welsh. Why not try to introduce it? Many of them would wince under 'English-Irish' and be spurred into action."[127] Henebry informed MacNeill that he wanted to offer some useful tips on managing the language movement because he had "learned a little about organizations, means of warfare, etc." during his time in England. Henebry's suggestion that the people of Ireland should be labeled on the basis of their allegiance, or aversion, to Gaelic culture seems to have been taken on board by MacNeill. Prior to Henebry's letter, the term *Irish Ireland* had not been used by Irish nationalists: a search of digitized Irish newspaper archives shows that the expression was almost nonexistent before 1899. Yet within a couple of years, it became the watchword of the Gaelic League and was used across the country as a congratulatory mark of "true" Irishness by those who saw Ireland's cultural distinctiveness being undermined by English influences. The most obvious example of this was D. P. Moran's newspaper, the *Leader*, which mercilessly castigated Irish people who were not Catholic or did not support Irish culture and Irish industry, labeling them "West Brits." Moran's *Philosophy of Irish Ireland*, published in 1905, made it clear that the clash between Irish Ireland and West Britain was a war of two civilizations in which no middle ground could be taken.[128] Of course, Henebry's letter did not create exclusionary nationalism in Ireland. But in offering up the example of "Welsh Wales," Henebry helped sharpen the language being used by orators and writers to cajole and shame the people of Ireland into accepting their vision of what an Irish nation should be.

It was within this context of a rigidly defined notion of Irish nationalism that the example of Wales was championed before the Irish people. Thus it is not surprising that Irish writers often presented an ambiguous message to their readers, at times celebrating the Celtic connection between the two peoples but also disparaging the Welsh for failing to express their nationhood as fully as they believed Ireland had done. Certainly the common Celtic heritage between the two countries was used as a way of encouraging the Irish people to emulate the Welsh in preserving their language, even before the formation of the Gaelic League. One writer who praised the success of the eisteddfod in Wales wrote that "those Celtic partiers [the Welsh] ought to teach a lesson to their Celtic kinsfolk in Erinn."[129] Isaac Butt, founder of the Irish home rule movement, lamented the attitude of the government toward the Irish language, noting that in making his way to London "we passed through another branch of the Celtic race, and there the Welsh tongue was patronized, was encouraged, was taught."[130] Michael Cusack, in demanding equal recognition for Irish and Welsh within the

British legal system, referred to the people of Wales as "our Welsh cousins."[131] When the Gaelic League was established in 1893, the *Freeman's Journal* believed it would do much good toward restoring Ireland's Celtic spirit, commenting:

> The object of the Gaelic League should be to substitute for this degrading and unnatural feeling, so foreign to the intellect and spiritual character of the Irish Celt, a just and natural pride in the possession of a language, which is at once, noble, powerful, and beautiful in itself, and the surest mark and best guarantee of national existence. In their efforts to re-Celtise the Celt the supporters of the movement will be borne up by many encouraging examples. The Welsh have made their language, once on the verge of extinction, a means of the highest mental culture, and a foremost factor in their national life, constituting it at the same time the ordinary means of intercourse throughout.[132]

It is not surprising that Gaelic Leaguers regularly commented on the Celtic connection between Ireland and Wales. Henry Murphy, in addressing a meeting at Clones, told his audience that the Welsh had saved their language and pointed out that "they in Ireland were another Celtic race, like the Welsh."[133] The noted journalist and politician Stephen Gwynn wrote that Wales was a fitting example for Ireland to follow in trying to revive its language because "Wales is, like Ireland, a Celtic country."[134]

At times, commentators could even collapse the national distinctions between the two countries. One correspondent to the *Nation* referred to the Welsh as "an offshoot of the Irish race."[135] Canon William Shinkwin told the Bandon branch of the Gaelic League that the Welsh people were "akin to the Irish" and that their "language is also akin to the Irish."[136] The journalist Richard Kelly, on visiting Wales, spoke of the Welsh and Irish as branches of "the vigorous and intelligent Gaelic race."[137] Meanwhile, in telling the story of the Welsh language to a crowd of Irish emigrants in Omaha, Nebraska, one Irish priest emphasized that the Welsh were the Gaelic descendants of the Irish by saying, "The Welsh Gaels, our Kymric brethren, began a hundred years ago this holy movement. To-day they have their annual meetings and their printed books, their papers and their reviews, and the tongue of the Gael Kymry is an honorable one on the literary markets of the world."[138] Hence, in depicting the Welsh as descendants of the Irish, writers were not only asking their readers to match the cultural achievements of the Welsh but also inviting them to bask in their success by virtue of their shared blood relationship.

Yet despite accepting the Welsh as ethnic relatives, some Irish observers found that Wales fell dismally short in terms of expressing its national identity in comparison with Ireland. Amid the political turmoil created by the Irish demand for home rule in the late nineteenth century, the lack of a similar demand from Wales was noticeable to those who measured nationhood solely in terms of political expression. In short, because the Welsh did not demand political autonomy as the Irish did, some questioned their right to be called a nation. William Patrick Ryan wrote that he did not believe that "Welsh nationality in the true sense is yet half what it ought to be. Wales . . . is not by any means so national as Belgium, or Bulgaria, or Bohemia. . . . We must hope for the best in the wide national sphere."[139] In his essay on what Wales could teach Ireland in terms of language, Peter MacGinley stated that while the Welsh had sovereignty they were not a sovereign people and that, unlike Ireland, Wales was indistinguishably part of England.[140] The greater vitality of the Welsh language did not prevent Irish commentators from asserting that Ireland was more of a nation than Wales. In Westminster, Willie Redmond, a Home Rule Party MP, said he was "rather amused to hear one of the Welsh members declare that the nationality prevailing in Wales amongst the people was superior to that prevailing in Ireland."[141] Another correspondent wrote that while "the Welsh have stuck steadfastly to the grand old Celtic tongue, they appear at present to have no distinctive nationality among them."[142] A Mr. M. Keating, writing to *An Claidheamh Soluis* about the need to politicize the Gaelic League, stated, "To assert that the existence of a language and literature is in itself sufficient to constitute a Nation is not true, because the Welsh people have a language almost entirely used in commerce, social intercourse, the pulpit, the press, and in public life; yet their highest instinct of National politics is to send a Radical to Westminster who may one day achieve the dignity of becoming an understrapper in a Liberal Government."[143]

Indeed, although the Welsh had preserved their national language far better than the Irish had, many jingoistic Irish writers noted that Welsh was less "pure" than Irish as a true Celtic language. Father Henebry warned Eoin

MacNeill that more attention had to be paid to the standard of Irish being printed by the Gaelic League because "if not then we shall hereafter have a dialect as they have in Wales—simply English with Welsh words."[144] The *Connaught Telegraph* commented in 1904 that "the Welsh language, though still purely Celtic, has become very much corrupted in the course of the ages."[145] Despite its declining linguistic relevance, Irish enthusiasts pointed out that philologists recognized "Irish as the leading Celtic language. It is the best preserved, the most capable and expressive, the most copious, the most cultivated, and endowed with the best and most abundant literature."[146] The Reverend Dr. Shahnan of the Catholic University of America referred to Ireland as "the home of the principal Celtic tongue."[147] Father James McNamee told a public meeting at Clones that "of the Celtic languages the most ancient referred to by the modern scholars is the Irish language. . . . The ancient Celtic alone remained almost in its original purity in modern Irish."[148] Occasionally, even the sounds of the Welsh language were sneered at. In the Gaelic League notes section of the *Anglo-Celt* newspaper the author referred to Machynlleth as "the unpronounceable village in Wales."[149] This particular League member apparently didn't appreciate the irony of his dismissive and Anglocentric attitude toward Welsh orthography, given that English people would probably express similar sentiments about Irish language place-names.

To some, the size of Wales also seemed to be a factor against considering the country a "real" nation like Ireland. One parish priest told a meeting of the Gaelic League that Wales was nothing more than "a portion of England."[150] Stephen Brown, after praising the ability of the Welsh to cling to their language, stated to an audience at Naas that "they in Ireland had far more reason to be proud of their ancient language than the Welsh people (hear, hear). Wales was nothing more than a Principality, but Ireland was a nation and is still a nation (applause)."[151] Even those who sought to praise the Welsh could not always contain a somewhat condescending attitude toward them. An article in *An Claidheamh Soluis* that urged the Irish to love their language as the Welsh did referred to Wales as a "tírín."[152] By adding the diminutive *ín* to the Irish word for country (*tír*), the writer implied that Wales was something of an infant nation and had not yet matured to full nationality as Ireland had. This view was no doubt owing to the much smaller size of Wales, as well as the lack of Welsh clamor for political autonomy. Therefore, while cultural nationalists admired the tenacity of the Welsh in maintaining their language, most of them were convinced that, in terms of culture and politics, Ireland was the superior Celtic nation.

Hence, as the Gaelic League grew in the early twentieth century, some members sought to play down the Welsh inspiration in the formation of the *feis ceoil* and the *oireachtas*. Within two years of the first *feis ceoil*, Edward Martyn wrote in the 1899 program notes that the event was successful because "its roots are in no foreign soils or systems, but in the ancient civilization and ancient art of Ireland. This is the secret of its true nationality. This will be the pledge of its lasting success."[153] Since the *feis ceoil* had been marketed as an Irish eisteddfod, Martyn's claim that it had no connection to foreign influences was extraordinary. But it demonstrates one of the internal tensions within the Irish cultural movement: a desire to celebrate Ireland's shared Celtic heritage while buttressing Ireland's claim to nationhood by denying that its distinct culture was based on any influences from outside the island.

Some insisted that Ireland had not borrowed the idea of the eisteddfod from Wales but rather Wales had borrowed it from Ireland. When Edith Oldham published her article crediting the Welsh inspiration for the *feis ceoil*, William Grattan Flood responded that she had ignored "how much Wales is indebted to Ireland for her Eisteddfodan." Grattan Flood claimed that the history of the eisteddfod dated back to the eleventh century when the Welsh king Gruffydd ap Cynan, who had been born and raised in Ireland, had brought Irish musicians and poets to Wales to replicate the musical festivals of Ireland. As a result of this, all Welsh music, as well as the Welsh standards for poetic meter and musical orchestration, came from Ireland, according to Grattan Flood.[154] Within a few years, others came forward to also deny that the *oireachtas* had really been modeled on the Welsh eisteddfod. In 1906 Pierce Beazley published an article to commemorate the ten-year anniversary of the formation of the *oireachtas*. Despite acknowledging that the *oireachtas* had been advertised as a festival "on the lines of the Welsh Eisteddfod," Beazley sought to play down the extent to which the Gaelic League had copied the Welsh festival. He wrote that "at no time did the Oireachtas really correspond to the Welsh Eisteddfod."[155] Beazley repeated the claim made by Grattan Flood on the origins of the eisteddfod as a way of underplaying any cultural debt that Ireland might have owed to

the Welsh institution. The basis for Beazley's claim was that the bardic ceremonies and picturesque traditional features had "nothing in common with
the essentially modern and practical character of the Oireachtas."

Certainly the Gaelic League did not include elaborate ceremonies as
part of the *oireachtas*, but the *oireachtas* remained a literary competition
that bore a striking similarity to the national eisteddfod. Indeed, one Welsh
cultural activist, Miss Mallt Williams, suggested that the *oireachtas* might
be a superior version of the national eisteddfod. Williams argued that the
eisteddfod was not doing enough to promote a Welsh national spirit when
compared to the *oireachtas*. Patrick Pearse, as editor of *An Claidheamh
Soluis*, noted that "Wales, too, has lessons to learn from Ireland."[156] Thus,
in less than a decade, the former clamor to emulate the success of the Welsh
festivals was being replaced by a desire to minimize the Welsh contribution
to Irish cultural nationalism. Ironically, as cultural nationalists gained confidence from their ability to emulate the Welsh and establish their own festivals, their willingness to acknowledge any Welsh influence declined, to be
replaced by a sense that the Welsh, even when it came to protecting their
traditional culture, were lagging behind the efforts of the Irish.

One of the best examples of this transition can be seen in the Gaelic
League's efforts to introduce bilingual education in Irish-speaking areas,
along the lines they believed already existed in Welsh-speaking Wales. For
much of the nineteenth century, Welsh children, many of them monoglot
Welsh speakers, had been educated solely in English. But after a campaign
organized by the Society for the Utilization of Welsh in Education, the
Education Committee of the Privy Council decided in 1890 to offer a financial incentive for schools to teach Welsh grammar.[157] While these gains
were modest, in that no school was required to use Welsh, members of the
newly formed Gaelic League told Irish audiences of the great concessions
made for Welsh speakers in education and argued that Irish speakers should
receive similar treatment. Irish cultural activists wanted to see the Irish language given a stronger footing in education because they believed that the
spread of English-medium schools had been responsible for the decline of
Irish. Maurice Healy, MP, told an audience in Cork that "the destruction
of Irish among the juvenile population" had arisen because teachers were
not permitted to use the language in the classroom.[158] Others argued that a
bilingual education was essential, not to preserve the language as such, but

to ensure that monoglot Irish children would not be failed by the education system as a result of being taught only through English.

One Gaelic League member wrote to the *Freeman's Journal* to complain "that the neglect of the Irish language in education has retarded and nullified those advantages for a large portion of the people, and that this evil result is in daily operation at present." In contrast, he noted, Welsh children who had been educated bilingually excelled in comparison to those educated only through English.[159] Occasionally, some warned that bilingual education might not be all it seemed in Wales and that its relevance to the struggle to revive Irish was negligible. Peter Toner MacGinley pointed out that many in Ireland believed Irish would die out unless introduced into schools but that in Wales, despite Welsh being ignored in schools for so long, the language still flourished.[160] But others saw in the Welsh system of education the perfect model for schooling in Ireland. Patrick Pearse, who visited Wales in 1899, wrote that those who opposed the introduction of Irish into the classroom needed only to look to Wales to see the practical utility of making a language a mandatory feature of the education system. He noted that in Cardiff, a cosmopolitan town where Welsh was very much a minority language, the citizens had voted by a large majority to make Welsh a regular part of the curriculum. He observed that the children in the school he visited appeared to be quite proficient in the tongue, though none of them spoke Welsh at home. Mr. J. J. Jackson, a member of the Cardiff School Board, told Pearse that the businessmen of Cardiff appreciated the advantages of having a bilingual workforce and hence wholeheartedly approved of the school board's measures. Given that similar suggestions by the Gaelic League had been dismissed as unrealistic, Pearse asked, "Which are the real practical men, and which are the dreamers? We, who are the most backboneless, and worst educated community in Europe, or the hard headed, clear-sighted Cardiffians, who have made the name of their town the synonym of all that is enlightened, prosperous, and go-ahead?"[161]

The core argument put forward by members of the Gaelic League for the introduction of bilingual education in Ireland was that they were simply asking for the same support given to Welsh. Joseph Carroll, a member of the Gaelic League branch in Warrenpoint, stated at a public meeting, "We urge upon the Commissioners of National Education, Ireland, that a system of bilingual education be introduced into the National Schools under their control in the Irish-speaking districts of this country, similar to that adopted in Wales with such eminently satisfactory results."[162] When an education bill for Ireland was introduced in 1900 without any provision for bilingual instruction, Irish-language supporters were deeply dismayed. Douglas Hyde wrote to the national education commissioners: "The desire of the people for a particular educational reform (a reform already conceded with the very best possible results to Wales) has been put forward with perfect propriety and absolute unanimity. . . . The demand thus put forward could not, and would not, be refused in any self-governing country in the world. It has not been refused in Wales. . . . We will be satisfied with absolutely no jot less than what Wales possesses already."[163]

This campaign eventually succeeded: a bilingual program was introduced into schools in Irish-speaking areas in 1904. Within a few years, some commentators began trumpeting the superiority of Irish bilingual education in comparison to the Welsh system. One visitor to Wales poured scorn on the idea that Ireland had anything to learn from the example of Welsh education. Aoidhmín Mac Gréagóir lived in Wales for a number of months in 1908 and noted that "Welsh teaching in Welsh primary schools cannot compare in any way with Irish bilingual schools, in efficiency, method, or results." He also observed that Welsh was almost nonexistent in intermediate education and that the University of Wales catered more to English students than to those who wanted to study Welsh.[164] Agnes O'Farrelly had a similar report on the state of education in Wales. She visited a number of primary schools in Wales and observed that "there is no such thing as a system of bi-lingual teaching, as we conceive it, at work in the Welsh schools. The ordinary subjects of the curriculum are taught through English in almost every case, and this notwithstanding the fact that the overwhelming majority of the children are Welsh-speaking."[165] She reported that while the Welsh had preserved their language at home, "they have not yet arrived in that country at as clear a conception of school-work on bi-lingual lines as that on which the work of the Gaelic League is based."

The notion that Ireland was pulling ahead of Wales in terms of the role the indigenous language played in education was given further credence with the formation of the National University of Ireland in 1908. A lengthy debate ensued about the suggestion that students should be allowed to enroll at the university only after passing an Irish-language exam. Those who were opposed to this measure pointed out that not even the University of Wales made such a demand upon its students. Not surprisingly, the response from some language activists was that this highlighted the failings of higher education in Wales. One priest, addressing a public meeting in Limerick, declared that it "was said that there was a National University in Wales, and that Welsh was not an essential subject. Then it was not a National University."[166] Welsh opinion on how Ireland could best preserve its language was no longer as highly valued as it had once been. In 1909, Sir Harry Reichel of the University College of North Wales wrote that, while he wished to see the Irish language prosper, he believed that a mandatory Irish exam for entrance to the National University would ultimately be harmful for the revival efforts.[167] Such opinions were not well received. Agnes O'Farrelly wondered, "Are we to take serious the advice of *foreign* educationists as to our action with regard to Irish in the new Universities? . . . We question the value of outside opinion."[168] In many ways, this comment epitomized the declining value that Irish cultural nationalists placed on learning lessons about nationhood from Wales. When the Welsh offered inspiration they were hailed as Celtic cousins, but they could be dismissed as "foreign" when their advice was out of sync with the vision Irish nationalists were trying to achieve for their country. Although ideas about Welsh nationhood were always somewhat mixed, there was a noticeable trend away from admiration of the Welsh in the late nineteenth century toward a feeling of Irish superiority in the early twentieth century. As this transition occurred, the Welsh seemed less a nation to be admired and more a misguided people to be pitied for flacking the strong nationalistic tendencies held by the Irish.

For much of the second half of the nineteenth century, the efforts of the Welsh to preserve their language and customs resonated with Irish observers because they saw in Wales a mirror image of their own struggle, namely a fight to retain their national identity in the face of growing anglicization. But by the beginning of the second decade of the twentieth century, shifting political currents in the United Kingdom caused Irish nationalists to view Wales less as a Celtic country battling the influence of perfidious Albion and more as an integral part of the British state. The rise of David Lloyd George to become chancellor of the exchequer was one reason for this. Once a prominent Welsh politician, indeed, a native Welsh speaker, was at the forefront of the Liberal government, it became difficult to view the Welsh as an ostracized minority within Britain. The reestablishment of the investiture ceremony for the Prince of Wales in 1911 further solidified the perception of the Welsh nation as an equal partner within the United Kingdom and British Empire. At Lloyd George's suggestion, Prince Edward was invested as Prince of Wales at Caernarfon Castle amid elaborate proceedings involving poems and songs in the Welsh language, with Lloyd George even teaching Edward some Welsh to use in the ceremony.[169] Thus Welsh culture had been formally embraced by the monarchy, and the expression of a distinct Welsh identity could now fit comfortably into a wider sense of Britishness. Meanwhile the passing of a Home Rule Bill for Ireland in 1912 meant that Irish nationhood had finally found a political expression. At the very moment that the Welsh nation affirmed its position at the heart of the empire, the Irish highlighted their distinctiveness in the United Kingdom through receiving a measure of self-government. Despite frequent comments to the contrary, political autonomy had always held more appeal to the Irish masses than cultural uniqueness, and in their eyes the first true measure of a nation was the control it exerted over its own affairs. The Welsh achievement of preserving their language now paled in comparison to the Irish achievement of attaining home rule. Indeed, Irish activists believed that a parliament in Dublin would be of immeasurable help in reviving the language, and hence the example of Wales in this regard became less relevant. To many in Ireland, then, it seemed rather that the Welsh should be looking to Ireland to learn how to develop a pure national spirit.

Nevertheless, the influence of the Welsh example on the cultural nationalist movement in Ireland should not be understated. The national eisteddfod directly inspired the development of the *feis ceoil* and the *oireachtas*, two festivals that restored a certain amount of pride in Irish culture and customs and that continue to flourish today. The vast quantity of Welsh printing material was the envy of Irish-language enthusiasts and convinced many that their language could not be successfully preserved unless Irish was being regularly printed and read. As a result, cultural nationalists placed a special emphasis on reading and writing in Irish, and, with the aid of competitions held at the *oireachtas* and local *feiseanna*, a modern Irish-language literature was born. The rights attained by Welsh speakers from local authorities encouraged Irish-language supporters to demand equal treatment for Irish speakers, particularly the extension of bilingual education to the Irish Gaeltacht. But the Welsh nation's most important influence was to offer a vision to Irish nationalists of what was possible in Ireland, namely the revival of Irish as the lingua franca of the country. It was not relevant that Welsh had never sunk to the depths Irish had, or that it was not as prevalent in Wales as commentators claimed. What mattered was that Irish-language supporters believed that Welsh had been saved from the abyss and that by extension such salvation could be achieved for Irish. Certainly, cultural nationalists fell short in their goal of making Irish the primary language of Ireland. But their belief, fueled by the Welsh precedent, that Ireland could be Gaelic once more proved to be the foundation upon which the modern Irish state was built.

CHAPTER 3

CELTS, CATHOLICS, CRIMINALS

Irish nationalists were not alone in looking across the Irish Sea in the nineteenth century to see what changes could be made to improve the character of their nation. Welsh nationalists also wondered if Wales would be better served by adopting the political and social agitation of their Irish counterparts. For much of the nineteenth century, the Welsh public had a generally negative impression of Ireland. Unflattering depictions of the Irish people were common in the Welsh press. For example, the *North Wales Chronicle* printed the following article in 1877:

> Another good typical instance of Irish wit has never to my knowledge been properly recorded. A certain Pat Callaghan had stolen and eventually killed and eaten a pig belonging to Widow Maloney. On hearing of his crime, his priest severely rebuked the offender, and set before him a fearful picture of the Judgment Day. "And there'll be the Judge in front, and to one side the Widow Maloney, and the pig in the middle, and you foreninst [*sic*] her, and what will ye say then, Pat Callaghan?" "Did yer Reverence say the pig would be to the fore?" "Well, yes, sure it will be—to testify agin ye [*sic*]—and what will you have to say for yourself?" "I'll say, plaze your Reverence, 'Widow Maloney, take your pig!'"[1]

In many ways, this short account perfectly encapsulates the general impression that the Welsh public had of Ireland and Irish people. Many Welsh people viewed the Irish as violent criminals, capable of any kind of lawlessness, in stark contrast to the law-abiding people of Wales. Ireland was seen as a land riddled with interfering priests, which only further prompted the largely Nonconformist population of Wales to perceive the Irish with disdain and suspicion. Yet, like Pat Callaghan, the Irish had shown themselves capable of defying authority in their own self-interest. Disobedient Ireland appeared to be rewarded with regular legislation to address its concerns, while Wales was largely ignored in Westminster. The Irish home rule movement in particular attracted attention in the Principality and helped shape an emerging political nationalist consciousness in Wales. As the Irish question came to dominate British politics, Welsh nationalists were excited at the possibility of creating their own political space, as the Irish had, within the United Kingdom. However, they wrestled with the question of how best to do this, because adopting Irish objectives and tactics threatened to undermine the foundation upon which their sense of Welshness was constructed.

The process by which one nationalist movement models itself upon the example of another has been an important element in the mobilization of ethnic groups the world over.[2] In this regard, the efforts of Irish nationalists to achieve a measure of self-rule from Britain served as an inspiration to other ethnic and nationalist groups. In the second decade of the twentieth century, African American leaders observed the nature of Ireland's struggle with Britain, hoping to learn lessons that might help further their own cause. Hubert Harrison, who founded the Liberty League, wrote in 1917 that "the new Negro race in America will not achieve political self-respect until it is in a position to organize itself as a politically independent party and follow the example of the Irish Home Rulers. This is what will happen in American politics." He called on black voters to "to disclaim allegiance to any and all political parties; to organize their votes independently, and by swinging them in their own interest, to play the same part which the Irish Home Rule party played in British politics."[3] Marcus Garvey, the creator of the "Back to Africa" movement and founder of the Universal Negro Improvement Association (UNIA), was also influenced by Irish political nationalism. Garvey insisted that all branches of the UNIA name their meeting place Liberty Hall, after the building in Dublin from which the Easter Rising had been launched. He insisted that the color green be part of the UNIA's flag, to show sympathy for the Irish freedom movement, and he regularly told meetings of his organization, "I would like to create an interest, create love in your breast for the native land, just as the Irishman born in this country loves Ireland as he loves no other place."[4] In India, the large number of Irish civil servants "stimulated and inspired Indian nationalism," and Annie Besant founded an Indian Home Rule League in 1916.[5]

In some regards, political advocates in Wales in the nineteenth century were similar to other, later, activists around the world in looking to Ireland for inspiration in achieving their own ideals. According to David Howell, "The Welsh radical movement was greatly stimulated by the Irish example, the newspapers of the late nineteenth century facilitating the spread of knowledge of Irish affairs."[6] As the Home Rule Party gained government attention for Ireland, political and social campaigners in Wales increasingly demanded that their country be recognized as a political entity separate from England. Legally, Wales had been indistinguishable from England since 1542, but as unique legislation was proposed to remedy Irish woes, many Welsh people called for similar accommodations for their country. The three main demands of Welsh nationalists, namely disestablishment of the Anglican Church, land reform, and a measure of local government, all mirrored major contemporary campaigns in Ireland.

Yet Welsh radicals differed from other international activists who admired various Irish movements from a distance, in that they had a great deal of personal experience with Irish people. A large number of Irish emigrants arrived in Wales during the nineteenth century, and tensions between them and the Welsh flared from time to time.[7] Furthermore, the Irish often appeared to be antagonistic toward the British state, a state that most Welsh people were proud to be associated with. While Irish cultural nationalists, most of whom had little experience or in-depth knowledge of Wales, placed the Welsh people on a pedestal for Irish-language enthusiasts to emulate, Welsh politicians were hesitant to do this with regard to Ireland. Knowledge of Irish affairs coupled with regular interactions with Irish immigrants meant that the Welsh population would not have been receptive to a romantic depiction of Irish struggles as motivation for their own assertion of political rights. As a result, a certain amount of tension developed within

Welsh radical circles as reformers sought to follow the Irish example in addressing Welsh problems while also reassuring their supporters that they were not in danger of becoming as Irish as the Irish themselves.

In general, the Welsh population had a very negative view of Ireland in the mid-nineteenth century. The arrival of poor Irish migrants to Wales, coupled with the Fenian bombings in 1867 and regular newspaper reports of violence in the Irish countryside, only entrenched the hostile attitude among the Welsh. This hostility did not begin to subside until the 1880s, when the Liberal Party, led by William Gladstone, championed the cause of Irish reform. As Welsh commentators and politicians displayed increased sympathy for the Irish struggle, they made comparisons between Ireland and the Principality, and some voiced the idea that the Welsh could learn from the Irish to the benefit of their own country. Yet even as Welsh perceptions of Ireland softened, the image of the Irish as violent, emotional troublemakers never fully disappeared, and those who were against social and political reform in Wales were always quick to charge their opponents with importing Irish tactics.

The famous Welsh bard Iolo Morganwg wrote in 1799 that "an Irishman's loves are three: violence, deception and poetry."[8] Throughout the nineteenth century, Welsh books and newspapers reinforced the idea that the Irish were hotheaded, violent vagabonds, lacking in basic human empathy for those they attacked. Another bard, Ieuan Gwynedd, wrote that Irishmen were as deceptive as devils. He declared that the Irish could switch from kindness to savagery in an instant: "Shoot a man! Bless you! What man is shot by an Irishman? He shoots his best neighbor seven times over, if he is ordered by some secret murder club, and he laughs having understood he mistook his prey in the end."[9] The *Baner ac Amserau Cymru* jeered when an Irish contingent arrived in Rome in 1860 to defend the city from the forces of Giuseppe Garibaldi: "Patrick did not care with who, nor why, nor where, the fight—fighting was his specialty! . . . On the first day of the arrival of the Irish volunteers . . . they appeared in endless riots. . . . Their proximity to the chair of Peter, had not tamed their turbulent spirits."[10] As rural unrest escalated in Ireland in the 1870s and 1880s, reports about the violent Irish increased in Wales. One writer for *Y Goleuad* said that the Irishman "is born to trouble like the sparks fly upward. . . . This most stubborn, ignorant creature is the most troublesome in all of the British Empire."[11]

Another writer, using the pseudonym "WFT," wrote in the *Red Dragon* that the chief characteristic of the Irishman was his "glorious uncertainty." "WFT" adapted Francois I's famous quote about women to highlight the untrustworthy nature of the Irish, writing, "Pat is fickle, and whoever trusts him is a fool."[12] "WFT" embellished the idea of the Irishman as inhuman, declaring, "If he cannot pay his rent he shoots his landlord instead of himself. There is a great deal of human nature in him, in a state of suspension, however, rather than solution." He further sarcastically highlighted the violence rampant in the Irish countryside by saying, "At least once a year he [the Irishman] has to decide a question which calls for the exercise of the highest judicial qualities. He must determine whether it is better to kill the pig to pay the rent, or to kill the landlord in order not to have to pay the rent."[13] One cartoon in the *Red Dragon* showed a picture of a stereotypical Irishman, clutching his shillelagh with a menacing look, under the title "Passionately Patriotic Patlander."[14] Welsh apologists for Irish agitation were few and far between, although one interesting effort was made to explain this violence as a Celtic tradition. The *Cymru Fydd* journal declared that while burning barns, plows, and hedges was illegal under English law it was a "legal method of reclaiming the land according to the law of the Celt. If a Celt goes a year and a day without burning the house and plow of someone on the land of his father, he has lost his right to that land."[15]

Many in Wales attributed the blame for the violence in Ireland not to the common man but to political leaders like Charles Stuart Parnell and Joseph Biggar, who they believed were whipping the Irish peasants into a frenzy for their own financial and political gain. One observer noted that those at the forefront of Irish agitation were "villains slyly fattening themselves upon an absurd, easily influenced nation." Left alone, the Irish peasant was of good character, and "the undeniable truth about the Irishman is, if he was not associating with unscrupulous contemptible fellows, professing love to him, but doing their best to destroy his character and his condition, he would be as good a member of the empire as the Welshmen or the Scot."[16] Another journalist, in an article entitled "The Irishman, His Field, and His Pig," similarly claimed that Irish turmoil stemmed directly from the manipulation of the peasantry. The trouble with the Irish peasant, he said, was "his willingness to listen, and to trust in close and disingenuous friends." The incendiary remarks of Parnell and John Dillon had made the Irishman's "condition more dissatisfied, and causing him to be . . . becoming every day more unmanageable. He is by nature tender—easily impressed, upset, and brought to a point of extreme stubbornness." As a result, the "law of the cudgel" ruled in Ireland and would continue as long as Irish leaders agitated "without cause to every type of villainy."[17]

Others imagined that priests were responsible for stirring the passions of the volatile Irish peasant. One Irish landlord, who was of Welsh descent, insisted that his family had been harassed by locals who were goaded into action by their parish priest. For the *Western Mail* this was "a typical example of the way in which Irish agitation was fostered."[18] Some in Wales believed the Irish problem stemmed from the failure of the population to identify those responsible for crime and violence. Articles in *Y Goleuad* highlighted that witnesses could never be found to prosecute those responsible for murderous attacks. According to the paper, it did not matter whether this was a result of "sympathy with the crimes, or fear of the perpetrators of the case. One is the same as the other in showing the low state of morality of society, and only a country of people who are too cowardly to go against murderers, could to some degree sympathize with their actions."[19]

As well as fearing the apparent lawlessness and chaos in Ireland, many Welsh observers were suspicious of the Irish on account of their Catholicism. Anti-Catholic sentiment had a long history in Wales. Gwyn Williams writes that "the pathological hatred of Catholicism, both in itself and in the tyranny it was taken to embody, rooted itself in Welsh Anglicanism and in the Dissent which later displaced it. The Irish, perceived as a quasi-permanent threat from Counter-Reformation Europe, were a human vehicle for this menace."[20] Thus some in Wales attributed the problems of Ireland to the faith of the majority of the people. *Y Goleuad* noted that the main problem with the Irishman was "the degrading influence, mentally, morally and religiously, of the religion he was raised through. When a man's religion demands he give up his personal opinion to any infallible authority, whomsoever outside of God himself, he is bound to begin a course of mental and moral deterioration." Catholicism, in the eyes of the writer, bred foolish superstitions among the Irish, so if peace was to be restored in the country, "the Irishman must be weaned from the papacy."[21] Other commentators in Wales perceived efforts to bring relief to Ireland as a cover for Catholic attempts to usurp Parliament. The *Baner* castigated efforts by Irish MPs to receive government funding for a Catholic university in Ireland: under no circumstances, the paper maintained, should government money ever be given to a Catholic institution, and it proclaimed in capital letters, "The Catholics are controlling the parliament of Great Britain already."[22]

Another writer claimed that the large numbers of Irish Catholics serving in the army were helping spread Catholicism across the British Empire. In short, the Irish, as agents of the pope, were manipulating the British state to further a Catholic agenda. Hence "while the Pope with all his energy aims to overturn Protestant and free institutions, he is making the greatest use possible of the most Protestant and Liberal country in the world to do it." The writer asked, "Is Protestantism sleeping?"[23] However, with the Liberal Party adopting a more sympathetic attitude toward Ireland in the 1880s, Nonconformist ministers followed suit, with some observers in Wales turning a blind eye to the religion of the Irish peasantry in order to highlight their economic and social suffering. When the Reverend Dr. Lynd, an Irish Presbyterian minister, sought support from the General Assembly of Welsh Methodists against Irish home rule in 1890, he found little was forthcoming. His claim that home rule would mean a Catholic tyranny in Ireland was met with complete silence. One reporter watching Lynd's speech noted that in the recent past his words would have evoked an enthusiastic, martial response. Now, the reporter lamented, "Roman Catholicism has become tolerable, nay, loveable, in the estimation of the Welsh political Nonconformist, and declamations against the 'prostitutions of Babylon' and the 'infernal mark of the Beast' have given way to complimentary references to the 'patience of the Irish Catholics' and the 'heroic sufferings of a downtrodden people.'"[24]

Within this context of anti-Irish and anti-Catholic sentiment in Wales in the nineteenth century, Welsh commentators came to see that, for all the problems that Ireland suffered, its status as a political entity within the United Kingdom also brought benefits that were not extended to Wales. The Welsh people had long taken pride in their language, which marked them out as a cultural nation distinct from England. However, the concept of Wales as a political nation, one entitled to separate legislation and administration from England, had few adherents. As late as 1886, one Welsh bishop claimed that Wales was "nothing more than a geographic expression," while the *Encyclopaedia Britannica* famously had the entry "For Wales, see England."[25] As the Irish question came to dominate British politics in the 1870s and 1880s, various administrations drafted legislation dealing solely with Ireland, in the hope of resolving social and economic unrest in the country. Following the Irish example, Welsh leaders began demanding recognition of their own political distinctiveness, seeking laws to address specific Welsh problems. The passing of the Sunday Closing Bill in 1881 marked the first time in over three hundred years that legislation had been created for Wales alone, recognizing the separate political character of the country. As calls for Irish home rule grew louder in the 1880s, so too did demands for more legislation to deal with Welsh issues, increasingly on national grounds rather than liberal principles.[26] The Irish example, coupled with a broadening of the franchise in 1867 and 1884, allowed, in the words of Kenneth Morgan, for "the emergence of a distinctly Welsh 'radical' style of politics, less bitter and less strident than the nationalist movement in Ireland, but in its quieter fashion perhaps the more effective."[27]

The catalyst for Welsh aspirations to attain a political distinctness similar to Ireland's came with the disestablishment of the Anglican Church in Ireland in 1869. The British Anti State Church Association, renamed the Liberation Society in 1853, had campaigned for the disestablishment of the church in Britain. From 1862, the Liberation Society focused on disestablishing the church in Ireland first, believing this was more likely to succeed than universal disestablishment. In Wales, where a large majority of the population identified as Nonconformist, the issue attracted great interest, as the tithe paid to the Anglican Church was deeply resented. In 1868, with the Liberal Party supporting Irish disestablishment, a general election was held. Viewing the election as a referendum on disestablishment, the Welsh electorate gave twenty-three out of thirty-three seats to the Liberal Party, who brought in legislation for Irish disestablishment.[28] With the Irish precedent set, Welsh Nonconformists hoped that the church would be generally disestablished in Britain. Yet as it became apparent that this would be unlikely, the idea of disestablishment for Wales alone gained popularity. The Welsh public rejected the claim that Ireland was a unique case, and slowly the demand for Welsh disestablishment, in line with what had been granted to Ireland, grew.[29]

When a measure for Welsh disestablishment was defeated at Westminster in 1870, with Gladstone among its opponents, many in Wales were disgusted at receiving different treatment from Ireland. In a letter to the editor of the *Baner*, a Mr. R. Jones of Bethesda rubbished the claims that there could be no Welsh disestablishment. He wrote, "I do not understand the expression 'There is no such thing as a Welsh Church. There is such a thing as an Irish Church.' I thought the Anglican Church was in Ireland as good as in Wales."[30] P. M. H. Bell notes that "Disestablishment in Ireland gave an impulse to a movement for Disestablishment in Wales, but . . . the conditions in which such a success was possible came about in the dozen years between 1880 and 1892."[31] As home rule became the burning issue in Ireland, Welsh ministers and politicians declared that the burden of supporting the Anglican Church was the great injustice under which Wales toiled. Arthur Humphreys-Owen, chairman of the North Wales Liberal Federation, said that "what the land is to Ireland, the Establishment is to Wales." Stuart Rendel, the MP for Montgomeryshire, declared that the Anglican Church was the Dublin Castle of Wales.[32] The nationalist *Cymru Fydd* proclaimed that the established church "in Wales is as great an anomaly and as great an injustice as that of Ireland was, and every plea for Disestablishment on the other side of the Irish Channel is an argument for the application of the same measure of equality and justice to the Principality."[33]

Many in Wales were infuriated by those who had supported Irish disestablishment but did not wish to see a Welsh equivalent passed. In a pamphlet advocating Welsh disestablishment, R. H. Morgan pointed out that those who supported Irish disestablishment did so because "they held that the Established Church in Ireland was a great practical evil." "Thus," Morgan responded, "the point at issue is yielded. What we insist upon, is that the Established Church in Wales 'is a great practical evil.'"[34] Another Liberal MP, George Osborne Morgan, told a cheering crowd in Chester that "the Church of Ireland was never so unpopular as the Church in Wales is today."[35] As Welsh protesters clashed repeatedly with police in the late 1880s over having to pay the tithe, at least one commentator cautioned that achieving disestablishment would not cure all Welsh woes. R. J. Derfel asked how much improvement there would be in the lives of ordinary Welsh men and women if the church was disestablished. "Not a single bit. Ireland is without the Anglican Church, and without the tithe, but not without its poverty."[36] Nevertheless, the disestablishment of the Anglican Church in Ireland was an important moment in the awakening of Welsh political consciousness. While Welsh disestablishment did not come about until 1920, the demand for it was the first time that Wales had sought to distinguish itself politically from England. Nor was this to be the last Irish political development to have an effect on Wales, as Irish calls for land reform and some type of self-government were soon being echoed across the Irish Sea.

The land problems that led to rural unrest in Ireland in the nineteenth century are varied and complex, but reformers usually blamed Irish landlords for the turmoil. Absenteeism, high rents, and a Protestant landowning class who were unsympathetic to Catholic tenants were believed to be the root of the problem. In some respects, this mirrored the landownership patterns in Wales, with landowners usually English speaking and Anglican, while their tenants tended to be Welsh speaking and Nonconformist.[37] When Welsh tenants were evicted in 1859, and again in 1868, for failing to follow their landlords' instructions on how to vote, many in Wales noticed a strong parallel with unjust evictions in Ireland. "For the first time," Gwyn Williams writes, "there was a major shift in Dissenting opinion towards the Irish struggle."[38] Not only did Welsh commentators preach about the common bond of suffering shared by Irish and Welsh peasants, some also advocated the adoption of Irish measures in Wales for dealing with unjust landlords. As a worldwide depression put Welsh farmers under increasing pressure during the 1880s, Thomas Gee, editor of *Baner ac Amserau Cymru*, decided to act. He founded the Welsh Land League in 1886, demanding that the rights granted to Irish tenant farmers in various land acts be extended to Wales. Gee's Land League shared a similar structure and philosophy with the Irish Land League and was at the forefront of anti-tithe activism and riots that resembled the unrest caused by the Land League in Ireland.[39] One of the men who advocated for greater cooperation between the Irish and Welsh on the issue of land reform was Tom Ellis. Ellis, a Liberal MP, had traveled to Ireland and had been present at Mitchelstown in 1887 when police opened fire at a Land League rally. He wrote to a friend, "We must work for bringing together Celtic reformers and Celtic peoples. The interests of Irishmen, Welshmen, and [Scottish] Crofters are almost identical. Their past history is very similar, their present oppressors are the same and their immediate wants are the same."[40]

Ellis, more than any other, emphasized the Celtic connection between Ireland and Wales to link their grievances and to call for unified action. He told a Welsh audience in Manchester in 1889 that "by the ancient laws of Wales and Ireland every Welshman and Irishman owned land, and the instinct is planted deep in every fibre of their nature. The leaders and the rank and file of the movement for land reform, which really means social reform, are Celts." He rejected the idea that land agitation was driven merely by greed: "It is a manifestation of a passion for social equality which characterizes every democracy. But with the Celt it is really not a question of the percentage of rent, but of the security and sacredness of the home, of the consciousness of the rights and duties of nationality."[41] One writer, using the pseudonym "Celt," believed that Welsh and Irish suffering emanated from the English conquest of their countries. He wrote, "One has to go to Ireland to find a parallel to the state of things that prevails in Wales. Welsh and Irish [*sic*] share the sad lot of living on sufferance on the land that should be their inheritance."[42] The *Cymru Fydd* journal also highlighted the similarity of the plight of Irish and Welsh peasants. "Nothing is so dear to a Welshman as his cottage—home of his fathers, favourite spot of his childhood. Willing to work through his life without charge, willing to stay in the dust, willing to regularly make sacrifices. . . . this is the same feeling in Ireland." The problem in both countries was that "the rights of farmers are not, neither in Wales nor Ireland, turned into law yet, and they can do nothing when the landlord comes to turn them out on the road."[43] The editor of *Cymru Fydd*, Thomas J. Hughes, wrote that with the mistreatment of Irish protesters by the British government "the Welsh people have been afforded fresh opportunity to exhibit the sincerity and depth of their good will towards Ireland. . . . They have not been slow to give expression to their feelings."[44]

However, sympathy in Wales for land reform in both countries was far from universal. Some observers among the Welsh press believed that the Irish Land League was a subversive organization. *Y Goleuad* proclaimed that the "Land League is an obstacle to the aims of our Government in the country. . . . The League champions secret conspiracies, like opposing the aims of the Government to restore peace and order. . . . These secret conspiracies are a great curse to the country." Ireland could not improve, the writer continued, until the Irish people turned to morality, but "it is difficult to promote and improve the morality of a people when their faith teaches them hypocrisy and deception."[45] Other journalists warned the Welsh people not to be gulled by Irish agitators who sought to establish a common bond with them. The *North Wales Chronicle* stated that the Irish "don't care a fig for the good of Wales, or of Welsh working men, though they will try to make you believe that they do." The Irish tenant was in a more favorable position than any tenant in the world, the paper proclaimed, and it scoffed at claims that Irish landlords were anything other than generous.[46] The *Western Mail*, meanwhile, mocked the visit of Arthur Williams of the South Wales Liberal Federation to Ireland on a fact-finding mission. When Williams claimed that Ireland suffered from tyranny as much as Poland did under the tsar, the paper retorted that he had been allowed to see in Ireland only whatever the Land League wished him to see. Resenting the growing sympathy for Ireland in Wales, the paper asked, "When *will* the Welsh people look to see further than their noses?"[47] The newspaper also rejected the idea that the Welsh Land League could be as influential as its Irish equivalent, claiming that the entire organization was the invention of Thomas Gee and that it had no political or popular support in Wales.[48]

In February 1886, Michael Davitt, the founder of the Irish Land League, was invited to Wales by a Baptist minister, Reverend J. Spinther James, to speak about the problem of landlordism in Ireland and Wales. In a speech given in the community of Ffestiniog, Davitt declared, "Welsh landlordism bore a very strong family likeness to landlordism in Ireland. They had many landlords in Wales who received large revenues, and spent most of their time away from the country . . . and he would advise them in Wales . . . to sweep away these aristocratic loafers." Although enthusiastic crowds greeted Davitt on his lecture tour, the reaction to his presence in the Welsh press was decidedly mixed.[49] One writer, E. J. Hewell, wrote that "in ancient times, it should be remembered, Wales was the teacher of Ireland, and Irish saints poured into Wales to learn the way of God more perfectly. Now, instead of Finnian of Clonard, Wales received Michael Davitt, who comes, not to learn, but to teach."[50] Yet many resented Davitt's presence. Thomas Gee and some older Welsh radicals tried to prevent Davitt from taking the platform at Ffestiniog, although he was eventually allowed to speak with the support of younger activists like David Lloyd George.[51]

Conservatives in Wales poured scorn on the idea that Davitt had any insight to offer to the Welsh people. One clergyman referred to Davitt as a "professional agitator" and "jaundiced spouter" who was trying to turn Wales into a "second Ireland."[52] The *North Wales Chronicle* commented that "the well-known Irishman and ex-convict, Michael Davitt, made a Quixotic tour through North Wales for the purpose ostensibly of setting the Principality ablaze on the land question." The paper asked why Davitt presumed that he knew anything about Wales, highlighting his lack of suitability to comment on Welsh affairs by sarcastically referring to him as "the learned Professor Michael Davitt Jones, of Bala." Davitt spoke openly about the opposition to his visit, saying he understood that the Welsh, like the Irish, wished to settle their own affairs without outside interference. However, he stated that he had received many kind letters and telegrams from across Wales asking him to speak at meetings and that consequently he did not feel like an intruder.[53]

The most scathing criticism of Davitt's presence in Wales came in the form of a satirical letter sent to the *Western Mail*. Purporting to be an account of a secret treaty made between Nonconformist ministers and Irish agitators, the letter emphasized the link between Irish protest and violence, as well as the lack of consideration among some Welsh radicals for the views of Welshmen who were English-speaking Anglicans. The letter, outlining the articles of the treaty "for the restoration of the ancient kingdom of Wales and the recovery of the lost liberties of the people," was signed by "Brian Llewhellyn Boirrhu Ap Cadwallader."[54] By combining the name of the Irish king Brian Boru with that of the famous Welsh king Llywelyn, the author was clearly mocking the supposedly ancient Celtic link between Ireland and Wales that had been implied by those like Tom Ellis. The first article of the supposed treaty, apparently written in Welsh and Irish, was "Mr. Michael Davitt to be first King of Wales," while the second article stated that "we will have no laws, as our first parents had none, and man was born free." This thinly veiled sneer implied that those who invited Davitt to Wales were aspiring to re-create the lawless chaos of Ireland within the Principality.

While the Irish land struggle elicited a mostly sympathetic response from rural Wales, the call for Irish home rule prompted many Welsh people to ask whether some form of political autonomy, including a measure of self-government for the Principality, might be the best way to govern the United Kingdom as a whole. Originally, there was little support in Wales for the Irish home rule cause. The obstructionist tactics in Westminster of the Home Rule Party, led by Charles Stewart Parnell, appeared to be another manifestation of Irish unruliness and barbarism. In 1875, the *Baner* stated that if someone needed "proof that the Irishman was a tumultuous creature full of lively unrest, we can refer them to a gathering held as recently as Thursday," in reference to a home rule meeting.[55] John Arthur Price, a Welsh member of the Conservative Party, wrote in 1890 that as "late as the year 1886, the belief was general that Wales detested Ireland; and . . . the attitude of Welsh voters to the Gladstonian Home Rule Bill was considered . . . to be exceedingly doubtful."[56] An editorial in the conservative *Western Mail* claimed that "when Mr Gladstone changed [his position on home rule in 1885] the Welsh Radical press changed also."[57] In a similar vein, Dr. E. Pan Jones, the prominent Welsh nationalist, said of Thomas Gee that "when the Irish were unpopular Mr Gee would have none of them, but when they became popular, the *Baner* changed also."[58]

Yet even when the Welsh press openly criticized the Home Rule Party for its parliamentary tactics, at times a certain sense of envy could be detected in the their accounts of Irish MPs' success in drawing attention to Ireland's problems. During the 1880s the *Red Dragon* ran a series of articles on the performance of Parliament that lamented the lack of vigor among Welsh members. The writer, using the pseudonym "A. Pendragon," noted that "'What will the Welsh members do?' is an exclamation never heard in anxious ministerial circles. Everything in relation to the gentlemen from Wales is taken for granted."[59] He wrote, "It is not easy to conceive Mr Dillwyn thundering sedition in the hat and boots of a Welsh Mr. Parnell; or Mr Henry Richards howling anathemas at the head of the Prime Minister in the spectacles of a Welsh Mr. Healy." As a result, "the Welsh Members enjoy an enviable reputation in the House of Commons. They are essentially a respected body of men, unaddicted to the licentious vices of their Irish brethren of the Legislature."[60] Throughout his commentary, Pendragon gave his readers the impression that while mimicry of the Irish MPs was not desirable perhaps Wales would be better served by representatives who had some of the national spirit of their Celtic colleagues.

The dramatic change in Welsh attitudes toward Irish home rule can be attributed to Gladstone's embrace of the cause after 1885. Gladstone lived in North Wales, was married to a Welsh woman, regularly attended the national eisteddfod, and had supported both the Welsh Sunday Closing Act and improvements in Welsh education.[61] Hence the split that occurred in the Liberal Party in England as a result of Gladstone's championing of

Irish home rule was not replicated in Wales, with most Welsh Liberals taking up Gladstone's cause. "All the people of Wales are Home Rulers," Dr. Evan Herber Evans, a Nonconformist minister, told a meeting in 1887, "and they could not see their brothers across the channel be treated with such wrongs." At the same gathering, another speaker declared, to cheers, that "there was much sympathy between the Welsh and Irish, and perhaps this originates from the fact that the two countries were governed by outsiders."[62] Thomas J. Hughes, in his first editorial of the nationalist *Cymru Fydd* journal, wrote, "Our struggling brethren across the Irish Channel cannot complain that Wales is backward in extending to them the right hand of sympathetic fellowship and goodwill. There is no ambiguity about Welsh feeling on the subject of Irish wrongs." Claiming that the Welsh people had been the first to support efforts to cure Irish ills, Hughes continued, "The agencies at work to destroy the nationality of Ireland have been recognized by us as precisely identical with those which have sought to kill the same patriotic sentiment in Welsh hearts."[63] Tom Ellis told a Welsh crowd that "Ireland was the country driven almost to rebellion in order to bring attention to its grievances; and out of the passionate sympathy of fellow sufferers, Wales has declared without hesitation in favor of Home Rule for Ireland."[64] Walter Foster, a Welsh writer, stated:

> The intense sympathy in Wales for the Home Rule movement in Ireland springs from the common sufferings of two peoples. Wales is in many respects a replica of Ireland. There is a somewhat similar religious separation between one class of the population and the other. The landowning and ruling class are out of sympathy in religion, in politics and nationality with the mass of the people. These conditions produce a social state not very dissimilar to that of Ireland, and not unlikely if ignored to have similar results. In the meantime, they engender among the Welsh masses a passionate enthusiasm in favor of the Home Rule struggle of their Irish fellow subjects.[65]

Another, anonymous writer commented that in relation to "the burning question of the day, Wales has spoken with no uncertain voice. . . . Wales . . . has suffered in a similar manner to Ireland, and so can and ought to sympathize with the unhappy sister-country in its struggle for freedom and independence."[66]

Yet despite the claims that Wales was now united behind the cause of Irish home rule, there were several vocal critics of the concept within the Principality. The *Western Mail* stated that while the Home Rule Party might enjoy popular support in Ireland "To us it seems a perfectly novel constitutional principle that any portion of the United Kingdom has the right to settle its own destinies without regarding the wishes of the other component parts of the Union."[67] The paper stated that Welsh people who supported home rule were "under the impression that, because Irishmen ask for self-government, it should be granted to them. Never was there a foolisher notion. The proposed remedy is worse than the disease."[68] The *North Wales Chronicle* meanwhile declared that "even in Liberal-ridden Wales" there were people who "honestly believe that the concession of Home Rule to the Sister Isle would prove a curse, and not a blessing."[69]

In 1889, Henry Tobit Evans, a journalist employed by the Liberal Unionist Party, published a pamphlet on home rule entitled *Y Berw Gwyddelig* (The Irish turmoil).[70] Evans said that he had visited Ireland to learn what was happening in the country because he believed the Welsh press was concealing the alarm of Irish Protestants at the prospect of home rule.[71] For Evans, religion explained all the problems in Ireland. The reason the country was in a constant state of unrest was that "almost all Irish nationalists are madcap and fanatical Catholics."[72] Evans recounted the grim history of religious massacres in Ireland, focusing almost exclusively on those committed by Catholics. Those in Wales who wondered why Irish Protestants were so opposed to home rule obviously did not understand that, as Evans wrote, "The Catholics cannot be trusted."[73] Protestants in Ireland understood, according to Evans, that home rule would lead to a Catholic tyranny, and "the result would be their possessions raided, their persecution in the country, and perhaps their murder."[74] Protestants whom Evans met in Ireland told him that "it would be preferable and easier for them to live in wildest Africa than to live in Ireland."[75] Evans tried to use sectarian language to dilute support for home rule in Wales. The message from Irish Protestants was that if "the people of Wales and England grant Home Rule to them [Catholics], we will have to depart and lose our property and homes that belonged to our forefathers for generations, or turn to Catholicism."[76]

These arguments largely fell on deaf ears in Wales. Welsh voters elected Gladstonian candidates in twenty-seven of the thirty-four seats in the 1886 general election, and thirty-one of thirty-four in 1892. While Welsh patriots like Tom Ellis and Dr. Evan Pan Jones supported Ireland's bid for home rule on national grounds, most in Wales favored home rule on the basis of their adherence to the principles of the Liberal Party. Since 1868, Welsh politicians and ministers had emphasized the concept of Wales as a rural, Nonconformist, and Liberal-voting nation.[77] Thus the appeal of those like Evans to the Welsh electorate not to subject Irish Protestants to a largely Catholic Dublin parliament presented Wales with the opportunity to show whether it was first a Liberal or a Protestant nation. Discussing the election of 1886, Stuart Rendel wrote that one might have "assumed beforehand that Nonconformist Wales would view with jealousy and alarm any large concessions of self-government to Catholic Ireland." However, regarding home rule, "Wales was guided in her political attitude and action by the unerring instincts of her purer Liberalism."[78] Thomas Hughes stated that Wales had not "abdicated or forgotten her Protestantism; it is *because* of her Protestantism that she has taken the worn and wasted hand of Ireland in her own. . . . The 'Enthusiasm of Humanity' has made Wales almost forget at times her own heavy legacy of injustice, in resentment at the oppression of Ireland."[79] This sentiment was echoed in the wake of the 1892 election. The *Oswestry Advertizer* declared that there had been a fear that appeals from Ulster Protestants "might influence the Welsh Non-conformist vote, but Welsh Liberals have proved once more that they are Liberals of the best sort, proof against the appeals of religious bigotry, able to understand the essential principles of Liberalism, and always ready to uphold them."[80]

Welsh commentators declared that Wales should take pride in its ability to set aside religious misgivings and judge the question of home rule on its merits. John Eiddon Jones, a Calvinist minister, contrasted the Welsh favorably against notable English liberals, who showed that in relation to home rule "their English nature overrides their idea of justice and fairness. They are great Liberals, but they are greater Englishmen."[81] Some observers in Wales hoped that once home rule was granted to Ireland liberal Wales would be rewarded with the enacting of Welsh disestablishment. The prominent Liberal MP Sir Edward Reed apparently disagreed with home rule in private, but he publicly championed the cause so that Parliament could move on to focus on other matters.[82] Yet numerous commentators chastised such utilitarian opinions on home rule and rejected the call for Welsh support for home rule to be conditional on the granting of Welsh disestablishment also. When the North Wales Liberal Federation passed a measure to this effect, the *Cymru Fydd* journal responded by stating that if "Irish Home Rule is right, and if the other measures of reform proposed by the Liberal party are right, then we ought to support them. . . . The doing of one right act should not be conditional on a *quid pro quo*."[83]

Similarly, the *Oswestry Advertizer* ran an article in 1890 that placed side by side two recent speeches, one by Mr. Griffith Ellis of the North Wales Liberal Federation and one by a Mrs. Tomkinson, a member of the White-church Liberal Club. Ellis had argued that Welsh voters should support the cause of home rule only if disestablishment would be granted in turn, while Tomkinson declared that true liberals would not behave in so petty a manner. The paper stated that if Welsh liberals thought like Mr. Ellis, this would be a cause for shame. However, the editor was confident that "Welsh-men are Liberals after Mrs. Tomkinson's lofty standard. . . . They are not prepared to haggle over their political convictions, or refuse justice to Ire-land until they are assured of the exact day on which their own wrongs will be righted."[84] In this regard, then, the question of Irish home rule was im-portant to the formation of a Welsh political identity. Through unwavering support for Gladstone's bid to pass home rule, in the face of sectarian ap-peals to side against Irish Catholics, Wales had shown that its commitment to liberalism was greater than that of any other part of Britain. There was now very clearly a Welsh political, as well as cultural, nation. But this flour-ishing of Welsh political consciousness against the backdrop of the Irish home rule debate led to the inevitable question: Should Wales itself seek some form of self-government?

The success of the Irish Home Rule Party in winning concessions for Ireland certainly prompted some Welsh politicians to consider adopting Irish tactics for the benefit of Wales. In Westminster, many of the younger Liberal MPs, led by Tom Ellis, formed a Welsh Party in Parliament. Al-though never organized into a formal political organization, the Welsh Party sought to have Welsh MPs vote in one bloc, as Irish MPs had done, with the hope of advancing the cause of Welsh disestablishment and other legis-lation focused on the Principality. According to Kenneth Morgan, the Welsh Party "helped to underline the similarities as well as the differences between the national movements in Wales and Ireland."[85] Meanwhile, the call for some form of Welsh home rule was raised by the Cymru Fydd

(Wales will be) society. Established in London in 1886, with Tom Ellis among the founding members, the movement became popular in Wales in the 1890s, and for a time it seemed that a vibrant home rule movement would develop in Wales as it had in Ireland.[86] Both of these developments were undoubtedly fueled by the inaction of former Welsh MPs in Westminster, as well as the desire to have the question of Welsh disestablishment treated as seriously as that of Irish home rule. "A. Pendragon," while disgusted with the "turgid stream of Hibernian complaint" in Parliament, wrote sarcastically of the Welsh members that "if it has not come to them to invest Wales with national importance, they may at least enjoy the consciousness of having obeyed the Whips with commendable docility."[87]

Another Welsh activist, Professor Henry Jones of the University of North Wales, claimed that Westminster had "paid to Wales the enormous compliment of treating it as if its people were perfectly altruistic and cared for everybody's affairs except their own; for they speak not of Wales and its needs, but of Ireland, England, and Scotland, and Ireland, Ireland, Ireland."[88] The writer Samuel Evans also called for a more militant Welsh attitude in Parliament. He stated that the Welsh MPs had been described as "good party men: always vote straight, even when it is against their own interest. Should [Gladstone] propose the removal of Snowdon from Carnarvon to Cornwall, I have no doubt the Welsh members would vote for it to a man."[89] Evans said he had been asked, "Why cannot you, Welsh people, send a few Irishmen to the house? Then you would get something." One farmer wrote to the *Baner* to say that it was Irish, rather than Welsh, MPs who advocated for small Welsh farmers. He wrote, "The Irish are our protectors. Would it not be better for us if the Irish were sent to parliament for Wales?"[90] Evans said that Wales as a nation had undertaken "great work for Liberalism, for Gladstone, and for Ireland. What would we turn to home, and do a little for ourselves now?" Parnell, according to Evans, understood that "God loves he who loves himself," and he believed that "Wales must follow [Parnell's] path if it is to rise from the ashes."[91]

The Cymru Fydd movement existed for about a decade, from 1885 to 1896. Originally, those who identified with Cymru Fydd wanted a distinct Welsh nationality to be cherished in fields like education, literature, music, and art. However, the failure of the Liberal Party to promote Welsh issues like disestablishment saw the movement increasingly focus on the political sphere. David Lloyd George led an effort to have Welsh Liberal organizations come under the umbrella of Cymru Fydd, which advocated self-government for Wales within the framework of the United Kingdom. Although the North Wales Liberal Federation agreed to this in 1895, its southern equivalent, fearful that the interests of South Wales would not be best served should Welsh home rule come to fruition, publicly rejected Lloyd George's advances in 1896.[92] Thus the Cymru Fydd movement collapsed, although after 1891, in the words of Kenneth Morgan, "there was an unreality about Cymru Fydd; it becomes a network of paper organizations rather than a reflection of a genuine national call for home rule."[93] Nevertheless, the influence of the Irish home rule struggle on this movement was obvious. From 1886 onward, several Welsh commentators and politicians drew a comparison between Ireland's call for home rule and the possibility of a similar demand from Wales. John Puleston Jones, writing in *Cymru Fydd*, said in 1888, "Look at Ireland crying for Home Rule, and Wales will be crying the same thing before too long."[94]

T. Walter Williams, who published a pamphlet on the need for Welsh home rule, stated that England could not rule Ireland appropriately because "the Irish are a nation, and therefore cannot be governed properly from the outside. The British Parliament must fail in its Welsh legislature for precisely the same reason that it has failed in its Irish legislation."[95] Thomas Gee, one of the most vocal supporters of Welsh home rule in the 1890s, declared that "the Welsh nation aspires to Home Rule, like the sister nation in the Emerald Isle."[96] Wales toiled under the same injustices as Ireland, according to some observers, and hence home rule was equally necessary for the Principality. One anonymous Welsh nationalist, writing an article entitled "What Young Wales Wants," commented, "Ireland justly complains of Dublin Castle, but Wales is in some respect worse off than Ireland. . . . She can never expect to be governed by a statesman who knows her history and her wants, as long as the current system prevails."[97] Tom Ellis, speaking at a meeting at Newport in 1888, echoed this complaint, stating that "by every democratic test, the Establishment in Wales is as indefensible as Dublin Castle." Ellis argued that, like Ireland, Wales needed its own assembly, because without "the symbol of unity and the instrument of self-government—her position as a nation cannot be secured, and her work as a nation cannot be done." To further this goal, he told his audience, and as "an immediate practical step, I think there should be in London, at least during the Parliamentary Session, a Welsh Parliamentary Office, similar to that of the Irish nationalists."[98]

Many supporters of Welsh home rule were quick to point out that Wales was as worthy of receiving self-government as Ireland. David Alfred Thomas, a Liberal MP and powerful industrialist, stated, "Home Rule for Wales must naturally follow the concession of self-government for Ireland whenever and as soon as the people of Wales as a nation demand it."[99] These sentiments were shared by Henry Williams, a laborer, who told a meeting in Denbighshire that "if Ireland can be trusted to govern its own affairs, the same right could safely be extended to Wales."[100] Indeed, some in Wales believed that their claim for home rule was more righteous than that of Ireland. David Lloyd George, addressing a meeting at Tonypandy, said, "There was not a single argument which was used against Home Rule for Ireland which was applicable to Welsh Home Rule. It was said that Irish Home Rule would mean the handing over of Protestants to Catholic government. That was not applicable to Wales. Ireland had been demanding separation, and they were using self-government as a kind of lever. That argument did not apply to Wales because they did not ask for separation."[101]

Another supporter of Welsh home rule, using the pseudonym "Morien," clearly implied a negative view of Irish nationalism when writing that it was a sad fact that "one cannot convince [Britain's] statesmen that people are in earnest unless they blow up with dynamite a number of houses and the people in them." The calm and peaceful nature of Welsh politicians was ignored, "Morien" complained, but "let a member obstruct the public proceedings of the House of Commons, and deliver rowdy speeches, spiced with personal abuse, and all the nimble fingers in the Press Gallery will take down his words with as much care as if they were flakes of manna!"[102] Professor Henry Jones argued similarly: "The fact that Wales has asked for the Disestablishment and Disendowment of the Church for a longer time than even Ireland has demanded Home Rule, and that its claim has hitherto received no practical response, exemplifies this truth in a very striking way." When comparing the merits of Irish and Welsh home rule, Jones sarcastically noted that "Wales is smaller, and its social disorganisation is not so great—we neither shoot each other, nor hate England, as yet. . . . This also diminishes the probability that Wales would make violent use of powers granted to it." He cautioned Welsh politicians on the dangers of following the path set by the Irish Home Rule Party, saying, "No country can force legislation on in this manner without falling into arrears with morality and injuring itself almost irreparably."[103]

Indeed, in spite of rising sympathy among the Welsh for Irish home rule in the 1880s, Ireland never fully shed its violent associations in the Welsh imagination. What is remarkable in many of the speeches, articles, and commentaries on Cymru Fydd that discuss Welsh home rule is not how often the comparison with Ireland is made but rather how often it is avoided. Obviously it is much more difficult to record the absence of a theme or idea than its presence, but it is striking that the speeches of the most prominent men associated with Cymru Fydd, certainly David Lloyd George, but even Tom Ellis, only sporadically, rather than consistently, make connections between the causes of Irish and Welsh home rule. To an extent, this should not be surprising; nationalist movements are frequently based on the narrative of a nation carving its own path in the world, and an overreliance on comparisons with other countries would diminish rather than enhance the image of the nation as unique and worthy of advancement. But while Irish cultural nationalists regularly brought up the example of Welsh tenacity in preserving the Welsh language as a model for Ireland to emulate, Welsh political nationalists were far less comfortable comparing their cause to that of Irish home rule. This was primarily due to the negative connotations that had become associated with the Irish home rule cause in the 1870s and early 1880s. An article in *Y Genedl Gymreig* highlighted this by saying, "Wonderfully frightening to many is the word Home Rule. It is in some ways linked to unhappiness—Fenianism, terrible machines, dynamite, the Phoenix Park murders, and so forth. And this has prevented some well-informed and sound minded brothers to look at this matter directly, and the weak taken over by horror and fear. It is imagined that a terrible fate awaits us if [the Welsh] are granted Home Rule, and alarmist fears are raised."[104]

One example of this reluctance among Welsh nationalists to make a strong connection between their home rule movement and the Irish equivalent is demonstrated by the anonymously written *Cymru Fydd, Gymru Rydd, or The Welsh Nationalist Movement*. The author talks at length about the qualities of Welsh nationalism and even writes an entire chapter on the necessity for some form of political expression of this nationalism, but Ireland is barely mentioned. The anonymous writer calls for the formation of an independent Welsh national party, clearly influenced in part by the existence of such an organization in Ireland, but makes absolutely no mention of the Irish Home Rule Party or its political successes.[105] Advocates of Welsh home rule were much more comfortable discussing the idea of "Home Rule All Round," that is, home rule for all four nations of the United Kingdom, rather than directly linking their cause with that of Ireland's. Irish home rule, in the eyes of many, had a strong association with independence from Britain, while Welsh commentators wished to stress their loyalty and commitment to the British Empire. *Y Genedl Gymreig* declared that some had tried to associate home rule with independence in order to "give the dog a bad name." However, "it is understood now that Home Rule does not mean withdrawing from England nor the breakdown of the British Empire." Indeed, home rule all round would improve the health of the empire: "When the Celts in Scotland, Ireland and Wales handle their own affairs, there will be so many more countries with true love for the Imperial parliament, and more of a true union with them and the great English nation."[106] In short, the relationship between Irish and Welsh home rule was complex. Clearly the Irish party served as an inspiration for the Welsh movement, but advocates of home rule who were drawn toward the Irish example also faced a kind of centrifugal pressure that simultaneously required that they lean away from it.

While many in Wales were lukewarm about acknowledging the Irish influence on the emergence of Welsh political movements, the turmoil generated in Ireland regarding home rule proved to be a useful barometer for Welsh writers to measure the intensity of their own demands. In particular, the call for Welsh disestablishment was regularly compared with the Irish cry for home rule as a means of asserting the sincerity of the Welsh nation in its claim. Henry Jones wrote in 1888 that "the Welsh people have demanded the Disestablishment of a Church which, whether the best or the worst in the world, it certainly does not want; they have demanded this with a unanimity and persistence to which Ireland can offer no parallel."[107] Welsh commentators emphasized that Wales deserved disestablishment because it demanded this more intensely than Ireland sought home rule. Griffith Ellis told a gathering of the North Wales Liberal Federation that Wales should receive disestablishment because "it is more united in demanding [it] than Ireland is demanding in Home Rule."[108] The *Oswestry Advertizer* supported the Welsh call for disestablishment along similar lines, arguing that the large victories won by prodisestablishment MPs in the 1892 general election showed that Wales was unanimous on the matter. "Even Ireland, with its remarkable demand for Home Rule, shows nothing like it."[109] So successful were Welsh writers in making this point that soon their cry was taken up by English members of the Liberal Party. John Morely, the former chief secretary for Ireland, made a speech in Westminster saying that Welsh demands needed to be listened to because "in Wales disestablishment is as much a national question as Home Rule is in Ireland."[110]

While supporters of Welsh home rule, and the Welsh Land League, trod carefully around comparisons with Ireland, opponents of these developments were quick to accuse their political adversaries of "importing" Irish methods to Wales. Owing to the prominent speeches made by Michael Davitt in Wales, the Welsh Land League was most open to these charges. The *North Wales Chronicle*, directly comparing the Irish and Welsh Land Leagues, concluded that they were organized by the same men, used the same tactics, and ignored the law of the land; further, "The scheme is the same in both countries: artificial and not spontaneous, the creation of the vernacular press and the Dissenting priesthood."[111] Henry Tobit Evans, the author of the anti-Catholic *Y Berw Gwyddelig*, claimed that he had been subjected to Irish-style harassment, and the *Western Mail* commented that "the evil the Irish Land League did is likely to live after it. Some of the seeds sown on the other side of St George's Channel appear to have blown over into Wales, and to be threatening to take root here."[112] Colonel William Cornwallis West, a Conservative MP, stated, "I am convinced that reasonable and sagacious Welshmen have no desire . . . to plunge headlong into a condition of things, such as we see going on in Ireland, where a National League has . . . only caused untold misery and created anarchy and ruin."[113] David Brynmor Jones, a Liberal MP, shared similar concerns, writing that there "was in the Wales of today a great unrest and mental activity which, if well directed, might be fruitful of much good, but if misdirected would be productive of evil . . . such as had been seen in Ireland."[114]

The Welsh home rule movement did not try to link itself to its Irish equivalent in the same way that the Welsh Land League had done. The criticism the Welsh Land League received may have deterred home rule sympathizers from doing so, although, with the Irish Home Rule Party in disarray after the Parnell divorce crisis in 1890, linking Cymru Fydd to the Irish struggle may have been even less appealing. Yet any mention of Ireland in relation to Cymru Fydd was seized by Welsh conservatives eager to discredit the Welsh home rule movement. When a pamphlet outlining the ideals of Cymru Fydd expressed a hope that "the new organization will do for Wales what the Irish nationalist societies have done for Ireland," opponents took note. The *Western Mail* asked whether "the author referred to the Fenian movement, the Clan-na-Gael, the Moonlighters, the Land League . . . some of these societies with which Ireland has been cursed from time to time?"[115] The *Cymru Fydd* journal, under a new and less nationalistic editorship, also criticized the Welsh home rule movement for copying Irish tactics. The new editor, R. H. Morgan, wrote in 1890 that a "host of screaming politicians have sprung up as of late. Their language is violent; and . . . they act as if they thought that a few yells would win the battle without any bloodshed. They make up for deficiency in argument by shrillness in tone."[116] Although the Irish Home Rule Party was not mentioned by name, Morgan clearly believed that Welsh home rulers were behaving just like Parnell and his followers.

In particular, Welsh conservatives repeatedly stated that Welsh liberals, in modeling their organizations and strategies after the Irish example, were destroying the social principles that made Wales a distinct nation in the first place. The *Western Mail* declared that "the vernacular press and the Nonconformist ministers have, by their association with and support of Mr. Parnell and his allies during the last five years, brought such discredit upon the fair fame of Wales that a generation of repentance will not wipe it out."[117] One could not ignore "the fidelity with which the anti-tithe agitators in the Principality have copied the Irish model. . . . The plain dictates of morality are unblushingly discarded—honesty and justice are mocked. . . . The traditions of Nonconformity in Wales are but as chaff driven before the whirlwind of political agitations."[118] One writer, using the pseudonym "Merion," criticized Tom Ellis particularly for attempting to make Wales a "second Ireland." He asked, "Who taught the Welsh people—the quiet, loyal, peaceful, law-abiding people of Wales—to . . . assemble by their thousands, bearing heavy and rough knotty cudgels, carrying lapfulls [*sic*] of sharp flinty stones in defiance of all law and in defense of the grossest lawlessness?"[119] Ironically then, those in favor of creating a political identity for Wales were accused of threatening the fabric of Welsh society in order to do so.

Yet despite the potential risk of associating Welsh causes with Irish ones it would be misleading to suggest that Welsh commentators never urged their countrymen to copy their Celtic brethren across the Irish Sea. Some writers and advocates openly called upon the Welsh people to take heed of what Irish activists had achieved. Thomas Gee noted that the "history of Ireland in previous years clearly shows that the country which raises a loud cry for her liberties only receives it when she asked for it and not one moment sooner." Wales had been waiting tranquilly for justice, but he believed that "it is not so likely justice will be brought in this way, nor does it appear she is willing to wait so long." If this meant that violence erupted in Wales, the writer said, he would place the blame "at the door of the parsons . . . and most important of all, on the Church Delegates, because of their cruelty, their brutality, and their hypocrisy, refusing to acknowledge the squeeze on the country under it is more substantial than empty words!"[120] T. Walter Williams wrote in 1888 that the "first step which Wales must take in order to obtain Home Rule is to return to Parliament a strong national party, and it is possible that this party will have to take a leaf out of the book of the Irish party, and practice a little Obstruction." Even though Parnell had largely abandoned obstructionism by this time, "It must never be forgotten that it was by Obstruction that he raised his nation to such a position of power that it is no longer necessary."[121]

Even David Lloyd George, who tended to avoid direct comparisons with Ireland and Wales, occasionally used the Irish example as a device to mobilize the Welsh people to follow his lead. He told an audience at Llanrwst in 1894, "We may need for the machine to consolidate the national awakening, so as to be made into a strong power. . . . The Irish had understood this, and had frequently gotten a 'round o beef' out of it. If Wales wanted something out of the parliamentary cauldron, it must rise."[122] The conflicted nature of Welsh nationalist views toward Ireland is best encapsulated in Stuart Rendel's article "Wales and the Liberal Party," published in 1888. On the one hand, Rendel praised the Irish struggle for home rule because it made Welsh disestablishment more feasible. The fight for Irish home rule was a Welsh fight also, Rendel wrote, because alone "Wales could never, perhaps, have secured a hearing from England. Ireland and Irish extremity were needed to develope [*sic*] and determine the Nationality issue with so masterful and self-complacent a neighbour." Yet while "Irish extremity" was necessary in Ireland, Rendel rejected calls for similar action in Wales, stating that the "analogy with Ireland does not hold good." There could be no Welsh extremity, Rendel argued, because "nothing could more serve the interests of our opponents, nothing could better fetter the hands of our friends than any organized exhibition of popular and public lawlessness."[123] Again, these examples reinforce the complex role that the image of Ireland played in the emergence of Welsh political consciousness in the late nineteenth century, both inspiring but also limiting Welsh political ambitions.

One of the more interesting aspects of the development of a greater political consciousness among the Welsh public in the later nineteenth century was the manner in which Welsh writers referred to the supposed Celtic connection with Ireland. Prior to the 1880s, Welsh commentators had sought to down play the Celtic link between the two nations and had preferred to make comparisons between England and Wales, rather than highlighting the "racial" link between the Principality and Ireland. This can be partially explained by the negative Welsh reaction to the report of an education commission in 1847 that claimed the Welsh adherence to their language and to Nonconformity had made the people immoral and barbaric. Known in Welsh history as the "Treachery of the Blue Books," it ensured that Welsh commentators tried to compare Wales favorably against England to prove Welsh civility.[124] Consequently, there was little desire to celebrate the Celtic bond with Ireland, as it would only connect Wales to Irish violence.

One of the best examples of this was the publication of an article entitled "The Celt of Wales, and the Celt of Ireland" in *Cornhill Magazine* in 1877. The presumably English writer asked how two nations, of the same racial stock and living in a similar climatic and geographic environment, could be so different. Using the pseudonym "F.P.C.," he wrote:

> Here are two branches of the same great Celtic family. . . . They have dwelt for several thousand years side by side as next neighbours, in countries under the same latitude, with a similarly pluviose climate. . . . For several centuries they have both been under the rule of

the same conquerors. . . . Yet instead of exhibiting such obvious and striking resemblances as might have been anticipated, under circumstances so similar, and instead of progressing together step by step in prosperity, the differences, or rather, contrasts, in the characteristics and fortunes of the two people are so much more salient than their likenesses, that nine Englishmen out of ten forget that they are anywise akin, and no statesman dreams that because one Act of Parliament is fitted for Ireland, it is likely to be needed in Wales.[125]

For the most part, "F.P.C." compared the Welsh favorably against the Irish. He praised the Welsh for avoiding political agitation: "Instead of a Home Rule meeting, there is an Eisteddfod." In terms of music, language, and native costume, "F.P.C." was confident that "Welsh nationality is better preserved and more pronounced at the present day than the nationality of Ireland."[126] The author also compared the physical features of the two peoples, writing that the beautiful Irish eye "has no analogue in the Welsh feature. On the other hand, the Irishman's frightful prognathous jaw, as seen in Munster and Connemara, is unknown in Wales; as is also the coarse lip which, in a lesser degree, is likewise distinctive of the Milesian race."[127]

"F.P.C." also borrowed heavily from Ernest Renan and Matthew Arnold in describing the Celtic nature of the Irish and Welsh, referring to their poetic nature, their powerful imaginations, their spirituality, and, of course, their inability to work with consistency and order. While he did claim that the Irish peasantry were more moral than their Welsh counterparts, "F.P.C" believed that Wales was more prosperous than Ireland because the Welsh were less reckless, more prudent, and more capable of forward thinking than the Irish. Despite this relatively positive assessment of the Cymric character, some in Wales were angered by the article. The editorial for the *North Wales Chronicle* proclaimed that the writer had shown "superficial flippancy and a cynical disregard for the facts."[128] The editorial then proceeded to compare Wales favorably with England in fields such as crime and religion, but it declined to evaluate the original comparison made with Ireland, pleading a lack of space. This editorial was representative of a general reticence to compare the Irish and Welsh as Celts. When making such comparisons, writers tended to view the Welsh as the more practical of the two. One writer wrote in 1883 that the "Welsh people are, like all of their brethren of Celtic origin, emotional, and their feelings are of great depth and strength." However, the writer added that the Welsh "are not, however, so easily excited as are the Irish."[129]

As Welsh sympathy for the Irish Land League and Home Rule Party grew in the 1880s, there was a greater willingness on the part of some to embrace the Irish as Celtic kin. By 1890, John Arthur Price was able to write that one "of the most remarkable signs in Welsh political life, at the present day, is the complete reconciliation of our old national feud with our sister Celtic nationality of Ireland."[130] When Timothy Sullivan, the Home Rule MP and lord mayor of Dublin, visited Wales in 1888, the North Wales Liberal Federation held a public reception for him in Holyhead. Sir Edmund Verney, a Liberal MP, welcomed Sullivan by saying that the Welsh were "like the Irish, a Celtic race, and . . . the Celtic race in Wales were in hearty and heartfelt sympathy with their Celtic brethren in Ireland."[131] The newspaper *Y Genedl Gymreig*, in supporting both Welsh and Irish calls for home rule, asked, "What is Home Rule? It is nothing more than an attempt by the Celt to discard everything Teutonic which is incompatible with his temperament."[132] Even David Lloyd George, in demanding home rule all round, acknowledged the Celtic connection of Ireland and Wales. He claimed that the unrest in both countries showed that the "objectives of the Celt and the Saxon are conflicting. . . . [The situation] is unbearable to the Celt, destroying the feeling of neighbourly good that should exist between the various nations that make up the United Kingdom."[133]

Yet while there was a more general readiness to acknowledge the Irish as close cousins, at times it appeared that even sympathizers were still a little wary of the Celtic connection. In 1889, Tom Ellis made a speech in Manchester entitled "The Influence of the Celt in the Making of Britain." It is notable, however, that Ellis spends more time trying to convince his audience of the mixed Celtic blood of the English people than discussing the common Celtic bond between the Welsh and the Irish. The anonymous "Celt" who penned *Cymru Fydd, Gymru Rydd* in 1895 wrote a chapter entitled "The Celt and His Mission" but did not make a single reference to Ireland. The Reverend A. J. Parry wrote an article discussing the support the Liberal Party received from the Celtic nations during general elections. Commenting on the nature of the three Celtic peoples, Parry wrote, "We tend to attribute stability in politics to the Celtic races, and loyalty to their parties, particularly their leaders, as their faith is stronger and more thorough." Parry continued that the Welsh, Scottish, and Irish were religious nations and that "although Catholicism is the religion of the latter, this allows their adherence to their political principles to be tight and unswerving."[134] Again, the fact that Parry sought to qualify Ireland's Catholicism suggests that he believed that some of his readers were unwilling to see the Irish as brethren.

The *Baner* went as far as to downplay the extent to which the Irish and Welsh shared the same bloodlines and tried to refute the popular notion that Irish unrest was the result of Celtic racial traits. Its editor, Thomas Gee, wrote in 1892 that people looked at the residents of Ireland and believed that "pure Irish blood is flowing in their veins." As a result, the British public understood that "these elements of the character of the population must entirely attributed to the discomforts and events in Ireland during the years." However, Gee declared, Ireland "is a mixed nation." Gee admitted that "the Celts had settled there, as in Wales and other countries in Europe; and it is not inappropriate to call them, because of this, as is often done, our 'cousins.'" However, he claimed that, owing to waves of immigrants and invaders over the centuries, it "would be difficult to think that there, by now, is not as much blood from other nations in the residents as Celtic blood."[135] Another writer, in trying to explain a series of riots at Mold and Ruabon, made a similar claim about the distinctiveness of Irish and Welsh genetics. The writer, using the pen name "One of Them," said that it must "be borne in mind that in the rioters in each case there was an admixture of Irish and Lancashire blood."[136] The implication the writer made was that the racial characteristics of the Welsh usually prevented them from resorting to violence. On the other hand, though many of the rioters had presumably been born in Wales, it was specifically their Irish blood, not their Welsh upbringing, that was said to contribute to the violent outburst. These examples best demonstrate many Welsh people's reluctance to acknowledge a racial link between Ireland and Wales. If Irish turmoil was due to the population's Celtic blood, then Wales would fall under the same suspicion of being somewhat less civilized than its Saxon neighbors. Hence Gee sought to deny Ireland an equal footing with the Welsh as Celts, emphasizing the racial purity of Wales while discrediting the idea that Celtic bloodlines produced an unmanageable nation.

If Ireland provided the inspiration for a politically focused sense of nationalism within Wales, it also served as a prism through which Welsh commentators could examine the superiority of their own nation. In this regard, Welsh nationalists were no different from their Irish counterparts, who claimed that Ireland surpassed Wales in terms of its national character. One source for this sense of superiority stemmed from the strength of the Welsh indigenous language compared to its Irish equivalent. As noted in the previous chapter, this was a sentiment shared by several Irish cultural nationalists. One commentator stated that, owing to the tenacity with which the Welsh had preserved their language, "The consciousness of national existence is deeper and stronger in the Welsh people to-day than it is among any of the other populations of the British Isles."[137] George Osborne Morgan told Parliament that the widespread use of Welsh meant that Wales had "a nationality more distinct from England than Scotland or Ireland, because Wales was separated from England not merely by a geographical barrier—a strip of sea or mountains, but by a greater barrier. In the everyday relations of life, the barrier of language."[138] The renowned nationalist Beriah Gwynfe Evans emphasized the strength of Welsh in making Wales a nation, writing, "In the manner of a separate language and literature, [Wales] is immeasurably superior to [Ireland and Scotland]. . . . While these sister tongues have dwindled, and been extinguished, or only retain a flickering existence, Welsh flourishes."[139] Henry Jones also argued that Wales was "a distinct nation, in a fuller sense of the word than even Ireland and Scotland, having not only its own racial characteristics, religious instincts and habits, literature and past history, but also, unlike Ireland and Scotland, its own living language."[140]

The success in maintaining the Welsh language was not the only reason many people in Wales felt a sense of national superiority compared to the Irish. Throughout the later nineteenth century, Welsh writers seemed to take great pride in the ability of the Welsh to endure injustice peacefully while Ireland responded with violence and chaos. Opinions such as these had a subtle parallel in Ireland, where some viewed the failure of the Welsh to engage in large-scale political agitation as proof of Irish patriotic supremacy. One writer noted, "Had Wales been able to behave as disloyally in agitating and disturbing as Ireland has done, she would have been granted more of her claims and rights ere now. There is no country under heaven so neglected and scandalized, and that with no cause, than the highly-civilized Welsh nation."[141] In 1884, the Irish Presbyterian newspaper *Witness* ran an article that compared the Welsh nation very favorably against Ireland. *Y Goleuad* translated the article into Welsh and published it, stating that readers would find it a "great joy" to see "the evidence given about our nation's high character." The article stated that the Welsh could complain that "they have received treatment much crueler than their Irish neighbours. While Ireland has received attention and kindness like a pampered child, they have received neglect and insults. . . . The Welsh bear their burden with amazing silence . . . but the Irish, after moving all of their complaints, are as dissatisfied as ever."[142] These sentiments, although written by an Irishman, reflected popular ideas in the Principality about the differences between Ireland and Wales. One popular story that demonstrated this was in relation to the death of Henry Rees in 1869. Rees was a Nonconformist preacher in Shrewsbury, and when he died the local Anglican parson refused to allow a Nonconformist minister to speak at his grave. The *Cymru Fydd* journal gave the following account in 1890:

> A good story is related of a conversation that occurred in the train between an Irish M.P. and a Welshman respecting this incident. The Irishman said, as he pointed to the spot where Mr. Rees is buried—"Wasn't one of your leading ministers buried there, and didn't the parson prevent any of your ministers speaking by his grave?" "Yes," answered the Welshman. "What did you do then?" "We simply submitted, and were silent; what would you have done under similar circumstances in Ireland?" "Oh!" replied the M.P., "We would have buried the parson first!" So they would, we know; for such is Ireland, and such is Wales. It is the influence of a generation of men like Mr. Rees that has taught the Welsh nation to bear insult patiently, and to seek redress of wrong by legal means, and not by the help of knives and revolvers.[143]

That these sentiments were being expressed in 1890 in a nationalist journal shows that while there was increasing sympathy for Ireland in the Principality, violence in the Emerald Isle was still viewed as anathema to the sensibilities of Nonconformist Wales. Indeed, Welsh writers at times had some difficulty in justifying the use of violence in their own history. In recalling the Rebecca Riots of the 1840s, the writer "One of Them" stated, "It was a wrong movement [as it employed violence] towards a right end. But for the movement, however, wrong as it was, the injustice might have continued."[144] This perfectly encapsulates the dilemma faced by Welsh observers in terms of adopting Irish methods of agitation in the late nineteenth century. Violence was wrong, but it often helped end injustice and thus was possibly justified.

Some in Wales believed that the religious differences between the countries explained why Wales did not suffer the disorder Ireland endured. Owen Morgan Edwards, who would become a famous educationalist in Wales, believed that the "influence of Geneva" explained why social chaos reigned in Ireland but not the Principality: "If Rome taught us to satisfy our passions, and to walk according to our imagination of our heart; to fight crazy wars and hopelessly agitate for our independence . . . Geneva taught us to restrain our passions, and to walk the narrow path of morality and law."[145] Professor Henry Jones of the University of North Wales echoed these thoughts, writing that Wales had "shown a power of self-restraint, deliberation, and patient perseverance, resulting in a peaceful continuity of development that is not easily surpassed in any country." With a clear reference to Ireland, Jones added that Wales had "national aspirations, which are not stained by a tinge of dislike to its neighbours, or by any foolish dreams of independence and isolation."[146] Clearly, then, Ireland served as more than a source of inspiration for the development of a Welsh political consciousness; it also existed in the Welsh imagination as the essence of national sentiment gone awry, thereby reinforcing the image Welsh nationalists had of their own country being based on a Nonconformist sense of justice, fairness, and civility.

In conclusion, Ireland played an important, if complex, role in the development of a greater political nationalist consciousness in Wales in the late nineteenth century. Irish cultural nationalists celebrated the preservation of the Welsh language almost uncritically, but the inverse did not occur among Welsh political nationalists. Welsh familiarity with Irish affairs and with Irish immigrants meant that an unrealistic depiction of the Irish struggle, like the romantic vision of the Welsh language that Irish-language enthusiasts disseminated in Ireland, was impossible. Yet the impact of Ireland on the Welsh nationalist conscience was greater than the influence of

Wales on the Irish nationalist mind-set. The achievement of Irish disestablishment alerted the Welsh Nonconformist population to the benefits that could accrue should Wales be recognized as a political nation within the United Kingdom. The struggles of the Irish Land League encouraged Welsh peasants to organize their own resistance to landlords and to obtain the same rights that Irish tenants had under the law. The demand for home rule in Ireland stirred a similar interest in Wales, although it arose from a desire to create greater justice in local government rather than to cleave Wales from the British state. Support for Irish home rule seemed to confirm that Wales was a singular nation united in its adherence to liberal principles and the Liberal Party, overcoming its dislike of Catholicism in the interests of true justice. Finally Ireland served as a useful foil against which Welsh nationalists could measure the quality of their own nationhood and feel satisfied that they far exceeded their Celtic brethren both in preserving their ancient language and in embracing the peace, stability, and civilization of a modern society. Nevertheless, to paraphrase Stuart Rendel, "Irish extremity" was required to rouse in Wales a sense of its own existence as a political as well as cultural entity.

CHAPTER 4

GATHERING THE CLANS

The growing acceptance among the people of Ireland and Wales that they shared a Celtic heritage fostered an interest among their respective populations in developments that took place in their "sister nation." For the most part, this meant that Irish and Welsh nationalists looked across the Irish Sea for possible solutions to the problems they believed hindered the development of a robust national identity at home. But others, in both countries, wanted to go beyond a cursory acknowledgment of their common Celticness and try to forge a deeper bond between the various Celtic nations. Advocates for promoting cross-Celtic ties often had different visions for what this would actually entail, from simple cultural exchanges to the possibility of a federal Celtic state. The challenges they faced included skepticism from nationalists who worried that a focus on Pan-Celticism would dilute their own distinctive sense of national identity, raise the scorn of English observers, and erase the linguistic, religious, and cultural differences that existed between the six Celtic branches. Pan-Celticism was a movement aiming to build cultural or political connections between Ireland, Wales, the Scottish Highlands, the Isle of Man, Cornwall, and Brittany. Its emergence in the 1890s was perhaps the inevitable outcome of the birth of Celtic nationalism in the latter half of the nineteenth century. Those who were most passionate about the Pan-Celtic project had ambitious dreams for what could be achieved by closer cooperation between the Celts, but they struggled to generate enthusiasm among the populations they viewed as their own people.

While historians debate whether nationalism is an ancient, medieval, or modern phenomenon, there is no doubt that pan-nationalism, or macro-nationalism, was a product of the nineteenth century. In its simplest form, pan-nationalism is the acknowledgment of an ethnic, cultural, or racial connection between one's own nation and groups outside one's state or territory. Louis Snyder has argued that pan-nationalism is an aggressive form of nationalism, with nationalists trying to expand the parameters of who should be included in the fatherland or motherland. Pan-nationalists "paint nationalism on a much broader canvas to include all (*pan*) those who by reason of geography, race, religion, or language, or by a combination of any or all of them, are included in the same group category."[1] Pan-nationalism emerged in the nineteenth century for many of the same reasons that a Celtic identity did: (1) the development of a racial sense of national identity, (2) linguistic studies that highlighted the relationship between certain languages (and therefore were taken to mean that the speakers of those languages came from the same racial stock), and (3) the rise of mass literacy, which allowed people to read about their ancient heritage and "imagine" the wider pan-nationalist community to which they believed they belonged. Drawing a hard distinction between nationalism and pan-nationalism can also be difficult. Historians usually label the driving force behind the formation of the Italian and German states as nationalism, but perhaps it would be more accurate to say that these states were pan-nationalist creations. In other words, pan-nationalism becomes simply nationalism once a pan-nationalist state is attained. Snyder himself provides a good example of how nationalism and pan-nationalism can be easily confused. Writing in 1984, Snyder declared that after the First World War the people of Czechoslovakia and Yugoslavia rejected Pan-Slavism because they wanted "freedom for themselves and not an unrealistic combination with 'foreign' Slavs."[2] But from the perspective of the twenty-first century it is evident that Czechoslovakia, and especially Yugoslavia, were in fact themselves Pan-Slavic states.

Indeed, Pan-Slavism was probably the most significant and most influential of all the pan-nationalist movements that came into existence during the nineteenth century. Two of the earliest Pan-Slavs were Jan Kollár and Pavel Josef Šafařík. Both were Slovaks and promoted a wider Pan-Slavic vision in order to win allies in an effort to promote Slovakian nationalism. Kollár's vision of the Slavic people was borrowed from the German writer

Johann Gottfried Herder, who believed that the Slavs were naturally peaceful, democratic, and humanitarian in their outlook.[3] This interpretation of Slavic identity fit well with how some Polish nationalists were beginning to view their own sense of nationhood. With Polish resistance to tsarist rule crushed in 1831, Polish writers imagined Poland as a messianic nation, sacrificing its children for the cause of universal liberty and freedom.[4] Such ideas were easily transferable to Pan-Slavism generally, and supporters of Pan-Slavism regularly put forward the idea that the Slavic peoples had a special mission to save humanity. To advance the agenda of the Slavs, two congresses were held, one in Prague in 1848 and another in Moscow in 1867. In truth these congresses did more to reveal the disparate political, social, and cultural aims of the various Slavic nationalities than provide a platform that could unite them in a single mission. Yet Pan-Slavism retained an appeal into the twentieth century. Its crowning achievement, at least in political terms, was the unification of the South Slavic people within the state of Yugoslavia in 1918, although the fault lines within this Yugoslav identity were brutally revealed when that state tore itself apart in the 1990s. Nevertheless, the early Pan-Slavs proved to be role models for the Pan-Celts, giving them both the idea to bring different nationalities together through formal congresses, as well as the mind-set that they could be a chosen people with a duty to save all of humanity.

Another vibrant pan-nationalist movement was Pan-Germanism, which, like Pan-Celticism, emerged in the 1890s. A General German League (Allgemeiner Deutscher Verband) was formed in April 1891. Its stated aims were (1) to activate patriotic consciousness at home and combat all tendencies opposed to national (*völkisch*) development, (2) to support ethnically German groups around the world in their efforts to preserve their German identity, and (3) to promote the acquisition of colonies by the German state.[5] The group renamed itself as the Pan-German League (Alldeutscher Verband) in 1894. Some Pan-Germans believed that a union of sorts should exist between the speakers of all Germanic tongues, including English and the Scandinavian languages. While this particular idea did not have many advocates, even the vision of more moderate Pan-Germans was, in the words of Roger Chickering, breathtaking: "The German community in *Mitteleuropa* was, by general consensus in the League, to include the German Empire, the Habsburg lands, Switzerland, Holland, Luxemburg,

Belgium, and—less out of ethnic considerations than because it lay at the mouth of the Danube—Romania. The League made no secret of its expectation that full political unity would be the end result, although in the short run political unity appeared impractical, owing not the least to the resistance of Swiss Germans and Flemish separatists to the idea."[6] The Pan-German League operated primarily as a right-wing pressure group in German politics, although their ideas were labeled beer-hall politics (*Bierbankpolitik*) and many within the German establishment dismissed them as cranks. The group's membership peaked at thirty-eight thousand in 1922, amid postwar disillusionment in Germany. Although it shared much of its ideology with the National Socialist Party, the Nazis distrusted the Pan-German League as a rival conservative faction, and the Gestapo forcibly shut it down in 1939.[7]

Several interesting comparisons can be drawn between the Pan-Germans and the Pan-Celts. Both groups believed their distinctive culture was under threat. The Pan-Germans saw threats everywhere to the German way of life, including the growing number of Polish speakers in Prussia, the adoption of foreign words in the German language, the perceived political marginalization of German speakers in Austria-Hungary, and the British annexation of the Boer republics in South Africa. The main objective of the Pan-Celts, meanwhile, was the preservation of the Celtic languages. The difference, of course, was that the Celtic languages were all undeniably in some degree of decline, whereas it is difficult to view German national identity in the late nineteenth century as anything other than thriving. Both Pan-Germans and Pan-Celts believed their respective races should play a greater role in world affairs, but in very different capacities. Pan-Germans wanted the German nation-state to be a major world power, and to this end they vigorously demanded the rapid expansion of the German navy and further German colonial annexations. The Pan-Celts, like the Pan-Slavs, believed their people had a special humanitarian cause and that if they could be properly organized they could serve humanity as ambassadors of peace. The Pan-Germans, to attain their goals, actively lobbied the German government to adopt certain policies, while the Pan-Celts, at least in their initial incarnation, avoided political debate or discussion. Finally, both the Pan-Celts and the Pan-Germans were dismissed by many in their respective countries as daydreamers and fantasists, although particular aspects of the Pan-German philosophy were transformed into a terrifying reality with the ascension of Adolph Hitler to the office of German chancellor in 1933.

Another pan-national identity that became increasingly prominent over the course of the nineteenth century was that of Anglo-Saxonism. Although a formal Pan-Anglo-Saxon society or league never emerged, there was certainly no shortage of writers or commentators who were willing to assert a white racial superiority based on an Anglo-Saxon or Teutonic ethnic identity. Nineteenth-century English historians like John Mitchell Kemble, Thomas Babington Macaulay, Edward Augustus Freeman, and James Anthony Froude all suggested that the distinctive character of the British people and the liberal and imperial achievements of the British state were due to the Teutonic origins of their Anglo-Saxon ancestors.[8] The Scottish philosopher Thomas Carlyle was a major proponent of Anglo-Saxonism, believing that the Teutonic idealism, moral intuition, and political institutions of the Anglo-Saxon race meant they were destined to control the uncivilized parts of the world. Such ideas had a profound influence on novelists like Charles Kingsley, poets like Rudyard Kipling, and politicians such as Benjamin Disraeli, Randolph Churchill, and Joseph Chamberlin.[9] These beliefs spread across the Atlantic to the United States as well, and the Anglo-Saxon origins of the American people were used to justify the institution of slavery, the expansion of white settlers into Native American lands, and the annexation of a sizable amount of Mexican territory.[10] From a social Darwinist perspective, those who adhered to Anglo-Saxonism could, in the late nineteenth century, consider the size of the British Empire alongside the growing economic and political might of the United States and Germany as irrefutable proof of their own ethnic superiority. But the conflation of Anglo-Saxon and British identities also provided an impulse to Celtic nationalists to forge a distinctive racial identity and to find a way to demonstrate their own historical and cultural achievements to their Saxon neighbors.

The story of Pan-Celticism begins with a French poet named Charles de Gaulle. Uncle of his more famous namesake, de Gaulle was a sickly child who turned toward the study of the Breton, Irish, and Welsh languages. In 1864, de Gaulle published an article entitled "Les Celtes au dix-neuvième siècle: Appel aux représentants actuels de la race celtique." He called for the establishment of a Celtic union that would promote regular contacts between the different Celtic nations. He also suggested creating a new

Celtic language, with words coined from the common roots of Celtic words, so that the Celtic people could communicate with one another without having to resort to English or French. De Gaulle helped bring together a Pan-Celtic congress in 1867, at St. Brieuc, Brittany, although he himself was unable to attend because of medical problems that dogged him his entire life.[11] The gathering attracted mostly Breton and Welsh guests, with no Irish visitors in attendance, but de Gaulle hoped that such congresses could provide the basis for creating stronger links between Celts. He wrote:

> Each of the four principal fractions of the race should convoke by turns a great national festival: representatives should be taken from all classes of the other countries. After an account rendered of the labors executed in each country since the last assembly, the most beneficial works for Celtic science should be solemnly rewarded, and recompenses should be bestowed, or at least public thanks be given, to all those whose efforts might have contributed to the moral or material welfare of their people. Poetical and musical assemblies should also form the common base of those festivals, to which expositions of art, agriculture and industry might be usefully added. The interest of business, equally with that of pleasure, would thus be united to the higher motives of patriotism, to attract a great meeting at these new Olympic games, serving as a national link between sister cities, separated by institutions like those of ancient Greece. One of these great reunions might take place every three years, so that in a dozen years, the Shannon, Clyde, Severn, and Laita, would successfully assemble on their banks a deputation of each of the members separated from the great Celtic family.[12]

Ill health prevented de Gaulle, who died in 1880, from organizing any further Celtic congresses. However, the idea continued to attract support. In 1882, for example, the Society for the Preservation of the Irish Language proposed holding its own congress and inviting "representatives from the Celtic societies of the Highlands and the principality of Wales" to discuss how the study and use of Irish might be best promoted.[13]

The growing interest in Celtic affairs in Ireland was marked by the establishment of the Pan-Celtic Society in Dublin in March 1888. Gerald Pelly and Augustine Downey, two medical students, along with Mathew

Daly Wyer, a Dublin barrister, were largely responsible for its creation.[14] The society was primarily focused on discussing Irish literature, and its membership included many of the up-and-coming Irish writers of the 1890s. Every Friday at eight o'clock, meetings were held where members delivered papers, read poems, sang songs, and critiqued one another's work.[15] The motto of the Pan-Celtic Society was "Do tháinig anam a h-Éirinn," which the society itself translated as "To Bring a Soul to Ireland." The objects of the society were:

1. To serve as a medium of intellectual intercourse for Irish littérateurs, with a view to the creation of a greater literary activity in Ireland.
2. To cultivate and spread a knowledge of the History, Language, Literature, Music and Art of Ireland.
3. To contribute to Irish Magazines and Periodicals, and to encourage the publication and sale of Irish Books.
4. By the publication of Original Poems, Essays, Tales and Sketches, to illustrate the national characteristics of Ireland, and thus "to treasure her legends, eternalize her traditions and people her scenery."
5. The establishment of an Irish Literary Magazine, if deemed practicable.[16]

The literary nature of the group was obvious, and the hope that the society would serve "as a medium of intellectual intercourse for Irish littérateurs" showed that its members did not envision a mass movement that would appeal to all members of Irish society. The interest in Irish history, language, and legends indicated that the members hoped to create an image of Ireland in their work that was based on a romantic vision of the country's past. Indeed, in taking up Denis Florence McCarthy's challenge to "people her scenery" there was an implication that the contemporary Irish man or woman was not romantic enough for the Irish landscape and needed to be supplemented by literary creations.[17] What was also apparent from these initial objectives was that members were primarily interested in discussing Irish material. The extent to which the group would function as a Pan-Celtic body remained to be seen.

Nevertheless, the structure of the Pan-Celtic Society demonstrated the value members placed on Ireland's Celtic past and their hopes to incorporate elements of this in running their organization. Membership was limited to those who had some literary work published, but the society's constitution also allowed those who had a "knowledge of the Celtic language" to join.[18] The fact that knowledge of "the Celtic language," rather than "a Celtic language," was prized by the society shows that members were largely conflating Celticness and Irishness. An Irish-language class for beginners was held once a week, though only those people who were introduced by a member of the society were permitted to attend.[19] There were six official positions within the society, and all of them were given a formal Irish title at the suggestion of R. J. O'Mulrenin, the teacher of the Irish-language class. Some of these positions, like *táisgeóir* (treasurer) and *rúnaíre* (secretary), were simply Irish translations of the titles one might expect to find in any society. Yet the names given to other offices suggests that members of the society imagined themselves as taking up the mantle of the ancient Gaelic poets and literati, borrowing various titles directly out of old Irish genealogies. One elected official was the *saoí*, or critic, who was charged with evaluating the poems and songs submitted by members. In medieval Ireland, *saoí* was the title given to learned scholars. The managing secretary of the society was known as the *seanachuidhe*, the keeper of traditions, while the title of the librarian was changed from the direct translation *leabhar-lannidhe* to *ollamh*, the honorary name given to master poets in Gaelic society. Interestingly, the Pan-Celtic Society also operated according to a Celtic calendar. The election of officers occurred not once but twice a year at general meetings that were held on the first of May and the first of November. These dates were significant because they marked two of the most important days in pagan Irish society: the feast of *Bealtaine* (spring festival) and the feast of *Samhain* (harvest festival).[20] The Pan-Celtic Society, then, distinguished itself from other literary clubs of the time by presenting the group as deeply connected to Ireland's ancient, pagan, exotic past.

For the most part, the society's members tended to be young men from a middle-class background living or working in Dublin. Of the society's eighty-four listed members, sixty-four were men and twenty were women, with seventeen of these women being unmarried. One member, Patrick Mc-Call, created a list with a little pen picture of each member, thereby allowing us some insight into the society's membership. Many of the men were university educated, and McCall listed several as members of the Royal Irish Academy or graduates of Trinity College. The members' occupations, with several barristers, solicitors, professors, and MPs listed, indicate that the society was primarily a middle-class organization.[21] Yet the leaders of the Pan-Celtic Society did not want their group to be a mere social outlet for the Dublin bourgeoisie. All members were expected to write literature, and in 1889 an amendment to the society's rules declared that "every member shall forward at least three contributions each half year, to be read at meetings of the Society."[22] By looking at the nature of the literature discussed at the society's meetings, it is possible to understand what interests and passions the members had. Although papers on the work of Ralph Waldo Emerson or Walt Whitman were occasionally delivered, poetry or songs related to Ireland usually dominated proceedings. Such work tended to focus either on the Irish landscape or on Irish history, with the titles of these poems and songs suggesting a strongly nationalist bent among the members. Songs such as "Imprisoned," "An Irish War Song," "An Irish Patriot," and "The Wind That Shakes the Barley," along with poems such as "The Saxon Shilling," "An Eviction Sketch," and "An Imprisoned Patriot," were typical fare at gatherings. McCall described several of the members of the society as "Fenians," and while not all members were politically active, it is clear that most were sympathetic toward nationalist politics. At the same time, the Pan-Celts' constitution insisted that "the society shall be non-politicised and non-sectarian but *National* in the broadest sense of the word."[23]

The most striking aspect of the Pan-Celtic Society was that there was nothing particularly Pan-Celtic about it. An occasional paper was delivered on the theme of Pan-Celticism, but Ireland was the almost exclusive focus of the society's writings and discussions. One might wonder, then, why the group named itself the Pan-Celtic Society. According to William Patrick Ryan, a journalist involved in various Irish literary groups, Wyer and Downey originally wanted to call the group the "Irish National Literary Society" but believed that the word *national* was too strongly associated with politics. In the end, Ryan wrote, the *Pan-Celtic* moniker was used because it was "appropriate and comprehensive enough."[24] It might be speculated that the title was adopted to suit the wishes of one member, Hugh H. Johnson. Johnson had been born in Dublin to an Irish mother and Welsh father but had been raised and educated in Wales. A fluent Welsh speaker, Johnson delivered a number of papers to the society discussing Welsh literature. McCall remembered that Johnson regularly amused other members with his impersonation of an Anglophobic Welsh parson.[25] Johnson tried to encourage his fellow members to take more of an interest in non-Irish affairs.

He asked the Pan-Celtic Society to celebrate St. David's Day, the Welsh national holiday, although little appears to have been done in this regard, and while Johnson's contributions were always received well they did not inspire others to take a similar interest in Wales.[26]

The focus of most members was never really Pan-Celtic in the truest sense, and perhaps it is no surprise that the group survived only three years. In the winter of 1890, the owner of the Temperance Hotel, where the group met, died. The hotel was sold off, and the society suddenly found itself bereft of a gathering place, as well as losing their private library, which apparently had been misplaced in the confusion.[27] With little enthusiasm for rebuilding, the Pan-Celtic Society dissolved in 1891, with many of the members joining the National Literary Society in Dublin.[28] The group had succeeded in introducing the label of Pan-Celticism to Ireland, but nothing else, as the title proved to be little more than a fashionable name for what was really an Irish literature society. Yet the desire to embrace a truer sense of Pan-Celticism did exist in Ireland. In 1892, William O'Brien, MP, wrote:

> Is it even too bold a vision of far-off years to dream of a time when passing the stormy Moyle once more into the Scottish isles and glens, the children of the Irish Gael might draw closer even than recent events have drawn those bonds of blood and clanship which once bound us to our Scottish soldier colonists who conquered with Angus and knelt to Columbkille?—Nay, spreading still further a-field and a-main, discover new nations of blood relations in our near cousins of the Isle of Man, and our farther cousins among the misty mountains of Wales and the old-world cities of Brittany; and combining their traditions, their aspirations, and genius with the ever-growing Celtic element with which we have penetrated the New World, confront the giant, Despair, which is preying upon this aged century, body and soul, with a world-wide Celtic league, with faith and wit as spiritual, with valour as dauntless, and sensibilities as unspoilt as when all the world and love were young.[29]

The man largely responsible for answering this call and creating an active Pan-Celtic movement in Ireland was Edmund Edward Fournier D'Albe. Born in England in 1868, Fournier came to Ireland in 1895 to take up the post of senior lecturer of physics at Trinity College.[30] Although a brilliant physicist, Fournier also demonstrated a passion for indigenous Irish culture. He joined the newly formed Feis Ceoil Association in 1896 in order to promote the study of Irish and international music. Fournier quickly mastered the Irish language. He published an Irish-English dictionary, as well as winning first prize at the *oireachtas* in 1900 for his essay in Irish entitled "The Qualities That Build Up a Nation."[31] It would appear that Fournier's interest in establishing relationships between the Celtic nations came from his own personal sense of connection to the different Celtic countries. Fournier maintained that while he was English born his family name was of Breton extraction, and he claimed to have had familial ties to the Scottish Highlands. The fact that he lived and worked in Ireland, and his ability to speak the native language, allowed Fournier to claim a sense of Irishness. His work with the Feis Ceoil Association provided him the opportunity to network with Welsh cultural nationalists, and he was made an honorary member of the gorsedd, the Welsh bardic institute, in 1897.[32] Fournier was of a romantic disposition, and given the bond he felt to these various Celtic lands it is no surprise that he began to think about how the different Celtic groups could be brought together in a more formal capacity. In his travels to Wales, Fournier also learned of an assembly of Welsh and Irish poets and musicians held in Wales in 1100, supported by the patronage of King Gruffydd ap Cynan. For Fournier, this was evidence of an ancient sense of a shared Celtic past between Ireland and Wales, and he hoped that this feeling could be rekindled among all the Celtic countries.

In his crusade for Pan-Celticism, Fournier found a generous and committed ally in Lord Castletown, Bernard Edward Barnaby Fitzpatrick. Castletown was a wealthy landlord, owning twenty thousand acres around Doneraile in Cork. A committed unionist who helped found the Irish Loyal and Patriotic Union in 1885, Castletown had also served in the British Army. Yet he equally embraced his Irish roots. As a Fitzpatrick, Castletown believed he could trace his lineage back to the ancient Gaelic rulers of Osraige and therefore felt a sense of duty to native Irish culture.[33] Newspaper portraits of Castletown often referred to the fact that he was an Irish speaker.[34] However, an examination of Castletown's personal correspondence reveals that letters written in Irish needed to be translated in order for him to read them, suggesting that he had no more than a limited command of the language. Yet he was more than willing to use his wealth to support Irish-language initiatives, and this enabled him to establish warm friendships with prominent members of the Gaelic League like Douglas Hyde, Patrick Pearse, and Agnes O'Farrelly. When Castletown gave a speech in London in 1898 on the excessive rate of taxation on Ireland, he commented that perhaps a "Pan-Celtic league" was required as a counterbalance to Anglo-Saxonism. Fournier read about this and wrote to Castletown, inviting him to join the Pan-Celtic movement.[35] Castletown became a committed Pan-Celt, and his financial support, combined with Fournier's energy and organizational abilities, allowed the Pan-Celtic movement to come to prominence.

Unlike the members of the defunct Pan-Celtic Society, Fournier and Castletown were interested in genuinely exploring what it meant to be a Celt in the broadest sense. Like many ethnic nationalists in Europe at the time, Fournier tended to accept that language was the best marker for understanding where racial boundaries between people lay. The fact that the Celtic languages were related linguistically was proof in the eyes of the Pan-Celts that the people who lived in the areas where the languages were spoken were also related by blood. Fournier believed that a Pan-Celtic association was required to assist with "the uplifting of a somewhat neglected and oppressed race."[36] The Celts were oppressed by Anglo-Saxons who judged them to be an inferior people and were neglected in the sense that the Irish, Welsh, and Scottish did not appreciate the true extent of their racial heritage.[37] Although primarily interested in promoting native Celtic culture, Fournier was adamant about distinguishing the Celts as a race. For example, speaking of Scotland, Fournier wrote that the notion of Scottish nationality was "indefensible from the racial point of view," owing to the division of the country between Celtic Highlanders and Germanic Lowlanders.[38] Hence only the Highlands, and not Scotland in its entirety, was recognized as a Celtic nation; as Fournier wrote, "We are primarily concerned with the Celtic population of Scotland—the Highland Gaels—and as Lowlanders are largely of Teutonic blood, they could hardly be regarded as an integral part of a Celtic nation."[39] The racial link was important because, culturally speaking, no real commonality existed between the Irish, Manx, Welsh, Scottish, and Bretons. Fournier, however, was confident "that the race is becoming conscious of a great and proud destiny." As a result, a Celtic organization was now necessary to facilitate "an exchange of counsel and information, and for an active collaboration in vital matters."[40]

This proposed Pan-Celtic body would not just be of benefit to those of Celtic stock. Both Fournier and Castletown believed that something of the human spirit had been lost in the industrial age. For Fournier, the Celtic race had a mission to save not just itself but all of humanity from the lack of spirituality and imagination that had developed in the modern world. He wrote, "The Celt will have to prepare himself, not merely for a leading position in his own country, but also for a great mission in the world at large, where his intense spirituality . . . will make him the advocate of the oppressed and the representative of moral force in the affairs of mankind."[41] The enemy in this case was Anglo-Saxon industrial capitalism, which, in Fournier's eyes, had caused people to crave material gain while losing out on the simple, spiritual pleasures of life. He hoped that the Pan-Celtic movement would develop a "militant Celticism, directed mainly against the deadening and demoralizing influences of modern Anglo-Saxondom."[42] The advantage the Celtic people had over the "less imaginative races" was their spiritual heritage, which was based on "the passion and love for all things beautiful."[43] According to Fournier, the Celtic love of beauty would save humanity from the soulless excess of the modern world: "The power of the Celtic race, when unified and brought into play, will exert a great and beneficent influence in the advancement of mankind."[44] Castletown shared these sentiments, declaring, "We of the Celtic faith are trying to preserve for the Celtic nationalities, and indirectly for all nationalities, some of the earliest, some of the most beautiful, and some of the most touching ideals of daily life and thought."[45]

Indeed, Castletown was the most outspoken in his criticism of contemporary society. He declared that "in earlier and simpler times man lived more according to nature, and was nearer heaven. Now, we may be more intellectual and more comfortable, but the sense of happiness is less."[46] The reality of the modern world was an "an awful thought, city upon city swallowing up the life, the beauty of the world, with increasing machine-like voracity with a pitiless calling for more. A city of the dreadful night where men write and sleep, but not the sleep of rest or the writing of joy."[47] The Celtic people would not suffer such a fate, however, because "as a purely descended race we are near to the great early imagination of primeval man, because having had little to do with the plain practical life of cities we have lived in closer commune with Earth and Nature and so our sensibilities have never been blunted."[48] Castletown believed that the strength of religious faith among the Celts was further proof of their resistance to the temptations of the modern world. He wrote:

> In the great waves of unbelief and doubt that sweep over the world, we see the Celtic race standing out pre-eminent in religious thought. I do not speak of one type of our Christian teaching, I say in all types. In Wales we have the powerful Church which appeals to many thoughtful minds, the Methodist—In Scotland the stern and vigourous Presbyterian stand out pre-eminent. In Brittany and in Ireland, and in many parts of Wales and Scotland, the great Catholic Church holds sway, while in Manx land and Cornwall religion is the guiding feature of the race.[49]

Furthermore, the Celtic people could shape the modern world through their respective diasporas. Castletown wrote that the millions of people of Celtic descent all around the world would rally to the Pan-Celts "if our cause is right, if our honour is pure and unsullied . . . If we can stand in this position no harm can come to us; we can have our say in the Councils of the world. We can mould the fate of these nations." Although Castletown believed that the spiritual superiority of the Celts would benefit humanity as a whole, he also noted that the countries in which the Celts lived, primarily France and Britain, stood to gain most from their loyal Celtic subjects and citizens.[50] The Celtic refusal to chase material gain meant that they provided the men required to build the great empires of France and Britain. Castletown wrote, "As other nations are, we are not content to sweat for gold, we look to higher attributes, we produce the fighting men of our different nations, we produce the generals, the administrators, the diplomatics, the Great Divines, the Leaders of men."[51] Castletown predicted that the everlasting glory of Britain depended on a spiritual reinvigoration of Anglo-Saxons by their Celtic neighbors. This would be, in Castletown's words, "the Celtic victory, pure minds over worldly matter—the spirits of the air so often disregarded coming again to triumph over the coarse worldlie [*sic*] mindedness of the ages yet unborn."[52]

For Fournier and Castletown, the combination of the various ideas they had on Pan-Celticism could be distilled down to one word: *Celtia*. Fournier gave the title of *Celtia* to the Pan-Celtic journal he established in

1900, but it was more than that. The word was, according to Fournier "formed after the analogy of Germania, Britannia, and Gallia, and denoting the personification of the Celtic race. The word has already become popular, and I have been present when toasts were drunk to 'Celtia' in Wales and Brittany. Dublin is recognized as the capital of 'Celtia.'"[53] Fournier, who wanted Castletown to be the figurehead of the new Celtic movement, addressed him as "Tighearna Celtia" (Lord Celtia) in their correspondence.[54] Bernard Doyle, editor of *Fáinne an Lae* and one of the most outspoken Pan-Celtic supporters, wrote at length describing Celtia as

> the name adopted at Cardif last year for the aggregate territory of the Five Celtic Nations, i.e., those nationalities whose surviving, or rather reviving, national languages belongs to the Celtic family of Indo-European languages. That definition leaves the questions of blood-relationship, of historical connection, of racial purity, and of present political status altogether on one side. "Celtia" has an actual existence in the hearts of those who speak and love their Celtic language, and are in sympathy with the parallel efforts of their kinsfolk across the sea. "Celtia" embraces the most mountainous regions of Ireland, Great Britain and France. It possesses all the rarest gems of landscape beauty in these countries. It is inhabited by the torn remnants of a once mighty race, which "shook every empire and founded none." Its people furnish some of the best soldiers and the boldest mariners and fishermen of Europe. And yet they have not founded an empire. They have not even formed a nation with all its attributes. Each of the five nationalities lives under the shadow of some central power, by which it has often been cruelly oppressed.

Doyle insisted that, through the existence of Celtia, "the five nations are linked together, however far apart they may lie [in] their political or religious tendencies." He quoted Heinrich Zimmer, the professor of Celtic at Friedrich Wilhelm University who said, "Whenever a signal fire is lighted in one part of the Celtic fringe, answering fires shine out in three other places." Furthermore, Doyle insisted that "Celtia has colonies too. Sixteen million of unabsorbed Irishmen dwell under the Stars and Stripes. Large colonies of Gaelic-speaking crofters have settled in Canada. Welsh-speaking colonies are stoutly maintaining themselves in Brazil and Patagonia, and hardy Bretons have sprinkled the iron-bound coasts of the north-east wherever the ocean is enlivened with their fishing fleets."[55]

Together Castletown and Fournier, with Doyle's newspaper in a supporting role, set about making Celtia a reality through the Pan-Celtic movement. Their main goal, according to Fournier, was to bring about the federation of all the linguistic and cultural organizations in the Celtic territories.[56] This, he hoped, would help preserve the indigenous language in these areas, which Fournier considered to be the most burning question at hand for all Celtic people.[57] Fournier envisioned a congress where philologists, linguists, musicians, and writers from across the Celtic world could come together and help reestablish a Celtic racial consciousness that was necessary for Celtic culture to be preserved. He also hoped that the Welsh gorsedd could come to Dublin and establish an Irish bardic institution, with poetic titles and elaborate ceremonies similar to those already in Wales.[58] Fournier wrote that the congress would mark an important epoch in "the annals of this Western Race, and its effects will be felt throughout the length and breadth of those beautiful lands which the Celt can still call his own. And it would be strange if this visible symbol of Celtic union did not put new heart into the gallant fighters of all the Celtic nationalities."[59]

Fournier brought together a group of like-minded Pan-Celts in 1898 in Belfast and quickly began taking steps to organize supporting committees in Wales, Scotland, and the Isle of Man. His aim was to hold a Pan-Celtic congress in Dublin in 1900 where common problems of the Celtic race could be discussed. In attempting this, Fournier was following in the path of the Pan-Slavists, who had organized congresses as a means of bringing about a greater unity between the different Slavic peoples.[60] At the same time, the influence of Charles de Gaulle's call for a kind of Celtic Olympiad was evident, as Fournier envisioned great demonstrations of Celtic pageantry, music, and culture accompanying these congresses. He also hoped that the festivals would be held triennially and would be hosted by each Celtic nation on a rotating basis. Fournier planned to install prominent men as president of each national committee in order to quickly raise the profile of the new movement, and he possibly hoped to win their financial support as well. Fournier planned to have Lord Aberdeen or Lord Campbell serve as the Highlands president, Lord Tredegar or the Marquis De Bute as the Welsh president, and the Duc de Rohan possibly as the Breton president.[61]

Although Castletown and Fournier were committed to building harmonious relations between the different branches of the Celtic race, both also believed that Ireland would play a special role in returning the Celts to global prominence. In their minds, Irish literature was older and more prestigious than that of any other Celtic country, the Irish language was the most Celtic, and the vigorous nature of Irish politics was a sign that Irish national spirit burned more strongly than that of the other Celtic peoples. Hence Irish leadership of the Pan-Celtic movement would be beneficial for the other Celtic nations but also for Ireland itself. Fournier wrote to Castletown, "I am also of opinion that Ireland is particularly adapted for taking the lead in this matter, and that its position at the head of the Celtic world will impart to the people a healthy sense of power and dignity."[62] To this end, Fournier sent a circular to potential Pan-Celtic supporters in Ireland in early 1899, asking them to consider the following questions for the upcoming congress:

1. The language or languages in which the general or sectional proceedings are to be conducted.
2. The holding of a Pan-Celtic concert
3. The possibility of producing plays in one or more of the Celtic languages
4. The means of cultivating and utilizing the living Celtic languages
5. The means of facilitating the publication of ancient Celtic MSS
6. The creation or extension of modern Celtic literature
7. The position of Anglo-Celtic or Franco-Celtic literature
8. The development of Celtic arts and crafts
9. The comparative study of Celtic archeology, ethnology and philology
10. The preservation of existing Celtic institutions and national characteristics
11. The means of fostering a close cooperation between the five Celtic nations
12. The position of the Celtic colonies in the New World together with any other points which may suggest themselves[63]

This circular caught the attention of Margaret Stokes, who had already agreed to serve on the Irish committee in charge of putting together the first Pan-Celtic congress in Dublin. Stokes was a well-known antiquarian in her own right, as well as being the brother of Whitley Stokes, a renowned Celtic philologist. Stokes wrote a scathing response to Castletown, pouring scorn on many of the points raised in the circular:

> The language in which the General or Sectional proceedings should be conducted is undoubtedly English—the language in which all educated classes and <u>most</u> of the uneducated speak. . . .
>
> It would be wholly impossible and foolish to produce a play in Irish-Manx-Welsh-Gaelic or Breton. I do not know what other Celtic languages to which you refer.
>
> There are two forms—the ancient and the modern—of the Irish language. One should be learned as any ancient language, containing literature is learned; the other is a mere patois which it may be useful for a few clergymen whose duty is to teach religion in the Western Islands to be able to talk in. . . .
>
> I do not understand what is meant by "Modern Celtic Literature" any more than I could understand what is meant by "Modern Teutonic Literature." Would you call a Dutch doll a Teutonic doll? . . .
>
> What institutions and characteristics are alluded to and where do these unmixed Celtic people exist. . . .
>
> I do not understand what is meant by "Celtic Colonies" in the New World.[64]

Stokes's letter was not a good omen for Fournier and Castletown in their efforts to promote Pan-Celticism in Ireland. If someone who had already agreed to be of assistance to the Pan-Celtic cause had such a vague idea of what "Celtic" meant and such a dismissive attitude toward the modern Celtic languages (calling Irish as a "mere patois"), then this did not bode well for efforts to win new supporters to the Pan-Celtic movement. As supporting the indigenous Celtic languages was one of the central pillars of Pan-Celticism, Fournier and Castletown probably expected a hostile attitude from those who had little time for the Welsh and Irish tongues. What was to catch them by surprise, however, was the fact that the fiercest resistance in Ireland to the idea of Pan-Celticism came from those who had already begun the fight of trying to save the Irish language.

CHAPTER 5

PROTESTANTS PLAYING PAGANS

In December 1923, Edmund Edward Fournier sent a letter to Lord Castletown to congratulate him on the successful publication of his memoirs. Twenty years previously, Fournier and Castletown had worked closely together in forming the Celtic Association, the Pan-Celtic body that promoted closer connections among the six Celtic "nations" of western Europe. The Celtic Association had long since become defunct, and the two men had not corresponded for a number of years. In writing his congratulations, Fournier also thanked Castletown for his kind words about him and the work he did on behalf of the Celtic Association. He wrote to Castletown that he, Fournier, might have been better off never becoming involved with the Celtic Association but confessed that he could not resist, as "the glamour of the Celtic Renaissance was too much for me." Yet Fournier lamented that the Celtic Association had not succeeded in its aim of solidifying the position of the Irish language in Ireland. He told Castletown, "I still think that the way we and the Celtic Association set about preserving the Irish language was the right one,—linking it up to the Welsh and Scots Gaelic and Breton. But the 'wild men' would not have it, and now there is little hope for it."[1]

The "wild men" that Fournier referred to were Irish nationalists who rejected the Pan-Celtic call to form a closer bond with their "racial brethren" in Britain and France and who opposed any kind of union between the Celtic Association and the Gaelic League. Though many prominent Gaelic

Leaguers, like Douglas Hyde, Eoin MacNeill, and Patrick Pearse, were sympathetic to Pan-Celtic sentiment, a large number of rank-and-file members expressed their disdain for the Celtic Association, and the Gaelic League hierarchy decided to avoid any connection with the Pan-Celtic movement. Ignored by the most powerful cultural organization in early twentieth-century Ireland, the Celtic Association failed to attract a popular following in the Emerald Isle and had all but disappeared by the outbreak of the First World War. The question we might ask is why the "wild men" were opposed to any links between the Gaelic League and the Celtic Association, especially as their goals of preserving the Irish language and promoting cultural distinctiveness between Ireland and England appeared to overlap.[2]

There were several reasons why the Pan-Celtic movement failed to win popular acclaim. Religion certainly played a part, with the prominent Protestant membership of the Celtic Association being distrusted by some Catholic clergy within the Gaelic League. Politically, the Celtic Association promoted a fidelity to the British Empire that was at odds with the anti-imperial mind-set aroused among Irish nationalists during the Boer War. The efforts of the Celtic Association to "import" Welsh cultural institutions like the gorsedd into Ireland provoked a negative reaction, as Irish cultural enthusiasts believed that Welsh influences were as unwelcome in Ireland as English ones, not least for their pagan associations. The rituals and processions of the Pan-Celtic movement struck many Irish people as completely unhelpful in dealing with Ireland's problems. In most capacities, the Gaelic League embraced modernity and progress, while the Pan-Celts yearned for a simpler, less materialistic Ireland. Therefore the Celtic Association not only failed to attract support from the majority of Irish nationalists but appeared to be working in opposition to the cultural revolution transforming the country at the beginning of the twentieth century.

As a member of the Gaelic League, Fournier was aware of both its growing popularity and its increasing influence on nationalist opinion in Ireland. He also understood that for the Pan-Celtic movement to succeed in Ireland, the support of the Gaelic League would be vital. As the Pan-Celts and the Gaelic League appeared to have similar objectives, Fournier may have imagined that such support would be forthcoming. Yet from the beginning it was evident that some members of the executive council of the Gaelic League were not enthusiastic supporters of Fournier's ideas. In September 1898, the executive council discussed what the League's position should be toward Pan-Celticism. They decided that the League "should remain neutral towards it for the present, as no scheme of any kind had been formulated in connection with it."[3] This neutral stance reflects the divided opinions that had formed among the council. Some members, like Eoin MacNeill, Douglas Hyde, and Patrick Pearse, were supportive of the sentiment behind Pan-Celticism at least. The opposition to Fournier and the Pan-Celts came primarily from three people: P. J. Keawell, manager of the Gaelic League newspaper, *An Claidheamh Soluis*; Norma Borthwick; and Mary O'Reilly. Keawell had been a member of the earlier Pan-Celtic Society,[4] and Borthwick boasted of her Scottish heritage,[5] yet this did not prevent them from having a negative view of Pan-Celticism. As Fournier's group continued to grow and pressure came on the Gaelic League to support Pan-Celticism, Keawell, Borthwick, and O'Reilly remained adamant that the League should stay aloof.

The first step Fournier took to bind the Gaelic League to the cause of Pan-Celticism was to invite Douglas Hyde to serve on the committee organizing a Pan-Celtic congress in Dublin. Hyde, as president of the Gaelic League, referred the matter to the executive council. The reply he received was that the council could not approve Hyde serving on the committee in his capacity as president. The council did inform Hyde that he was free to act in whatever way he saw fit as a private individual but stated that "they would be sorry that any of their members should give time or money to an enterprise that could not help the Irish language."[6] Hyde acquiesced to their wishes and told Fournier that he was unable to be of assistance.[7] Fournier asked Hyde a second time in January 1899, but after a vote the executive council again rejected the idea, informing Hyde that "the committee did not consider any useful end would be gained by his joining as President of the Gaelic League."[8] Desperate to gain some measure of support from the League, Fournier tried again, this time asking the executive committee to simply appoint an official representative of the League to the Pan-Celtic congress board, and again the reply was in the negative.[9] The attitude of the League hierarchy toward the Pan-Celts upset some of the rank-and-file members. In particular, members of the Belfast branch voiced their displeasure at the failure of the League to offer assistance to the Pan-Celtic congress.[10]

The most outspoken critic of the anti-Pan-Celtic wing of the Gaelic League was Bernard Doyle, the editor of the bilingual *Fáinne an Lae*. Doyle used his newspaper to support Pan-Celticism at every turn. He believed that those opposed to Pan-Celticism were guilty of "parochialism" and would "confine our efforts within the confines of Ireland, and even within the limits of one organization in Ireland, [which] is one of the many evidences of that slavishness that, foully born in the ruins of Limerick, has marked us more deeply than the sun has burnt the American negro." In trying to convert the skeptical, Doyle simultaneously tried to play to the vanity of Irish nationalism to support Pan-Celticism while implying that opponents had succumbed to colonization:

> Such narrowness was unknown in Erin as long as even the fragments of our social system remained. Both the spoken and written Gaelic is evidence of the quick and wholesome interest we took in our neighbours' affairs until the blighting influence of English came, not to join us in community of thought with the Continent, but to cut us off from the rest of the world forever. It would be stupid, as well as ungenerous, to shut our eyes to what is going on among the neighbouring nations, which are so closely allied to us in blood and language. There would be a meanness in such action, seeing that we are, even in our weakness, the greatest of the Five Nations.[11]

Those who opposed the Pan-Celtic ideal remained steadfast, however, and soon began openly criticizing Fournier and the Pan-Celts. Margaret O'Reilly, a member of the executive committee of the Gaelic League, blasted the Pan-Celtic movement in the pages of the *Freeman's Journal*. She wrote that while on first glance Pan-Celticism might appear to be inconsequential, "closely regarded the Pan-Celtic Congress is not harmless. It is unreal, there is no force behind it, it is the mere parasite of a serious movement." O'Reilly noted that the Gaelic League had thrived "with no material resources" and had been formed by "nine men, among whom there was not one man of wealth." In doing so, O'Reilly was trying to emphasize that the Pan-Celtic leaders were aristocrats who knew nothing of the struggle of the Gaelic League. Indeed, she sarcastically commented that one member of the Pan-Celtic committee "has actually done a man's share for the spread, if not the preservation, of Irish. For many a peasant who might be speaking Irish by his Clare fireside to-day finds himself and his language in America owing to Lord Inchiquin." O'Reilly observed that apart from "a few stray members of the Gaelic League" most Pan-Celts did not speak Irish and had not offered financial assistance to the Irish-language movement. "You would look in vain down the list of subscriptions for a half-crown from the noble and entitled president, or from the very energetic secretary, or from the overwhelming majority of the Irish Committee of the Pan-Celtic Congress." O'Reilly referred to the proposed Pan-Celtic congress as a plan to bring "foreigners" to Dublin. She stated that the reason that Pan-Celticism was so out of touch with Irish cultural nationalism was that "the gentleman with whom this grand idea originated is not Irish at all, and has lived in this country for less than three years. Only a foreigner would so mistake the trend of the times."[12] O'Reilly's letter highlights the flexible nature of Celtic identity among Irish nationalists. Members of the Gaelic League could simultaneously celebrate their Celtic heritage while dismissing other Celtic nationalists who planned to attend the Pan-Celtic congress as foreigners. Of course, this flexibility was also possible for Irishness, with people like O'Reilly condemning Irish people who did not learn Irish as unpatriotic and at the same time labeling Fournier, who had thrown himself into the study of Irish, as a foreigner.

This attack on Pan-Celticism was only the beginning. In May 1899 an editorial (presumably written by Keawell) in *An Claidheamh Soluis* ridiculed the Pan-Celtic movement and declared that the Gaelic League should have nothing to do with it. The article referred to Pan-Celticism as a "scheme" organized by Edmund Fournier, "who is not a native of this country." The writer also mocked the lack of a clear objective on the part of the Pan-Celts, labeling them "vague," and noted with glee that Fournier's efforts to win the support of the Feis Ceoil Association, the National Literary Society, and the Gaelic League had failed. The author insisted that the Pan-Celtic movement was alien because "it was based on no native element, was due to no native impulse; it was owing to one man, and that man a stranger in our country." The writer commented that while there were many "humourous" elements to the Pan-Celtic ideal, it also was a dangerous development for Ireland and needed to be opposed. In particular, the author worried that money that might otherwise be donated to the Gaelic League would instead find its way into the coffers of the Pan-Celtic group. The article expressed concern that the Pan-Celts were trying to bring about "a reversion to the bad old tradition of seeking foreign aid instead of trying to help ourselves," and it poured scorn upon Fournier's boast that the Pan-Celts would bring "vast and powerful forces to aid the struggling Gaelic language." Finally, the entire historical premise behind Pan-Celticism was rejected out of hand, with the author blasting that "it is absurd to talk of the reunion of the Celtic nations."[13]

In the wake of these articles, the Pan-Celtic question was ignored by the League hierarchy for a number of weeks but came to the fore once more when the national eisteddfod requested that representatives of the Gaelic League be sent to take part in the annual Welsh cultural festival. At the same time, a delegation of Pan-Celts, led by Lord Castletown, was also planning to attend the national eisteddfod in Wales in order to invite the gorsedd to the Celtic congress in Dublin the following year. Some within the League's executive committee were worried that their Welsh hosts would believe that their organization and the Pan-Celts were the same body. Keawell told his fellow committee members that "there was mention in the newspapers of a united delegation of different societies in Ireland under the headship of Lord Castletown, and he objected to anything identifying the Gaelic League with these societies at Cardiff."[14] Patrick Pearse was chosen to go to Wales and to give an address on behalf of the Gaelic League. John St. Clair Boyd, a member of the Belfast branch of the League, as well as a supporter of Pan-Celticism, offered to join Pearse. Boyd's offer was accepted, although the committee wrote to him emphasizing that the League was quite distinct from the Pan-Celtic movement and that he was not permitted to represent any other organization at the eisteddfod.[15] The actions of Pearse and Boyd while in Wales, however, provoked fury among those opposed to Pan-Celticism. Despite the disdain some League members had shown for the Pan-Celts, Pearse had a number of informal meetings with Lord Castletown during the eisteddfod. Pearse and Boyd also took part in certain ceremonies with the bards of the gorsedd and had honorary distinctions bestowed upon them.[16] Norma Borthwick later accused Pearse of drinking to the health of Queen Victoria at one eisteddfod function, something she believed violated the nonpolitical stance of the Gaelic League.[17] Those in the committee who opposed Pan-Celticism believed that Pearse and Boyd had disobeyed their instructions not to fraternize with the leaders of the Pan-Celts.

As usual, Bernard Doyle provided the retort for those in favor of Pan-Celticism. An article that appeared in *Fáinne an Lae* in July reminded those Gaelic Leaguers who objected to the presence of Pearse and Boyd at the national eisteddfod that the Irish had much to learn from the Welsh. It stated that the Welsh had put up the best fight among all the Celts to retain their language. "They had a complete victory in English speaking areas, and they restored their language fully across the country. If we desire such a victory, we must learn a lesson from this race. . . . Nothing will be better than to get to know them and talk with them."[18] The author of the article noted that the Welsh had shown themselves to be willing to embrace the Irish but that the failure of some members of the Gaelic League to reciprocate this feeling was a source of embarrassment. He wrote, "Irish people were greatly ashamed for lacking suitable interest in this friendship between the Welsh and the Gaels, but, indeed, it would be a great wonder if we were not so disinterested, for a while at any rate, because disinterest is the first thing given to anything useful in Ireland. For our own sake we must extend our heartfelt thanks to the group that gave a foundation to this friendship and we don't have anything for the group that was against this except scorn and contempt."[19]

Despite such sentiments, a scathing article appeared shortly afterwards in *An Claidheamh Soluis* that mocked the behavior of the Pan-Celtic delegation at the eisteddfod. In particular, the invitation of the Pan-Celts to the gorsedd asking them to visit Dublin was the subject of much derision. Keawell once more questioned whether the Pan-Celts were really Irish, writing, "We ask our readers to look down the names of the Pan-Celts given with the invitation and to analyse their claim to be styled the 'men of Ireland.'" Fournier was labeled "an Englishman of Huguenot extraction now resident in County Dublin." Keawell pointed out that of the nine men who signed the invitation only three were Irish and only one could read or write in the Irish language, although he neglected to mention that the one who could speak Irish was in fact Fournier, the "Englishman of Huguenot extraction."[20] Fournier's declaration that the coming of the gorsedd to Dublin would "be the signal for the awakening of the country to its Celtic traditions" was similarly mocked. Keawell wrote that the Irish people "were under the impression that Ireland did not need this signal from abroad to arouse it to its duty, and that a very lively awakening has been for some time in progress here." This highlights how Keawell, O'Reilly, and others felt the

League was already doing much of the work that Fournier's organization promised to do. On this point, the very right of the Pan-Celtic committee to invite the gorsedd to Dublin was questioned. In his attack on the Pan-Celts, Keawell observed that "the Gorsedd . . . is a Welsh national institution. As such it should have received a national invitation." The general committee of the Pan-Celtic congress, he maintained, had no moral authority to issue such an invitation, and as a result the gorsedd, and the Irish nation as a whole, were both being insulted, and would be further embarrassed if and when the gorsedd arrived in Dublin.[21]

This article provoked an angry response from those who were sympathetic to the efforts of Fournier and Castletown. Eoin MacNeill wrote a letter to the nationalist daily *Freeman's Journal* disassociating himself from the offending articles and claiming they had been printed without his knowledge.[22] Others privately expressed their disgust. Pearse wrote to Fournier that it had been a "painful surprise" for him to read these articles, and he assured Fournier that he had immediately telegraphed Dublin repudiating their publication.[23] Boyd was similarly upset. He wrote to MacNeill, "I may say that any attacks on P.C. Congress appearing in the *Claidheamh* show a great want of ordinary good manners." He asked MacNeill to carefully supervise future articles in the newspaper because "attacks frequently appear in the *Claidheamh* alienating many who might be of great service to us." Boyd believed that the criticism of Pan-Celticism was really a personal attack on Lord Castletown, owing to his unionist politics. He told MacNeill that Father Hayde, president of the Cardiff Gaelic League, had met Castletown in Wales and believed he was "sincere and most anxious to do all he can for the Language movement; he has left behind him here a very deep impression of his patriotism and personal worth."[24] A showdown among the Gaelic League executive committee on the issue was inevitable. At their next meeting, MacNeill raised the question of the articles in *An Claidheamh Soluis* and produced a number of letters that League members had written in protest. Meanwhile Mary O'Reilly defended their publication and criticized MacNeill's letter to the *Freeman's Journal*. O'Reilly and Keawell both resigned immediately from their positions on *An Claidheamh Soluis* and the committee.[25] Norma Borthwick would also resign from the executive committee a few weeks later.

With the departure of these committee members, some of the most hostile voices against Pan-Celticism in the League hierarchy had been removed. As senior figures like Hyde, MacNeill, and Pearse had shown themselves to be receptive to the overtures of Fournier, the path had seemingly been cleared for closer cooperation between the Gaelic League and the Pan-Celts. Fournier wrote in Irish to MacNeill, "I hope that a 'Celtic Peace' will come to our country, as it has come to the other four countries."[26] Fournier was to have his wish in seeing peace develop between his group and the Gaelic League, but an alliance between the two was to prove elusive. Pearse declared to Fournier, "I am making a great effort to convert the Committee to Pan-Celticism. . . . Frankly, however, I have little hope that the League will see its way to take part in the movement."[27] The executive committee reasoned that the wider membership was as divided on the question of Pan-Celticism as they themselves had been. While a majority in the committee was now sympathetic toward Fournier's ideas, they decided that in trying to support the Pan-Celtic movement they would destroy their own. At the end of August 1899, the executive council released a statement outlining the official position of the League regarding Pan-Celticism. It stated that "taken as a whole, the objects comprised under the title of Pan-Celticism extend beyond the scope of the Gaelic League. The Gaelic League, as a body, is therefore precluded from joining in a Pan-Celtic movement. It is also precluded, as are its organs and branches, and official meetings, local and central, from either adopting a Pan-Celtic movement as a whole, or taking up an attitude of hostility towards it."

Individual members were allowed to participate in the Pan-Celtic movement in any manner they pleased, so long as it did not interfere with the business of the Gaelic League. The League's own commitment to having a positive relationship with Welsh and Scottish cultural enthusiasts was re-affirmed, as the committee proclaimed, "We desire to maintain the fullest and most cordial friendship between the language movement in Ireland and in the other countries that have retained their Celtic speech." They emphasized, however, that they now considered the issue closed as far as the Gaelic League was concerned. The executive council acknowledged that the Pan-Celtic question had the potential to divide their own organization, stating, "We consider that the agitation of this question, favourably or unfavourably, with the League is hurtful to the progress and solidarity of the Language Movement and destructive of the concentration necessary to attain the objects of the movement."[28]

This was a bitter blow for Fournier, Castletown, and the Pan-Celtic movement. Without the support of the Gaelic League, it seemed unlikely that Pan-Celticism could flourish in Ireland. This would undermine the Pan-Celtic project completely. Fournier believed that Ireland would be the center of the Pan-Celtic world and that the other countries would take their lead from Dublin.[29] In response to the Gaelic League's decision, Bernard Doyle wrote, "The 'Fágfaimíd súd mar atá sé' [we will leave it as it is] attitude of the Gaelic League Executive towards the Pan-Celtic movement ought not to surprise anyone who knows the history of the Gaelic League so far . . . a primitive organization that has not yet adopted even the simplest form of a national and representative constitution."[30] One observer, using the pen name "Old Sincerity," compared the logic used by the Gaelic League to that of a priest who might refuse to join any organization whose purpose extended "beyond the scope of the priesthood." Challenging the authority of the League to even rule on the matter, the writer asked, "Is not all this too pettish, too girlish, too much tying to the apron string? Could the Tsar of all the Russians have issued a more daring, a more sweeping ukase? Let me suggest to the Executive, with 'the fullest and the most cordial friendship,' that liberty is like to an elastic ball, the more you press it the more it will resist, but too much pressure may burst it."[31]

Fournier and Castletown made one last effort to bring the Gaelic League over to their side, hoping that Castletown's wealth might sway the executive committee. In October 1899 Castletown offered to donate fifty pounds to the Gaelic League. The offer came with two stipulations, however. First, Castletown asked that twenty other donors be found to contribute a similar amount. Second, he requested that three or four of the contributors be allowed to form a small committee to "watch over the movement and the disposal of the funds thus contributed."[32] Fifty pounds was a substantial sum at this time, and few outside the Irish aristocracy would have been in a position to donate so generously. Given that any such contributors would likely have had some social connection with Lord Castletown, he was in a position to gain considerable influence in the Gaelic League if the offer was accepted. The proposal, however, was rejected out of hand. Charles MacNeill, brother of Eoin, wrote to Castletown saying that the conditions "could not be becomingly accepted by such a body as the Committee of the Gaelic League." MacNeill pointed out that the committee had already been elected by members of the League to oversee the movement and its finances. It could not, MacNeill stated, "relinquish its functions and responsibilities into the hands of any others."[33]

Hoping to avoid any further unrest, the committee permitted *An Claidheamh Soluis* to print a notice of Castletown's offer to contribute to the League's funds, although his stipulations were not mentioned. This angered Canon O'Leary, a priest from Cork who was made aware of the full contents of the letter by Norma Borthwick and Mary O'Reilly.[34] O'Leary complained to Charles MacNeill that "the public admire the *generosity*. The *stipulation* is *not* published. The public get no chance of seeing how the *insolence* outweighs the *generosity*." He also warned MacNeill that Castletown was not the ally he had tried to depict himself as. O'Leary wrote that some within the League had sought to embrace "as a friend a man who is in reality a subtle and a dangerous enemy. I have known that man for 15 or 16 years. I would not sit at the same table with him to save my life. The less we have to do with him the better."[35] O'Leary did not have his way, and the full details of the letter were not published. Nevertheless, the Gaelic League had drawn a line under the question of Pan-Celticism. Never again would the issue be discussed at length, despite Fournier's continuing efforts to curry favor with the executive committee.

Bernard Doyle continued to lament the indifference of the Gaelic League toward Pan-Celticism, believing that this attitude was actually hindering efforts to revive the Irish language. In an editorial in *Fáinne an Lae*, he claimed that the example "set us in Brittany, in Wales, and in Scotland, but above and beyond all in Wales, ought to make us anxious to direct the eyes of the Irish people, who treat this language movement so coldly, to these countries in which language movements have been crowned with success." Most importantly, Doyle believed, "It is men of our own Celtic stock that have so triumphed over the grosser tendencies of the age, and proved the might of the intellect and patriotism at a time when half the world bows down to the spirit of materialism." The Gaelic League was making a mistake in limiting its focus to Ireland because "if they do not lift their eyes to the Celtic horizon what prospect does a semi-Anglicised Ireland afford them?" Doyle was adamant that "example was a million times more forcible than precept" and that if the people of Ireland would take note of what their Celts were doing "we shall supply an incentive to labour in our own field more effective than all the counsel of our sages combined." On the other hand, "If we are so bog-buried as to believe that nothing is to be gained by studying the achievements of our brother Celts, they on their part, as men of experience will not be hindered by flimsy prejudices from studying our efforts and judging them on the merits."[36]

Doyle's urgings had little effect. Indeed, news of a minor scandal in Wales had traveled to Ireland and unfurled a fresh round of bitter exchanges between supporters and opponents of Pan-Celticism. The *Freeman's Journal* reported that at a meeting of Welsh bards the presiding archdruid, Gwilym Cowlydd, had invoked "the blessing of the Almighty on British arms in South Africa in the war against falsehood, iniquity and error, and announced that the Gorsedd Sword would never again be sheathed, till the triumph of the forces of Righteousness over the hordes of Evil." This, the newspaper believed, would be of interest to the Gaelic League in light of the recent Pan-Celtic debate.[37] Such reports were a black eye for the Pan-Celtic movement in Ireland. There was deep sympathy among mainstream Irish nationalist opinion for the Boers, and this incident served to remind people that whatever cultural and racial similarities might exist between Ireland, Wales, and Scotland, there were significant political differences as well. Furthermore, Lord Castletown was an officer in the British Army, and his imminent deployment to South Africa would serve to reinforce the idea that Irish cultural nationalism was incompatible with Pan-Celticism and its imperial tendencies. Indeed, when *Fáinne an Lae* reported that Castletown had been sent to South Africa in February 1900, Bernard Doyle tried to soften his imperial image by noting that his "opinion on this unholy war is not a secret" and expressing the hope that "he will live to undo some of the vast harm wrought by this memorable conflict."[38]

Whatever Castletown's private opinion, Fournier was certainly opposed to the war. He told Castletown in December 1899 that "all the enthusiasm of a fight for liberty, most of the skill and preparedness, and 90 per cent of the justice are on the Boer side. It is a fight of Empire against nationality, in which the latter stands to win."[39] Furthermore, once Castletown was sent to South Africa, Fournier informed him that he could not put the term "Orange River Colony" on the address of the letters he sent to Castletown because "I have an invincible objection to that title."[40] Hence as soon as the report of the gorsedd blessing appeared in Ireland, Fournier knew it had to be countered. He immediately wrote to the *Freeman's Journal* pointing out that Gwilym Cowlydd's group was an eccentric breakaway sect from the national gorsedd, which remained politically and religiously neutral.[41] Bernard Doyle also tried to limit any potential damage to the Pan-Celtic movement from the incident. He reminded his readers that the "Welsh Bards, are, however, not the Welsh people, whose sacrifices on behalf of the Irish Nation in their periodic struggles for some measure of constitutional freedom are too little known and too little appreciated in Ireland."[42] He pointed out that Welsh voters who had supported the Liberal Party in the election of 1868 on the question of Irish disestablishment had been evicted in large numbers and that the Welsh were "the most active supporters of the Home Rule cause, when another opportunity was offered them of helping Ireland."

These efforts to make the incident blow over as quickly as possible were for naught. For members of the Gaelic League who had been sidelined because of their hostility toward Pan-Celticism, this was a glorious opportunity to crow that their suspicions had been correct all along. Canon Peter O'Leary wrote that true Gaelic Leaguers were very intrigued to hear about the affair, claiming that their interest was akin to that "a person takes in a very ugly cesspool into which he barely escaped walking head foremost." The behavior of the Welsh bards was "the lowest and most disreputable form of English cringing to the powers that be." O'Leary stated that "the Gaelic League would now present a nice figure to the world if it had permitted itself to be made part and parcel of the Pan-Celtic humbug!" He declared that the Gaelic League would have been quickly extinguished had it become involved with Pan-Celticism, and that "we all owe a deep debt of gratitude to the foresight and energy of those who warned us in time." O'Leary believed that the attacks on Fournier and his associates in various newspaper articles in 1899 had been completely vindicated. He was confident that even at the time these criticisms had reflected the feelings of many in the League, whereas after the gorsedd incident "I think there are very few members of the Gaelic League whose feelings and convictions they do not represent now."[43]

Fournier responded instantly. In a letter to the *Freeman's Journal* he noted that O'Leary, "the valiant Gaedhilgeoir of Castlelyons," had fallen victim to an "illusion." He stressed that the blessing had been performed by a dissident group of bards who were not part of the national gorsedd of

Wales. Fournier resorted to what had become the standard defense of the Pan-Celts, namely that those who opposed their movement were being misled by deliberate English efforts to divide the Celts. He wrote that the entire affair was "another example of that prejudice of kindred Celtic nations, and that ignorance of each other's feelings and doings, which the London Press has been at such pains to create, and which forms part and parcel of the system of Anglicization."[44] Fournier went further, claiming that the fact that "Father O'Leary himself should have walked into the trap explains to a great extent what some of the lesser lights of the Gaelic League uttered and wrote last year about the Pan-Celtic movement, before they were overruled by the better-informed Executive Committee." He emphasized repeatedly that those who sought to use the incident to disparage the Pan-Celts were guilty of the old Irish weaknesses of accepting at face value news "made in England." Fournier expressed the hope that O'Leary would eventually be an honored guest of the Pan-Celtic congress upon which "he at present pours out the vials of his honest but misinformed wrath." He sought to remind O'Leary and his allies, however, that cooperation between Irish and Welsh organizations, as well as between Irish and Welsh MPs, was the surest way of advancing the cause of the Irish language: "There is no need 'to fall back upon Macroom' any longer."[45]

Fournier's remark about "Macroom" was vague. Macroom was the site of the first *feis* organized under the auspices of the Gaelic League in 1898, and Fournier may have been trying to say that the Gaelic League did not need to be so self-reliant in pursuit of its goals. However, seemingly unbeknownst to Fournier, Macroom was also the hometown of Canon O'Leary, and some saw Fournier's comment as a personal barb against the esteemed cleric. One retort, penned under the name "MacGhiolla Brighde," said that Fournier's comment was "of very questionable taste." "MacGhiolla Brighde" referred to Fournier three times as "Monsieur Fournier," playing the "foreign" card in the exact same way that Fournier had done when he claimed that opposition to the Pan-Celts stemmed from English efforts to encourage divisiveness among the Celts. However, "MacGhiolla Brighde" was firmly on the side of the Macroom man, writing, "Father O'Leary's work for the language is worth more to us than all the parliaments of Europe, and we would no more think of bartering his help for theirs than we would exchange our Irish Oireachtas for an Imperial Gorsedd."[46] These sentiments were echoed in another letter to the *Freeman's Journal* by Margaret O'Reilly, who had resigned from the executive committee of the Gaelic League as a result of the Pan-Celtic controversy. Calling Fournier's Macroom remark "pernicious and degrading," O'Reilly blasted that "it is from the hearthstones of Macroom and of places like it, and not from Wales or Westminster, that we seek and find our strength. When we do otherwise, the Gorsedd in green petticoats may dance a death-dance over the Irish language movement."[47]

Like "MacGhiolla Brighde" and others before her, O'Reilly cast Fournier in the role of a foreigner by repeatedly referring to him as "Monsieur Fournier." It is interesting that Fournier's enemies tried to depict him as a Frenchman, on the basis of his ancestry, rather than as an Englishman, even though he was born and raised in London. It suggests that these hard-line Gaelic League members felt that highlighting Fournier's Englishness would not be sufficient to cast him as an outsider. Even when Keawell referred to Fournier as an "Englishman," he qualified this with "of Huguenot extraction." Ironically, English attitudes may have been so pervasive in Irish society that even these champions of resistance to anglicization could not help but view Frenchness (as opposed to Englishness) as the ultimate mark of foreignness. Nevertheless, O'Reilly sought to discredit all of the reasons that the Pan-Celts put forward for why Irish nationalists sought support for their endeavors. If the blessing for the British war effort was carried out by a group falsely representing itself as the national gorsedd, "Why has not the real Gorsedd protested? Why indeed." She said that Irish-language supporters didn't have time to worry about which gorsedd was which. "Have we not stern reality enough here at home? Our language question is no holiday affair for us; it is a life and death struggle for us, and we are not in the temper to be bothered by humbug—Pan-Celtic or otherwise." O'Reilly laughed at those who suggested that the Welsh and Irish were natural allies: "But we are told that 'the Irish and Welsh democracies have fought too long under the same banner of religious and political freedom.' The same banner! In the name of mush, where and when? Was it in 1798, when the Welsh regiment of 'Ancient Britons' wrote their name in blood all over Wexford, or was it last summer, when the street preachers of South Wales had to be protected by police in Waterford?" Going further, she asked if the supposedly shared democratic sentiment between the Irish and Welsh was reflected in the annual cultural festivals of both countries: "Would English imperialistic speeches be tolerated at the Oireachtas? They are applauded at the Eisteddfod." She noted that Lord Castletown himself had given one such speech at the eisteddfod the previous summer when he declared that "Scotland, Ireland and Wales poured forth their battalions to fight for empire in all corners of the world and in every climate." As far as O'Reilly was concerned, then, the Welsh and Irish were not naturally allies, and Welsh institutions like the gorsedd, tainted with imperialism and pointless pageantry, had nothing to offer the Irish-language movement.

These rumblings eventually produced a response from Wales. Edward Thomas was a member of the gorsedd, and he had visited Dublin twice the previous year. He referred to the blessing ceremony involving Gwilym Cowlydd as a "disgusting farce" and declared that the real gorsedd would never "countenance a ceremony . . . favouring the shedding of the blood of their fellowmen." Thomas also tried to assure skeptics that the Welsh bards were allies of the Gaelic League. Referring to the proposed visit of the gorsedd to Dublin as part of the Pan-Celtic congress, Thomas stated that "no set of people will ever visit Ireland who will understand and so thoroughly sympathize with the aims of the leaders of the Gaelic League as the bards."[48] This letter seems to have ended the argument about the gorsedd blessing, but both sides remained as divided as ever. The editorial for the *Gael*, a monthly bilingual journal published in New York, stated that Irish Americans had viewed the Pan-Celtic debate with dismay:

> The League has for its definite and ultimate aim the practical use of Irish as the spoken tongue of Ireland. The object of the Pan-Celtic Congress, according to the declaration of the leaders, is rather philological, academical, and international than popular. It is not easy to see why there should be any friction between the two organizations. But it is, unfortunately, a most regrettable trait of the Irish nature—and this conviction is forced upon any serious thinker and observer of the Irish race—that there is a woeful lack of brotherly spirit in Irish work, whether it be political, literary, or what not.

"Unfortunately," the editorial concluded, "it is an old saying, and a homely one, but none the less true: 'Put an Irishman on the spit and another will be always found to turn him.'"[49] Naturally, this assertion did not go unchallenged. Edward Hynes, a member of the Gaelic League, wrote, "I am confident we are quite capable of reviving our own language and have no need to give foreigners an opportunity of claiming the credit of having assisted us." Hynes did not feel any racial sympathy toward his fellow Celts, stating, "The organizations of Wales and Scotland are largely composed of Imperialists." The very fact that the Pan-Celtic movement "has the support of some Irish Imperialists should, in my opinion, be sufficient to warn any Irishman against it, for I am fully convinced that any movement that has the support of any of the 'English garrison' in Ireland is, if not injurious at least, not beneficial to Ireland." The breach between the hard-line nationalist element of the Gaelic League and the Pan-Celts was irreconcilable, and the proposed Dublin congress would go ahead without the assistance of the League.

Nevertheless, Fournier and Castletown continued to promote Pan-Celticism. The outbreak of the Boer War forced the postponement of the Pan-Celtic congress in 1900. In the wake of the gorsedd scandal, Fournier was probably correct in believing that the uproar over the war would overshadow "all festive enterprises" and therefore decided to delay the Pan-Celtic gathering until 1901.[50] Yet he also took steps to enhance the position of the Pan-Celtic movement. Fournier helped establish the Celtic Association in October 1900, under whose auspices the Pan-Celtic congress would take place. Castletown was chosen as the president of the Celtic Association, with Fournier taking the office of honorary secretary. The objects of the association were defined as "the furtherance of Celtic Studies, and the fostering of mutual sympathy and co-operation between the various branches of the Celtic Race in all matters affecting their language and national characteristics."[51] Fournier also launched *Celtia*, a monthly Pan-Celtic journal, in 1901. This was the organ of the Celtic Association, and its purpose was to allow cultural and language enthusiasts to keep abreast of developments in other Celtic countries. *Celtia* was truly a multilingual journal, with articles, poems, and songs appearing in all five Celtic languages, as well as English. The journal featured an Anglo-Celtic dictionary, with English words translated alphabetically into Irish, Scots Gaelic, Manx, Welsh, and Breton.[52]

Preparations continued throughout 1901 for the first ever Pan-Celtic congress in Dublin. Fournier declared in *Celtia* that the congress "will be the most important Celtic business meeting of centuries, and will be an event of the greatest significance."[53] The Celts who were coming to the congress were to "forswear their racial jealousies and prepare their united forces for a career of intellectual conquest—not a conquest of strange territories, but a re-conquest of what is rightfully their own."[54] Fournier commented that some in England and France appeared alarmed that the Pan-Celts had political ambitions. He refuted these ideas, however, by writing, "No, ours is a very different task. We have to foster and give expression to the growing sentiment of kinship which animates those five small nations who have retained their Celtic speech. We have to emphasise the points they have in common, and respect their differences. We have to assist them in maintaining their struggle for national existence by a full exchange of information on all questions affecting their national language, arts, customs and characteristics." The Pan-Celts did not have a political goal, Fournier asserted. Their aim was merely "to save what remains of the Celtic race as such from being swept into the Atlantic."[55]

Bernard Doyle had expressed similar sentiments the year before in an editorial in *Fáinne an Lae*. He did not entirely rule out some kind of political alliance between the Celts when he wrote, "It would be premature to assume that any Congress could immediately lead to the federation of the five nations. That must be a matter of slow growth." Doyle insisted that Ireland had a special role to play as the leading Celtic nation. He declared, "Ireland has, beyond all her sister nations, most steadily guarded her great ideal, her 'rêve eternel.' She is freer than the others from subjugation to an overshadowing power, freer in spirit if not in body. That fact, together with her numerical superiority, must give her a certain leadership which the others cannot aspire to. But that leadership must not be *claimed*. It must be voluntarily and spontaneously conceded."[56]

The first steps toward bringing about this Celtic unity were taken when the Pan-Celtic congress took place in Dublin from August 20 to 23, 1901. The proceedings began with an assembly of the Celtic nations at Mansion House on the morning of August 20. The lord mayor of Dublin, Timothy Harrington, welcomed the delegates with a short speech in Irish. A meeting of the gorsedd then took place on the lawn. The archdruid, Hwfa Mon, stood on a stone altar and pronounced the ancient gorsedd prayer in Welsh. Another bard addressed the assembled Celts in English, saying that the Welsh "rejoiced now that efforts again were made to bring them together to make for common improvement of the Celtic family."[57] A procession of the Pan-Celts through the streets of Dublin then followed. Dressed in various national costumes, this collection of bards, druids, ovates, pipers, choirs, aldermen, councilors, and mounted police must have made an impressive sight. Over the four days, several papers on Celtic topics were read, many issues were debated, and numerous concerts were held. Delegates discussed Celtic commercial possibilities, music, and games and traditions.[58] A spirited debate took place on whether Cornwall should be declared a sixth Celtic nation. When the issue was put to a vote, however, Cornwall's application was rejected, with some wishing to restrict membership in the Celtic club to countries where a Celtic language was still spoken.[59] Nevertheless, Fournier believed that a giant step forward had been taken for the cause of Pan-Celticism. He wrote that "when a Breton was heard cheering a Highlander for whistling the Welsh National Anthem in the streets of Dublin, the bond of fraternity appeared strong enough to withstand the shocks of all time."[60]

Amid this Celtic celebration, the Gaelic League remained aloof. It was left to the Society for the Preservation of the Irish Language to deliver a report on the status of the Irish language to the Pan-Celtic congress. Regardless, Fournier decided to try and offer an olive branch in choosing to generously praise the Gaelic League in an address to the congress. He said that, owing to a "misunderstanding," the Gaelic League was not officially represented at the Pan-Celtic congress.[61] Fournier declared that "the work done by the Gaelic League had put a new soul into the Irish nation." He told the assembled Pan-Celts that he hoped someday the "great gap" caused by the League's absence would be filled, but he noted with pleasure that many individual members of the Gaelic League had decided to attend the congress.[62] Judging from the list of subscribers and guarantors published in the congress's program, many Gaelic Leaguers donated money to support the Pan-Celtic venture. Patrick Pearse, Edward Martyn, John St. Clair Boyd, Thomas William Rolleston, Thomas O'Neill Russell, Maxwell Close, and William Gibson were all prominent Gaelic League activists who contributed financially to the Pan-Celtic congress.[63] The fact that some League members were willing to donate to the Celtic Association suggests that many more Gaelic Leaguers may have had a positive opinion on Pan-Celticism. One week after the congress concluded, Patrick Pearse told Bernard Doyle that the attitude of the Gaelic League had been disastrous:

I agree with you as to our proper attitude towards the Pan-Celts. The fact is that the League made a gigantic blunder two years ago in deciding to have nothing to do with the affair. The result is that the foreign visitors and delegates, seeing nothing of the real language movement, have gone away with the impression that the Gaelic League is a fraud, and that there is no language movement in Ireland. One of the Highlanders publicly stated as much. Some may say, of course, that it does not matter after all what the foreigners think. Still it is regrettable that the leaders of kindred movements as well as such men as Zimmer, Kuno Meyer and Robinson, should leave Ireland with the impression that no effort is being made to save the language. That they have this impression is not the fault of the Pan-Celts here, who did the best they could, but of the Gaelic League.[64]

Yet without the backing of the Gaelic League the Pan-Celtic movement was doomed to fail. The congress attracted very little attention in the national press and was a financial failure. Although a more successful congress was held in Caernarfon in Wales in 1904, the Edinburgh congress of 1907 left Fournier and Castletown with large expenses.[65] With membership of the Celtic Association never rising above a couple hundred people, it was clear to both men by the end of the decade that Pan-Celticism had failed to take hold, and Fournier and Castletown ended their involvement with the movement.

The question that remains, however, is why some within the Gaelic League were so opposed to cooperation with the Celtic Association. Religion was undoubtedly a factor. Many of the most prominent Pan-Celts, Fournier and Castletown among them, belonged to the Anglican Church. Fournier was aware that some Catholics would hold this against the Celtic Association, thereby limiting the appeal of Pan-Celticism in Ireland. He tried to counter this by inviting Cardinal Logue, the most influential member of the Irish clergy, to attend the Pan-Celtic congress. Logue politely declined, citing a prior engagement, although he wrote, "I can . . . express my warmest sympathy with the Congress, its aims, and work, and wish it every success."[66] Fournier published Logue's letter on the front page of *Celtia*, hoping it would sway skeptical priests to support Pan-Celticism. The Gaelic League, according to Fournier, had flourished after Logue and the Catholic

Church gave their support to it, "and the same great authority has now expressed approval of the efforts of the Celtic Association to draw the Celtic race into a closer union. It is a proof, if proof were needed, that the aims of both organisations are consistent with each other."[67]

Yet privately Fournier had his doubts that the Catholic clergy could be won over to his side, thereby removing a major obstacle to an entente with the Gaelic League. He wrote to Castletown, "It is no use trying to get the Gaelic League to work with us. Dr. Hyde is as friendly as he can be, but he is a mere puppet in the hands of the clerics on his Committee, who terrorise him into submission on every occasion."[68] Fournier, it appears, was correct in his belief that clerical opposition to Pan-Celticism prevented the Gaelic League from adopting a more supportive position. Three of the most vocal critics who wrote to the MacNeill brothers expressing their concern about associating the League with Castletown and Fournier were priests. Father John Hogan, a member of the executive committee of the Gaelic League, wrote a lengthy letter to MacNeill explaining his opposition to Pan-Celticism. The first point Hogan made was that the relationship between Ireland and the other Celtic countries was satisfactory as it was and that no closer union was possible. There was no common language between the Celts, Hogan noted, and "we do not belong to the same Church." For Hogan, Pan-Celticism lacked appeal in part because it promoted a sense of common identity divorced entirely from religious affiliations. He was also not enamored with the idea of working with Castletown and his associates. He told MacNeill that the Pan-Celtic committee "cannot give us any help. . . . The day of Castletown and his peers is gone."[69] Indeed, the noble status enjoyed by Castletown and some other Pan-Celtic supporters made Gaelic Leaguer supporters leery. Margaret O'Reilly wrote, "The piping of a peer will not get the peasant to dance now, much less will it get the sons of the peasant to do so, and it is the sons of the peasant who form the backbone of the Irish movement."[70]

The fact that Lord Castletown was the figurehead of the Pan-Celtic movement was also problematic for Canon Peter O'Leary. He was the parish priest of Castlelyons in County Cork, not far from Castletown's estate at Doneraile. O'Leary, who was also a prominent member of the Gaelic League, expressed his distrust of his neighbor in a letter to Charles Mac-Neill, saying he could not remain on the executive committee if any attempt was made to bring Castletown on board. In an attempt to establish what role sectarian tension played in the rejection of Pan-Celticism, it is at times difficult to precisely identify religious bigotry. For Fathers Hogan and O'Leary, Castletown's unionist politics, as much as his religious background, could have explained their distrust of him. Father Richard Henebry, however, was open about his religious prejudices in his correspondence with Eoin MacNeill. He boasted to MacNeill that he had rejected the efforts of the New York Gaelic League to create a nonpolitical and nonsectarian constitution.[71] Henebry wrote "I said 'Dock that!' I explained that I thought the Gaelic League was political and Catholic."[72] Henebry was also skeptical about efforts to establish a Pan-Celtic congress. He wrote to MacNeill, "What do you think of the Pan-Celtic Congress people? . . . What do they mean? I notice many of the names are 'the right sort,' i.e. Anglo-Irish Protestants."[73]

Indeed, within the Gaelic League itself, many Protestant members were becoming troubled by the growing influence of Catholicism. J. H. Lloyd complained to Eoin MacNeill that "religion has been introduced." In particular, Lloyd was upset that the Gaelic League insisted on having meetings on Sundays. He told MacNeill that "no good Protestant believes in such a thing."[74] Other Protestants had noticed that some Gaelic League publications appeared to be written for a Catholic audience only. When in 1901 the Gaelic League published a pamphlet authored by Father Ford hinting that Gaelic culture was only the preserve of Catholics, many Protestant League members were angered. T. W. Rolleston described the publication as "very unfortunate." Rolleston acknowledged that the vast majority of Irish speakers were Catholic but said this did still not justify attacks on Protestantism. He complained that nationalist rhetoric increasingly associated with the Gaelic League was compelling Protestant members to withdraw their support.[75] To many within the League, even those who rejected sectarian division, there remained a lingering sense that Protestants did not fit so easily into the vision of what an ideal Irishman should be. A few years after the Pan-Celtic affair, Agnes Young wrote to Castletown to tell him he was mistaken when he claimed that religious discrimination existed within the League. Castletown had indicated to her that he was disliked because of his faith. Young acknowledged that there was a "distance" between Castletown and most members of the League but wrote that this was "not on the score of religion."[76] Yet in the same letter she told Castletown that the principal of Midleton College, a Mr. Baker, to whom she had recently been in troduced, was "an interesting man . . . an Irish Church clergyman but a good Gael—very keen and sensible." The "but" that Young used in this sentence speaks volumes about how Protestantism was typically assumed to be outside the realm of Gaeldom and how an "Irish Church clergyman" was not usually imagined to be "a good Gael."

Those who rejected the Pan-Celtic movement out of religious bigotry risked dividing the Gaelic League along religious lines and driving Protestant members into the Celtic Association. Rolleston told MacNeill that he had once believed that the Gaelic League would help foster a sense of Irish identity that accepted all religious traditions. He warned, however, that "if the League deliberately turns its back on the task, the latter must either be abandoned, or some other means created for carrying out the object in view."[77] As the Pan-Celtic congress approached in the summer of 1901, the possibility existed that the Celtic Association would steal the thunder of the Gaelic League. Some in the League hierarchy feared that the Protestant membership might leave en masse to join the Pan-Celtic ranks. Douglas Hyde, himself the son of a Church of Ireland minister, believed the possibility was real. He had received a letter from Rolleston warning that there would be "consequences" if the "sectarian or intolerant party retain the upper hand in the League."[78] Rolleston told Hyde that "it would be very easy to form a strong party with Lord Castletown at its head, who would take up the Celtic Association and make it the Gaelic organization for all Protestants who are interested in Gaelic matters and for all Catholics who dislike the introduction of sectarianism into the matter." Hyde took the threat seriously, believing it would do a great deal of harm to the League. He wrote, "If I had a free hand I would prevent this threatened secession under Lord Castletown by taking part in the Pan-Celtic business, coaxing him and the rest into the Gaelic League."[79] Nevertheless, Hyde believed that the "furious partisans" who were opposed to Pan-Celticism would tear the Gaelic League apart if he attempted this course. Faced with the possibility of upheaval no matter what he did, Hyde decided to bow to the "partisans" and did not take part in the Pan-Celtic congress. The threatened secession never took place, but questions about how welcome Protestants were in the League continued to linger.

While the faith of the leading Pan-Celts was a problem for some priests within the Gaelic League, the political leanings of Lord Castletown meant that the Celtic Association was viewed with suspicion by many nationalists.

The Pan-Celtic debate took place during the Boer War, when anti-British and anti-imperial feelings ran high in Ireland.[80] The fact that Castletown was well known for his unionist politics and fought against the Boers in South Africa did little to endear the Pan-Celtic movement to a wider Irish audience. For some Gaelic Leaguers, the Pan-Celtic idea of strengthening the cultural connection between Ireland and other parts of Britain implied that political connections between Ireland and Britain should also be strengthened, at the expense of Irish political autonomy. One anonymous League member wrote to Eoin MacNeill highlighting this implication. Commenting on the differences between the Gaelic League and the Pan-Celts, he wrote, "The Gaelic Leaguers are like the Irish Home Rulers and the Pan Celts are the Imperial Federalists. What would the Home Rulers say if in the struggle for Home Rule they were invited to join as an organization an Imperialist Federation League?"[81] The leaders of the Pan-Celtic movement wrestled with the issue of trying to appeal to mainstream Irish nationalists while remaining unequivocally supportive of the union between Ireland and Britain. Prior to the first Pan-Celtic congress, Boyd asked Castletown about the thorny question of toasting the queen during official functions: "How are you going to leave out the toast to the Queen? I am sorry to say that I am afraid it would not be acceptable to some of the Irish present, so I suppose all toasts must be omitted at all its gatherings!"[82] Other Pan-Celts wanted a more prominent connection between their group and the crown. When King Edward VII visited Ireland in 1903, W. J. Dennehy wrote to Castletown asking him to try and win from the king an expression of approval for the Pan-Celtic movement.[83]

Both Fournier and Castletown hoped that the Celtic Association would strengthen the British Empire, not undermine it. Fournier had a vision for a new Ireland that would take pride in both its ancient culture and its role within the British Empire. Hence he chose Castletown as the leader of the Pan-Celtic movement, a man whose royal Gaelic lineage and service in the British Army embodied the dual identity he hoped all Irish people could embrace. In various letters to Castletown, Fournier encouraged his friend to view himself in this role. Fournier told Castletown that in doing his military duty in South Africa he had done Ireland as a whole a great service: "Let me tell you, Mac Giolla Phádruig of Osraight, that it was _you_ who showed that Ireland united is Ireland irresistible, who called forth memories of the Irish Volunteers in one short flash of glory, and foreshadowed the magnificent conception of an Imperial Celtic Ireland as queen of her race."[84] Fournier hoped that Castletown would be a strong leader not only for the Pan-Celts but for the Irish people as well. He told Castletown that he wanted to take him to some remote Irish-speaking area and "and to 'de-anglicize' you completely . . . let you drink the wisdom of your ancient race."[85] The purpose of this exercise, according to Fournier, would be for Castletown to "come forth from the rebirth like a King by divine right, fit to lead and rule a long suffering but patient and strong race."[86] Hence it is clear that Fournier believed Castletown to be the man Ireland needed to preserve its native culture while embracing its supporting position within the empire, thereby creating an "Imperial Celtic Ireland."

Castletown likewise saw the Pan-Celtic movement as having the potential to promote both an appreciation of Irish culture and British imperial splendor. Although others viewed him as part of the ruling English class in Ireland, Castletown took great pride in his Irish identity. He wrote that his parents had "made me proud of my native land, taught me what my nation had done in the past and what we ought to try for in the future."[87] The dawn of the twentieth century, Castletown claimed, marked an era when all small countries of the world "claim an equal right to be considered, to have a history and a literature of their own. Like Bohemia and Hungary, Denmark and Poland, they all have the desire to make themselves heard in their own language."[88] He hoped that Ireland, like the other nations of Europe, could have a history, literature, and language of its own, but not, of course, political independence. Castletown believed that Ireland, as a Celtic land, could never stand alone. He had a romantic notion of all Celtic people as tragically doomed to defeat when they attempted to resist conquest by a stronger people.[89] Therefore Ireland and the other Celtic countries were compelled to work with the English, whom Castletown termed "the necessary though utilitarian Saxon."[90] If English practicality was combined with Celtic imagination, prosperity would be forthcoming in what some Pan-Celts referred to as "our composite Anglo-Celtic Empire."[91] Castletown believed that a thriving local culture in each nation of Britain would improve the empire overall, something he termed "the principle of the liberty of the subject nation." He wrote, "As every subject of the Sovereign has a right to pursue his own heritage and develop his own capacities and resources, so every subject nation has the right of fostering its national traditions. As the liberty of the subject makes for the well-being and advancement of the Kingdom, so does the liberty of the *subject nation* make for the progress of the Empire."[92] Yet the idea of Ireland being a "subject nation" was anathema to many Irish nationalists. Given the anti-imperial climate in Ireland at the height of the Pan-Celtic debate, the imperial connection that Castletown gave to the Pan-Celtic movement did little to entice Gaelic Leaguers to support it.[93]

Religious and political differences, however, cannot alone explain why some Irish nationalists opposed Pan-Celticism. Many saw the movement as little more than Fournier's attempt to introduce foreign, specifically Welsh, elements into the Irish cultural mainstream. Fournier was certainly an admirer of the gorsedd, as well as its pomp and ceremony. After he had been made an honorary member, he began to take steps to form a similar institute in Ireland. In 1897 he wrote to the executive council of the Gaelic League, asking that he be allowed to discuss with them the possibility of creating a "Gaelic Gorsedd."[94] For Fournier, this was not merely an attempt to ape Welsh cultural nationalists. The entire premise behind the Pan-Celtic congress was to recreate the gathering of Irish and Welsh bards convened by Gruffydd ap Cynan in 1100. The Pan-Celtic congress and the creation of an Irish gorsedd were not attempts to invent tradition but, in Fournier's eyes, efforts to reestablish practices lost but not forgotten in Ireland.[95] Nor were his ideas immediately rejected. Eoin MacNeill was cautiously supportive of the gorsedd idea. He asked Fournier about the historical records of the old Irish bardic institutes, how he imagined a Gaelic gorsedd would serve the national interest, and what titles would be bestowed upon members.[96]

Others, however, balked at the idea. Father John Hogan wrote to Mac-Neill declaring, "The establishment of a 'Gaelic Gorsedd' is repugnant to me, I would as soon have English Institutions here as Welsh ones. I admire the Welsh but do not love them."[97] Hogan also worried that the creation of an Irish gorsedd would hinder the growth of the *oireachtas*, the Irish cultural festival recently established under the auspices of the Gaelic League. He asked MacNeill, "Do they mean to supersede the Oireachtas as well as catch for themselves whatever money should be available for Irish language purposes? Is the Gaelic League going to aid them in doing this? Surely you are not in favour of a Gaelic Gorsedd and the suppression of the Oireachtas?"[98]

Meanwhile P. J. Keawell was scathing in his assertion that "[t]here is no historical union between this country and Wales. . . . Wales and Ireland have developed on entirely divergent lines. For instance, no two countries could well be further apart in the matter of religion. Without community of religion or language there exists no such thing as innate racial sympathy."[99] He also condemned the idea of forming an Irish gorsedd: "We most strenuously protest against such a thing. We have been fighting against anglicisation, we should fight as determinedly against unnative institutions unsuited to the conditions and temperament and needs of the Irish people."[100] Fournier's attempt to bring a Pan-Celtic congress and the gorsedd to Dublin was labeled another example of the tradition of seeking foreign aid. In contrast, the Gaelic League "inculcates self reliance and self help. It teaches the Irish people that the future of the Irish language is in their own hands, that the language cannot be saved or destroyed by foreign influences."[101] "Sinn Féin Amháin" was the catchphrase of nationalists, and while most were content to describe their "race" as Celtic, in cultural terms they saw themselves as exclusively Irish.[102]

But the Pan-Celtic movement also failed to win the support of Gaelic League members because most of the Pan-Celts were interested in performing rituals rather than trying to achieve tangible social goals. The Pan-Celtic congress that took place in Dublin was most notable for the colorful pageantry that accompanied it. The Pan-Celts organized a ceremony in which a "Celtic Peace" was officially declared. The ceremony borrowed heavily from rituals usually employed by the gorsedd. The archdruid raised the gorsedd sword before the assembled delegates, and all officers and bards touched its sheath. The archdruid then called out three times in Welsh, "A Oes Heddwch?" (Is there peace?), to which all assembled replied, "Heddwch" (Peace).[103] Another sword ceremony was arranged to signify the reunification of the Brythonic nationalities, the people of Wales and Brittany.[104] Fournier enjoyed this symbolic gesture of unity so much, he established another ceremony to represent the coming together of all the Celtic people. He created the Lia Cineil, or "Stone of the Race." A giant granite rock, weighing one ton, was carved into five pieces. Each piece denoted one of the five Celtic nations, with the first letter of the nation that owned the piece being engraved on the front. An ogham inscription, reading "Baile Átha Cliath" (Dublin), was carved on the side of the stone. Whenever the five Celtic nations came together, they were to bring their section of the Lia Cineil. The stone would then be assembled into a five-foot-high pillar, symbolizing peace and unity among the different nations.[105] Kaori Nagai has suggested that the Lia Cineil was "a phallic pillar, undoing . . . the 'castration' and feminisation of the Celts by their Saxon neighbor." She has also stated that Fournier was trying to re-create a Celtic Tower of Babel, symbolizing a return to the era before the Celtic languages became unintelligible from each other.[106]

One aspect of identity that was important for the Pan-Celts was the question of traditional Celtic clothing. For Irish Pan-Celts, the distinctive outfits of the Scottish Highlanders and the Bretons, as well as the costumes worn by the Welsh gorsedd, gave the impression that Ireland's lack of unique clothing was a sign of decaying national spirit. Bernard Doyle wrote, "We have no national dress. . . . We have been so long wearing English cast-clothes that we have nearly forgotten what a national garb can be like."[107] Some were concerned that Ireland itself would be embarrassed at the Pan-Celtic congress in Dublin when the lack of representative clothing compared to the other Celtic peoples would become apparent. One commentator, using the name "Scolaire Bocht," wrote that "we have no wedding garment for the festival. We cut a very poor figure last July at Cardiff, where our nation was the only one that had no national costume. . . . If the same thing is repeated in August our neighbours will make a laughing-stock of us."[108] Naturally, this led to calls for a national outfit that could best represent the historic distinctiveness of the Irish people. Doyle suggested that "the costumes selected might differ by provinces, by counties, or by any of the old historical divisions of the Kingdom. In one particular, however, they should all agree. The costume should be Gaelic, and the designer of the same should derive his knowledge and inspiration from the history of the Gaelic nation."[109]

Fournier was a passionate supporter of creating, or reviving, a traditional Irish outfit. He attended Gaelic League meetings in clothing he had deemed to be traditionally Irish, and in 1902 he gave a lecture to students of University College Dublin on the importance of reestablishing native Irish attire.[110] At the Pan-Celtic congress, each delegation was encouraged to come attired in their "national costume," and those who wore modern clothes, like most of the Manx delegation, were criticized for sporting "the garbs of de-nationalization."[111] A long and contentious debate regarding national dress took place during the congress. Castletown declared the issue of national costume to be "one of the most difficult questions" to be addressed by the Pan-Celts.[112] Fournier argued that it was impossible to reverse modern trends and compel people to wear a national costume in their everyday lives. Thus he wanted a national costume that would be worn "on certain occasions only . . . [as] the wearing of it on all occasions would somehow defeat the end of wearing it altogether." Others, such as Captain Otway Cuffe, wanted a national costume that would be worn every day "which would remind them of their national life, and be a mark that they belonged to one people, and be an outward sign of what is the true inner sense of the spiritual unity of these races." W. B. Yeats suggested that there was no need to decide in favor of one way or the other and that it was indeed healthy to see costumes evolving from two different but "necessary" directions.[113] The pages of *Celtia* were also filled with suggestions regarding what the national costume should look like and from when it should be derived. Fournier wrote, "The best plan will be to select a period at which native Irish dress reached its highest stage of development. That period is the eleventh century."[114] He advocated the development of a festive costume that consisted of a long tunic, a cloak worn over the shoulders fastened with a brooch, and pantaloons, with buttons being prohibited.[115]

In most matters of business, symbolism trumped functionality. For example, when Fournier sought to bring the gorsedd to Dublin, he sent a delegation to Wales to deliver the invitation in person. As Fournier wanted to establish a connection with the assembly of Irish and Welsh poets in 1100, he asked Lord Castletown to deliver the invitation in a speech in medieval Irish. Fournier assured Castletown that he need not worry about being accurate in his pronunciation because "nobody knows how it was really pronounced. Read it as you would Italian."[116] It was this Pan-Celtic obsession with ceremony and costume that irked many members of the Gaelic League. There was a fear among some Gaelic Leaguers that donations would be diverted from the League to the Pan-Celts "to be frittered in masquerading and banqueting and processioning [*sic*]." Keawell appealed to the readers of *An Claidheamh Soluis* not to support Pan-Celticism because the money would "be spend on a week's junketing in Dublin." The Pan-Celtic movement offered no practical assistance to the goals of the League, Keawell maintained, because "the Irish language will not be saved by picnics to Tara Hill, or by the eating of big dinners in a Dublin hotel."[117] Keawell and his allies in the executive committee of the Gaelic League were also concerned that the Pan-Celtic movement was too focused on medieval, rather than modern, Irish culture and that this could harm the goals of the League. Keawell wrote, "Once let the movement get a vague, a fantastic, or anti-quarian character, and the edge is taken off our sword. . . . The rank and file up and down the country would lose faith in a 'golden age' and 'tenth-century Irish' movement."[118] Father Hogan echoed these thoughts when he complained to MacNeill that the coming of the gorsedd would be a "set-back" for the Irish language, owing to "the old world air of the business, the strange rites and ceremonies, the 'bards' quaintly not to say absurdly robed marching thro the streets of our city."[119] When Fournier suggested organiz-ing an "imposing ceremony" on behalf of his own branch of the Gaelic League to declare Douglas Hyde the "King of Dalkey Island" in 1901, the executive committee shot down the idea.[120]

Another League member, W. H. Brayden, was equally scathing about the Pan-Celtic congress. He wrote that the movement's membership con-sisted of "the intellectual who is too lazy to undertake the study but yet pro-fesses sympathy, and who is prepared to explain in English the philosophy of the Gaelic avatar; the Irish landlord who wants to be a patriot in every-thing except rent reduction and the nationalization of the government; and the social butterfly in search of a new sensation."[121] In particular Brayden criticized the influence of Welsh rituals on the congress, writing, "There was a good deal of mummery introduced into the proceedings by the Welsh contingent, whose archdruid and chief bard had much hoary ceremonial to get through." Brayden noted that the watching press and crowds struggled to keep a straight face because there was "so much that was merely ridicu-lous introduced by the Welsh contingent that it was calculated to kill the whole movement in laughter." The costumes worn by the delegates also came under fire, with Brayden labeling the congress a "display of millinery." Referring to the procession through the streets of Dublin, Brayden wrote, "The Welsh contingent appeared in their ceremonial robes, the Scots in their kilts and plaids, and the Bretons in their national costume. The Dub-lin Lord Mayor and town council . . . looked quite drab in the rear of this display of colour."[122] He also had a theory as to why elaborate dress was so popular among the Pan-Celts, declaring that "the ordinary Gaelic leaguer is content to work in the trousers that prevail from San Francisco to Athens, but the Anglo-Irish Pan-Celt needs a crimson cloak and a saffron waistcoat to make up for his little skill in Gaelic." According to Brayden, the Pan-Celtic movement could be a success in Ireland only if it would "purge itself of its excrescences."[123] The ceremonies and costumes would remain at the heart of the movement under Fournier's stewardship and therefore alienated many Irish nationalists who wanted to concentrate on contemporary social and economic problems rather than glorifying the past.

The divide between the Pan-Celts and the Gaelic Leaguers in relation to the question of national dress highlighted the fundamentally different attitudes of the two groups regarding modernization. In essence, the Gaelic League embraced modernity and wanted to promote a modern, industrial Ireland, while many of the Pan-Celts believed that something of the human spirit had been lost in the industrial age. The Gaelic League has often been misrepresented as an antimodern organization. R. F. Foster writes that Gaelic League "zealots" did not think of Ireland as economically backward but rather "saw the remnants of a Celtic 'civilization' that implied a spiritual empire far greater than England's tawdry industrialized hegemony."[124] Yet from an examination of the Pan-Celtic furor it is evident that many Gaelic Leaguers were very much in favor of "tawdry" industrialization.[125] Members of the League believed that the Pan-Celts were only serving as a distraction from the real problems facing Ireland. When asked by a Breton poet how her organization viewed the Pan-Celtic congress, a female member of the League responded, "The Gaelic league has to think about education, emigration, intoxication and leather. It is not time just now for ornamentation."[126]

Irish-language activists strongly believed that their efforts to revive Irish were essential to the eventual economic and social prosperity of Ireland as a whole. William Patrick Ryan, a member of the Gaelic League who also had socialist sympathies, wrote:

> The spirit which language revivals infuse into the most wretched and hopeless nations; the fine material and spiritual energy that results as they advance; the large and heartening opportunities that come forth for native power and talent, once the people, through the illumining

and creative force of the language, and all that it enshrines, are filled with the ideal of making the most of their land and their place in the onward movement of the world; how industry growing spacious brings social prosperity, and art becoming beautiful gives the nation new distinction; how speedily the language fits itself to all the requirements and developments of modern life; how, when minds are educated and trained in it, they assimilate any outer culture that they will need without loss of individuality.[127]

In other words, much of the Gaelic League membership was committed to an Ireland that was not Gaelic merely but industrial as well. For example, at the annual *oireachtas*, an industrial exhibition always took pride of place.[128] This is also evident in the programs of the various *feiseanna* that were organized by the Gaelic League around the country. The rules for competing in these *feiseanna* reflected the desire of the League to promote Irish manufacturing. Almost every *feis* had a rule declaring that "all competitors will be dressed in materials of Irish manufacture, and any prize-winner who does not comply with this condition will run the risk of having the prizes withheld."[129] Writing competitions were frequently part of a *feis*, and occasionally written submissions were required to be made on Irish paper and written with Irish ink.[130] Indeed, the titles used for the *feiseanna* essay competitions demonstrate the importance the Gaelic League attached to developing an industrial Ireland. At the Féise Uibh Ráthaigh in Cahirciveen in 1908, two pounds was offered for the best essay on "the best way to advance Irish manufacturing."[131] Meanwhile the recitation competition saw League members compete for ten shillings for the best response to the prompt "Is it possible for the people of Iveragh to conduct their business solely in Irish?"[132]

Competitors at a *feis* in Tullamore were offered one pound for the best essay in Irish on "what the industrial movement means for Ireland." At the same competition, fifteen shillings was on offer for the best essay in English discussing the topic "Our Greatest Industry" or "A Suitable Industry for the Midlands."[133] Ten shillings was the prize at another *feis* in Listowel for the best Irish or English essay written under the title "The Most Suitable Industry for Listowel, and the Best Means of Promoting It."[134] The fact that the organizers of both *feiseanna* were willing to accept entries in English on this topic shows that there was a genuine interest in tapping into local ideas about industry. Organizers were satisfied to sacrifice the usual deference to the Irish language in these cases in the hope of stimulating new ideas for developing Ireland's industries. Although less common, competitions promoting local craftwork were also held at some *feiseanna*. At the Mitchelstown *feis* in 1908, aside from offering one pound for the best essay on "Irish industries," thirteen "industrial competitions" were held for those who lived within a sixteen-mile radius of Mitchelstown. Prizes between five and ten shillings were offered for, among other things, the best piece of domestic furniture, the best quilt, the best cotton or wool shirt, and the best crochet collorette. All thread used had to be of "guaranteed Irish manufacture."[135] The *feiseanna* demonstrate that the League was committed to promoting a modern industrial Ireland. What the Pan-Celts sought to reject, the Gaelic League wholeheartedly embraced.[136] It is no wonder, then, that many in the League had little time for what they viewed as "a parasitic organization, which seeks to divert to itself Irish energy and Irish money, and which cannot give in return any practical work."[137]

The Pan-Celtic idea was rejected by Irish nationalists because the movement appeared to be little more than Protestants playing as pagans. The debate regarding Pan-Celticism came at a time when some nationalists viewed Protestantism as increasingly incompatible with "Irishness." That the leaders of the Pan-Celtic movement were Protestant served to make Pan-Celticism less appealing to one segment of the Gaelic League, as well as the fact that the Pan-Celts promoted stronger links with countries where Catholicism was resented. Castletown's position as a landlord, unionist politician, and imperial soldier meant that he personified the "un-Irish" caricature some Catholic nationalists had of all Protestants. Indeed Castletown's politics allowed Irish nationalists to view Pan-Celticism as an attempt to provide a cultural justification for unionism, and therefore as being at odds with their vision of a politically and culturally autonomous Ireland. The attempt to introduce Welsh traditions into Ireland further alienated Irish cultural nationalists who believed the country needed to expunge all foreign influences, not encourage new ones to emerge. The pagan overtones of the druidic rites and ceremonies associated with the gorsedd did little to encourage influential Catholic clerics to throw their weight behind Pan-Celticism.

Most importantly, the Pan-Celtic movement portrayed itself as interested in playing games rather than tackling Ireland's problems. The costumes, the color, the pageantry and processions appeared to some within the Gaelic League as irrational and irrelevant. Furthermore, the antimodern attitude of the leadership of the Pan-Celts meant that they were distinctly at odds with the Gaelic League and its desire to see an industrial and agriculturally progressive Ireland. The failure of Fournier to win the support of the League meant that Pan-Celticism would remain a marginal influence in Ireland. For the Gaelic League itself, an ugly precedent had been set. The leaders of the League, men like MacNeill and Hyde, had been sympathetic to Pan-Celticism but had been cowed by nationalist hard-liners into withdrawing their support. The Pan-Celtic debate marked the beginning of a long struggle within the League between those who wanted to maintain the organization as a strictly cultural entity and those who wanted the League to support Irish political autonomy, culminating in a victory for the latter in 1915. The Pan-Celtic moment had offered "a multinational movement for others, thus providing a space in which support for the Irish language could be expressed without that inevitably entailing a commitment to the goals of Irish nationalism."[138] Its defeat meant that Irish cultural activists increasingly insisted on the separate and distinct nature of Irish nationality from Britain, culminating in the rise of the Sinn Féin movement. Irish nationalists, in other words, proclaimed themselves members of the Celtic race, but only to distinguish themselves from Anglo-Saxon England, not to acknowledge their connection with the rest of Britain. The opportunity for an alternative, broader, retelling of Ireland's past remained a tale untold, while the story of Ireland's cultural, national, and racial separation and distinction from Britain remained the master narrative of the country for much of the twentieth century.

CHAPTER 6

DANCING TO A DIFFERENT TUNE

When Edmund Fournier conceived the idea of a Pan-Celtic alliance, his vision was centered on Ireland. He believed that, with Irish leaders and a base in Dublin, Ireland would be "at the head of the Celtic world" and that the Pan-Celtic movement would grow on the basis of Irish enthusiasm.[1] The mixed reaction of the Gaelic League to Fournier's proposals, however, meant that the Pan-Celtic ideal received a cool reception in his adopted homeland. In contrast, there appeared to be a genuine groundswell of support for Pan-Celticism in Wales. At the two Pan-Celtic events held in Wales, namely the Pan-Celtic national eisteddfod in Cardiff in 1899 and the Pan-Celtic congress in Caernarfon in 1904, thousands of Welsh well-wishers took part in the celebrations. The visitors, from across the Celtic world, were warmly received by local dignitaries, who fêted their guests as long-lost family members. Fournier was undoubtedly pleased that his ideas were supported in Wales at least. His interest in Pan-Celticism had been sparked by a visit to Wales in 1897, and he regularly proclaimed that Wales, by preserving its native language so effectively, was the role model that the other Celtic nations should aspire to. The passion the Welsh appeared to show for a closer social and cultural bond with their fellow Celts encouraged Fournier to believe his dream could survive Irish indifference.

However, a closer inspection reveals that the Pan-Celtic ideal may not have been as popular in Wales as it initially seemed. Certainly there was no public campaign against Pan-Celticism in Wales, as had taken place in Ireland. The Pan-Celtic congress held in Caernarfon proved to be the only event of the Celtic Association that was a financial success, with the congresses held in Dublin and Edinburgh resulting in heavy losses. Welsh writers, with a few exceptions, warmly welcomed the Pan-Celtic initiative. Yet all of these factors, in addition to the large crowds that attended the Pan-Celtic gatherings of 1899 and 1904, do not provide conclusive evidence that the Welsh public were as committed to the cause as Fournier hoped. The Pan-Celtic meetings held in Wales certainly captured public attention, but it is possible that many were attracted merely by the entertainment value of viewing the elaborate and exotic costumes of the Pan-Celtic delegates. Welsh nationalists who championed the movement did so in part because they saw it as an opportunity to enhance the dignity and respect of the Welsh nation. With Fournier proclaiming Wales as the exemplar for all Celtic nations, and with proposals afoot to export the Welsh gorsedd to other Celtic lands (an idea that alienated Irish nationalists from the movement), Pan-Celticism was naturally appealing to many in Wales. Yet certain cultural misunderstandings between the Scottish and Irish visitors and their Welsh hosts did little to encourage a deeper commitment to Pan-Celticism. Indeed, when Fournier stepped away from the Celtic Association after the 1907 congress, much of the movement's energy went with him, despite the strong support seen in Wales. In many ways this best summarizes the involvement of Welsh nationalists with Pan-Celticism: willing participants, but with little desire to direct and lead.

Although the Pan-Celtic movement was greeted with skepticism in Ireland, Irish scholars have been quite willing to analyze its role in the evolution of modern Irish nationalism. Rather surprisingly, Welsh historians have not followed suit. Little attempt has been made to explore the impact of Pan-Celticism in Wales or to understand why the ideas behind the Pan-Celtic initiative were more popular in Wales than in any of the other Celtic countries. One of the few writers to discuss Pan-Celticism in Wales is Clive Betts. His book, *A Oedd Heddwch?*, contains one chapter dedicated to the 1899 national eisteddfod in Cardiff, which was attended by a Pan-Celtic delegation. Betts states that the eisteddfod brought discord, not unity, among the delegates, writing that the Celts "were all great friends until they looked closely at each other."[2] He focuses on the controversy regarding the

Highland dance (discussed in detail below) and the radical political views of Patrick Pearse, the Gaelic League delegate, to highlight how disappointed the visitors were in "seeing through superficial Welshness to all pervasive Britishness lying under the surface."[3] Yet Betts says almost nothing about how the Welsh viewed Pan-Celticism, and some of his assertions, such as claiming that Pearse abandoned Pan-Celticism after visiting Cardiff and discouraged the Gaelic League from supporting it, are patently false. Marion Loffler, in her article "Agweddau ar yr Undeb Pan-Geltiadd, 1898–1914" (Aspects of the Pan-Celtic Union, 1898–1914) and her *Book of Mad Celts: John Wickens and the Celtic Congress of Caernarfon 1904*, discusses the Pan-Celtic congress held in Wales.[4] Loffler points out that while scholars remember the Celtic Association as a literary movement, many Pan-Celts were deeply interested in the question of fashioning a distinctive national costume. She notes, however, that most of the Welsh attendees at Caernarfon wore normal clothes and claims that this was because their middle-class inclinations made the idea of wearing an outfit modeled on the clothes of the Welsh peasant very unappealing.[5] Yet Loffler, like Betts, does not explore the impact of Pan-Celticism on the Welsh national consciousness. It is this omission that this chapter hopes to begin redressing.

While the impetus behind the Pan-Celtic movement came from Ireland at the turn of the twentieth century, efforts had been made in Wales throughout the nineteenth century to solidify ties with Brittany. The distinct culture of Brittany owed its origins to the migration of Brittonic speakers from Britain to Armorica between the fifth and seventh centuries.[6] As a result, the Welsh and Breton languages stayed very similar into modern times, highlighting the strong historical and cultural ties between Wales and Brittany. Thomas Price, also known by his bardic name as Carnhuanawc, was instrumental in fostering closer cultural relations between the two countries. Price won a prize at the Carmarthen eisteddfod in 1823 for his essay on the connections between the Bretons and the Welsh, and he convinced the British and Foreign Bible Society to finance the translation of the Bible into Breton.[7] He began a long correspondence with the Breton scholar Théodore Claude Henri, which culminated in the visit of a Breton delegation to the Abergavenny eisteddfod in October 1838. The Bretons, led by Henri, the vicomte Hersart de la Villemarqué, and Alexis-François Rio, were warmly received at a public banquet held in their honor. During the course of the banquet, Henri sang a Breton song, with the lyrics so resembling the Welsh language "that they were plainly understood by the audience, and gave them unbounded pleasure."[8] Several speeches were made calling for closer unity between the two countries, and competitions were held to show the similarity of the two languages.[9]

Despite the sentiments shared at Abergavenny, interactions between cultural nationalists in both countries were sporadic. In 1863 Sir Watkin Williams, a Liberal politician, said to a cheering eisteddfod crowd in Rhyl, "I am told that the Welsh language [Breton] is spoken very much in France and I am given to understand that there are no better soldiers and sailors serving under the French Government than the Bretons."[10] The seeds of Pan-Celtic idealism had been sown in Wales, however, and when Edmund Fournier sought to develop a Pan-Celtic movement, the Welsh looked upon his proposals favorably. Fournier attended the national eisteddfod held at Blaenau Ffestiniog in 1898, helping establish a Welsh Pan-Celtic committee to be based in Cardiff. He also announced that an "influential Irish delegation" would attend the national eisteddfod in Cardiff in 1899 and would invite the Welsh bards to come to Dublin to form an Irish gorsedd.[11] It was from the idea of sending Irish visitors to Cardiff that Fournier conceived of turning the Welsh national eisteddfod into a distinctly Pan-Celtic affair. By February 1899, a circular from the Pan-Celtic Association referred to the Cardiff event as a "Pan-Celtic Eisteddfod."[12] The concept of Pan-Celticism was beginning to attract attention in Wales. One Welsh newspaper, reporting on the establishment of a branch of the Gaelic League in Cardiff, noted that the development was "very significant of the wide spread movement towards Pan-Celticism."[13] Fournier was invited to be the president of the North Wales eisteddfod at Llandudno in March 1899, and he reported to Lord Castletown that "every reference by myself and other speakers to the Pan-Celtic Congress was received with marked applause."[14]

Fournier's plan to grow Pan-Celticism was based on holding congresses every few years that would bring Celtic scholars and enthusiasts together to discuss matters of common interest. With plans for the first Pan-Celtic congress still in the works, Fournier saw the visit of the Celtic delegates to the Cardiff eisteddfod as an ideal opportunity to advertise the movement and generate enthusiasm for developing stronger bonds between the Celtic countries. For Fournier, Wales was a natural choice of location for the first major Pan-Celtic event. Speaking at Llandudno, he told his Welsh audience, "I always return from Wales with renewed courage. Wales is the great object lesson for the Celtic race. The Irish language movement is firmly established and vigorously pursued, but in Wales we have a kindred language in all its strength and beauty, the envy of Ireland and Brittany and Gaelic Scotland." He urged his listeners to maintain their hold on their native language, declaring:

> Wales does not, perhaps, even yet realize what her responsibility is in this all-important matter. Wales is in this respect the standard-bearer of the Celtic race. A victory for Welsh is a victory for Irish Gaelic, and Breton as well. Millions of Celts in the old world and in the new look to Wales for inspiration in their own language struggle. The Welsh are the vanguards. None of us other Celts have a mayor like the Mayor of Conway, who can address us in a Celtic language, or who cares to do so, if he can. Welsh is being studied and learnt in Ireland and in Brittany. And it is not only in Wales that the fervent prayer is heard, "O bydded i'r hen iaith barhau" [Oh may the old language endure].[15]

Although Fournier had already begun advertising the national eisteddfod as a Pan-Celtic gathering, the committee organizing the event in Cardiff had not formally announced the attendance of the Celtic visitors. In May 1899, three members of the national eisteddfod committee, Edward "Cochfarf" Thomas, Thomas "Awstin" Davies, and Gwilym Hughes, traveled to Dublin to meet with Fournier and discuss the aims of the Pan-Celtic movement.[16] While it is unknown what exactly was said at the meeting, the Welsh visitors returned to Cardiff impressed by Fournier's vision. Edward Thomas, for one, embraced the Pan-Celtic spirit. When interviewed upon his return from Ireland, Thomas pointed "to a hundredweight of literature, with some writing materials on the table, [and] said 'I am learning Irish.'" Thomas was asked about the Gaelic League branch in Cardiff, where Irishmen like Father Hayde spoke fluent Welsh, and whether he found a similar interest in the Welsh language in Ireland. He replied, "I found in Ireland a greatly increased interest in the Welsh language and literature, and many people well able to converse in Welsh. Mr. E. Fournier, for example, addressed us in fluent Welsh."[17] Thomas also made a supportive speech for the

Irish-language movement at the *oireachtas* in Dublin and joined the Cardiff Gaelic League.[18] Thomas Davies declared that the presence of the Celtic delegations in Cardiff would create scenes "as romantic as Arthurian legends."[19] On the day the eisteddfod began, Davies wrote:

> Two years ago, the idea of a real Pan-Celtic re-union was so nebulous that some matter-of-fact folks exclaimed in my presence, in the words of the Good Old Book, "Thou shalt not hearken unto that dreamer of dreams," but, with more faith in the ultimate realization of our object, I remind my unbelieving friends that the same Good Old Book says, "Your sons and daughters shall prophesy; your old men shall dream dreams; your young men shall see visions." They only smiled and yet the "coming of the Celts" to Cardiff in such numbers is an early fulfillment of the most sanguine dream that "that dreamer of dreams" Mr. Fournier, ever conjured up in his mind.[20]

At least one voice, however, was somewhat skeptical about the arrival of the Pan-Celts. Samuel Coupe Fox had been born in England but moved to Cardiff in 1890. He would become one of the best-known journalists in Wales through his "Man about Town" column, which appeared in the *South Wales Echo*. He was also the most ardent Welsh critic of Pan-Celticism. Although he wrote that the "Pan-Celtic revival should prove useful and broadening in its influence, and to that extent it should be encouraged," Fox had his doubts about the movement's purpose. He observed that while race and patriotism were important, it should not be forgotten that "Saxon and Scot, Irish and Welsh, we are all part of that great amalgam the British nation. The Pan-Celtic revival should not be permitted to foster a spirit of parochialism or caste of race or draw about it a barred fence of nationalistic sentiment."[21] The irony is that whereas some Gaelic Leaguers in Ireland were suspicious of Pan-Celticism precisely because they feared it would foster a British rather than Irish sense of identity, Fox was concerned that Fournier and his allies could potentially create racial divisions within the British state.

The national eisteddfod took place between July 17 and July 22, 1899, with the visit of the Pan-Celtic delegations forming only part of the wider celebration of Welsh culture and nationality. Unlike the vitriolic attacks upon Pan-Celticism that had appeared in some Irish newspapers prior to the Pan-Celtic congress in Dublin in 1901, the Welsh press exuded sympathy and admiration for the movement. Leading the way in this regard was the *Western Mail*. The *Western Mail* was a major sponsor of the national eisteddfod, printing the bulky hundred-page program for the event.[22] The newspaper employed three journalists, Thomas Davies, the Reverend "Golos" Jones, and Owen "Morien" Morgan, to write about the eisteddfod. Each day of the festival, long and detailed reports filled the pages of the *Western Mail*, with great attention paid to the activities involving the Celtic visitors. The highlight of the week in this regard was the ceremony to welcome the Pan-Celtic delegations into the gorsedd circle. The Welsh poets, wearing their bardic robes, assembled in front of the Cardiff Town Hall and marched to Cathays Park, where a stone circle had been erected for the gorsedd ceremony. Half an hour later, the Celtic delegates followed along the parade route. Most notable were the Scottish and Breton pipers, who, clad in their native costumes, alternated in playing "The Campbells Are Coming" and "Seziz Gwengamp" (The Siege of Guingamp) on their respective bagpipes and binioù.[23]

Within the gorsedd circle, the sound of the approaching music was the signal for the Pan-Celtic reception ceremony to begin. Fournier, wearing the green robe of a gorsedd ovate, stepped forward and formally asked the archdruid, Hwfa Môn, for permission for the Celtic delegates to enter. Hwfa Môn gave his consent by uttering the biblical verse "Lift up your heads, Oh ye gates," and the Irish delegation walked into the gorsedd circle. Lord Castletown, president of the Pan-Celtic Association, then delivered a speech in medieval Irish asking the bards to come to Dublin to establish an Irish gorsedd.[24] The Breton delegation entered next, led by Breton pipers and followed by two groups bearing two halves of a sword on separate silk cushions. The Breton leader, François Jaffrennou, made a speech in fluent Welsh, declaring that this Pan-Celtic reunion safeguarded forever the distinctive nationality of the Celts. The Scottish delegation, led by bagpipe players and, to a man, wearing kilts, were the next to enter, while the more moderately dressed Manx delegation brought up the rear.[25] Once all speeches had been concluded, the procession returned to the main eisteddfod pavilion in Cardiff. Hwfa Môn stood on the stage with one half of the split sword as the Bretons marched up onto the platform, playing Breton tunes and carrying the other half of the sword. Jaffrennou approached Hwfa Môn with the Breton half of the sword and, speaking in Breton, requested a "marriage of the swords." Hwfa Môn consented to this, and the two halves were bound together with ribbons, symbolizing the union of the Celtic nations.[26]

Judging by the size and demeanor of the crowd, it seems fair to say that the concept of Pan-Celticism was welcomed by the general public in Cardiff. Unlike reports from the Pan-Celtic congress in Dublin in 1901, where onlookers were described as struggling to keep a straight face, all accounts state that the Welsh audience was intrigued by the Celtic visitors. One writer noted that the people of Cardiff "turned out in thousands, and about 8.30 [a.m.] the main thoroughfares through which the procession was to march became a dense mass of human beings."[27] The *Western Mail* had two pictures of the proceedings in their report, one showing the procession to Cathays Park, and the other showing the sword ceremony on the eisteddfod platform. Both pictures show very large crowds in attendance, but an exact figure is hard to know. The *Cardiff Times* estimated that five or six thousand people watched the gorsedd ceremony, while the *Wrexham Advertizer* stated that fifteen thousand people were in attendance.[28] Whatever the size, it appears the onlookers approved greatly of the proceedings. Thomas Davies wrote that the "enormous multitudes that assembled . . . bore an attitude of gentleness leaving nothing to be desired."[29] The sword-binding ceremony was also well received by the spectators, with one observer stating that it "was manifest from the demeanor of the audience that so far from resenting the innovation they awaited it with eagerness. . . . There was a deafening outburst of applause," and when the Bretons appeared "the vast audience rose en-masse to greet them, and a mighty cheer of welcome was raised."[30] Davies believed the throng was openly embracing Pan-Celticism: "'Erin go Bragh!' was shouted, and the response promptly came 'Cymru am byth.' . . . There was neither levity nor lightness: but the 'hands across the sea' had been grasped so warmly as to make all feel, as one congratulated the other, 'Thy people are my people.'"[31] Yet while the crowd may have approved of the Pan-Celtic gathering, this is not to say that everyone was an expert on Celtic affairs. One wag noted that as "the kilted Highlanders went up to be presented an enthusiast in the crowd shouted out 'Ireland forever!'"[32]

While it might be tempting to view the presence of a large and vocal audience as proof that there was a deep interest among the Welsh public for establishing closer connections with their Celtic relatives, this would be an overly simplistic assessment. It is possible that most of the crowd came to view the novel national costumes worn by the visitors, in particular the Scottish Highlanders and the Bretons. This appears to be borne out by the extensive coverage that the Scottish and Breton delegates received in the media, in contrast to the scant comment made regarding the Irish and Manx parties. Thomas Davies made the connection between the crowd size and the more exotically dressed visitors, writing, "The bards and literati assembled at the Town-hall as . . . the Scottish Highlanders and the Breton contingent mustered outside, so that a great crowd was attracted long before the procession was formed."[33] Owen Morgan also commented on the appearance of the Highlanders, writing that they "wore kilts, with the thistle of their native moors or straths as silver clasps pinned to their tartans on their shoulders. In their midst were two tall figures who might have very well represented Wallace and Bruce." Morgan was most impressed by another "venerable sire, with long hair and beard, both grey, and wearing a costume of the Stuart period, who seemed, with his bonnet and feather, as if he had just stepped out of an oil painting of a Scottish king at Holyrood."[34] The Bretons also caught the attention of the bystanders, as they "were attired in their national costume, and naturally excited a great deal of curiosity."[35] Morgan commented that the "amiable and highly intellectual little Bretons were received with thunders of applause."[36]

In contrast, the Irish and Manx visitors, dressed in modern clothes, remained very much in the background. Of course, indifferent attitudes toward the Irish were not uncommon in Wales. Thomas Gwynn Jones, a well-regarded Welsh poet, noted in relation to the visit of the Pan-Celtic enthusiasts that "there was a time, and not that far back, when there was not close intercourse in terms of feeling and desire between the Celts of Ireland and the Welsh of the Principality."[37] Certainly Patrick Pearse, the representative of the Gaelic League, did not appear to receive the same level of fanfare that the Breton and Scottish representatives did. Pearse gave a speech at a reception held by the mayor of Cardiff for the visitors, with the Reverend Jones rather snidely recording that "Mr Pearse had an audience of one as he expressed his felicitations in Irish."[38]

While the speeches of Pearse may not have attracted much attention, the Pan-Celtic aspect of the national eisteddfod was popular, and Hwyel Edwards's assertion that the addition of the Celts "proved unsuccessful" is wide of the mark.[39] As has already been noted, the Welsh media was almost devoid of the negative commentary toward the Pan-Celts so evident in the Irish press in 1901. The *Cardiff Evening Express* ran a cartoon on the first day of the eisteddfod, under the title "Back to the Old Home," that best encapsulated the positive spirit generated by the arrival of the Celts. It showed an Irishman, a Scotsman, a Manxman, and a Breton, all stereotypically dressed for their nationality, rushing, with exuberance on their faces, to be embraced by a traditionally dressed Welsh peasant woman.[40] Henry Lacelles Carr, editor of the *Western Mail*, was similarly optimistic, writing, "Today commences what is unquestionably the grandest eisteddfodic gathering of modern times. . . . So far as outward show, popularity and public enthusiasm are concerned, this meeting at Cardiff will, no doubt, eclipse all previous gatherings."[41] In particular, Carr believed that the visiting Celts could impart a certain "vivacity" that the Welsh spirit was lacking. He wrote that "Welsh poetry . . . has been too prosy and matter-of-fact, and devoid of that dreaminess and haziness which constitutes the chief charm of Breton and Gaelic poetry and legend." He hoped that "intercourse with Brittany and Ireland, not forgetting Manxland and the Highlands, will open up the ancient founts of Celtic inspiration afresh."[42]

At the end of the eisteddfod week, some believed this had been achieved, with the *Cardiff Times* stating, "The meeting this year will be memorable for the revival of the Celtic spirit, which has been so characteristic a feature of the gatherings."[43] There was a broad consensus that the event had been a success. Thomas Gwynn Jones wrote, "Certainly that which makes the Cardiff Eisteddfod stand highly among the national eisteddfods of Wales was the welcome given to the representatives of the Celtic tribes from Scotland, Ireland, France, and the Isle of Man."[44] Another writer declared that the national eisteddfod would be "characterized in the historical records as the one with the largest meeting of the Celtic tribes in one place since their dispersion to different countries. . . . The Pan-Celtic Congress is very much likely to become strong in the future, and . . . to be an effective means to unite the Celts more than ever."[45] The *Tarian y Gweithiwr* stated that "every visitor to the town—from the most ardent eisteddfoder to the littlest Dic Shon Dafydd—testified that this was the greatest day in the history of the old festival."[46] Fournier himself seemed to sense the positive reaction to Pan-Celticism building in Wales, telling Lord

Castletown that "the Welsh seem anxious to go ahead with their part of the movement now."[47] In short, the Celtic visit to the eisteddfod was an encouraging experience for both participants and audiences and gave great hope to those behind the movement that Wales could be fertile soil for a Pan-Celtic flowering.

While the Pan-Celtic aspect of the Welsh national eisteddfod was successful, one incident highlighted the cultural and religious differences between the various Celtic nations cooled the ardor of some Welshmen for Pan-Celticism. On the afternoon of Wednesday, July 20, the ceremony for the chairing of the bard was due to take place. This ceremony recognizes the best entry in the *awdl* competition, with the *awdl* being a long poem composed in accordance with a strict meter form. For the Cardiff eisteddfod, however, the judges decided that no entry was worthy of being declared the winner, and an announcement was made to the expectant crowd that no ceremony would take place. What happened next is somewhat unclear. The Scottish delegation had expressed their desire to give an exhibition of a Highland jig, although the eisteddfod secretary, Vincent Evans, afterwards said he had no knowledge that a show of dancing was planned.[48] At any rate, with the canceling of the bardic ceremony, the Scottish representatives, all wearing kilts, walked out on the eisteddfod platform. Two swords were crossed on the floor of the platform, forming four triangles. One young Highlander began dancing, jumping between the blades of the sword, while a piper played a tune on the bagpipes. Once this "sword dance" was concluded, two more pipers and four more dancers entered the fray and performed a "Highland fling" for the audience. Satisfied with their demonstration of a prominent aspect of Scottish Highland culture, the pipers and dancers withdrew from the stage.[49]

The Scottish delegation was unaware that in dancing upon the eisteddfod platform they were committing a serious faux pas. Nonconformist Wales, strongly influenced by Calvinist principles, had little appreciation of dancing. In Scotland, where Presbyterianism was the faith of the majority, Highland dancing had not been proscribed, and the Highlanders never imagined that their demonstration could cause offense to their hosts. Irish cultural nationalists who complained about too much dancing at *feiseanna* did so only because they believed it was distracting from people learning Irish. They certainly agreed that dancing was an integral part of Ireland's

Gaelic heritage, and at the national cultural festivals of Ireland (the *oireach-tas*) and Scotland (the *mòd*) dancing took a central place in the competition curriculum. But Wales was different. The national eisteddfod consisted of various singing and literary competitions, but dancing was excluded. Welsh attitudes toward this particular activity were best demonstrated by the op-position shown to a proposal to introduce dancing in the school curriculum in Caernarfon in 1904. The *North Wales Observer and Express* commented, "The proposal to include dancing in the County School curriculum will not find much favor among parents, we fear." The writer himself supported the proposal, stating, "It is a healthy and innocent exercise, one too that is natural to the Celtic temperament. . . . Perhaps, when we have outgrown the old-world notion that dancing leads to the devil, the old reels and jigs, together with the modern waltzes and polkas, will be yet done justice to by the light fantastic toes of the children of Wales."[50] Yet objections certainly existed to this proposal. One writer, using the pseudonym "Sylwedydd" (Observer), declared, "In the name of all reason, what possible point is there to teaching dancing to children?"[51] Thus, when the Scottish gave an exhibition of national dancing to honor the Welsh, a mixed reaction was inevitable.

The crowd, for the most part, seemed to thoroughly enjoy the exhibi-tion of dancing. The *Liverpool Mercury* hinted at one obvious reason the audience appreciated the gesture when it stated that the "disappointment of the crowd at the non-award of the chair prize was, however, considerably ameliorated when the conductor announced that the Highlanders would give an exhibition of characteristic Highland dances."[52] Recalling the reac-tion of the crowd, Owen Morgan exclaimed, "Shade of Burns, how the au-dience seemed to enjoy the fun," while Thomas Davies remarked, "The thousands expressed their enjoyment of the scene they had witnessed by thunders of applause."[53] *Tarian y Gweithiwr*, a newspaper aimed at the la-boring classes, commented that during "the afternoon, there was a dance and music by the Scottish pipers, and others, in their national costume, causing great delight to those present, and a completely new thing to the Eisteddfod platform."[54] The *Baner ac Amserau Cymru* similarly noted that the masses were greatly entertained, saying it "was a very interesting scene, and attracted attention, and it played to the feeling of the crowd because of its novelty. . . . Great fun was had for a number of minutes, and the crowd enjoyed the treat undoubtedly."[55]

The audience, it appears, were unaware that their sensibilities should have been offended. The *Sheffield Independent* highlighted this by stating that among "the uninstructed mob who thronged the building this friendly exhibition of a picturesque custom belonging to another Celtic race excited applause, but in the ranks of the elect it produced groans."[56] As this report indicates, while the majority of the audience was quite pleased with the exhibition, some discontent was also evident. Various accounts acknowledged that the event was "loudly, though not universally, applauded" and that the dancing was "very popular with the audience, who cheered heartily, but there were some who gravely shook their heads and whispered colloquies of an excited character showed that the departure from the beaten track had filled some minds with dark foreboding."[57] Owen Morgan admitted that some people "seemed to regard the whole thing as ungodly," while Thomas Davies feared that "the novel scene would cause a religious earthquake."[58] One writer for the *Tarian y Gweithiwr* had little sympathy for those upset by the display, believing the audience had been entitled to some compensation with the chairing ceremony not taking place. He noted that "the pipers and dancers understood their work, if not the bards."[59]

Nevertheless, there was strong resentment among some as a result of the Scottish display. At the forefront in this regard was William Abraham, best known by his eisteddfod name, "Mabon." Abraham was an MP for Rhondda, and as president of the South Wales Miners' Federation was one of the most famous and influential men in the Principality. Abraham was present at the eisteddfod pavilion during the Highland jig, and he made his displeasure known instantly. Owen Morgan observed that as soon as the Scottish had ceased dancing, "Mabon" rushed to the platform "with a leonine expression on his face, and roared an englyn in what seemed to me some unknown tongue."[60] An *englyn* is a short Welsh poem, which Abraham clearly uttered as some kind of rebuke to the Scottish, although what he said exactly is unknown. The *Sheffield Independent* described his retort as "an extempore couplet, which is understood to be too full of indignation to translate."[61] Later that same evening, there was a joint meeting of the national eisteddfod and gorsedd committees, with Abraham again taking the opportunity to voice his opposition to dancing on the eisteddfod platform. He declared that the exhibition had "prostituted the Welsh national gathering to the level of a dancing saloon."[62] Abraham was furious that the eisteddfod stage had been allowed to be "begrimed by the feet of anyone dancing a Highland jig" and insisted that the introduction of pipers and dancers "was the beginning of the decadence of the Eisteddfod."[63] One observer of the meeting noted that "the feelings of the others were only too plainly on the side of Mabon."[64]

Owen Morgan and Thomas Davies had been the two most prominent champions of the Pan-Celtic presence at the eisteddfod, and with this unexpected criticism they both sought to downplay the significance of the dancing controversy. Owen Morgan tried to claim that the exhibition of dancing had met with the approval of the archdruid, Hwfa Môn. Having the approval of the archdruid was important because Hwfa Môn was, in a sense, the personification of Welsh culture and heritage. Should he approve of the dancing, it would imply that the Welsh nation had no cause for offense. Hence Morgan declared that Hwfa Môn, "who sat within a couple of yards of the jigging, seemed to see the light of other days, and actually stealthily moved one of his feet, as if in sympathy with the spirit of the Highland jig."[65] Another writer in the *Western Mail* claimed that the archdruid had watched the performance with "amused astonishment" and that after "a little while the effect was seen. Hwfa's heel rose and fell, the movement quickened, the hand followed suit, and before long Hwfa's feet were actually joining in the jig as far as they could with the owner sitting down."[66] Morgan said that after the display, a friend exclaimed to him, "'That was fine! We have too few dances in Wales these days.' His fine face, as he passed out of the building wore a smiling expression." Thomas Davies tried a different approach, citing scripture to defend the dancing: "Although David dancing before the Ark may be cited as a precedent, I feel sure the scriptural allusion will not satisfy the people who contend that such a proceeding is not compatible with the dignity of the eisteddfod."[67] Morgan echoed Davies when speaking at the meeting of the national eisteddfod and gorsedd committees, declaring, "David danced before the Ark, and it was only fair for David Jones to have dancing before the Gorsedd." He also felt that the protest of "Mabon" was too harsh, saying that the Welsh "had invited other nationalities there, and each nationality had its own predilections. It was unfair to the Highlanders to condemn them for what they excelled in."[68]

Despite these efforts to downplay the incident, many Welsh people were upset by the display and adamant that dancing in the national eisteddfod should never be allowed to happen again. Evan Rees, a Calvinistic Methodist minister and prominent attendee at the eisteddfod, had been horrified by the dancing, saying, "I felt ugly [*hyll*] when it was on. It made me feel dismal and miserable. Mind you, I could look at such an exhibition elsewhere without qualms, but not at an eisteddfod. It was out of place. I did not like to see it, and I sincerely hope I may never see it again."[69] Vincent Evans, the secretary of the national eisteddfod, shared this outlook. Evans said he had been unaware of any plans for an exhibition until the Scottish took to the stage, and stated, "My personal opinion was that it was an innovation that was un-Welsh and un-eisteddfodic."[70] One man in attendance at the eisteddfod, Enoch Davies, was appalled by what he saw. He wrote that he supported "every word—aye, every letter—spoken by our worthy member 'Mabon' in the Gorsedd committee. . . . Who are to be blamed for thus reducing our sacred National Eisteddfod to the level of the tap room?" Davies believed that the dance was "a degradation of our national gathering" and exclaimed, "In the name of everything that is decent, in the name of Wales and its religion, I condemn in the strongest possible terms the actions of those responsible for the modesty, the purity, and the elevation of our nation through the medium of the National Eisteddfod in allowing such things."[71] Thomas Gwynn Jones agreed, writing, "The Cardiff Eisteddfod has brought in a practice that should not, to say the least, happen again."[72] The *Gwyliedydd* newspaper, published by the Wesleyan Church, concurred with this view, saying that while it welcomed the Celtic visitors the Welsh people should not "be willing to take up any vulgar practices of theirs. We seriously hope that the last dance on the Eisteddfod has taken place."[73]

Interestingly, while Owen Morgan and Thomas Davies believed that any objections to the dancing were on religious grounds, many of those who criticized the Highland exhibition did so on the basis that the eisteddfod was a platform for intellectual, rather than physical, prowess. Edward Anwyl, the professor of Welsh at the University of Wales, commented:

The incident in question doubtless originated in an outburst of sympathy on the part of the Highlanders with what appeared to them the national characteristic of the Eisteddfod; but the general question of using the platform of the Eisteddfod for the display of physical as well as artistic and intellectual perfections is one upon which a strong difference of opinion might well be expected. I confess that it seems advisable to me on the whole to have a separate arena for the display of physical perfections as distinguished from those which are intellectual and artistic. It scarcely seems in keeping with the history of institutions to leave those arenas undifferentiated.[74]

Thomas Charles Edwards, principal of University College of Wales, saw the incident in a similar light. He believed that the goal of the national eisteddfod was "the moral and intellectual advancement of the people." As a result, Edwards wrote, "I did not like the sword dance and the jig. Of course, I thought they were going to play some tunes. That would be quite in keeping with the objects of the Eisteddfod, which is intended for moral and mental advancement, and not as a place for the display of physical feats."[75] Thomas Gwynn Jones also questioned whether dancing was of any benefit to the goals and aspirations of the Welsh cultural festival. He commented, "It is said somewhere that the aim of the Eisteddfod is developing the mind . . . [to] develop the talents of the Welsh, and to use every other means likely to promote the social, moral, and intellectual condition of the Welsh! This, as we can see, is what should be the main aim of the Eisteddfod." With this in mind, Jones asked, "Is dancing on the platform of the Eisteddfod likely to assist in the realization of this high aim? We answer unhesitatingly no; and for this reason, we unhesitatingly say, dancing should not be tolerated on the platform of the Eisteddfod."[76] Of course, one might question whether objecting to the physical nature of the activity was a cover for opposition based on social and religious, rather than intellectual, grounds. After all, a singular display of dancing was unlikely to undermine decades of tradition associated with the festival.

Nevertheless, while resentment of the dancing was clearly evident, some people in Wales urged a more measured and understanding response to the misjudgment of their Scottish guests. After the Highland jig, Hwfa Môn said, "I do not object to dancing, and I think too much has been made of this incident. I see no harm in letting these visitors give an exhibition of skill in what is with them a national pastime." He believed that while the Welsh themselves did not dance, "there is no reason we should object to other people dancing if they wish." David Alfred Thomas, the MP for Merthyr Tydfil and a powerful coal magnate, stated, "I was not against the dance myself, and I am sorry to hear so much about it. I think a great deal too much has been said, and what has been said is in very bad taste." These sen-

timents were shared by D. W. Evans, the local honorary secretary of the national eisteddfod. He said that he had "no objection" to the dance, believing
"it is right that we should become acquainted with these things." Evans
pointed out that the Scottish "came to us in a national capacity, and wished
us to see what was predominant with them," and as such "I think we can
tolerate things of that sort."[77]

Others were more critical of the hostile response toward the Scottish
dance. A man named Wmffa Huws wrote a letter to the *Tarian y Gweithiwr*
saying that "Mabon was too reckless in burning his two lines of unforget-
table poetry on the corner of the stage. Surely displaying the national custom was the main aim of the Scottish patriots?" Huws asked, "What is
wrong with a little starlit dancing? More dancing, and less ceremonial hypocrisy, does a great deal of good in many circles outside of the Eisteddffod."[78] The *London Kelt*, meanwhile, dismissed the behavior of William
Abraham as "naked bigotry." The paper stated that, despite the audience's
appreciation of the dance, "a number of people narrowed their mind raising
a great cry against such a thing. They see nothing but "the hand of the 'evil
one' in everything, and they see dancing on the festival platform as fire on
the skin of the long faced man." The writer declared that "it would be better
for such people to quickly dispense with such thinking and give to others
the same freedom to sing as they prefer just as we wish to speak freely and
sing our national songs."[79] Samuel Coupe Fox commented, "It is difficult
for the majority of Cardiffians to understand why so much fuss should be
made over the incongruous innovation of the sword dance, because they do
not realize the horror with which dancing in any form is regarded in the
Hills. What many people look upon as innocent diversion and an aid to social enjoyment is held to be a matter of grave evil, for participating in which
members of churches are threatened with excommunication."[80] Bernard
Doyle, following events from Ireland, struck a similar note. Writing in
Fáinne an Lae, he asked, "Seriously now, isn't it a little late in the day for
turning away the face from a dance or even for talking about cultivating
the heels at the expense of the head?" Doyle said he hoped Mabon would
not visit Ireland, as he would be deeply troubled "if he looked into the Feis
at Milltown-Malbay and found reel and jig in full swing. At Ballyvourney
Feis he would certainly get a fit, for there's a hornpipe to be added to the
other horrors."[81]

The Scottish response to the whole affair was one of bemusement. Edward Thomas, who had played an important role in bringing the Pan-Celts to Cardiff, spoke to a well-known Scottish Presbyterian minister about the controversy and reported, "He told me that even in Presbyterian Scotland it is looked upon almost as a religious duty to be able to do a Scotch reel."[82] A. S. McBride, the man who brought the pipers from Scotland to Wales, attempted to explain away the misunderstanding while also making it clear that he was not pleased with the Welsh response to the Scots' unwitting mistake. McBride wrote, "I have to express our regret that any act of ours should have given offence to the feelings or even prejudices of Welshmen at their great national gathering." Causing offense, he explained, was obviously far from the intention of the Scottish visitors: the pipers had traveled a great distance, at considerable expense, to be at Cardiff and they had believed "that an exhibition of our Highland dancing, which we consider an art, and which we cultivate as such, would be something new and entertaining to the vast audience of the Eisteddfod." McBride admitted that when he first suggested that a dance be performed on the eisteddfod platform he had noticed some hesitancy among officials, but he had assumed that this was due to the already overcrowded nature of the festival program. Had he known the dance would create such upheaval no performance would have taken place, but the pipers "did not deserve to have showered on them any harsh, insulting, or ungentlemanly terms for what in the innocence of their hearts they thought would please the people to whom they claim a Celtic kinship."[83]

John Mackay, president of the Highland Association and the leader of the Scottish Pan-Celtic delegation, was even more forthright in expressing his displeasure at the treatment of the pipers and dancers. Quoting the poetry of Robert Burns, Mackay said the controversy had developed because of the attitudes of the "unco guid" (extremely virtuous), the "Holy Willies," the "rigidly righteous." The jig "was intended by us as a compliment to the eisteddfod, not as a show of agility in dancing." This, Mackay maintained, was how the audience had viewed the performance; thus they had "lustily cheered and applauded." However, he noticed that the jig for William Abraham was "like a red rag upon an infuriated bull," and that Abraham had "looked sternly at me as if I were the concoctor of the 'disgrace' thrown on the eisteddfod." The Scottish delegation, Mackay claimed, were not aware that any offense had been caused until after they had departed from the eisteddfod platform, but Mackay had no intention of apologizing. Echoing McBride, he stated that the dance was "a compliment we wished to pay to the eisteddfod, and I do not regret having been a party to it. As a compliment it was understood by the great multitude assembled, who, as you know, loudly applauded the performance." His only regret was that the incident "should have any other effect than showing up the 'Holy Willies' to public contumely."[84] Such strong language did not go unnoticed. Gwilym Hughes, who had journeyed to Dublin two months previously to secure the presence of the Pan-Celts at Cardiff, refuted the idea that Welsh protests had been couched in anything but "the most respectful of language." He regretted that Mackay and McBride had not responded with an "equally gracious spirit" and stated that the problem had arisen only because "some of the visitors forgot that they were guests, and displayed an anxiety to themselves wield the reins."[85]

Despite this sharp exchange of words, the general sentiment in Cardiff at the close of the national eisteddfod was that the Pan-Celtic celebration had been a success and that as a movement Pan-Celticism was worthy of support. Several people commented that the misunderstanding regarding the Highland jig should not be allowed to undermine greater Celtic harmony and cooperation in the future. Edward Thomas hoped that the incident would not lead to any further "bad feeling which seem to dog the steps of every Celtic movement."[86] Henry Lacelles Carr similarly sought to downplay the furor about the Scottish dance, writing that the "little misunderstanding which took place on one of the evenings is now forgotten, and has left no sour feelings behind."[87] The newspaper *Y Cymro* believed the incident was "proof of the dangers" faced by the Pan-Celtic movement in trying to bring together five countries of differing religious, linguistic, and cultural backgrounds. Nevertheless, the newspaper hoped the dancing difficulty would be forgotten, as "the Pan-Celtic idea is so beautiful, it should be given every fair play."[88]

There remained a great deal of sympathy for Pan-Celticism in Wales in spite of the misstep of the Scottish delegation. Yet after the national eisteddffod, several commentators suggested that the Welsh cultural festival might not be the best vehicle for spreading the popularity of the Pan-Celtic movement. This foreshadowed a similar development in Ireland two years later, when the Pan-Celtic congress took place in Dublin. In Ireland, a number of cultural nationalists suggested that the Pan-Celtic event threatened the future growth of the *oireachtas*. These concerns were also raised in Wales in relation to the national eisteddfod, although it is notable that in Wales these worries came to the fore only after the Highland jig, whereas in Ireland members of the Gaelic League warned of the potential threat to the *oireachtas* well in advance of the arrival of the Pan-Celts. Henry Lacelles Carr wrote that if a Pan-Celtic exhibition were to return to the eisteddfod, efforts needed to be made to ensure that the event itself was not overshadowed. Carr stated that by "paying so much attention to strangers there is danger of losing sight of the distinctively Welsh character of the Eisteddfod." Visitors, he believed, "of course, must be in the picture, but they should be in the background, and not in the forefront." Any attempt to create an "international eisteddfod" would lead to "failure and disaster." In short, Carr was adamant that the "only way to make the Eisteddfod interesting . . . is to uphold as much as possible its traditions and its Welsh spirit and character."[89]

Gwilym Hughes held similar views. He wrote that he was unsure if the Cardiff festival "cannot be better described as a Pan-Celtic festival than as an Eisteddfod." Many people, he reported, had observed that the Pan-Celtic display "so overshadowed all other as to largely efface the Eisteddfodic features of the gathering." Hughes also cautioned that the gorsedd should not rush to enroll all Celtic visitors in its ranks, as "the Welsh bards, unless they are not very watchful, may soon find themselves ousted from all authority in their own Gorsedd." While he was not opposed to future Pan-Celtic events, Hughes maintained that "if these Pan-Celtic displays are to be continued, they must be held apart from the Eisteddfod."[90] In one regard, this thinking was not a problem for the growth of Pan-Celticism; Fournier had always envisioned a Pan-Celtic congress as an independent event. However, such attitudes did demonstrate that, just like many of their Irish counterparts, Welsh cultural nationalists could support Pan-Celticism while also being concerned about its potential impact on established national institutions.

The first Pan-Celtic congress had been scheduled to take place in Dublin in 1900, but the outbreak of the Second Boer War and the deployment of Lord Castletown to Africa scuttled that plan. Instead, Fournier rescheduled the Congress for 1901, with the Welsh gorsedd traveling to Ireland to take part in the celebration. As already noted, not everyone in Ireland was welcoming toward the Welsh. The *United Irishman* poured scorn on Welsh claims of a distinct nationality, declaring, "There was a Wales one time, which we civilized and taught music—a Wales which brought forth Rhys Ap Griffith and followed Llewellyn to battle for liberty. But that Wales is as dead as Julius Caesar."[91] Such comments did not go unnoticed in Wales. Sir John Gibson, a well-respected Welsh journalist, reported that one Irish newspaper had mocked Hwfa Môn for wearing his gold ornament in the wrong place. Gibson exclaimed, "O Ireland, Ireland, how can you be so cruel." Although Gibson was himself skeptical about the importance of bardic rituals, he noted that "it is a safe game."[92] The criticism by members of the Gaelic League of the Pan-Celtic Association also attracted attention. In response to Father Peter O'Leary's stinging attack on the congress, the *North Wales Express* declared, "Of the Pan-Celtic movement we have heard a great deal, but we must confess that the existence of the Gaelic League was altogether unknown to us." The paper sought to defend the Pan-Celtic ideal by belittling the League, calling it an "insular organization . . . suffering from crabbed old age," while labeling O'Leary's writing "puerile." The *Express* issued a tongue-in-cheek warning to the gorsedd: "The Welsh bards, who will go in large numbers to Dublin next week, must beware. The Gaelic League is going to keep a sharp eye on them! They will be marked men for the rest of their days!"[93]

Although Irish writers like W. H. Brayden were adamant that the Dublin crowd viewed the Pan-Celtic celebration as preposterous, Welsh commentators reported that the efforts to create hostility toward the visitors failed. The *Weekly Mail* noted that the "prophets who foretold disaster to the Pan-Celtic demonstration at Dublin belied their office. The people of the city on the Liffey turned out in their thousands to witness the procession that was formed at the Lord Mayor's Mansion House on Tuesday morning."[94] Similarly, the *Cardiff Times* commented that the "absurd prophecy of the extremists among the Gaelic League section . . . has been falsified, and the ridicule then predicted as awaiting the congress by the citizens of Dublin has fallen upon the heads of the false prophets themselves." The writer concluded that "those who came to curse remain to bless, and each succeeding day and each succeeding meeting proves that the hopes of the promoters of the movement have been more than justified."[95]

Not surprisingly, the Pan-Celtic congress in Dublin attracted less attention in Wales than the Pan-Celtic celebration at the national eisteddfod in Cardiff, and certainly the critical comments about the congress that were heard regularly in Ireland were absent in the Principality. In *Y Celt*, the congress was described as "an Eisteddfod—and also not an Eisteddfod." The anonymous writer noted that the Pan-Celtic movement owed its origins to the Cardiff festival of 1899, believing that that eisteddfod would achieve "great fame" for birthing a "big idea" that would influence many nations.[96] T. C. Evans, a well-known figure in eisteddfodic circles, seemed similarly pleased that the congress highlighted a growing Welsh influence among the other Celtic nations. He stated that it was a "very pleasing duty" of the Welsh bards "to give the Irish every helping hand to regain the ground which they seem to have lost in the retention of the national language of their country, and to revive the national customs, traditions, the literature, and the poetry of old Ireland." For the most part, however, the Welsh press adopted a passive attitude toward the Dublin congress, content to report upon proceedings with little analysis or commentary. This passiveness may have been shared by the Welsh representatives in Dublin: the *Weekly Mail's* special correspondent noted that few Welsh delegates attended the afternoon sessions, which he believed "contrasted very unfavorably with the unquestionably earnest disposition of all the other delegates."[97] Yet the discussion of Celtic national costumes at the congress, which seemed farcical to many of the Gaelic League observers, attracted the attention of Henry Tobit Evans. Evans, who had authored the anti-Catholic and anti–home rule pamphlet *Y Berw Gwyddelig* in 1889, appeared to be quite sympathetic to the Pan-Celtic movement. Reflecting upon the debate on Celtic costumes, Evans declared that "dress is much more important than we have thought." He continued, "There are so many commonalities regarding material and form of the Welshman and the Englishman that it is impossible to say which one is the Celt without talking to him. It should not be. It is obvious that the Celt is filling places so important in the history of this world that he deserves an outfit that will make him immediately well known." Evans proposed that a Welsh national committee of tailors should work together to create a distinctive Welsh outfit, believing that the members of this committee would "immortalize themselves."[98] Little came of Evans's suggestion, and while the Dublin congress was noticed in Wales, it seems that interest in Pan-Celtic affairs was more muted when the festivities were taking place in another country.

The one Welsh journalist who did pay close attention to the Pan-Celtic congress in Dublin was Samuel Coupe Fox. To Fox, the congress appeared to be nothing more than "symbols and costumes, greetings and handshakings, feastings and fraternisings, with compliments galore." However, the problem with Pan-Celticism in his view was it was easy "to dream dreams; not quite so easy for the visionary to work, and there must be research and study, the spending of laborious days and nights with the use of the 'midnight oil' if Pan-Celticism means anything but a new excuse for a holiday."[99] Fox's criticisms of the practicality of Pan-Celticism sounded very similar to those put forward by the hard-line Gaelic League members in Ireland. However, Fox was no ally of the Gaelic League. He questioned why the Pan-Celts were seeking to revive the Irish language because "Irish is a dead language to literature and modern life. . . . Erse is not the language of the newspapers, nor of trade, nor is it the language of the Church. Ireland's brilliant orators and writers know not Erse, but English."[100] Fox's main criticism of the congress was that Pan-Celticism was about making vague speeches, without any tangible goal. He asked, "How are they [the Celts] to be united and the process of race absorbtion resisted?" Pan-Celticism was pointless because "the Celt . . . will advance not by keeping behind his native hills or at the head of the tributary springs of the broad river of human progress and advancement, and setting up race distinctions and social prejudices but by plunging into the stream and becoming a Citizen of the World, a worker and a thinker."[101] He was confident that the movement would not take hold in Wales because "the young Welshman does not desire to see Five Celtic Nations—Welsh, Irish, Scotch, Manx and Breton— parading in a style of costume a few centuries old, a style which the world cast off before history began. . . . There is no danger. The young Welshman is becoming practical."

For the most part, however, Fox's commentary was one of the few negative opinions voiced in Wales regarding the Pan-Celts. Meanwhile, during the congress in Dublin, Lord Castletown revealed that the congress was to be held triennially and would return to Dublin in 1904.[102] As time passed, however, it seems Fournier believed that Wales would be a better location for the next gathering of the Pan-Celts. The fact that the Gaelic League refused to assist Fournier in developing Pan-Celticism, which in turn led to a rather indifferent reaction among the Irish public to the Dublin congress, may have influenced this decision. In addition, Fournier needed the next Pan-Celtic congress to turn a profit, as the costs of running the Celtic Association were already proving beyond his means. From his regular visits to the Principality, Fournier knew that the Welsh were quite successful in organizing such cultural festivals. In 1903, Fournier travelled to Caernarfon, addressing the town council and asking them to host the Pan-Celtic congress in 1904.[103] Fournier chose Caernarfon as a potential location because it would be only a short journey from Rhyl, which would host the 1904 national eisteddfod. He no doubt hoped that the close proximity to the Welsh national festival would help boost the attendance and prestige of the Pan-Celtic event. Fournier also may have believed that the town of Caernarfon best embodied the ideals of Pan-Celticism. The writer Ernest Rhys stated that "Carnarvon [*sic*] . . . is the one Welsh town best fitted perhaps for a gathering of this kind. There, the ideas for which the Celtic Association has worked, and especially those bearing on the maintenance of a national spirit and a Celtic tongue, have all the while been quietly followed without any external stimulus."[104] The Caernarfon town council agreed to host the congress, deciding to hold it the week before the national eisteddfod.[105] The two local secretaries for the Celtic Association were Thomas Gwynn Jones, and Robert Gwyneddon Davies, a solicitor and son of Thomas Davies, a noted journalist.[106] Together they began planning for the visit of the Pan-Celts to the heart of Welsh-speaking Wales the following year.

The second Pan-Celtic congress opened on Tuesday, August 30, 1904. With rain falling, the various delegates assembled at the railway station and followed a group of Irish and Scottish pipers who led the Celtic procession toward Caernarfon Castle. Once again, the Scottish visitors dressed in their national costumes, while the mayors of Dublin, Caernarfon, Conway. and Bangor wore their official regalia. The Bretons, however, decided to wear bardic outfits similar to those worn by the gorsedd. Ernest Rhys believed that because of this decision the "public pageantry" was "shorn of something of its effect."[107] Nevertheless, the *North Wales Express* declared that "it is doubtful if a not only more picturesque but also more stately and impressive cavalcade ever passed through the streets of Carnarvon [*sic*] before."[108] In the courtyard, the delegates assembled the Lia Ceneil, the stone pillar made up of five blocks, each one representing one of the Celtic nations. After this opening ceremony, the mayor of Caernarfon, Mr. W. G. Thomas, hosted an official reception for the visitors, with six hundred guests in attendance. Lord Castletown presented Thomas with a shillelagh of black bog oak, with Caernarfon's mayor jokingly responding that this gift implied he might have to use the shillelagh to keep order during the course of the congress.[109]

During the plenary sessions, each delegation gave a report on the status of their indigenous language, outlining the steps being taken to strengthen and preserve it. The liveliest discussion was in relation to the question of Cornwall, with Henry Jenner and L. C. R. Duncombe-Jewell petitioning to have the English county included as one of the Celtic nations. Some representatives, like William Gibson, son of the Lord Chancellor of Ireland, objected to Cornwall being included because Cornish was not a living language. However, when the issue was put to a vote, Cornwall was unanimously accepted as the sixth Celtic nation.[110] Other discussions addressed the cultural connection between ancient Egypt and ancient Britain, and the eastern origins of the Scottish kilt. The constable of Caernarfon Castle, Sir John Henry Puleston, hosted another reception for the visitors, and the congress concluded with two Pan-Celtic concerts on Wednesday and Thursday evening.[111] After the congress, many of the visitors traveled to Rhyl for the national eisteddfod, and the Pan-Celts received an official welcome during the course of the celebrations.

The program for these Celtic concerts featured singing, music, and of course, dancing. This included Irish dancing, the Highland jig, and the Scottish sword-dance.[112] As this dancing took place on the Pan-Celtic stage and not upon an eisteddfod platform, it was warmly received by the Welsh audience. However, one observer was not overly enamored with the dancing display, writing that "the Irish and the Scottish found great fun dancing and singing, and displaying the remnants of paganism remaining in the Celtic blood."[113] It also appears that one prominent Welshman had not forgotten the dancing incident in Cardiff. William Abraham, who had led the protest against the Highland jig in 1899, was due to be a conductor at the national eisteddfod. However, when it became clear that the Pan-Celts would visit the eisteddfod on the same day he was to be in attendance, Abraham withdrew his services, possibly as a protest against the inclusion of the visitors.[114] Nevertheless, the presence of the Pan-Celts at the national eisteddfod passed off without incident this time. The ceremony of joining the halved sword took place, receiving the approval of the large crowd in attendance. Lord Mostyn, president of the national eisteddfod, praised the Celtic Association for the progress it had made and spoke positively of his interest in Celtic unity. All of the visiting delegates hailed the character and resolve of the Welsh in preserving their culture.

One of the most notable features of the Caernarfon congress was the decision to adopt a song that could serve as a national anthem for the Pan-Celts. The Celtic Association had chosen heather as the symbol of Pan-Celticism in 1901, and Fournier had suggested that a Pan-Celtic flag would be unveiled at Caernarfon,[115] though apparently this did not occur. As for choosing a representative Celtic song, the poet Alfred Graves announced that the executive committee of the Pan-Celts had decided to adopt the Welsh national anthem, "Hen Wlad Fy Nhadau," as their own. Graves declared that "the anthem would be engrossed and illuminated in each of the six Celtic languages on vellum by Celtic artists, and then handed over to the safe-keeping of the Mayor and Corporation of Carnarvon."[116] A verse of the song was sung in each of the Celtic languages, with the chorus being sung in Welsh. Fournier wrote that the first time it was attempted the song was sung "in a remarkable manner. Four Celtic singers, representing Ireland, Wales, Brittany and Cornwall, each in turn sang the solo of the anthem in the native tongue of each country, while the thousands of assembled Celts thundered out the chorus in Welsh. Their faces were transfigured, and their eyes were streaming with tears of joy."[117] This Pan-Celtic version of the song was repeated when the group attended the national eisteddfod the following week, in which the audience "all heartily joined."[118] Commenting on the Pan-Celtic adoption of the song, Samuel Coupe Fox sarcastically remarked that in the future, "when Mabon sings its inspiriting strains, we must think of the Land of Scotland, Ireland, Manxland, Cornwall, and Brittany. It is the National Anthem of the whole Celtic race henceforth, and is to be engraved on vellum in the six Celtic languages. So much has been accomplished."[119]

Indeed, Fox, through the medium of his "Man about Town" column, launched daily attacks on the Pan-Celtic congress. When it was announced that Cornwall had been accepted as a Celtic nation, he wrote, "The syrens round the Land's End are singing, the fish in St. Ives Bay are flapping their fins with joy, the ghosts of St. Michael's Mount are pleasantly excited, even the old smugglers are turning in their graves."[120] Fox questioned the entire purpose of the congress, stating, "There is so little in common between the Irish and the Welsh, the Scotsman and the Breton."[121] Taking aim at those participating in the congress, Fox declared:

> It is well for the world that so many can detach themselves from the every-day realities of a busy generation and devote themselves whole-heartedly to such subjects as the study of Gaelic and Welsh. There is an old-world romantic flavor about the doings of the Pan-Celtic Congress already, although it is only a few years old—a mere puling infant among National and International Societies, and crying in the night. What does all this toying with sentiment, the revelry in symbolism, the talk about Gaelic, Erse, Manx, and Welsh, the erecting of the "stones of the nations" mean? To what end?[122]

As in 1901, his criticisms were very similar to some of those leveled by Irish opponents of Pan-Celticism, depicting the movement as a collection of backward-looking people obsessed with symbols and rituals. The congress, according to Fox, was "seeking to revive the dead past, to check the mutations of time, the irresistible tendencies of the age. . . . Is it not pure Celtic dreaming?"[123]

Fox aside, most of the Welsh public responded enthusiastically to the presence of the Pan-Celtic visitors in 1904, although perhaps not immediately. One attendee recalled that the town of Caernarfon "was somewhat frigid at the beginning of the notable week . . . [but] we all know what scenes of enthusiasm were witnessed before the last of the Celtic brethren bade us good-bye."[124] It is possible that such initial indifference on the part of the local population may have been due to uncertainty about the purpose of the Pan-Celtic congress. After all, unlike the gathering of 1899, it was not associated with the national eisteddfod, and perhaps the people of Caernarfon did not know what to make of it. However, most press reports at the time emphasized the positive reception given to the Celtic guests. Thousands of people lined the streets to watch the Celtic procession to Caernarfon Castle, with the *North Wales Observer and Express* exclaiming,

"Carnarvon [*sic*] has been entirely dominated by the Pan-Celtic idea this week, and is a captive, but a willing one, at the chariot-wheel of the Celtic conquerors."[125] The streets of Caernarfon were decorated with bunting for the occasion, with the Welsh flag and other Celtic emblems displayed in public buildings. At the Pan-Celtic concert on the final night of the congress, an audience of four thousand people attended.[126]

Such public enthusiasm led one anonymous observer to state that the "present movement has undoubtedly caught the popular imagination, and though the man in the street may not rise in every instance to Mr. Fournier's interpretation of it as a 'literary and linguistic manifestation of racial kinship,' something of the real meaning of it all has been realized." The reason for this, he speculated, was that the Pan-Celts showed that Wales was not alone in its struggle to preserve its native language, and this realization by the townspeople led to "the 'homeliness' of the Congress, the warmth that has permeated this reception of brothers and sisters from far away by their elder sister of Cambria."[127] Alexander Carmichael, leader of the Scottish delegation, said he had been "struck by the innate courtesy of the Welsh people." Carmichael observed that wherever the Scottish Highlanders went in Caernarfon, "they had never been greeted or followed with a rude stare or rude remark, but always everywhere with friendly courtesy and ready hospitality—and there were not many towns in Scotland of which the same might be said."[128] The *London Kelt* was confident that "the delegates would testify they had spent some of the happiest days of their lives" during their stay at Caernarfon.[129] Some members of the Welsh public were equally impressed by the occasion. One female reader of the *North Wales Observer and Express* said that in reading about the congress she "perused and devoured each speech, and a huge wave of Celtic enthusiasm swept over me. I wept copiously, such large Celtic tears." She regretted not being able to attend the event but had no doubt that "Carnarvon [*sic*] was in its glory. Oh, for the wings of a dove!"[130] Fournier himself was ecstatic about the Caernarfon event, writing, "The first Pan-Celtic Congress has been completely outstripped by the Second, and the triumph of Carnarvon marks a step in advance in the Pan-Celtic movement . . . the most imposing gathering the Celtic race has seen since its imperial days."[131]

The greatest proof regarding the success of the Caernarfon congress is shown in the profit made from the event. Initially, fund-raising had not gone well. In 1901, Fournier and his associates had raised £365 to offset the cost of the congress, but this proved to be insufficient as the costs exceeded the money taken in.[132] In 1904, Fournier called for a smaller fund of only £200 to be raised, but as the congress drew closer he had failed to raise even half of this.[133] Faced with the possibility of a serious financial reversal, Fournier was relieved to discover that the event was a modest financial success. In total, the Pan-Celtic congress had a net profit of £150, split equally between the Celtic Association in Dublin and the Welsh Pan-Celtic committee.[134] This compared very favorably with the financial loss from the Dublin congress in 1901 and the calamitous loss of £352 resulting from the final congress Fournier organized in Edinburgh in 1907.[135]

It is possible to interpret these figures as evidence that Pan-Celticism as a movement captured the popular imagination in Wales in a way it never did in Ireland or Scotland. However, it may also be that this profit can be explained merely as a result of the greater Welsh experience in organizing events like the Pan-Celtic congress. Comparing the success of eisteddfods in North and South Wales, the *Rhyl Journal* noted that "the upper classes in North Wales give more encouragement to the Eisteddfod. . . . That is one reason, perhaps, why meetings in North Wales as a rule are attended with greater success. . . . It is very seldom a North Wales Eisteddfod leaves a balance on the wrong side of the ledger."[136] Another commentator believed that the success of the Celtic congress highlighted "Carnarvon's knack of making these undertakings pay."[137] In addition, almost all of the Welsh performers at the Pan-Celtic concerts were well-established singers and musicians in the Principality, so it is difficult to say for sure whether audience members were attracted by the Pan-Celtic element of the concert or merely the Welsh presence.[138] Nevertheless, it appears reasonable to view the financial success of the Caernarfon congress as an indication that Pan-Celticism held some appeal in Wales. It also provided a vital lifeline to the movement as a whole. In 1904 the Celtic Association had debts amounting to seventy pounds, which worried Fournier so much that he had come to think that "life was hardly worth living."[139] The money from Caernarfon cleared these debts in an instant, although it proved to be only a brief respite in the troubled financial history of the Celtic Association. The £352 bill for the Edinburgh congress had to be split between Fournier and Castletown. As Fournier had an annual salary of only £180 for teaching physics at University College

Dublin, this was quite a financial blow to him and led to him stepping away from the movement shortly thereafter.

In addition to the revenue generated, the congress attracted a great deal of media attention, with journalists themselves acknowledging that newspapers did not just record the events in Caernarfon but dedicated editorial comments to them as well.[140] The congress could also be deemed a success for avoiding the type of incident that had marred the Celtic gathering in Cardiff in 1899. That being said, the tensions between the differing worldviews brought together by the Pan-Celtic congress were at times evident. The fascination of the Celtic visitors with the gorsedd alarmed those in Wales who viewed the bardic institution as a romantic fabrication. The newspaper *Y Celt* warned against exporting the gorsedd to other countries, declaring, "Dear Celts, walk away from the children's toys of the old Celts [Welsh]." The same writer believed that the Pan-Celts needed to move beyond conversations on Celtic costumes and Celtic cuisines or they would "soon be subject to the ridicule of the nations of the world."[141] Meanwhile, during one discussion, the question turned to whether a common language understood by all could be found to use during the Celtic conferences, as not all delegates were eager to use English or French. Fournier suggested Esperanto, believing its international character would not offend any nationalist sensibilities. However, the suggestion was ridiculed by others in attendance, with Welsh, Cornish, and even Turkish suggested as better alternatives.[142] This incident showed that while there was undoubtedly genuine warmth among the delegates, differences of opinion were never far from the surface.

This was best demonstrated by a couple of minor incidents that took place on the night of the second Pan-Celtic concert. Halfway through the concert, David Lloyd George tried to slip unnoticed into a seat reserved for him. He was quickly recognized, however, and the crowd rose to acknowledge him, with some demanding he make a speech. At first, Lloyd George declined to do so, but eventually Lord Castletown went down into the audience and led the reluctant MP to the stage. The crowd continued to call for a speech, and *Y Celt* humorously described what happened next: "A speech had to be delivered, even if the program of singing and dancing must go to pieces. Someone protested the giving of a speech at the concert, and the disregarding of the order of the musical program. Some Welshwoman, who showed much more zeal for speeches than singing, took an umbrella, and smote the protester. This item was not on the program either."[143]

Fournier described the same incident in a more diplomatic way, writing that Lloyd George "did speak, and in his own mother tongue. And then a voice from the Gods thundered in the same tongue (which we long ago declared to be that of Paradise), and after a few more words, the tired man, nothing loth, resumed his seat."[144] The intervention of the woman and her umbrella amused those in attendance, but a second disturbance at the end of the night showed how the "Celtic peace" did not always smooth over political differences among the Pan-Celts. As the concert came to a close, a pianist began to play "God Save the King." Loud murmurs of protest could be heard around the hall, and one unnamed Irish representative apparently leaped to his feet, kicked his chair, and stormed out in protest.[145] This was not the first time the question of loyalty to the crown had to be addressed among the Pan-Celts. In 1899, John St. Clair Boyd, a member of the Gaelic League who also supported Pan-Celticism, wrote to Lord Castletown saying that toasts might have to be omitted from Pan-Celtic gatherings, as traditional toasts to the monarchy might offend Irish nationalists who were present.[146] Indeed, at one gathering in Caernarfon, two Scottish delegates refused to drink to the health of the king, maintaining that as Jacobites they believed in the divine right of the Stuarts to the English throne.[147] Hence the reaction to "God Save the King" being played is not surprising. One journalist wrote that an "Irish representative jumped up, and kicked a nearby chair—was there not an Englishman close enough for him to kick, I wonder?" He questioned whether the incident showed the failure of Pan-Celticism, stating that the "objective of the large Celtic conference was to create fraternity, but the conference of fun was spent fighting, and fighting for fun, and ended in a violent altercation."[148] Similarly, the *Western Mail* opined:

> In view of the exciting scene witnessed at Carnarvon on Thursday the question suggests itself whether it is possible to hold a Pan-Celtic gathering in Wales without some jarring incident. At the Pan-Celtic gathering in Cardiff a few years ago the Puritan element in the Welsh character revolted against the exhibition of Scotch dancing on the platform, and the Picts gathered up their bagpipes and returned North in

a huff. The Carnarvon meeting, also, was destined to witness an unfortunate incident. . . . These "scenes" do not add to the dignity of the congress, and must be avoided in future.[149]

Others felt that the whole incident had been overblown. The *North Wales Observer and Express* acknowledged that some people were not happy with "God Save the King" being played but denied that any kind of scene as described in other newspapers had taken place.[150]

An interesting insight into whether this incident did any damage to the reputation of Pan-Celticism in Wales can be found in a letter from William Gibson to Lord Castletown. Gibson, upset with the inclusion of Cornwall within the Pan-Celtic movement, had left the Celtic Association immediately after the Caernarfon conference. Thus Gibson intended his letter to the president of the Celtic Association to be discouraging, and it should be read with a certain amount of caution. Nevertheless, Gibson does give credence to the idea that not everyone in Wales was enamored with the Pan-Celtic movement. He wrote that certain incidents "have created bad blood in important quarters." This undoubtedly was a reference to the discontent shown at the playing of the national anthem. Gibson admitted that there was popular support for Pan-Celticism in Wales, describing the crowds who greeted the Pan-Celts as "enthusiastic" and commenting that "public opinion seemed to be interested" in the movement. But potential leaders of the movement in Wales were not so sure. Mr. Thomas, the mayor of Caernarfon who had been so accommodating to the visitors, was concerned for the long-term future of the Celtic Association. Gibson told him that the main problem was that the "Gaelic League boycott" prevented popular support for the movement in Ireland, causing Thomas to "have his doubts about the whole thing."[151]

Gibson's exchange with Castletown also revealed that some of the Pan-Celts were beginning to question one important aspect of the movement, namely the revival of national costumes. Gibson told Castletown that one member of the gorsedd told him that he did not want to become involved with the Pan-Celtic movement because "he did not want to make himself ridiculous," while Gibson also felt that Welsh "university men" viewed the Pan-Celts as "a circus." While members of the gorsedd wore elaborate costumes themselves, this particular bard may have felt that the bardic robes had a historic legitimacy in a way the Pan-Celtic outfits did not. Gibson himself recommended that in future "papers on such questions as that of *costume*, should be delivered at least a third of their extent, in a Celtic language. (This would ensure the question being made subordinate to that of language, which is paramount.)"[152] Gibson was a noted costume enthusiast, but clearly even he was coming to feel that the pantomime associated with the congress was opening the Pan-Celts to ridicule and distracting from the practical work of language revival. Castletown appears to have come to a similar conclusion. He replied to Gibson that "as to costume I look upon that as foolishness and have said so. I consider as I conclude you do that language, customs, dances, music and games [are] the best means of keeping up" a Celtic identity.[153] It appears that Castletown, as president of the Celtic Association, tried to rein in some of the excesses associated with Pan-Celticism. With preparations for the next congress in Scotland gathering pace, Fournier assured Castletown that "the Edinburgh Congress will be more scholarly, literary, serious and weighty than any of the others."[154] When the Scottish committee proposed a street procession of the Pan-Celts, as had taken place in Dublin and Caernarfon, Fournier wrote to Castletown, "I have told them you will have nothing to do with that, and that they must curb their enthusiasm."[155] Evidently, the criticism of the Pan-Celtic pageantry was hitting home with the leadership of the Celtic Association.

At the same time, it should not be overlooked that the Welsh press generally had a more favorable view of Pan-Celticism than their Irish counterparts. One factor that might explain these different attitudes was the focus on Welsh cultural achievements among the Pan-Celts. In Ireland, nationalists were outraged with the suggestion that an Irish gorsedd be established at the Pan-Celtic congress in Dublin. This appeared to be an attempt to import foreign customs, and as such it ran counter to the philosophy of mass movements like the Gaelic Athletic Association and the Gaelic League, which sought to promote indigenous Irish culture. In Wales, the population received a very different message. The Pan-Celts came to the Principality to learn from the Welsh, to admire the strength of the language and the eisteddfod, and to understand how this success could be replicated. In short, Pan-Celticism was an appealing idea in Wales because it massaged Welsh nationalist pride. Despite the Irish leadership of the movement, some in the Principality claimed Pan-Celticism would not have been possible without Welsh inspiration. The Reverend Thomas "Gwynedd" Edwards said that "the idea of a Pan-Celtic Association owes its origin" to the national institutions of Wales, such as the eisteddfod and the gorsedd. He suggested that Pan-Celticism was really about the other Celtic nations copying Wales, writing that "if all the Celtic races were to follow their Cymric brethren in these respects, the objects of the Pan Celtic Association would be well advanced."[156] W. G. Thomas, the mayor of Caernarfon, echoed these sentiments. Addressing the crowd at the Rhyl National Eisteddfod, he declared, amid much applause, that he "believed that the enthusiasm of the Welsh in keeping alive their own language had acted as an incentive to the other branches of the Celtic race and he hoped they would continue to lead the way."[157] Commenting on the fact that the Welsh example had a tremendous influence on their fellow Celts, including inspiring the Irish to relearn their language, Edward "Idriswyn" Thomas wrote that Pan-Celticism "will strengthen the United Kingdom, not weaken it; and there is no doubt that Wales will carry great influence in future in all government circles of Great Britain."[158] Indeed, the *Western Mail* went as far as to claim that, in the wake of the Pan-Celtic national eisteddfod in 1899, French journalists who had been in attendance were so impressed by the show of unity that they wrote a number of articles encouraging a rapprochement between Britain and France, eventually leading to the entente cordiale between the two states in 1904.[159]

The Pan-Celtic visitors constantly expressed their admiration for all that had been achieved in Wales in terms of cultural preservation, flattering the Welsh as an exceptional nation among the Celtic countries. Arthur William Moore, speaker of the House of Keys on the Isle of Man, was amazed on visiting the national eisteddfod in 1899. He wrote, "I have been delighted with everything I have seen, but the music is the one thing that astonishes me more than anything. . . . This is simply magnificent, and I have no words to express my admiration of it." Count Plunkett, a member of the Irish delegation, was impressed by the manner in which all Welsh people celebrated their culture. He commented, "What strikes a stranger most is the fact that the whole Welsh people are parties to the celebration, and . . . one is struck with the fact that . . . the common sentiment moves them all."[160] Brendon Rogers, the organist at St. Patrick's Cathedral in Dublin, shared Plunkett's views, telling a Welsh journalist, "The enthusiasm shown by your people for everything Welsh is beyond praise." François Jaffrennou, the leader of the Breton contingent, said of the gorsedd that "it was grand—it was magnificent." He was similarly complimentary toward the eisteddfod, exclaiming, "It was all very beautiful—I never saw anything so beautiful."[161] The Welsh were quite conscious of how impressed their guests were. Owen Morgan, observing some of the Pan-Celts at their first eisteddfod, described their reaction by saying that the "Highlanders, standing in kilts on the seats of the orchestra at the back of the platform, seemed amazed. Ireland seemed dumbfounded at the extraordinary scene before her." It seems likely that this admiration for the achievements of Wales encouraged the Celtic delegates to adopt the Welsh national anthem as the official Pan-Celtic anthem at Caernarfon in 1904.

The delegations from other countries did not come to Wales merely to praise the Welsh, as they also hoped to learn from them and return home with ideas on how to safeguard their own indigenous cultures. This was especially true of the Irish visitors. During his speech at the national eisteddfod in 1899, Patrick Pearse said, "I come . . . to study your ways and methods. You whose native speech is the everyday spoken language of all your people are not in a similar position to us, who are commencing to bring our mother tongue into popularity once more. You saved your language, your literature, and your music from death. All honour and glory to you for it. We are now setting ourselves to save our language, our literature, and our music, in the same way."[162]

Pearse was not alone in declaring that Ireland had much to learn from Wales. Douglas Hyde told Thomas Davies that it was the Welsh "whom we in the Gaelic League always have before us as our ideal, and who are, to us, indeed a shining light, teaching us how to preserve the core and essence of our individuality, apart from our politics."[163] Count Plunkett said he would return to Ireland "with a message of encouragement to his people to feel that if those of their blood could gain such triumphs it was time for the Irish to emulate them. He would go back with the feeling that the hearts of the Welsh people were with them in the old country." He added that the example of Wales was "a great incitement to the Irish people, so as to utilize it for national purposes in Ireland."[164] In coming to Wales, Plunkett stated, the Irish delegation "found what they yet hoped would be found in Ireland—that the culture of the race would not be repressed by circumstances. They found in Wales hard-handed men, possessed of fair opportunities, cultivating a gift that lifted them near the angels." In particular, Plunkett wanted Ireland to copy Wales regarding the manner in which all classes embraced Welsh culture. He told his Pan-Celtic audience that he "wished he could take back to Ireland some of the feeling that dominated all classes in Wales. He wished he could say to the landlords and the Irish tenants, 'Why do you not unite and form one nation, as the Welsh have done?'"[165] Lord Castletown believed that the Welsh offered lessons not just for the Irish but for all Celtic people. Castletown had been appointed honorary president at the Cardiff eisteddfod, and in his speech he stated:

> If he was asked, as a stranger, what was their eisteddfod, and why pilgrims and admirers came from far-away lands to attend, he would answer that the eisteddfod is the embodiment and bulwark of Welsh nationalism. It was the consciousness that they had solved the problem that they and others were still struggling with—how to reconcile their material and intellectual advancement with the retention of their national characteristics, their Celtic language, and all those treasures of Celtic tradition which had been bequeathed to them by an immemorial past, and for the due preservation and cultivation of which they or their children's children would surely at some future time be called fully to account.[166]

Not only did Pan-Celticism bring visitors to Wales who were eager to learn how to maintain their national traditions, but it appeared to be a movement through which Welsh cultural institutions would be established overseas. Naturally, by copying the eisteddfod and the gorsedd, the Pan-Celts bestowed a level of prestige upon Wales that made the movement as a whole appear very attractive to Welsh cultural nationalists. When Fournier visited in Cardiff in 1899, he requested "a contingent of the Gorsedd bards to visit Dublin in August, 1900, to establish a Gorsedd there, subject to the rules and regulations of the Gorsedd of the Bards of the Isle of Britain."[167] Thomas Davies made several references to the golden ribbons worn on the arms of some Irish delegates in Cardiff, claiming that it represented the color chosen for the Irish gorsedd.[168] As has already been noted, this idea was not well received in Ireland, and an Irish gorsedd was never established. But the Breton delegates were very enthusiastic about establishing their own version of the Welsh institutions. Jaffrennou declared in Cardiff that the Bretons "were going to organize an eisteddfod on the same pattern in Brittany."[169] Such enthusiasm for a distinct Breton culture was believed to be a direct result of Welsh influence, with one newspaper declaring "the nationalistic wave that has passed over Wales has crossed 'the silver streak' and gained fresh strength among the Breton Celts."[170] A Breton gorsedd was established by Jean le Fustec and Erwan Berthou in 1899. Other Celtic countries also created their own national festivals, with commentators describing these efforts as imitations of Welsh institutions. Thomas Davies attended the *feis ceoil* in Dublin and wrote, "The eisteddfodic spirit which is so prevalent in Wales is catching on in Ireland."[171] The spread of Irish cultural festivals, or *feiseanna*, caught the attention of the *London Kelt*, which noted that "75 local eisteddfods are held in Ireland. Wales is to thank for this."[172] Arthur William Moore admitted that the Isle of Man had also taken inspiration from Wales, saying, "We have started a movement of this kind in the Isle of Man, known as a guild, and for the last fifteen years it has been worked greatly on the lines of the Eisteddfod."[173]

Welsh cultural nationalists reveled in the admiration of their Celtic peers. The *North Wales Express* commented that "for the first time in modern history Welshmen have stretched their hands across the sea to brother Celts, and Ireland, Manxland, Scotland, and Brittany have alike responded. The Eisteddfod has influenced these even more perhaps than those have influenced the Eisteddfod."[174] Thomas Gwynn Jones believed that the Pan-Celtic delegates "were struck then with surprise by the possibilities of the National Eisteddfod as a means to elevate the moral standings, and foster the spirit of research within the nation." He wrote that the Celtic visitors "almost went home in tears because they did not have an organization whose impact was so incisive and broad; and the outcome is, that the 'eisteddfodic spirit,' now, has arrived, not only to Ireland and Scotland, but as stated already, to the Isle of Man and Brittany."[175] Another commentator stated that there was "no better proof of the popularity of the Eisteddfod than the fact that the other branches of the Celtic race hold annual gatherings on lines similar to the great Welsh festival. The Irishmen hail their Feis Ceoil, and the Scotchmen their Mod and . . . they show signs of vitality."[176]

To an extent, this explains the popularity of Pan-Celticism in Wales. While in no way questioning the sincerity of those in the Principality who wanted to help foster the language and traditions of other Celtic countries, there can be little doubt that the acknowledgment of the Irish, Scottish, Breton and Manx delegates that they had failed where the Welsh had succeeded fostered a sense of Welsh national superiority. This contributed to the appeal of Pan-Celticism in Wales, albeit possibly as a subconscious rather than a conscious factor. Yet while the Pan-Celtic ideal was popular in the Principality, the decline of the Celtic Association with the resignation of Fournier in 1908 also meant the cessation of Pan-Celtic activities in Wales.

Edmund Fournier had grand visions for the role Ireland would play in leading the Pan-Celtic movement. In reality, Pan-Celticism enjoyed far more success and popularity in Wales than it ever did in the Emerald Isle. Whereas some Irish nationalists were extremely critical of the Pan-Celtic movement, it appears that many in Wales were open to the idea of building stronger connections between their own nation and those countries that identified as Celtic. This is most evident in the size of the crowds and the financial success that Pan-Celtic events had in Wales compared to the Celtic congress held in Dublin, even if it must be acknowledged that such success was partly due to the well-established Welsh practice of organizing such festivals. Nevertheless, there appears to have been genuine enthusiasm for Pan-Celticism in Wales, judging not only by the positive reception afforded the visiting Celtic delegates by the Welsh crowds but also by the fact that there was far less criticism of the Pan-Celtic movement in the Welsh media, in either Welsh or English. To be sure, questions were asked about how the Pan-Celtic movement should be received in Wales. When certain Welsh commentators voiced their concern about allowing the Pan-Celtic reception to be a central feature of the national eisteddfod, they echoed those in Ireland who feared that a Pan-Celtic congress posed a threat to the recently established *oireachtas*. The contrast in this regard was that Welsh concern was voiced after the national eisteddfod, when certain logistical problems had been highlighted, whereas Irish critics attacked Pan-Celticism before a single event had been held because of ideological differences.

While it is fair to label the Pan-Celtic movement a success in Wales, it was very much a qualified success. The uproar connected to the Highland jig demonstrated that Welsh understanding and tolerance in trying to build a bond with their Celtic neighbors could only go so far. Aside from religious differences, some minor incidents at Caernarfon in 1904 revealed that the Welsh were often on a different political wavelength from some of their Irish and Scottish guests. But for the most part, Welsh writers and commentators were content to speak in glowing terms about Pan-Celticism. This is not necessarily surprising. Unlike in Ireland, where Pan-Celticism was quickly associated with an effort to form an Irish gorsedd along the lines of the Welsh bardic institution, Pan-Celticism did not threaten to bring any "foreign" intrusion into the Welsh cultural landscape. After all, the Pan-Celtic congress decided to use the Welsh national anthem as the movement's own song. Indeed, the Welsh public read of how the other Celtic nations had created, or were seeking to create, their own eisteddfods and gorsedds. Pan-Celticism seemed to mean the exportation of Welsh institutions, not the importation of new cultural traditions. This highlights one of the main reasons that Pan-Celticism was appealing in Wales, in that the movement allowed for very favorable and flattering comparisons between the Principality and the other Celtic nations. The praise of the visiting delegations for the way the Welsh had preserved their language and traditions inevitably led to Pan-Celticism being viewed positively. The fact that the movement petered out after its leadership stepped aside heightens the sense that Welsh nationalists were only superficially interested in Pan-Celticism and had little interest in establishing long-lasting bonds with the other Celtic nationalities. A new Celtic Association was to emerge in 1917, but by then Ireland, Wales, and Pan-Celticism itself had dramatically changed.

CHAPTER 7

BRINGING THE MOON
AND MARS TOGETHER

By the outbreak of the First World War, Pan-Celticism was dead. Once Edmund Fournier and Lord Castletown withdrew from the movement, they took most of the energy and financial support that had allowed Pan-Celticism to come to prominence in the first place. During the war, however, Pan-Celticism was reborn under the leadership of Edward Thomas John. A Liberal MP for East Denbighshire, John was labeled an "optimist" in one interview with the *Western Mail*, and it was certainly an apt description.[1] He labored tirelessly and with utmost confidence in the inevitable triumph of his twin passions, Pan-Celticism and Welsh home rule. John's vision of Pan-Celticism, however, differed from Fournier's in two important respects. First, the pageantry, costumes, and rituals that had delighted Fournier and many of his contemporaries had no place in John's reformed Pan-Celtic movement. More significant, however, was the differing attitudes to the role of politics between the first and second waves of Pan-Celticism. Fournier's Celtic Association had been a strictly nonpolitical body, with Fournier fearing that allowing political discussion would only serve to accentuate the differences, rather than the commonalities, between the respective Celtic nations. John, on the other hand, believed that a political dimension to Pan-Celticism was necessary, as he ultimately hoped that greater collaboration between Irish, Welsh, and Scottish nationalists in particular would lead to a federal United Kingdom. But the Irish War of Independence made John's vision of a Pan-Celtic political body almost impossible. Unionists, particularly in Scotland, were outspoken in their criticism of Irish rebels and rejected any efforts to include Sinn Féin supporters in the Pan-Celtic congresses. Irish nationalists, many of whom remembered Fournier's Pan-Celtic movement, were suspicious of the revived organization and felt it did not demonstrate enough sympathy with the plight of Ireland during its struggle for independence. Indeed, the Irish conflict only served to radicalize John's own political views, and he tied his demands for Welsh autonomy to those of Ireland, essentially arguing that whatever measure of independence was granted to Ireland should also be extended to Wales. In the end, John's efforts to blend nationalist politics and Pan-Celtic sentiment failed, with Welsh political nationalism and Pan-Celticism of interest only to a small minority by the time of his death in 1931.

Edward Thomas John was born in Pontypridd in 1857. He had a successful career in the field of ironworking, and once he retired from business he decided to enter politics. John was elected MP for East Denbighshire in 1910 and would hold the seat for eight years, until the conclusion of the war. It was John who would take up the cause of Cymru Fydd, becoming the first political figure of note to call for Welsh home rule since the 1890s. John formed a Welsh National League with the goal of campaigning for home rule and introduced a private member's bill at Westminster calling for Welsh political autonomy in 1914.[2] This legislative attempt to introduce Welsh home rule was swept away by the deluge of the First World War, mostly because it was a one-man campaign.[3] Nevertheless, John soldiered on and remained a passionate advocate of Welsh self-rule for the remainder of his life. One notable feature of John's campaign for Welsh self-government was his willingness to lean on the example of the Irish home rule campaign to justify Welsh demands. The Cymru Fydd movement of the 1880s and 1890s had certainly hoped that Welsh home rule would be granted in tandem with any arrangement made in Ireland, but, as noted in chapter 4, the leading Welsh home rulers had mixed opinions about explicitly linking their cause with Ireland's. Certainly David Lloyd George was keen to avoid mentioning Ireland when arguing the merits of Welsh self-rule. But Edward John did not shrink from drawing a connection between the Irish and

Welsh campaigns. He stressed that Irish and Welsh calls for home rule were equally meritorious and that any measure of autonomy granted to Ireland should simultaneously be awarded to Wales and Scotland also.

In a speech he prepared to mark the occasion of the introduction of the Irish Home Rule Bill of 1912, John noted that Wales had always supported the cause of Irish self-rule, declaring, "It is because we have always perceived that Self Government for Ireland implied sooner or later—and sooner rather than later—the recognition of the separateness of the Welsh Nationality, that Wales has, with an unerring instinct, countenanced and supported, through its many vicissitudes, the Irish movement."[4] Thus John's support for Irish home rule was unwavering because he felt that it would inevitably lead to some form of autonomy for Wales as well. John rejected the claim that Irish home rule supporters were separatists bent on the destruction of the United Kingdom. He pointed out that "nowhere is the national language, the national heritage, its literature and history more warmly cherished than in Wales, while, at the same time, no part of the country could be more entirely exempt from Separatist Sentiment." John hoped that the granting of home rule to Ireland would "do much to assimilate the nationalism of Ireland—in the past too often disgruntled and declamatory—to the Nationalism of the Welsh people."[5]

However, John was not an uncritical cheerleader of Ireland either. Indeed, in his speeches on home rule he regularly made the point that Ireland had garnered far too much government attention at the expense of Wales. He noted that "the liberal treatment of Irish Agriculture by Great Britain has made the Irish farmer a far more formidable competitor of the Welsh Agriculturist." When it came to the dedication of government resources to local issues, John felt "Ireland has least to complain of, and Wales most. The expenditure of Parliamentary time, of Imperial resources and credit, upon Ireland has been extremely lavish—upon Wales it has been absolutely negligible."[6] He drove this point home at a speech on home rule in Colwyn Bay in 1913, stating, "As a matter of fact, apart from the paucity of mineral riches in Ireland, the need for self-government is vastly more acute in Wales—Ireland has for 45 years been the spoiled child of Imperial Parliament—both parties vying in legislative and administrative attention and in the most lavish financial assistance—while Wales has been neglected with the most unqualified completeness—with absolutely disastrous results in all the purely rural counties."[7] Privately, John could be even less complimentary in his opinions on Irish home rule. When Edward Hughes, the former mayor of Wrexham, wrote to John expressing his fear that efforts to introduce Welsh home rule would lead to strong resistance, John assured him that there was no possibility of the emergence of an "Ulster in Wales." John was confident that "there will be infinitely less opposition to give Home Rule to Wales, and its people are undoubtedly far better fitted to exercise the functions of Self Government than the very indifferently educated Catholic population of Ireland with their hosts of illiterates."[8]

The unfolding political crisis regarding Ulster's position under a Dublin parliament was of significant interest to Welsh nationalists generally. The claim of unionists that Ulster was a politically distinct nation held obvious implications for the demand for Welsh home rule. E. V. Arnold, the professor of Latin at University College Wales, Bangor, told Edward John that "the relation of Wales to England appears to me like that of Ulster to Ireland."[9] Another friend of John, Percy Watkins, believed that Cardiff was developing a distinctly different character from the rest of Wales. He told John, "I am dreadfully afraid of this corner of Wales becoming a second Ulster in its relation to the rest of the nation."[10] Indeed, John exchanged a robust correspondence with a man named E. A. W. Phillips on the question of Welsh and Ulster nationalism. Phillips asked John, "Has Ulster no better right to consideration than Wales [regarding home rule]? "How about the Protestants of Ulster? You know how tyrannical a majority can be, yet you, belonging to a free race, are helping to subject another free race to a majority of 3 to 1. How can you justify it? If small states, as I firmly believe, are good, then Ulster is nearly as big as Wales and nearly as populous."[11] John responded that the fears of Ulster Protestants about potential mistreatment really stemmed from the way they had treated the Catholic minority in their midst. He wrote, "On grounds of nationality I do not see that Ulster has any claim to separate treatment, for there is no substantial element of distinction other than religious prejudice." John denied that Ulster had the right to deny home rule for all of Ireland but acknowledged that if "Ulster, in good faith, asked for separate treatment, it would, in all probability, be acceded."[12] Phillips retorted by reminding John of the physical similarities between Wales and Ulster, writing, "Wales has an area of 7,370 square miles, Ulster an area of 8,300 square miles; Wales has a 1911 population of 2,027,610, Ulster of 1,578,572. In 1901 the difference was far less.

If Wales, by her historical and local variations has a claim to home-rule, Ulster has quite as strong a claim."[13]

The challenge that faced John was not to persuade Ulster unionists to accept Dublin rule but rather to convince the British public that Wales was worthy of its own parliament. To paper over the fact that there wasn't evidence of significant support for home rule in the Principality, John focused his efforts on reviving the old idea of home rule all around. He told an audience of young Welsh nationalists, "Federal Home Rule implying separate national legislatures for Scotland and for Wales as well as for Ireland, is thus a policy in being; is indeed the avowed policy of the Ministry itself, and explicitly or implicitly has been endorsed by the formal votes of the great bulk of the representatives of Wales,—for it is scarcely conceivable that any Welsh Member will desire to withhold from Wales that which he is willing to concede both to Scotland and Ireland."[14] When John Redmond, the leader of the Irish Home Rule Party, visited Holyhead in Wales in 1911, John delivered a welcoming address, telling the esteemed guest, "We are entirely with the Irish Party. Our desires and aspirations for Wales are identical, and those of us who are urging Wales and Scotland alike to claim similar privileges do not consider that we are thereby rendering Ireland any disservice." John called on Redmond to declare himself "a Federal Home Ruler, who desires to see extended to Wales, to Scotland and to England every privilege he seeks for Ireland."[15] John went as far as to claim that Wales and Scotland deserved stronger home rule parliaments than Ireland because "both countries properly repudiate many limitations and restrictions unhappily imposed upon Ireland by reason of the somewhat violent divergences of opinion which exist in that disturbed and distressful land."[16] This was a particularly disingenuous claim by John, as he knew full well that vocal opposition to home rule in Wales or Scotland was lacking because the prospect of home rule being introduced was extremely unlikely.

For John and other supporters of Welsh home rule, a federal settlement of the home rule question was the only way a Welsh parliament could feasibly come into existence, and John unceasingly sought to present a link between Irish home rule and its Scottish and Welsh equivalents. His desire to promote a joint political cause between the three nations led to his taking an interest in their common social and cultural issues, which eventually progressed into an exploration of the possibility of reviving the defunct

Pan-Celtic movement. John decided to put together a gathering of those interested in Pan-Celtic affairs. He invited delegates from Ireland, Scotland, the Isle of Man, Cornwall, and Brittany to attend the national eisteddfod in Birkenhead in 1917. Those invited were told that papers on the language and literature of the various Celtic countries would be delivered and that "it is proposed to arrange for the formation of a permanent organization to ensure the holding of an Annual Conference of Representatives with a view to more effective co-operation in the future among Celtic peoples." However, the point was made that as "the War may render the representation much less complete than is desired, it may only be possible at this stage to bring into being a tentative and provisional organization."[17] A similar gathering was held the following year in Neath, again in conjunction with the Welsh national eisteddfod. John had hoped to hold a conference in Ireland in 1919, but the outbreak of violence in the Emerald Isle meant the Pan-Celtic conference was moved to Edinburgh. As it happened, a railway strike meant the Scottish conference was pushed back until 1920, and the fourth Pan-Celtic gathering was held in 1921 on the Isle of Man. In 1919, the executive committee of the Pan-Celtic movement published their constitution. Declaring that their society was to be known as the "Celtic Congress; alternatively, the Celtic Federation or Celtic League," the executive committee outlined the objectives of their organization as follows:

> To promote intercourse and co-operation between the respective Celtic nations and all Celtic communities wheresoever situated, through the instrumentality of an International Union of Celtic Societies, consisting of representatives of affiliated Societies, with provision for the inclusion of individual Celts and Celtic sympathizers finding membership of an affiliated Society not readily practicable.
>
> To promote by the holding of an Annual Congress and other convenient methods the comprehensive and exhaustive study of the internal history, the external influence, the literatures and languages of the several Celtic nations; the maintenance and development of the indigenous Celtic culture of the respective Celtic countries by the wider and more habitual use of the Celtic languages; the more adequate provision in their educational systems of facilities for all phases of Celtic

studies; the effective encouragement of current Celtic literature, art, drama, and music; the maximum development of all the intellectual and artistic resources of the Celtic peoples, and the examination and amelioration of the social conditions obtaining in the various Celtic countries.[18]

Thus the end of the First World War witnessed the rebirth of Pan-Celticism, although there were some important differences between this new movement and its predecessor. First, the Pan-Celtic gatherings were to be held every year, not triennially as the original congresses had been. Second, Fournier and Castletown, who were both still alive, were not involved in the new Celtic congress. John claimed that several invitations had been sent to Castletown before the Birkenhead conference but that Castletown never replied. When the Scottish Pan-Celts proposed inviting Castletown to their congress in 1919, John wrote to Agnes O'Farrelly "to be quite sure that such an invitation to him [Castletown] would not be displeasing to our Irish friends generally." No effort seems to have been made to invite Edmund Fournier, and this may have been because he was deemed responsible for the "excesses" of the first Pan-Celtic movement, namely the elaborate costumes and rituals. Indeed, the programs for Celtic congresses of the John era are notable for the lack of any papers discussing national dress, and the Lia Cineil, the symbolic centerpiece of the original Pan-Celtic conferences, was also absent. This was not an accident. Tomás Raithde, living in Dublin, advised John and David Rhys Phillips, who served as secretary for the Celtic congress, that if they wanted Irish support for Pan-Celticism "I am inclined to think that mere theatricality—weird costumes, symbolic rites and so on—had better be avoided; they are useless and only give people the idea that the movement is a mere bit of stage work to give its leaders a chance of posing before the public."[19] Meanwhile, the *Welsh Outlook* said of the first incarnation of Pan-Celticism, "One always felt that the serious were inclined to regard the whole affair as a crank's game."[20] Of course, while getting rid of the costumes would allow the reformed Pan-Celtic movement to put itself on a more serious footing, it also meant that attendances, and hence, profitability, would be reduced. The Reverend William Cooke, who attended the 1920 gathering in Edinburgh, wrote to John hoping to improve the aesthetics of the Pan-Celtic congress to be held on the

Isle of Man in 1921. Cooke stated, "If the Bards of the Gorsedd could be secured it would give the Congress a great boon on the popular side, and a few Welsh harps & Irish pipes—as well as Scotch—would give distinction and colour. They are done to death in Douglas with mere cinema & variety hall appeals."[21]

Despite Cooke's pleas, John's Pan-Celtic movement steered clear of the pageantry. But this is not to say that the new Celtic congress did not share some philosophical similarities with its predecessor. In particular, John and some of his supporters strongly echoed Fournier from years before when they alluded to the Celts having a special mission to save humanity. In a speech at the Pan-Celtic congress in Edinburgh in 1920, John said of the postwar world that "materialism reigns rampant—increased production of material wealth being well nigh the sole and all sacrificing gospel of publicists of every description, it being rarely recognized that even maximum industrial productiveness is primarily a problem of the spirit." In effect, John was repeating the same ideas espoused by Fournier and, before him, Matthew Arnold and Ernest Renan, namely that Celtic spirituality was an important counterbalance to Teutonic pragmatism. He declared that the "real need of the age is most assuredly not so much the due appreciation of material and materialist conditions, so readily appealing to the Saxon and Teuton spirit and tradition, but rather the sympathy and comprehension which have ever been the intuition and instinct of the Celt."[22] Indeed, in the wake of the horror of the recent war, John felt that the Celtic nations were uniquely positioned to lead a global push for pacifism. He told his audience:

> None are better entitled by the bitter experience of centuries of oppression—by complete immunity from designs of territorial aggrandizement—from the passion of domination—to plead for the complete elimination of the element of physical force from the solution of all problems of national and international government. In regarding this, as the first and foremost of Celtic ideals, we will prove profoundly faithful to the oldest and most fundamental tradition of our race. . . . It is perhaps difficult to conceive an organization better fitted to consider dispassionately the philosophic problem of the interaction of internationalism and nationalism than the aggregation of

the Celts of the world—so habitually practicing a concurrent and triple loyalty to nationality, to the State and to the race—at once intensely nationalist and perfervidly cosmopolitan. We claim that Celtic nationalism—always aiming at achieving the highest standards of individual, communal and national rectitude, at securing the physical and social wellbeing of the people and their maximum intellectual growth and progress, never menaces in any way any other nation.[23]

Nor were such ideas confined to Edward John. The Reverend John "Dyfnallt" Owen was a Welsh poet and enthusiastic Pan-Celtic supporter. Owen wrote that there "was evidence on every hand that Celtic civilization and culture had a message to a world bleeding to death under a Teutonic and materialistic conception of life." This, according to Owen, led to the resurgence of Pan-Celticism, since the "consciousness of cultural development, the definite acceptance of the principle of nationality as the greatest factor in the life of New Europe, and the spiritual outlook of the Celt, created a longing in the heart of every true Celt for a movement to embody these ideals in a permanent form."[24]

If John's reformed Pan-Celticism shared some of the idealism of Fournier's movement, it also faced some of the same challenges in trying to bridge the significant political differences between those eager to label themselves Pan-Celts. As Fournier had insisted that his Celtic Association adopt a strictly nonpolitical approach, he had largely avoided any political squabbles, although there had been grumblings about the appropriateness of toasting the monarchy and playing "God Save the King" at those initial Pan-Celtic congresses. But the Easter Rising had amplified the political differences between some Irish nationalists and potential Scottish and Welsh supporters of Pan-Celticism. Even before the new Pan-Celts assembled at Birkenhead in 1917, John had received warning signals that any revived Pan-Celtic movement would struggle to accommodate both Irish republicans and British unionists. Tomás Raithde had declared that if the new Pan-Celtic movement "wants to get Irish support it must eschew completely 'Rule Britannia,' 'God Save the King,' and all that kind of thing."[25] Similarly, Victor Collins, an avowed Irish nationalist and teacher at Mount St. Benedict in Wexford, told John, "Of course we do not agree with you in remaining within the Empire. As well try to get oil and vinegar to mix as

Teuton and Celt. It matters not whether you call the Teuton English, German, or (as the fashion is) Hun; he is at heart a domineering, course, materialistic animal. He is, in a word, *vulgar*: that the Celt never is. Even when he is a blackguard he has some delicacy always left."[26]

Ruaraidh Erskine was a Scottish nationalist who became involved with the revived Pan-Celtic movement. He wrote to the Welsh poet Thomas Gwynn Jones in 1917 asking him to attend the Pan-Celtic event at Birkenhead. Erskine told Jones that he believed the conference would allow for "an exchange of views of real importance." Erskine made his political leanings clear when he wrote, "We can reasonably expect no peace till that monster John Bull is fired out of both our countries," and he warned Jones that "diluted Celts, of the Lloyd George type, should be cabaled against, so as to neutralise that mischievous power."[27] This comment best represents the challenge that faced John in his efforts to build a cohesive Pan-Celtic movement. Those of a nationalist disposition would dismiss those who were not as "diluted Celts," asserting that only those of a certain political persuasion could claim to be truly Celtic. On the other hand, those who professed loyalty to the crown were inclined to view nationalists, especially those with Sinn Féin sympathies, as traitors. Trouble was perhaps inevitable.

From the moment he started to revive the Pan-Celtic movement, John was forced to attempt a political balancing act. He told David Rhys Phillips that picking which Irish delegates to invite to the first conference at Birkenhead would be a "delicate matter," alluding in particular to potential problems if Lord Castletown or Lord Ashbourne were asked to come.[28] Liam Ó Briain was an Irish representative at the Pan-Celtic meeting at Neath in 1918. Ó Briain was the professor of romance languages at University College Galway and had taken part in the Easter Rising. His political views did not sit easily with everyone. By Ó Briain's own admission, "Nobody raised more awkward questions at Neath than I did." His statements in favor of radical Irish nationalism greatly annoyed Eleanor Hull, an Irish-language scholar from an Ulster Protestant background.[29] Indeed, the following year Ó Briain declined to deliver a paper because he felt "his views on modern Ireland would be too vitriolic for the Conference."[30] When John suggested to Ruaraidh Erskine that someone might deliver a paper on the contributions of various Celts to the British Empire, Erskine responded that he would "rather listen to a paper by Sir O. M. Edwards on teaching methods in Wales than I would to any amount of 'gush' about what Celts have done to build up John Bull's rotten Commonwealth, and I fancy you might find most Scots Celts of the same opinion as I am."[31] He also told those organizing the Edinburgh conference that "there could be no Rule-Brittaniaising at the Congress."[32] Nor were nationalists the only ones stirring up political trouble among the Pan-Celts. Present at the first meeting of the Scottish Pan-Celtic committee in Glasgow in December 1917 were the Reverend Neil Ross and Professor William Watson. Ross was a Presbyterian minister and a native Scots Gaelic speaker who had earned his DLitt for the study of Irish and Scottish Gaelic literature, while Watson was the chair of Celtic at the University of Edinburgh and another native Gaelic speaker. According to Angus Henderson, a Scottish nationalist who was also at the meeting, "Ross got up and asked if it was intended to invite Irish 'Shirkers' to the Conference. If so, he would refuse to 'rub shoulders with Sinn Feiners and Pacifists who aimed at the defeat and destruction of the British Empire.' Professor Watson homologated these sentiments."[33]

One of the reasons that political tensions emerged was that Edward John himself seemed to be uncertain what role, if any, politics should play in the reformed Pan-Celtic movement. When John first proposed reviving the Celtic congresses, he told Ruaraidh Erskine that it would be possible to form an organization on a "'no-politics to exclude' basis," which Erskine interpreted as meaning that politics should not be discussed.[34] But when David Rhys Phillips told John that the Pan-Celts "can never hope—and therefore should not try—to agree on either politics or religion. Therefore both must be barred outright," John disagreed.[35] He replied that "a Celtic movement which excludes any reference to Politics and Religion would very indifferently represent the Celt, who has always been absorbed in both essential phases of National life."[36] When Philips created an advertisement for the 1920 congress in Edinburgh, he included the line "In case of any misapprehension, it may be stated that the Congress is absolutely non-political in its aims."[37] However, John requested that this be amended to read, "In case of any misapprehension, it may be pointed out that the whole of the subject matter of all the papers read will be absolutely non-political. The precise scope of the future operations of the Congress will be considered at its business meetings."[38] Of course, defining what exactly was to be deemed "political" was not so straightforward. When Erskine suggested that "God

Save the King" should not be played at the Celtic gatherings if they were to be truly nonpolitical, John retorted that attendees "would doubtless be staggered at the suggestion that the National Anthem involved any political issue."[39] In some ways, John was trying to simultaneously steer the Pan-Celtic movement in two different directions. On the one hand, he told Erskine that he wanted the congress in Edinburgh to "proceed on lines of comprehension and catholicity, seeking to exclude neither persons nor organization nor subject matter."[40] Yet in another letter to Erskine, written on the exact same day as the one above, John suggested that "a private Conference of the advanced nationalists of Ireland, Scotland and Wales might be held in Glasgow" in the days after the Edinburgh meeting.[41] Undoubtedly John believed that holding a private conference of nationalists in Glasgow after the main congress had taken place in Edinburgh was maintaining Pan-Celtic neutrality in the strictest sense, but it conveyed something of a mixed message. In short, John was proposing that the Pan-Celts not adopt any formal political position but not exclude any political opinions from the congresses either. Whether such a policy might have helped foster a Pan-Celtic unity among the different national representatives at another time is debatable, but John failed to understand that permitting diverse political opinions in the context of the developing conflict in Ireland could only lead to rancor.

The first fissures in the new Pan-Celtic movement emerged in Scotland. At the Birkenhead meeting, a Miss Cameron, who was involved with the Highland Land League, was appointed convener of the Scottish Pan-Celtic committee. An invitation had also been extended to the Scottish committee to organize a Pan-Celtic congress in Edinburgh for 1918. However, at the December 1917 meeting in Glasgow, when Neil Ross and William Watson made their opposition to Sinn Féin sympathizers apparent, the Scottish committee felt that given the political divisions among themselves they could not organize a congress in Scotland, and the Pan-Celtic gathering took place in Neath in 1918 instead. Furthermore, according to Angus Henderson, Ross and Watson had worked to make Cameron's position untenable, because of her political leanings, and she resigned from the convenership.[42] The Scottish committee remained divided throughout 1918 between unionists and nationalists. Erskine had been elected president of the Scottish committee, but he claimed that other members interrogated him on his sympathies for Sinn Féin and his opinion on conscription.[43] In early 1919, Erskine wrote to John, complaining, "It is not possible for me to work with Watson or with the Comann Gaidhealach crowd, who are coalitionists and imperialists to a man. . . . I think the only way to deal with them is to fire them out at once and to reorganize the Congress on a definitely political, Celtic basis."[44] With conflict appearing inevitable, the Scottish committee invited John and Phillips to travel to Edinburgh in March 1919 to try to unify the Scots. At the meeting arranged between the Welsh guests and the Scottish committee, John presented a letter from Erskine in which he claimed he wanted to resign as president of the Scottish Pan-Celtic body. The outcome of the meeting, according to John, was that the Scottish committee decided that Erskine had not actually resigned officially and remained president.[45] Henderson, however, claimed that for four hours "Mr. Erskine's politics were dissected and analysed with great minuteness and assiduity." Meanwhile, during the meeting, the Reverend Dr. John Norman MacLennan, a Presbyterian minister from Inverness, stated boldly, "If a Sinn Feiner shows himself at the Congress, out he goes—or I shall go out."[46] For the nationalists on the Scottish committee, the failure on John's part to censure MacLennan for his comments was the final straw. Erskine, Henderson, and Donald MacPhie, the committee secretary and editor of the Gaelic journal *An Gaidheal*, all resigned.

While these resignations purged the Scottish Pan-Celts of their most outspoken Sinn Féin sympathizers, they still left John with the difficulty of trying to avoid any problems between Irish Pan-Celts, who were likely to have sympathies somewhere on the nationalist spectrum, and Scottish unionists. John wrote to Agnes O'Farrelly, lecturer of modern Irish at University College Dublin, asking if someone from Ireland could deliver a paper at the congress in Edinburgh on "the Celt in Modern Times." John hinted that O'Farrelly should be careful in choosing who should speak on this topic, writing, "As you will quite readily appreciate our Scottish friends are very wishful that this paper should not be of a very aggressive character."[47] John also had to worry about any offense the Scottish committee might cause their Irish visitors. The Scottish Pan-Celts decided to ask Baron Strathcarron, Ian Macpherson, to preside over the Celtic concert to be held at the congress. The IRA was waging war with the British government at this time, and since Macpherson was the chief secretary for Ireland his presence would not endear Pan-Celticism to Irish nationalists. John wrote to Lachlan Macbean, the new convener for the Scottish Pan-Celtic committee, and commented, "The choice is not likely to be particularly acceptable to our Irish friends." However, John expressed the hope that the Irish visitors "will not want to impose their prejudices upon Mr. Macpherson's countrymen."[48] Indeed, John began to think that Macpherson's presence might present an opportunity to promote Pan-Celticism. He wrote to O'Farrelly suggesting that the president of the self-proclaimed Irish republic, Éamon de Valera, should visit the congress alongside Macpherson.[49] While acknowledging that this was probably "too much to hope," John undoubtedly believed that having these two in attendance would bring worldwide attention to the congress and possibly peace to Ireland in one fell swoop. O'Farrelly quickly shot down the idea, writing, "You might as well think of bringing the Moon and Mars together as to suggest the possibility of De Valera and MacPherson uniting for any purpose under the Sun. Where have you been living recently? Not in Ireland certainly."[50]

As John struggled to ensure civility between Irish and Scottish Pan-Celts, his movement received another blow when the executive committee of the Gaelic League decided not to send representatives to the Edinburgh congress. Of course, this provided something of a historical echo with the earlier Pan-Celtic congresses, which the Gaelic League had boycotted. The decision was largely based on the recommendation of Art Ó Briain, the president of the Gaelic League in London. Ó Briain wrote to John and told him that he had made the recommendation for several reasons. First, John's Pan-Celtic movement had been in existence for almost three years but had not produced a constitution outlining its objectives (the constitution of the Celtic congress was not written and published until two months after Ó Briain's letter). Second, when the Celtic congress had organized a meeting of interested parties in London in early 1919, the Gaelic League of London, "the most important Celtic organization in London," had not been invited. However, Ó Briain also suggested that ideological differences were another reason he did not believe that Gaelic League representatives should travel to Edinburgh:

Whilst the leading Celtic country was in a life and death struggle for the maintenance of its own civilization and culture, the other Celtic countries were doing nothing to render any effective assistance to their sister nation and . . . if the Congress had any real life it should be able to, in some way, restrain and control the nationals of the various Celtic countries and not allow men like David Lloyd George and Ian Macpherson to serve the enemy of all the Celtic countries by their persecution and bullying of Ireland without any restraint or criticism from a body which in name, at all events, would seem to unite for some good purpose all the Celtic nations.[51]

Liam Ó Briain, who was also at the Gaelic League's executive committee meeting, told John that there was another reason for the reticence of the League: the Scottish schism. Liam Ó Briain insisted that while other matters were raised as reasons why delegates should not go to the Pan-Celtic congress, the only reason the League had decided against supporting the event was that "the meeting in Edinburgh would be held by only a section of Scottish language revivalists, that one whole society the Cumann na Gaedheal had withdrawn from it and [that] we might give some umbrage to them, who were the section most in sympathy with us, if we participated."

John was naturally disappointed at this turn of events. He expressed dismay to Art Ó Briain that he had not brought his grievances to him before he sought to turn the Gaelic League against the entire Pan-Celtic movement. John reminded Ó Briain that as the Edinburgh conference would be the first "true" Pan-Celtic congress (the events at Birkenhead and Neath having taken place under the umbrella of the national eisteddfod), this would be the first suitable opportunity to craft a constitution. Furthermore, John told Ó Briain that "that political action of any controversial nature" could not have taken place at the first two Pan-Celtic meetings, as the attendees were guests of the national eisteddfod. John revealed the limits of his Celtic patience when he wrote, "If you will pardon my saying so, it really is very Irish to decline to attend a meeting which is the first entitled to deal with the constitution of the Celtic Congress, because no such constitution is already in place."[52] Ó Briain was not moved, however. He replied that neither he nor the Gaelic League was hostile to "any movement that will genuinely work for the emancipation, both political and intellectual, of the Celtic nations but we are not prepared to support any movement which, by its invertebrate nature, is a hindrance and not a help to the other existing movements of a healthy character in the different countries."[53] However, Ó Briain felt it had yet to be seen whether that description could be applied to the Pan-Celts. John responded by sending copies of various speeches he had made in favor of Irish home rule and told Art Ó Briain that the unpleasant feelings that had arisen in Scotland had largely subsided.[54] Ó Briain in turn replied that the reports of a split in Scotland had nothing to do with the Gaelic League's decision (contrary to what Liam Ó Briain had told John) and clarified the comments in his earlier letter, declaring, "I am distinctly hostile at the present moment to a movement which is purely academic in its nature as, in the present crisis, it merely acts as a red herring for a number of our people."[55]

Art Ó Briain may have denied to John that the split in the Scottish committee had anything to do with his recommendations to the Gaelic League, but he was undoubtedly in communication with some of the Scottish nationalists as he corresponded with John. William Gillies, who would go on to form the Scottish National League with Erskine the following year, wrote to Art Ó Briain saying, "We must write up (or rather, <u>down</u>) the Pan-Celtic affair at Edinburgh. It will be chock full of writers and absurdities."[56] Ó Briain also received a letter from Angus Henderson claiming that "at the present moment the Scots Committee is wholly and frankly anti-Irish." Henderson also made a request: "With respect to the Irish Gaelic League, if I may presume to offer an opinion, I would strongly urge that it send delegates to Edinburgh. The Pan-Celtic movement as guided from Scotland cannot survive the Edinburgh Congress. If you and your friends come to Edinburgh we may be able to take effective measures to place the movement on a more useful and satisfactory basis."[57] Erskine, however, praised Art Ó Briain's intervention to prevent the Gaelic League from sending representatives to Edinburgh, proclaiming, "I trust the Gaelic League will use the opportunity to extract guarantees from John. . . . If we had not abstained from Edinburgh, it would not have been so easy as it now should be to bring John to his senses, and the view of the Congress to Celtic priorities."[58] At the same time, Liam Ó Briain tried to assure John that the Gaelic League was not permanently opposed to collaborating with the Pan-Celts, writing: "I consulted the President of the G.L. Mr. O'Kelly, and the President of the Committee for the annual Congress or Oireachtas. . . . We would still be very pleased to see the Congress in Dublin next year and to co-operate with it in every way."[59]

However, the whole Scottish quarrel caused some of the Irish and Scottish nationalists to have doubts about John himself, even though his political convictions were largely in sympathy with their own. Liam Ó Briain felt John had misled him by telling him that Angus Henderson was to take part in the Edinburgh congress when Henderson had already resigned from the Scottish Pan-Celtic committee. Liam Ó Briain told his namesake Art that "John is too Lloyd Georgeish by half."[60] Erskine also compared John to David Lloyd George, telling Art Ó Briain, "I think John is fairly sound at heart, but his methods are as full of shifts and ticks as are those of the other man from Wales."[61] This flurry of correspondence on the question of the Gaelic League's participation in the Edinburgh conference highlighted once more how national fault lines often lay just beneath the surface in any effort to foster Pan-Celticism. John accused Art Ó Briain of being "very Irish" regarding his attitude about the lack of a Pan-Celtic constitution, an ironic insult in many ways given what John's movement was trying to achieve. Ruaraidh Erskine and Liam Ó Briain, for their part, suggested that there was something deceitful and innately Welsh about John's political maneuvering. By comparing John to the prime minister, David Lloyd George, the pair were implying that there was an element of untrustworthiness about the Welsh generally. Such attitudes, especially on the part of enthusiastic Pan-Celts like John and Erskine, demonstrated the difficulty in bringing about any meaningful cooperation between the various Celtic nationalities.

The Celtic congress of 1919 was postponed because of a railway strike and eventually took place in Edinburgh in June 1920. It was rather poorly attended. The Scottish Pan-Celts who were sympathetic toward Sinn Féin boycotted the event, while only Douglas Hyde and Agnes O'Farrelly traveled from Ireland. John confessed to O'Farrelly that "the representation of Wales at Edinburgh was painfully inadequate and in the main resolved itself into a few people from the vicinity of Swansea who had come up out of regard for Mr. Phillips."[62] Ever the optimist, John declared to Beriah Evans, a fellow Welsh nationalist, "I must say that in spite of a very limited attendance from each of the Celtic areas we managed to make a respectable show at the meeting, and that in every other respect the Congress was a most notable success."[63] Not everyone was convinced of this, however, David Rhys Phillips noted that the "Scottish Left" had remained aloof from the conference and that recent correspondence had alerted him that "they [the "Scottish Left"] have designs of their own, and it is believed that one of them is to start a new Celtic movement with a Scots Professor as President. Apparently some Sinn Fein people are to some extent behind this."

Phillips continued, "Someone unnamed is forcing the pace, but I don't know who it is. I am told however that some bitter comments have been already published in Gaelic on the last Congress."[64] It appears that the person "forcing the pace" was Ruaraidh Erskine, who wrote to Thomas Gwynn Jones to say, "There is a project on foot to form a union of Welsh, Scots and Irish with a view to action on behalf of Celtic communism." He asked Jones to suggest some Welshmen who could be invited to London "with a view to drawing up a programme suitable for the Celts of the 3 nations, the basis of which programme being Celtic Communism." Erskine stressed to Jones that "it is highly desirable of course that only Celtic Communists be invited."[65]

Whether this meeting of Celtic communists ever took place is unclear, but no organization emerged to challenge John's movement as the foremost Pan-Celtic body. However, the division among the Scottish Pan-Celts continued to disrupt the Celtic congress. Up until the conclusion of the Edinburgh conference, the infighting amongst Scottish representatives was known only in private circles. This changed when Angus Henderson, whom John described as "a very loyal personal adherent of Mr. Erskine," published a scathing article in *Welsh Outlook* in August 1920, unveiling the bitter Pan-Celtic disputes before the public.[66] Henderson declared that the recent history of Pan-Celticism had been a "history of manoeuvring. The wrinkled thread of party politics has been a constant and troublesome feature in the history of the organization."[67] He recalled the meeting of the Scottish committee in March 1919, which had prompted the withdrawal of the Scottish nationalists, proclaiming, "More wrinkled and knotted than ever, the Teutonic thread showed itself a fast feature in the texture of the committee." Henderson felt that John had failed to tackle this "Teutonic thread" at the meeting, writing, "It must be confessed that Mr. John's attempts at its elimination were singularly injudicious." Recalling John's conduct at the meeting, Henderson commented, "Pandering to strangers that happened to be present, and sneering at friends who happened to be absent, were not the actions of a heaven-born leader."[68]

Henderson also criticized those who had attended the conference in Edinburgh. He described Douglas Hyde and Agnes O'Farrelly as people "believed to be in favour at the 'Castle'" and said that when the suggestion was made that Eoin MacNeill and others "of the wrong political colour" be invited, the Scottish hosts were uninterested at best. Noting that almost no mention was made of the Irish conflict at the Edinburgh meeting, Henderson stated that "the Congress shrank from offending Teuton susceptibilities" and claimed that the Pan-Celts had decided to hold their next conference at the Isle of Man instead of Ireland: "Unfortunate Erin was shunned because she dared to resent Teuton domination." Continuing his attack, Henderson suggested that the "nonpolitical" aspect of the congress was bogus: "Ostensibly, it has been non-political from its inception. The difficulty is to define the term politics. Hitherto it has been construed as anything suggestive of Nationalism. On the other hand, condemnation of Nationalism and laudation of Imperialism have been held to be entirely non-political in their meaning and application." Suggesting that John should resign as president of the Celtic congress, Henderson concluded his missive by declaring, "At the present moment the Congress is a political body of the Primrose League pattern. Let us strive to make it purely and gloriously Celtic in aim and outlook; to loosen the Imperial bonds that impede its progress and development, and to make it worthy in some measure of the noblest Celtic tradition."[69]

Henderson's article once more showed that tension was inevitable in any effort to meld distinctive national identities under a broader, supranational identity. Henderson's attitude was that only those overtly in favor of political autonomy for Ireland, Wales, and Scotland could be considered "Celts" and that those who professed loyalty to the British state were irreconcilably "Teutons." Even those who undeniably had made enormous contributions to "Celtic" scholarship, like Douglas Hyde and Agnes O'Farrelly, had questionable loyalties in Henderson's view. Edward John believed that all of the Scottish unrest had one source, writing that "the whole trouble had ranged round the personality of one highly respected but very advanced Scottish nationalist."[70] John was clearly referring to Erskine, and there is evidence to suggest that Erskine was behind Henderson's attack. Prior to the Edinburgh meeting, Erskine told Art Ó Briain that Ireland would not be represented in Scotland "save by one or two . . . court imperialists, who don't count."[71] Although Erskine didn't mention them by name, this seemed to be a direct reference to Hyde and O'Farrelly. This opinion of the Irish representatives, which most contemporaries would have considered deeply unfair to Hyde and O'Farrelly, bore a close resemblance to Henderson's description of them as people "in favour at the 'Castle.'" Erskine also had motivation for the attack on Pan-Celticism, namely a desire to discredit John's movement and potentially win support for his own fledgling plans for some kind of Celtic communist league.

Whatever the true reason for this attack on the Celtic congress, a response was not long in coming. In his own article in *Welsh Outlook*, John replied that his movement had never expressly excluded politics and pointed out that Henderson "evidently considers that a non-political Celtic Congress should rigidly exclude all supporters of the present Government, otherwise the organisation becomes, to use his phrase, a political body of the Primrose League pattern." Although the Pan-Celtic constitution did not include political objectives as part of its aim, John pointed out that this could be amended if members so wished. He also noted that in his own draft of the constitution he had proposed including within the objectives "the assertion and accomplishment of all legitimate Celtic national aspirations." John recalled that this "proved to be meat too strong for the majority of my colleagues." John criticized Henderson for publishing his account of what had taken place at the Scottish committee meeting of 1919, writing that "it has been wholly unnecessary, not to say mischievous, to canvass in so much detail, the proceedings at a gathering which was intended on all hands to lessen existing friction, and where it was almost unavoidable that the acute disagreements of preceding months should find expression." John denied that there had been any kind of political statement in the decision to hold the 1921 congress in Man rather than Ireland, recalling:

> There was no invitation from Ireland, but, on the other hand, a very pronounced expression on the part of the Irish delegates that under present conditions it was inadvisable, and, indeed, impracticable, to embark upon the preliminary arrangements for a Congress to be held next year. As regards the attitude of the impenitent Celtic leaders, one of the most representative Scotsmen repeatedly stated that if the Irish delegates were in any degree wishful that the next Congress should be held in Ireland, he was perfectly prepared to propose that it should be held there. The suggestion that there was the smallest lack of sympathy for unfortunate Erin is without justification of any kind.

John's severest rebuke to Henderson referred to the comments made about Hyde and O'Farrelly. He wrote, "I must deprecate most profoundly the suggestion that Miss O Farrelly and Dr. Hyde were believed by anyone to be in favour at the 'Castle.' . . . To such distinguished and devoted adherents of the Gaelic cause, no suggestion could possibly be more hurtful and offensive." John hoped that after making such remarks "Mr. Henderson is now appropriately garbed in sack-cloth and ashes."[72]

Agnes O'Farrelly was more than capable of coming to her own defense, also through the medium of *Welsh Outlook*. Her opinion of the entire affair was that it was "a deranging shock to stumble over what is evidently a two-year-old quarrel in the Scotch household."[73] O'Farrelly declared, "I was quite unaware the garments of Celtic courtesy and the decent clothing of Celtic brotherhood needed washing so badly. The particular method adopted by Mr. Henderson will, to my thinking, leave them in a more bedraggled condition than before." Her main concern was Henderson's comments about herself and Douglas Hyde. Describing Henderson's depiction as a "libelous statement," O'Farrelly noted that the "Castle in Ireland represents a British Government, hateful in itself and hated by us all. We who have spent the greater part of our energy in trying to loosen its death-grip." Answering Henderson's claim that those who opposed conscription were not allowed to attend the Edinburgh congress, O'Farrelly wrote, "Well, I opposed conscription. Not only that, but I was secretary to the Women's Anti-Conscription Movement in Ireland. Nay, more—and this is, I suppose, the crowning crime of all,—I was opposed to recruiting in Ireland." O'Farrelly tried to bolster the Sinn Féin credentials of the Irish Pan-Celts by pointing out that their secretary, Liam Ó Briain, "was in prison a great part of the year and right down to the time of the Edinburgh Congress." She rejected Henderson's suggestion that the Scottish committee did not wish to invite Eoin MacNeill to come to Edinburgh, pointing out that Edward John had expressed a "strong desire" to have MacNeill speak.[74] O'Farrelly denied that there was any effort on the part of the Edinburgh delegates to prevent the congress taking place in Dublin the following year: "I got the impression the whole Congress wanted to come, and I felt rather ashamed we were not in a position to invite them yet." However, O'Farrelly did acknowledge that "the majority of the Scotch delegates I met in Edinburgh are decidedly Conservative" and that the Duke of Athol had "made a decidedly jingo speech," although this apparently "was resented by many of the delegates." Nevertheless, she maintained that to exclude opinions as

Henderson suggested would result in "an emasculated Inter-Celtic debating society. . . . Bereft of vitality from its very nature, such an organisation could never benefit the language movement in any of the countries concerned."[75]

In a letter to Lachlan Macbean, published in *Welsh Outlook*, Henderson admitted that "in introducing names, I probably made a mistake."[76] However he was adamant that "I must entirely disown Celtic Reform from a Coalition point of view," referring to the coalition government then in power and implying once more that those who supported the British state, or at the very least, the Conservative Party, could not be considered true Celts. Macbean responded that Henderson's opinion that "Mr. Edward T. John and Professor Watson, whose advanced views are well known, and with men like Dr. Douglas Hyde and the Rev. G. W. MacKay taking part, should be presented as a political body of the Primrose League pattern, must be regarded as astounding." Furthermore, while Macbean acknowledged that it would be false to claim that there was perfect harmony within the original Scottish Pan-Celtic committee, he believed that "our besetting sin was not politics. The fiercest of all our storms, lashing through three meetings, raged around—music!"[77] At this stage, Erskine himself waded into the public row, in defense of "my friend" Henderson. Erskine clarified that the reason he had resigned from the Scottish committee was that when MacLennan proposed excluding Sinn Féin members from the congress, no one had spoken out against efforts to exclude people on the basis of their political opinion. He also criticized O'Farrelly, who had said that Henderson was "trying to have it both ways" in boycotting the Edinburgh conference and then complaining that only Scottish unionists were in attendance. Erskine sneered that it was O'Farrelly who "would appear to have designs in the direction of the manoeuvre in question, and that is a privilege which Miss O'Farrelly, in spite of the immunities commonly indulged her sex, cannot have."[78]

The public Pan-Celtic feuding ended at this point, but significant damage had been done to the movement by the drawn-out Scottish spat. Nor was it the only challenge to John's leadership. When Henderson's article was published, David Rhys Phillips wrote to John to tell him, "I had had some idea, though a very vague one, that mischief was brewing, but the virulence and unreasonableness and unfairness of it, as revealed in this article, I had until now no conception." Phillips recommended that "the best thing that can occur is to hold up the Celtic business until local Parliaments have been set up all round and people have returned to their ordinary senses."[79] John, however, was starting to doubt Phillips's loyalty to him. The national eisteddfod took place in Barry in the first week of August, and John learned that a Pan-Celtic meeting had taken place in his absence. Present at this meeting were Phillips, William Gibson, now Lord Ashbourne, Lachlan Macbean, Pierre Mocaer from Brittany, and a Mr. Reynolds from Cornwall. John came to believe that this meeting had passed some "resolutions" in his absence and learned that Lord Ashbourne had delivered a "very incoherent tirade" concluding with a threat that "he had already helped destroy one Pan-Celtic movement and was quite prepared to render a similar service to the present effort."[80] In taking credit for destroying the first Pan-Celtic movement, Ashbourne seemed to be implying that his departure from Fournier's Celtic Association in 1904, due to Cornwall's admission as a sixth Celtic nation, had been the reason that the movement dissolved. This was an overly generous assessment of his own importance to the Celtic Association and ignored the fact that the organization carried on for several years after his departure.

To John, however, the meeting at Barry looked like an effort to usurp his authority, and the fact that it coincided with the publication of Henderson's attack on the movement caused him to believe that the two were connected. John forwarded Phillip's letter proposing a suspension of the movement to Lachlan Macbean, writing, "You can see for yourself what preposterous stuff Phillips constantly inflicts upon me. It is difficult to imagine anything more stupid than 'a suspension for two or three years seems to be the only remedy.' Or that we should wait until Home Rule all round is in operation." John was concerned that Phillips and Lord Ashbourne were conspiring to turn those organizing the 1921 congress on the Isle of Man against him.[81] John also raised the matter with Phillips directly, telling the secretary that he had "noticed Mr. Henderson [in his article in *Welsh Outlook*] expresses himself very much in sympathy with you," adding that "your letter and its conclusions together with all that happened at Barry make it very difficult for me to feel that I can count upon your cordial cooperation in conducting the business of the Celtic Congress." John revealed that there had been tension between himself and Phillips about how their organization should conduct itself, writing:

You suggest, not for the first time, that the Congress should be held triennially, or in your own words that "a suspension for two or three years seems to be the only remedy." I have felt that like others connected with the old Pan-Celtic movement, your sympathies are entirely with the methods then pursued rather than those which I have adopted in connection with the present movement. I think you can very readily see that I cannot be very sanguine as to active and strenuous assistance from a colleague who appears continuously to think that the policy of the Congress should be triennial rather than annual gatherings.

John declared that he cared little for Ashbourne's opinions but that "his action and utterances at Barry together with the very virulent outburst by Henderson indicate sufficiently the kind of difficulties I have to deal . . . without being compelled to feel that the General Secretary . . . is completely out of sympathy with the clear policy of the Congress and with my personal purpose and methods."[82]

Lachlan Macbean, who had been present at Barry, tried to persuade John that no mutiny was afoot. He denied any secret "committee meeting," describing what had taken place as two "informal consternations" that were "quite normal endeavours to help clear away misconceptions that must arise when we are so scattered." Macbean pointed out that at these gatherings "we regretted your absence and I jotted down the report of our talk for your information." Macbean felt John had been far too quick to suspect Phillips of treachery, writing "his [Phillips's] mere suggestion of triennial conferences hardly deserved it." Ashbourne had made some kind of threat, Macbean admitted, "but only in the event of our becoming a political society."[83] Although it is unclear what exactly Ashbourne said, given his Irish nationalist leanings it must be assumed that he was warning against the Celtic congress becoming a movement sympathetic toward unionism and imperialism, as alleged by Henderson. John responded that he was pleased to hear that Phillips "took no really overt and hostile part in all that transpired at Barry" and that Phillips himself had tried to convince him "that his attitude towards myself has been less hostile than I imagined."[84] John's fear of a Pan-Celtic rebellion passed, but the events of August 1920 revealed the limitations of the movement. The eruption of the festering Scottish boil in public highlighted that it was impossible to promote Celticness without stumbling into political disputes, especially in the context of the ongoing Irish conflict. At the same time, the distrust between the president of the Celtic congress, John, and its secretary, Phillips, revealed a certain amount of dysfunctionality at the core of the new Pan-Celtic movement. Given these factors, John's Celtic congress remained a minor academic interest group without any ability to instill a broader and deeper sense of Celtic identity among the populations of the Celtic nations.

However, although John's Pan-Celticism bore some similarity to Fournier's movement in that both struggled to overcome the perception that they had a proimperial, antinationalist agenda, John's Celtic congress tried to link the Pan-Celtic cause with nationalist politics in a way that Fournier and Castletown would never have dreamed of doing. While John preached the need to avoid excluding any political views from the Celtic congresses, in reality he was always trying to explore ways in which Pan-Celticism could be used to develop ties between political nationalists in Ireland, Wales, and Scotland. Before the Pan-Celtic gathering in at the national eisteddfod at Neath in 1918, John admitted to Ruaraidh Erskine that "the Neath Conference would present itself as an opportunity of arranging a modus vivendi between Ireland, Scotland and Wales." Reflecting on the purpose of bringing the Irish, Welsh, and Scottish together, John stated, "My own feeling is that we are entitled to insist upon, and to enforce the immediate grant of a substantial measure of self-government to the three countries."[85] Clearly, in John's mind, the revived Pan-Celtic movement had a role to play in promoting some kind of legislative independence for the three Celtic countries. John made this connection more explicitly during a speech to the assembled Pan-Celts at Neath. After noting that there was support in Wales for Welsh home rule, John commented, "While the Conference might not consider itself called upon to deal with every aspect of National life in the Celtic countries, there could be little doubt that the problem of securing adequate attention to the Celtic languages, literature, and history would be more readily achieved under systems of national autonomy—intellectual development being so indubitably a fitting subject matter for separate control by the four nationalities constituting the United Kingdom."[86]

John also expressed his sympathy for Irish nationalism, saying, "Celts the world over intensely desired for Ireland, an immediate surcease to her troubles through the ungrudging and instantly effective acknowledgment of that right of national self determination, which was the ostensible cause of an infinitude of sacrifices and suffering." Immediately after the Neath event, John was thinking of how to expand this political form of Pan-Celticism. As noted earlier, he hoped that a political meeting of Pan-Celts could take place after the Edinburgh congress, telling Erskine, "We might hold . . . a purely Political gathering at which all political organizations working for the fuller expression of Celtic Nationalism would be represented. At such a gathering we could speak and act with full freedom without being hampered by the timorous academic elements." When Fournier was the champion of Pan-Celticism, he spoke of the Celtic people being a part of "Celtia," a vague concept that implied some kind of unspoken, spiritual bond between the disparate Celts. For John, however, there was no imagined Celtic homeland but rather a tangible, political goal for Pan-Celticism, namely, home rule all around.

John's efforts to use the Pan-Celtic movement to promote political autonomy for all the Celtic nations coincided with his attempts to revive the cause of Welsh home rule. Traditionally, the Liberal Party, for whom John stood in the 1910 election, was the only party that gave any support to the concept of Welsh home rule. As the Labour Party gained in strength in Wales, John came to believe that the causes of socialism and nationalism were closely intertwined. He felt that that hopes of gaining a Cardiff parliament would best be realized by cooperation with the Labour Party. In the "coupon election" of 1918, John had decided not to contest his seat in East Denbighshire in order to unify opposition to the government candidate around a representative of the Labour Party. Yet when the Labour candidate for West Denbighshire withdrew, John took his place, running on the Labour Party ticket. John was heavily defeated, something he claimed he knew was inevitable before he took up the offer.[87] Despite this, John believed an alliance with Labour was the only hope for the cause of Welsh home rule, telling one friend, "There is no alternative but to induce all sincere Welsh Nationalists to join the Labour Party, making, however, such arrangements as may be considered necessary for emphasizing the Nationalist side of the matter in Wales."[88] John explained the logic of this position to Beriah Evans, stating that since there was no Welsh national party in existence "I have throughout felt constrained to act with Labour. I am in complete sympathy with their social aspirations and all that is immediately practicable in their industrial and economic policy. I regard them as much the most sincere supporters both of sane nationalism and enlightened internationalism."[89]

As he had before the war, John insisted that the extension of some form of self-government for Ireland would have to be matched with autonomy for Wales. He was appalled when a conference was proposed in Cardiff in 1919 to explore the possibility of creating a secretary of state for Wales. John blasted: "With all the minor nationalities of Europe asserting their claims most vigorously, with the demands of Ireland advancing from the emasculated Bill, which remains on the Statute Book in a state of suspended animation, first to Dominion Self-Government and now to the position of a completely Independent Republic, it is lamentable that any Welsh Nationalist should be content to claim for Wales merely an arrangement conceded to Scotland nearly 30 years ago, which has proved entirely unsatisfactory and insufficient, which would continue to subordinate the interest of Wales to the caprice of England."[90] Indeed, what is notable about John's utterances on Welsh self-government after the First World War is that the extent of autonomy he demanded for Wales was always linked to what Ireland might be offered. Though John himself was author of the bill seeking Welsh home rule in 1914, he acknowledged that "the Welsh Bill is now almost as insufficient for the present situation as the Irish Act. The war and its outcome has so revolutionized the situation that nothing short of Dominion Self Government will meet the requirements of Scotland and Wales."[91] John's claim to dominion status for Wales of course reflected one of the suggestions mooted to resolve Ireland's demands for independence. He lamented that if Welsh MPs "knew the alphabet of their business they would be preparing an overwhelming case of self-government for Wales virtually on Dominion lines."[92] When the Government of Ireland Act of 1920 established parliaments in both Dublin and Belfast, John felt that the case for Welsh autonomy was strengthened: "That Ireland should demand Dominion status as a minimum, and that six dissident Ulster counties should be accorded a Parliament, jointly place the claims of Wales to virtually complete self-government in domestic affairs in a position of incontestable strength."[93]

John's calls for Welsh self-government did not generate much interest within the wider Welsh public. Nevertheless, he maintained his position and continued to look for ways to link Pan-Celticism with the promotion of Celtic political autonomy. As the war in Ireland dragged on, John considered that the Pan-Celtic congress, due to take place in July 1921 on the Isle of Man, could present an opportunity to solve the Irish crisis. Just as he had proposed a meeting of Éamon de Valera and Ian Macpherson at the Edinburgh conference, John suggested that the Man gathering could be a forum to bring the warring parties together. He wrote to Douglas Hyde hinting that he would like to see "the personnel of the two Irish Parliaments or a delegation from each to meet at Douglas on the 15th or 16th of July after the termination of the Congress proceedings." John also thought that the Irish representatives could meet with MPs from Scotland and Wales, although he admitted, "This is, I doubt not, too visionary for words."[94] The approach used by John was identical to the suggestion he had made to O'Farrelly the year before in proposing the meeting of de Valera and Macpherson, in that John admitted both were highly unlikely. Nevertheless, it seems that John really did hope his suggestions would be taken seriously. Hyde replied that it was a "brilliant idea," although he thought it was too "premature" for any such meeting yet and pointed out, "I am not in touch with any of the parties."[95] John was encouraged by Hyde's response and suggested that a conference involving representatives from both Irish parliaments, as well as Scottish and Welsh nationalists, be held on the Isle of Man in September. He told Hyde, "I know the idea commends itself very strongly to the more advanced elements both in Scotland and Wales."[96] When rumors of a possible cease-fire emerged at the end of June, John began to think the Man conference could still play a role in an Irish peace settlement, and he wrote to Hyde, "Some consideration should be given and action possibly taken at Douglas with regard to the problems of Celtic National Self Government in general and the position in Ireland in particular."[97]

One reason John was so eager to have the Celtic congress play a role in resolving matters in Ireland was that some people still believed the Pan-Celts had not done enough to support the Sinn Féin cause in Ireland. William John Gruffydd, the professor of Celtic at University College Cardiff, had been invited to deliver a paper at the Man congress. However, he told John, "I cannot possibly take part in any Pan-Celtic Congress while Ireland is passing through its agonies. It would, if you will allow me to speak frankly, be in me sheer hypocrisy. . . . I could not possibly take part just now in a *non*-political Pan Celtic Meeting and keep my self respect."[98] John responded to Gruffydd by pointing out that some the Irish delegates who were coming represented an advanced position among Irish nationalists. He also confided in Gruffydd his proposal to use the Pan-Celtic congress as a forum to try to resolve the impasse in Ireland.[99] Of course, John's proposal came to naught, especially since he was making it to Hyde, who, by his own admission, had no influence upon the leadership of the Irish revolutionaries. Yet John continued to urge for peace in Ireland. In his presidential address to the assembled Celts on the Isle of Man, John hoped that "completely cordial and mutually satisfactory relations may be forthwith established between the democracies of Ireland and Great Britain."[100] Meanwhile, Lachlan Macbean proposed the following motion, seconded by John "Dyfnallt" Owen: "That this Congress having watched with prayerful interest the present negotiations for settlement of Irish questions express the earnest hope that such an issue may be reached as shall secure for Ireland development on truly national lines, which shall satisfy the noblest historical aspirations of her people, and give them their unrestricted share in the best life of the commonwealth and of the world."[101]

Coincidentally, a truce was announced in Ireland just as the conference ended, eventually leading to the signing of the Anglo-Irish treaty in December 1921. When the treaty was signed, John telegraphed Éamon de Valera that "confident Celts the world over will most unfeignedly rejoice that the desire of Douglas Conference has been so largely realized."[102] This again is evidence of John's unrealistic eagerness to insert the Pan-Celtic movement into mainstream Irish politics. He sent the exact same message to David Lloyd George, adding, "May I add my personal felicitations combined with the confident hope that 1922 may bring both to Scotland and Wales status, dignity and freedom fully equal to that now achieved by Ireland."[103]

The settlement of the Irish question spurred John to renew his promotion of Welsh political autonomy. This is not surprising. Since the 1890s, the major hope for Welsh nationalists was that the granting of self-government to Ireland would create an opportunity for a Welsh parliament to be formed as well, so the Anglo-Irish treaty meant that John and his supporters had to strike while the iron was hot. It is interesting that John's demands for Wales changed in tandem with the Irish political situation. When Irish MPs sought home rule for Ireland before the war, John wanted Welsh home rule. When various commentators suggested dominion status for Ireland as war erupted in the country, John called for dominion status for Wales as well. Naturally then, the establishment of an Irish Free State led John to call for the creation of a Welsh Free State. John tried to organize a Welsh convention on home rule in 1922, based on the proposal "that advantage should be taken at the present juncture to secure for Wales forthwith a measure of self-government which will give to a Welsh Legislature status, power and authority fully equal to that enjoyed by the new Irish Free State and also enable Wales to take her proper place with Ireland and Scotland as members of the Council of the League of Nations."[104] Equating the demand for Welsh home rule with the independence granted to the Irish Free State was unlikely to win supporters in Wales. John failed to appreciate that the form of self-government bestowed upon Ireland had been won by force of arms. As such, the Irish Free State was a treasonous entity in the eyes of many people in Britain, and linking the cause of Welsh autonomy to the Irish situation could scarcely advance the cause. Herbert Lewis, a long-standing Welsh MP for the Liberal Party, told John, "In my judgment such a proposal [a Welsh Free State] would be ruinous to the prospect of carrying such a Devolution Bill through Parliament."[105] John had invited Sir Charles Leolin Forestier-Walker, the Conservative MP for Monmouth, to preside as convener at the proposed home rule convention, but Forestier-Walker replied, "I regret that it will not be possible for me to act as a Convener of the Convention on several grounds, the chief of which has reference to the position you give to the new Irish Free State."[106]

Despite these warnings, John insisted that Wales demand the same measure of freedom that Ireland had obtained. He told David Rhys Phillips that the main goal of the conference "would be to deal mainly and really exhaustively with the Educational Policy of the contemplated Welsh Free State."[107] John urged Beriah Evans to speak to Owen Thomas, the Labour MP from Anglesey who had once espoused Welsh home rule rhetoric, and see if he could get him to support the "conception of the Welsh Free State."[108] John himself tried to convert George Maitland Lloyd Davies, an independent candidate in the 1923 general election, to the cause of the Welsh Free State, promising him that "the Welsh Free State alike pacifist and nationalist from its inception, declining absolutely to expend one penny piece upon preparation for war and equally withholding the services of its sons, would be a working demonstration of the attitude, which a nation so committed, at any rate, to institutional Christianity should take up."[109] Indeed, in the run-up to the 1923 general election John, in his role as president of the National Union of Welsh Societies, issued a questionnaire to all candidates running in Welsh constituencies asking the following questions:

1. Will you, if elected, cooperate with representatives of the National Union of Welsh Societies in preparing and submitting to Parliament next Session a Bill securing for Wales a measure of Self-Government, which will give to a Welsh Legislature status, power and authority fully equal to that enjoyed by the Irish Free State; and granting to Wales similar representation in the League of Nations to that accorded to the Irish Free State. . . .

2. Should you not be prepared to claim for Wales rights equal to those enjoyed by the Irish Free State, will you support a measure granting to Wales powers similar and equal to those granted to Northern Ireland?[110]

Only nineteen of the eighty-one candidates in Wales responded to the questionnaire, six of them Liberal candidates, three Conservative, and ten from the Labour Party. Thirteen of the nineteen respondents indicated that they supported the idea of a Welsh Free State, with another three saying they supported Welsh aspirations generally, and one Conservative candidate saying he supported some measure of Welsh autonomy, but not along Free State lines.[111] Charles Ellis Lloyd, a representative of the Labour Party, declared, "I am strongly in favour of Home Rule for Wales. . . . I do not, however, stand for a Sinn Fein policy, which seems to me to be one largely of isolation from the political life of Great Britain and the Colonies."[112] Although most of the people who responded to the questionnaire were in favor of Welsh political autonomy, it is safe to assume that the large majority who did not reply were against the idea. The lack of support for Welsh self-government can be indicated by John's own failure at the ballot box. Running as a Labour candidate for Parliament in Brecon and Radnorshire (1922), Anglesey (1923), and Brecon and Radnorshire once more (1924), John was thrice defeated, unable to win much more than 30 percent of the vote each time. John wanted a Welsh Free State, but Welsh voters had other concerns.

Nevertheless, John continued to combine his efforts in aid of Welsh political autonomy with Pan-Celticism. One way he felt he could successfully do this was through the establishment of a Celtic federal union. John first mentioned this idea in an article in the *Welsh Outlook* in 1919. He wrote that the "mission of the Celtic races" could only "be discharged by the achievement of virtual independence by Ireland, Scotland, Wales and by Brittany, constituting eventually an informal Celtic Federal Union, naturally assuming the leadership of Celts the world over in the peaceful evolution of human destiny."[113] Although vague, this idea offered the possibility of radically reimagining the relationship between the Celtic nations. The fact that John emphasized that Ireland, Wales, Scotland, and Brittany should attain independence first hints that he may have considered a Celtic state, organized on federal lines, to be a possibility. John tended to have grandiose ideas, and something along these lines may have been his ultimate aim for the Pan-Celtic movement. In 1921, the idea of a Celtic federal union surfaced again in a letter from John to Douglas Hyde. John was discussing the possibility of a Celtic congress in Ireland, and wrote that he wanted the congress to finish on Tuesday and then "devote the Wednesday and Thursday to meetings of a Celtic Federal Union, which I have had in my mind for some years, as a body to be organized for the purpose of ventilating the political aspects of the life of the Celtic Nations everywhere, with the fullest freedom to take such action as may be considered desirable. This will relieve the Celtic Congress itself of much difficulty and controversy, leaving the cultural activities of the Celtic races as its main subject matter."[114]

Of course, the proposed "Celtic Federal Union" in this letter appears to be a much more modest vision than that mentioned in his 1919 article. It appears that John had learned the lessons of the Scottish controversy and felt that the best way to handle the question of politics in Pan-Celticism was to create an entity that would meet in tandem with, but separately from, the Celtic congresses. A year later, John was still mulling over the possibility of a "Celtic Federal Union," telling Agnes O'Farrelly, "This is a body which I have long contemplated organizing to deal frankly and more or less exclusively with political questions." He added, "I contemplate that the activities of the Congress will continue to be mainly cultural, but to discuss either the past, present or future of the Celtic races without continual reference to Religion and to Politics is in no sense practicable."[115] By 1923, John had envisioned the "Celtic Federal Union" as an entirely separate entity, with the federal union holding meetings in different countries and at different times of the year from the Celtic congresses. He told O'Farrelly that "our clientele would be perhaps rather different, as the gathering would be purely political." He hoped that the audience to attend this political Pan-Celtic meeting would come from "Members of Parliament and candidates for the two Irish Parliaments, the Manx House of Keys, the Members for Scotland and Wales in the British House of Commons as well as the unsuccessful candidates and the representatives of Brittany in the French Chambers."[116]

Like a few of John's other ideas, the Celtic federal union never came into existence. But clearly he had envisioned some form of Celtic political alliance, be it collaboration between elected representatives of the various Celtic nations or the eventual possibility of a federal Celtic state. Of course, if the latter were ever to become a reality, all of the Celtic nations would need to attain some level of independence first, and John continued to use his Pan-Celtic platform to advocate for this. Delivering his presidential address at the Celtic congress in Quimper, Brittany, in 1924, John spoke of the ongoing battle in Wales to secure political autonomy. He declared that "in Wales the struggle was being waged daily with increasing intensity and indeed growing audacity—the most acute controversy among the younger leaders of Welsh Nationalism being whether in the coming Welsh Free State Welsh and English should rank equally or whether Welsh should be its official language and English secondary." Attempting once more to draw a connection between Pan-Celticism and Irish politics, John claimed that "Douglas [site of the Celtic congress on the Isle of Man in 1921] virtually saw the initiation of the agreement to create the new Irish Parliaments, bringing into existence two additional Celtic States and making now five Celtic Parliamentary bodies in existence, four in Ireland and the ancient House of Keys in the Isle of Man." Looking optimistically to the future, John proclaimed, "Feeling in Scotland and Wales was now so pronounced and the Government of the day so completely sympathetic that it is not unreasonable to hope that when they meet in Dublin next year we might find ourselves well on the way to the immediate creation of both the Scottish and the Welsh Free States."[117]

Since Ireland had already been granted self-government, it is not surprising that it was the role model for nationalist ambitions in Wales and

Scotland, at least in John's eyes. Hoping to capitalize on Irish independence as a boon for Celtic autonomy elsewhere, John was eager to host a Celtic conference in Ireland as soon as possible. Francis Taldir Jaffrennou, who had taken part in the old Pan-Celtic movement under Fournier's stewardship, explained the allure of Ireland to the other Celtic nationalists. In the weeks before a cease-fire in Ireland in 1921, Jaffrennou observed, "If Ireland is erected a Nation, it seems purely natural to the Celts and Gaels of the world to turn their eyes towards this centre of National life and freedom, and to accept its moral and intellectual sovereignty. Then the Celts could at last provide for themselves a General Headquarter, far from the intrusion of the Strangers. Ireland is in a special situation among the Celtic nationalities, she is worthy of her independence."[118] John planned on having the Pan-Celtic congress take place in Ireland in 1922, but as early as May 1921 Douglas Hyde warned that "there is not, so far as I can see, at present, the ghost of a chance that the Congress can meet in Ireland next year."[119] The declaration of a truce, followed by the Anglo-Irish treaty, raised hopes that a conference could take place in Ireland in 1922 after all, with David Rhys Phillips telling John, "The Irish news is really very splendid, and I hope that things will now so shape themselves that we shall have a real Congress of all Celts in Dublin this coming year."[120] Those in Ireland were more cautious, with O'Farrelly informing John, "I see a fair prospect now of holding the Congress here during the coming summer, though there are still many difficulties to be overcome."[121] But with a civil war breaking out in Ireland shortly after, holding the congress in the Emerald Isle in 1922 became impossible.

John was content to wait, however, believing that it was important that the next Pan-Celtic gathering should take place in Ireland. He informed O'Farrelly, "No great harm is done by missing this year as you will remember happened in 1920. To my mind it is far more important that when the Congress is held, it should be held in Dublin and that the arrangements generally should be on a scale consonant with the conspicuous place Ireland had occupied, and occupies to-day more than ever, in the Celtic confraternity. Both Edinburgh and Douglas, in their way, were delightful gatherings. I want Dublin to eclipse both, and this, I am sure, is equally the desire of yourself and your colleagues."[122] As a result, the Celtic congress planned to hold its next meeting in Dublin in 1923 instead. But this plan was also undermined by the continuing conflict in Ireland. In May 1923 O'Farrelly gave John a grim account of the circumstances in Ireland, telling him, "Our ministers can only emerge as a rule in armoured cars. How on earth could we hold a national Congress in Dublin under such circumstances? Our museum and our picture galleries as well as our National Library are closed and fortified." Ruling out any possibility of a congress in 1923, O'Farrelly lamented that "we would be ashamed to have the Celts of other countries see us in our national rags."[123] John and Phillips were forced to change plans again, deciding to hold the next congress in 1924 in Dublin and pushing the congress due to be held in Brittany back until 1925. However, the Breton Pan-Celts refused this proposal, insisting that the 1924 congress take place in Brittany as originally planned.[124] O'Farrelly was "very disappointed" with the "Breton embargo,"[125] and John felt "very perturbed,"[126] but both agreed that waiting until 1925 to bring the congress to Ireland was, at that stage, the best option.

With the conclusion of the Irish Civil War and the holding of a successful conference in Brittany in 1924, the way was finally clear for the Irish congress to take place. O'Farrelly told John, "I feel that Ireland—the mother country—should welcome all the Celts in a great hearted way after the long, long separation,"[127] and "I have my mind made up that this is to be a memorable Congress worthy in some way of the motherland of the Old Celtic Empire."[128] John used the occasion of the congress to once again stress that Ireland's political freedom was something that other Celtic nations should aspire to. Speaking to the assembled Celts, he said, "Ireland had thus unquestionably effected in the political domain a triumph of the spirit, the outcome of an unflinching national persistence confronting the grim Goliath of English domination." He suggested that the Pan-Celtic movement could learn from the triumph of Sinn Féin, declaring, "The Celtic Congress emulating the Sinn Fein movement in its initial stages, would be wisely advised if it devoted more ample attention to the economic condition and outlook of the Celtic nations, as well as their cultural prospects and aspirations." John believed that "politically, what Ireland had brought about should be equally feasible for Brittany, Scotland and Wales and at infinitely smaller cost." Indeed, he claimed that the settlement in Ireland, which involved retaining a link with the British crown, showed that nations could be free while retaining "sentiment and enlightened interest."

This offered an obvious path for the other Celtic nations to follow, and John predicted that Celtic nationalism would soon be fulfilled by "the inevitable and probably early establishment of national self-government on Free State lines."[129]

In many ways, however, the Celtic congress of 1925 was the high-water mark of John's dream for Pan-Celtic political cooperation. His proposed "Celtic Federal Union" remained a pipe dream. In Wales especially, the call for home rule was growing fainter, not louder, as evident from John's own failure at the ballot box. John had placed his hope for the advancement of Welsh nationalism in the Labour Party. While this party did indeed grow in size and strength, it never viewed self-government for Wales or Scotland as any kind of political priority. John seemed to have given up on any possible Celtic political nationalism by the time of his next presidential address to the Celtic congress, at Bangor in 1927. He claimed that the idea of "Celtic fraternization . . . greatly transcended the more restricted ideals of nationalism—political and economic—and connoted rather racial kinship." The Celts, John said, had more in common with "the notable homogeneity of the Hebraic people than with the political federation of differing races constituting both the British Commonwealth and the great Republic of North America."[130] This was a remarkable turnaround for someone who, only four years previously, had still been looking for ways to create a platform to bring political activists from the various Celtic countries together. Perhaps this change had been brought about by his own electoral defeats and a realization that he was not going to see a vibrant Welsh home rule movement in his lifetime. John died in 1931, and his dream of political Pan-Celticism died with him.

Edward John, however, had done much to revive the Pan-Celtic movement. The Celtic congress survived his passing, led ably by Agnes O'Farrelly, and Pan-Celticism continued in various manifestations throughout the twentieth century. But the grand hopes that John had for the movement never materialized because of a combination of unfortunate timing, indecisive leadership, and unrealistic ambitions. That the early years of John's reformed Pan-Celticism coincided with the Irish War of Independence did little to facilitate a greater appreciation of a broader sense of Celtic identity, as impassioned national sentiments and tensions could not be avoided. John compounded this difficulty by sending mixed signals to potential supporters of the Pan-Celtic movement regarding its position on politics generally and Irish independence in particular. John's efforts to not exclude anyone based on his or her political opinion ultimately ended up alienating him from advanced nationalists in Scotland, Ireland, and even Wales. While allowing the Celtic congress to adopt a more overtly nationalist position would have been unlikely to broaden its appeal to the masses, it would have enabled him to work with a larger group of like-minded individuals who were equally interested in some form of Celtic political cooperation. What this cooperation could have yielded, however, is difficult to say. In his speeches, John regularly spoke about political autonomy for Wales and Scotland as if it were on the cusp of being achieved, something far removed from political reality. His hint at some kind of political rapprochement among independent Celtic nations in the future was beyond the realm of the fantastical. John undoubtedly viewed the establishment of the Irish Free State as the first step towards self-government among all the Celtic nations. He didn't appreciate that, in political terms, the arrival of the Irish Free State had widened the distance between the Welsh and Scottish, content in their status as British subjects, and the Irish, self-confident in their newly acquired independence. Ironically then, from John's point of view, Irish secession from the United Kingdom marked an end, rather than a beginning, to Celtic political cooperation.

CHAPTER 8

CELTIC HEROES AND
CELTIC VILLAINS

The late nineteenth century had been a period of great agitation but ultimately disappointment for Irish and Welsh nationalists, as their demands
for Irish home rule and Welsh disestablishment were not granted. But by
1914 both countries appeared to be on the verge of realizing their nationalist legislative ambitions. The Parliamentary Act of 1911, curtailing the veto
of the House of Lords, removed the rock upon which Irish and Welsh aspirations had previously perished. That such a feat had been achieved by the
preeminent Celtic statesman David Lloyd George, chancellor to the
exchequer, only embellished the victory enjoyed by longtime advocates of
home rule and disestablishment. The passage of the Irish home rule and
Welsh church bills in 1912, with both acts to become law in 1914, satisfied
the ambitions of the majority of nationalists in both countries. It seemed
that once these were implemented the Irish and Welsh people would finally
be fully content with their position within the United Kingdom, and nationalist energies could be redirected to embracing a more inclusive sense
of Britishness.

Of course, some matters remained to be resolved before the successful
implementation of both acts. In particular, the vociferous and increasingly
militant opposition of Ulster unionists to home rule presented an ominous,

and seemingly intractable, obstacle to Irish political autonomy. The outbreak of the First World War, however, forced a postponement of the issue. Royal assent was given to the Irish and Welsh acts on September 18, 1914, the same day that the Suspensory Act was also signed into law by George V, suspending the implementation of home rule and disestablishment until after the war. Nevertheless, supporters of both measures remained confident that the changes would be enacted and that Britain would be better off if they were adopted in all parts of the United Kingdom. Dewi Morgan, a renowned Welsh poet and journalist, wrote, "We no more believe that Irish Home Rule will weaken imperial unity than we believe that Welsh Disestablishment will weaken religious unity. There will have to be Disestablishment all round, just as there will have to be Home Rule all round. Both reforms are absolutely essential if there is to be national and international progress."[1]

The war changed everything. The Easter Rising of 1916 and the attempt to introduce conscription into Ireland in 1918 radicalized Irish nationalist opinion, leading to a paramilitary campaign that sought complete independence from Britain. The opposition to this struggle was led by Lloyd George, the former leader of the Welsh home rule movement who had become prime minister. This public juxtaposition of Celtic nationalisms raised intensified questions about what ideals were paramount to the national identity of Ireland and Wales. While Irish nationalists were primarily focused on the achievement of a political nation, the prominence of the Welsh language prompted a deeper consideration of what role the Irish language should play in a new state. Irish prisoners at Frongoch were inspired to learn Irish by the example of the Welsh-speaking heartland that surrounded their internment camp. Yet as Lloyd George regularly boasted that the Welsh language was much stronger than its Irish equivalent, members of the Gaelic League used his taunts as a rallying cry to encourage the adoption of Irish; they also questioned whether the Welsh language was really as vibrant as the League had once claimed.

In the aftermath of the Easter Rising, hundreds of suspected rebels were shipped off to Wales for incarceration. Liam Tobin, who would go on to lead the abortive army mutiny in the Irish Free State in 1924, was one of the rebels arrested by crown forces. He recalled that he and some of his comrades were taken to Dublin port and "were put aboard a vessel, and brought down very far in one of the holds. It was some sort of a collier or something." He also recalled that "the crew of that vessel, as far as I can remember, were mostly Welsh, and were very hostile to us. We made the journey to Holyhead, and certainly it was not a comfortable journey."[2] Transportation across the Irish Sea gave men like Tobin an opportunity to learn more about the Welsh nation when many of them were interned at Frongoch prison camp. Frongoch was a former distillery in Welsh-speaking north Wales that had been converted to house German prisoners, many of whom were perplexed by the fact that some of them spoke better English than the local inhabitants.[3] The German prisoners were moved elsewhere to accommodate the 1,800 Irish internees who were kept at Frongoch from July to December 1916. While interactions between the prisoners and locals were kept to a minimum, it is possible to attain some insight into how the Irishmen perceived their fellow Celts. William Brennan-Whitmore was one of the men arrested by authorities and imprisoned at Manchester before being sent to Frongoch. He described the train journey with his fellow prisoners as follows: "At every English railway station we sang the most seditious of Irish songs, and the crowd gazed at us pretty much the same as they would at a party of aborigines from Kamchatka. In a few cases we were jeered. We answered taunt with taunt. Why should we not? It was nation against nation."[4]

However, Brennan-Whitmore notes that this attitude changed once the train moved into Wales. He writes that when "we crossed the border our hearts warmed to Wales. 'It's so like Ireland!' one of my comrades pathetically remarked. We seldom sang at the Welsh stations. We greeted the people in a friendly tone and invariably received a cheery reply."[5] Brennan-Whitmore's colleague was not the only Irish prisoner to observe the physical similarity between Ireland and Wales. Joseph McCarthy, a prisoner from Wexford, recalled that the prisoners were taken on daily marches out of their prison camp. He noted that "the country road was picturesque and resembled Wicklow or Kerry. Little streams were tumbling down crags, everywhere fuschia was growing by the roadside."[6] Sean Prendergast was a Dublin man who had taken part in the Easter Rising. Commenting on his train journey through Wales on his way to Frongoch, Prendergast noted that the landscape "was so much like our own lovely Ireland."[7] From a geographical standpoint, it is hardly surprising that the prisoners noticed a great deal of similarity between rural Ireland and rural Wales. It is also possible, however, that this desire to identify Wales as a kind of second Ireland may have been something of a coping mechanism for the internees, who were dealing with the stress of being incarcerated in a foreign land. Several of the witness statements given during the 1940s by the Frongoch internees emphasized the similarity between the Irish and Welsh peoples, in terms of their "racial" heritage and their language.

Sean Prendergast described his excitement at being in Wales despite the circumstances. He wrote:

> What a thrill indeed to feel that we were in a Celtic country inhabited by a Celtic people who had withstood the ravages of time to preserve their own national characteristics, traditions and culture. What a delightful experience it would have been to us were we journeying in better and freer circumstances to make human contacts with a race which we had learned was akin to our own. How often was one forced to make comparison between our own hard lot, the hardships imposed on our dear land so cruelly and arbitrarily deprived of not merely independence but national culture and tradition as well, and their lovely Wales which remained true to everything that was racy of the soil, nationhood and national consciousness in the face of an proximate presence of an all pervading and overpowering foreign culture.[8]

Prendergast clearly believed there was some kind of bond between the prisoners and the land they had been sent to, a "Celtic country" filled with "Celtic people" like themselves. Like many Irish nationalists before him, Prendergast was deeply impressed with the strength of the Welsh language and culture, certainly when compared to Ireland. He imagined that if he had been in Wales in "better and freer circumstances," he could form friendships with a race that was "akin to our own." Assumptions that the desire for Celtic brotherhood would be reciprocated could be misplaced. When Captain Jack White, the man who had trained James Connolly's Citizen Army, fled to Wales in 1916 to try to organize a strike to prevent Connolly's execution, he found little support and was promptly jailed for "trying to sow the seeds of sedition."[9] White's barrister explained his logic in coming to Wales, namely that "the Welsh, being Celts, he thought he could rouse their sympathies more quickly." Indeed, even Prendergast, while celebrating the fact that the Welsh were also Celts, noticed differences between the Irish and Welsh. He admitted that the Irish internees had poked fun at the Welsh names of the train stations, "names which we in our ignorance thought so peculiar."

Beyond place-names, however, Prendergast hinted that the prisoners also saw fundamental differences between the Welsh and the Irish. He declared, "Yet we could not help thinking that the country of Wales was less free than that which we aimed and desired our Ireland to attain. Why was it that the English exercised such unremitting and deliberate care to prescribe our national institutions, customs and culture, while at their doorstep stood Wales, a country that was permitted and encouraged to live its own life somewhat free of interruption and oppressions? We pondered on these questions and thoughts as we made our forced journey on our way as prisoners to the Welsh portion called Frongoch."[10] The implication of Prendergast's words is clear. Welsh culture thrived in part because the British state allowed, indeed, encouraged the Welsh people to embrace their traditions. Irish customs, on the other hand, were repressed. The reason for this, as far as Prendergast could see, was that Ireland wanted freedom and that the "English" felt that in order to curtail this desire they had to eliminate all elements of a distinct Irish nationality. Welsh culture flourished because the Welsh people did not desire political freedom. Paradoxically then, Prendergast interpreted the markers of Welsh national distinctiveness as indicators of subservience to English imperialism, in marked contrast to the patriotism shown by the Irish rebels.

Other internees saw signs that the Welsh people shared the same independent-minded spirit as themselves. One example comes from the statement of Frank Hardiman, an internee from Galway. Hardiman wrote about the marches the prisoners undertook around the Welsh countryside, recalling, "My friend, the late Seamus Carter, was usually near me on all those marches. Seamus was a well-known Irish scholar. His wonderful knowledge of Irish enabled him to translate the Welsh road signs which were very interesting and like our own Irish names of places usually referred to some noted object in the localities we were passing through. Another thing that attracted my notice was a stone tablet on a house pointing out— All the material used in the building of this house was got on this estate: Sinn Féin Amháin."[11]

Two things in this statement are noteworthy. The problem with Hardiman's account is that the Welsh and Irish languages, while related, are mutually unintelligible. There is no reason to doubt that Seamus Carter thought he was translating the Welsh correctly, particularly if there was no one to correct him, but his Irish-language skills would have been of little use in this. But again, the story highlights the desire of the Irish prisoners to imagine a linguistic and ethnic connection between the locals and themselves. This was not confined to the Irish in Frongoch either. The *Irish Independent* reported in August 1916 that the "Welsh people fraternised with the Irish prisoners and spoke and sang with them in Gaelic."[12] Not only was this report incorrect in indicating that the locals could have fraternized with the Irish had they so desired, but also it assumed that the Welsh language was so close to Irish that the locals were able to speak and sing Gaelic with the internees.

The fact that Hardiman also saw the Irish nationalist motto "Sinn Féin Amháin" engraved on a stone tablet on a house is interesting for a number of reasons. Hardiman viewed the sign as an indicator of the similarity between the Irish and Welsh people: just as the Sinn Féin movement sought to build a new Ireland through Irish self-sufficiency, these Welsh people were constructing their houses in the same independent spirit. Hardiman probably interpreted the use of the phrase "Sinn Féin Amháin" as either proof that the motto and its meaning had become known in Wales or possibly that since the two languages were so similar (according to Seamus Carter), the phrase "Ourselves Alone" looked the same translated into Welsh or Irish. If Hardiman's account is correct, then this stone tablet could be evidence that some of the locals sought to show their support of the rebels with a subtle gesture. Alternatively, it is possible that the engraving was making fun of the ideology of the internees—although if this was so the joke was lost on Hardiman. There is also the strong possibility that the engraving was entirely in Welsh, given that the house was a Welsh-speaking area, and that Hardiman's recollection of what it said was based on a translation by Seamus Carter. If that is the case, then we might question whether it had been accurately translated at all, just as we might question Carter's ability to translate the meaning of Welsh place-names using his Irish-language skills. Regardless of what the sign actually said, what Hardiman remembered it saying demonstrates that the prisoners were eager to imagine that they were among a people who sympathized with them on the basis of their ethnicity and their politics.

Therefore, it appears that the Irish prisoners embraced the idea that they shared an ethnicity with the Welsh and expected empathy from Welsh people they might encounter. Opportunities for interaction between the prisoners and the local population were confined to food deliveries and to instances of prisoners being taken out for a haircut or tradesmen coming into the camp to tend to repairs. One internee, Michael O'Flanagan, remembered that the local people exhibited warm feeling toward the Irish prisoners. He wrote that when the group of internees he was traveling with reached Frongoch "We got a very friendly reception from the Welsh people who had assembled in large numbers on the platform. They were particularly anxious to obtain souvenirs from us and sought diligently such personal belongings as Rosary Beads and other religious emblems."[13] It is odd that the Frongoch locals sought religious items from the prisoners, as Welsh Nonconformists generally were not enamored with Catholicism, but perhaps their curiosity overcame any potential religious prejudices. Jon Parry writes that the local population was sympathetic to the prisoners' plight, as opposed to their political convictions, noting that "some monoglot Welsh speakers who saw the prisoners were later to serve in the hated Black and Tans in the forthcoming war in Ireland."[14] Reports circulated in Ireland that the locals were quite friendly with the prisoners, although released prisoners pointed out that camp regulations made such interaction rare indeed.[15] Despite this, it does appear that there were some friendly encounters between the Welsh and Irish at Frongoch, and when the prisoners were released in December the *Freeman's Journal* noted that at the train station "the Welsh people gave them a hearty send-off, which was gratefully reciprocated. In a sense it did not surprise the men. While the local residents were not allowed to have any undue communication with the prisoners at the camp, yet a friendliness sprang up between them, and the children frequently approached the recreation ground. On the mutual sympathy engendered as the outcome of racial and language characteristics, very friendly intercourse prevailed, but eventually the youngsters were scared off by the military guard."[16] This account was corroborated, at least in part, by Thomas Leahy. Leahy had been a member of the Irish Citizens' Army who was interned at Frongoch. He remembered that the prisoners were notified suddenly that they were being released and "we had no time to wire home to tell our friends to expect us or meet the boat. However, we got a good send off in a way from the guard and a few Welsh people who lived near the camp."[17] Like the report in the *Freeman's Journal*, Leahy's report recalls a good send-off, though it qualifies this by saying "in a way." Interestingly, Leahy remembers that it was the guards who gave them this send-off, as well as "a few Welsh people." Whether the locals came to wish the prisoners a safe journey home because they felt some kind of bond with them or simply were curious is difficult to say.

There is evidence, however, that not all locals were sympathetic toward the Irish interned in their midst. According to Frank Hardiman, "During one of the early marches we noticed a woman standing at the door of her house and shaking her fist at us. We were rather surprised at this sign of hostility, and to show there was no ill-feeling between the Welsh people and ourselves, I suggested to a few of those near me to strike up the Welsh National Anthem. Soon we were all whistling it, and in all our marches afterwards we included it with our own patriotic tunes."[18] There are a couple of things worth unpacking here. First, Hardiman was surprised at the show of hostility. This, I believe, is because Hardiman and his comrades imagined that, as fellow Celts, the Welsh would be sympathetic toward the Irish. Confronted with the reality that at least some of the locals resented them, Hardiman decided to appeal to their nationalist sentiments, perhaps believing that this would emphasize that a kind of common bond between them existed. Unfortunately, Hardiman doesn't say whether whistling the Welsh national anthem brought an end to the vigorous fist-shaking in their direction! Joseph McCarthy, on the other hand, had more positive memories of the fleeting encounters between Frongoch natives and the Irish prisoners while they were out marching. He wrote, "After walking a mile or two before returning, there would be a halt and the piper played a hornpipe or reel for some of the more expert dancers. Sometimes a shepherd or two would come to view the scene and Liam O'Briain would engage them in a conversation in the Welsh language which would be mingled with hearty laughter."[19]

Of course, McCarthy's recollection hints at one obstacle to friendlier relations between the Irish internees and the local population, namely, that of language. At the same time, it appears that the Irish rebels were quite impressed with the vitality of the Welsh tongue in the area. One of the prisoners, M. J. O'Connor, wrote that he first realized he had entered Wales when he saw the bilingual train signs, and he questioned why the Irish Railway Company didn't follow this example by using the Irish language on its notices.[20] Batt O'Connor, another internee, wrote, "One thing at Frongoch greatly impressed us. All the workmen who came to carry out any plumbing or repairs at the camp spoke the Welsh language. This was a great surprise for most of us. We marvelled at the fine national spirit of those men, and their love for their native tongue, that they should have been able to preserve it, and they living alongside the English without even a bay between them."[21]

O'Connor was not alone in admiring the proficiency of the Welsh in their native language. According to Rex Taylor, Michael Collins "interested himself keenly in the Welsh tradesmen who came to do jobs in the camp and who spoke their native language with the pride of the undefeated. Hearing them speak, seeing them at their work, determined him yet again to seek out the true value of his native tongue."[22] The prisoners at Frongoch organized classes to occupy their time, and one of the most popular classes was instruction in the Irish language. Sean O'Mahony writes that the Welsh example inspired the men to learn Irish.[23] To what extent all the prisoners were impressed by the Welsh example is difficult to say. William Brennan-Whitmore doesn't mention the Welsh language in his memoir, whereas Batt O'Connor says it "gave us a feeling of wholesome humility beside those Welsh fellows to hear them chatting away to each other without a word of English, while we were laboriously re-learning the language of our fathers."[24] Some of the prisoners even tried their hand at learning Welsh. Johnnie Roberts was a fifteen-year-old local boy who was employed in the camp canteen. Years later he recalled that Michael Collins had paid for Welsh dictionaries and other Welsh material and that these had been used for a Welsh-language class for the internees.[25] While it is unlikely that any prisoner mastered Welsh while at Frongoch, other lessons were learned. Many of those interned at the camp went on to become active members of the Sinn Féin movement in its struggle for Irish independence, and there seems little doubt that their quest for an independent, Irish-speaking Ireland was partly inspired by what they had witnessed in the hills of North Wales.

Of course, the Easter Rising served as the precursor for the Sinn Féin revolution in Ireland, culminating in a military conflict between the IRA and the British Army from 1919 to 1921. An interesting subplot in this clash was the juxtaposition of two conflicting concepts of Celtic nationality. On the one hand, Sinn Féin wanted to form a state that was, in Patrick Pearse's famous words, "not merely free, but Gaelic as well," thereby justifying the Irish demand for independence on the basis of its distinct culture from England. At the same time, the crown forces in Ireland answered to the prime minister, David Lloyd George. His very presence in Downing Street was the embodiment of a very different conception of nationalism, of a Welsh nation that was as comfortable in its Welshness as its Britishness, and moreover a nation that spoke a Celtic language, as opposed to aspiring to speak one. While there was much interest in Wales about events unfolding in Ireland, Irish nationalists virtually ignored the Principality during this time period. However, they were quite aware that Lloyd George was a Welshman, and throughout the Irish War of Independence Irish commentators and the prime minister exchanged barbs regarding which country had a greater claim to nationhood over the other.

At the same time, Lloyd George was not the only Welshman that Sinn Féin supporters encountered. As the conflict escalated in Ireland, the British government sought to assist the Royal Irish Constabulary by raising special reserve and auxiliary divisions for the force in Britain. Many of these were soldiers who had fought in the First World War, and naturally some came from Wales. Although the evidence is slight, there is some indication that Welshmen who served in Ireland believed that the Irish would recognize them as fellow Celts and not English invaders. One example of this is found in a tale told by Patrick Mullooly, an IRA volunteer from Roscommon. Mullooly recalled an incident that had taken place in Dublin during the war:

> One night Mick O'Connell and I went into a public house opposite the Castle. The place was full of Auxies and soldiers. O'Connell was drinking a bottle of stout and I a mineral. A little Welsh soldier came over and said to me that he would sing a song in Welsh for me. I told him to go away, that I did not want any singing. He went away but returned again with the same request, and again I told him to go away. He returned the third time and taking off his tunic said he would sing whether I liked it or not. I gave him a slap—more a push than a slap— and he fell on the floor. Immediately every Auxie and soldier left the place in a hurry. Things now seemed nasty and the barman was show-

ing vivid signs of great fear. We left the premises and went down Dame Street. Here we were held up by Auxies who ordered us to put our hands up. O'Connell's reaction was to stick his hands down into his pocket. We were put under arrest and brought to Dublin Castle.[26]

Of course, it is impossible to say what exactly the Welsh soldier was trying to do in offering to sing, especially when one considers that his judgment may have been clouded by alcohol. Yet it appears he may have believed that by offering to sing in Welsh he was making the point that he was also a Celt, like Mullooly and O'Connell. Or perhaps it was intended to be something of a mocking gesture, similar to those voiced by David Lloyd George during the war, a reminder that Welsh was far more widely spoken than Irish. Whatever the case, Mullooly clearly wasn't filled with a sense of Celtic kinship toward the soldier and pushed the Welshman to the ground when his attempts at singing became too persistent.

Another case of a Welsh soldier who tried to turn his Welshness to his advantage while in Ireland is recounted by Donnacha O hAnnagáin. Serving as an IRA volunteer in Limerick, O hAnnagáin captured a British soldier who was cycling near the village of Kilteely. The soldier "pleaded that he was a Welshman and not an Englishman. He cursed the English nations and said that thousands of Welsh coal miners were then on strike against conditions imposed by their British taskmasters."[27] No doubt this soldier hoped that his captors might treat a fellow Celt more leniently than an English soldier. His nationality may have saved his life, for he was released, but it didn't save his bicycle, which O hAnnagáin kept. Of course, a Welsh connection could be worked both ways. Isaac Conroy was brother of the renowned Irish-language writer Pádraic Ó Conaire and was married to a Welsh woman. His wife's brother worked as a miner in Wales, and through him Conroy was able to secure about thirty pounds of gelignite, four hundred detonators, fuses, an electric detonator and cable, and a box exploder, all to be used in IRA operations.[28] While some Irish and Welsh people tried to gain an advantage through their shared Celticness, some English observers found it hard to tell the Irish and the Welsh apart. Mícheál Ó Droighnáin, from Connemara, was arrested and sent to England along with other Irish Republican Brotherhood volunteers in February 1917. Eventually, some of the men were placed in towns near the Welsh border, where they were free to move about. Ó Droighnáin recalled that a group of IRB men, including Terence MacSwiney and Tomás MacCurtain, "were having a snack together one day in a hotel in Presteign in Wales, conversing in Irish, as we nearly always did—we were all Irish speakers with the exception of Dick Murphy who didn't know much of the language—when a big burly Englishman jumped up, and began to abuse us—Welshmen—for not being out at the front, helping Britannia in her troubles. He took it that we were speaking Welsh. We laughed him out of the room, in good Irish."[29]

However, it was at the level of high politics, because of the premiership of David Lloyd George, that the differences between Ireland and Wales were most apparent. One of the most interesting insights into how Sinn Féin supporters viewed Lloyd George comes from Kevin O'Shiel. A Tyrone man, O'Shiel served as a judge on a Sinn Féin court during the Irish War of Independence, and, having been educated in England, he had closely followed the rise of David Lloyd George. O'Shiel felt that David Lloyd George was a "different cup of tea" from the rest of the British political establishment because, "to begin with, he was not English. He was a Welshman, a Celt, with all the emotionalism, the excitability, the tendency to hyperbole and a very liberal share of the trickery and unreliability of his race. He was a full-blooded peasant and had an abundance of vitality and high natural intelligence, indeed genius, that, despite his meagre education—only that of a national school—enabled him, an unknown, penniless and obscure Welshman, to carve out for himself a meteoric career that swept him . . . eventually to the Premier's chair."[30] Not only was Lloyd George a Celt, but he had supported the cause of Welsh home rule. O'Shiel noted, "Indeed, he was all his life a protagonist of Home Rule—for Wales wholeheartedly; for Ireland, yes, but very half-heartedly." The reason for Lloyd George's indifference to Irish home rule was, according to O'Shiel, that "Lloyd George was, deep down in his Nonconformist peasant heart, anti-Catholic and anti-Papist." O'Shiel believed that "this conviction, this prejudice of his, coloured all the critical approaches to Home Rule that he was called upon to make."[31]

In other words, Sinn Féin supporters did not expect the prime minister to express any kind of Celtic sympathy with their cause. Indeed, Lloyd George regularly attacked the central tenet of Sinn Féin ideology, namely that a people with a distinct culture were entitled to complete self-determination. Lloyd George was not afraid to question how Ireland could claim the right to independence on the basis of a language that most nationalists could not speak, and he made several comments during the Irish War of Independence to this effect. Part of this was undoubtedly propaganda, but Lloyd George was also probably genuinely bemused at the idea that speaking (or wanting to speak) a language other than English was grounds for exiting the United Kingdom. In the House of Commons in July 1918, Lloyd George stated that Ireland could not consider itself a nation, as it had lost its national language. This prompted William Gibson, the former Pan-Celt who was now known as Lord Ashbourne, to criticize Lloyd George in Irish in the House of Lords.[32] But the prime minister was not deterred. Speaking in Caernarfon in 1920 about the use of Welsh in Welsh county council meetings, Lloyd George sneered, "Go to an Irish Co. Council in Ireland, and I have no doubt Mr. [Arthur] Griffith would be presented with an address in Gaelic which neither he nor anyone else in the place would understand."[33] During a debate on the Government of Ireland Bill in 1920, Lloyd George questioned Joseph Devlin, the leader of the remnants of the Home Rule Party, as to why Ireland was dissatisfied with the bill when Wales or Scotland would have welcomed it. Taunting Devlin, he said that the Scottish and Welsh were as much proud patriots as the Irish, and "I say with regard to one of them, more than Mr. Devlin can say, it has conserved its language (Cheers)." Continuing along this line, Lloyd George referred to the alleged Sinn Féin plot to conspire with Germany in 1918, declaring, "Why the very treasonable documents we found in the pockets of the gentlemen, who were trying to strike a blow at Britain, when we were fighting in March 1918, were all written in the language of the oppressor. There is an attempt—an artificial attempt—to revive the language in Ireland, and for putting up names at street corners to the confusion of every honest patriot (laughter)."[34]

Interestingly, the most disparaging comments Lloyd George made in comparing the status of the Welsh language to that of the Irish language came in August 1921, after a truce had brought the conflict in Ireland to an end. Speaking at Barnsley, Lloyd George told his audience that if Ireland had a right to separate from Britain, then so did Wales. He said, "I belong to a small nationality of these islands. There are a far larger number of people in that small country talking the native language of the race than you have got in Ireland talking their language."[35] Seeking to undermine

Sinn Féin's justification of its independence claim based on the Irish language, Lloyd George pointed out that Wales "is an emphatic nationality; it is a distinguished nationality; it is a proud nationality; and if it is claimed for us to set up an independent Republic we have got a greater claim than anybody in the whole British Empire to do so." However, Wales had realized that such an idea was "folly," and as for the idea of breaking up the United Kingdom, Lloyd George was adamant that "no Welsh patriot outside a lunatic asylum—and Welsh patriots don't go there (laughter)—would ever dream of demanding it."[36]

The words of Lloyd George stung Irish nationalists, largely because there was a great deal of truth in them. Over the course of the Irish War of Independence, various commentators sought in different ways to answer the prime minister's jibes. The most common was to highlight how speakers of the two languages were treated differently by the British state, the same sentiment that Sean Prendergast had felt when imprisoned at Frongoch. Even prior to the outbreak of hostilities in 1919, the Gaelic League had been suppressed by the government, in part because the organization had been controlled by Irish republicans since 1915. Support for Irish had become synonymous with supporting Sinn Féin, so Gaelic League meetings were broken up and fund-raising efforts harassed. Not surprisingly, Irish writers declared that the Irish language was outlawed while Welsh was encouraged. The *Irish Independent* highlighted that Cathal Brugha, a Sinn Féin MP, had been arrested for giving his name in Irish to a policeman, while another police commander in Cork banned the singing of Irish songs in his district. In contrast, the paper noted, Lloyd George regularly attended the national eisteddfod, where singing in Welsh was a central feature. In short, Welsh nationhood was being encouraged by the state, "while the Irish, for fear they might become a nation, are prosecuted and imprisoned for speaking Irish. If an Irish Prime Minister attempted to treat the Welsh people this way we know what would be said."[37] Timothy Harrington, editor of the *Irish Independent*, criticized Lloyd George for taunting Ireland for failing to retain its language as Wales had done. Harrington pointed out that "Mr. George on such occasions failed not to conceal the loving care with which his government has helped to preserve the Welsh language while his agents in Ireland have arrested our Gaelic teachers, prevented the holding of collections for the language fund, broken up Gaelic classes, and actually proclaimed as 'a dangerous society' the one organization that has as its objective the revival of its ancient tongue."[38]

Harrington stressed that the Irish bore no ill will toward the Welsh language being supported by the government but wondered why a similar stance was not adopted for Irish. He asked why government forms were bilingual in Wales but not in Ireland and noted that a recent government job posting for Caernarfon had made fluency in Welsh a mandatory requirement for the applicant. Harrington marveled that this should be so, as Caernarfon was "by no means a Welsh speaking town," while fluency in Irish had never been a requirement for government jobs even in Irish-speaking districts.[39] In claiming that Caernarfon was not a "Welsh speaking" town, Harrington was incorrect, demonstrating once more how Irish opinions on Wales were rarely based on experience or knowledge of the country. Meanwhile, in response to the proscription on singing Irish songs, one anonymous Welsh MP suggested that the same songs be sung in Welsh. He believed this would be an appropriate test to see "whether the Prime Minister would give his sanction to the application of penal measures to the language of his forefathers still spoken in Wales."[40] Though a few of the prisoners at Frongoch had learned some Welsh, it does not appear that this suggestion was ever put into effect.

Other commentators questioned whether the Welsh language was really as vibrant as Lloyd George claimed when he mocked Sinn Féin's vision of an Irish-speaking republic. This of course marked a notable shift away from the manner in which Gaelic Leaguers had praised the tenacity of Welsh in the past, but by 1920 there were signs that usage of the Cymric language was beginning to decline. The report of the Welsh Intermediate Education Board in 1920 commented that in many schools "Welsh is not accorded the place to which, as the national language, it is entitled."[41] The report stated that parental indifference and teacher hostility were to blame for this state of affairs. With tongue firmly in cheek, the *Irish Independent* advised that if the prime minister wished to reverse this trend, "he might consider the advisability of having class-rooms for the study of Welsh raided by Crown forces, having the teachers arrested, compelling shopkeepers to remove native signboards, and seizing all documents in the Welsh language." Once this was done, Lloyd George "would then succeed in making the study of Welsh as popular in his own land as he has made the study of Irish in this country by similar methods."[42]

Irish writers also seized on census figures to show that Lloyd George's depiction of the Welsh preserving their language might not be accurate. Timothy Harrington pointed to the census returns of 1901 and 1911 to claim that the "tame" Welsh "were falling off in linguistic patriotism." Harrington noted that while there was a decline in the percentage of monoglot Welsh speakers during this time, there was no rise in the percentage of bilingual speakers of English and Welsh, by which he deduced that fewer people were speaking Welsh. Harrington concluded, "Taffy, in short, is falling in his glory and assimilating the English speech as his ruler, Mr. George, is assimilating the English manner."[43] Other Irish nationalists questioned whether Lloyd George could truly call himself a Celt. Liam De Róiste, a Sinn Féin representative of Cork, stated that the prime minister "talks once more of 'Celtic nationalities' and 'national feeling' while he is endeavouring to stamp out with fire and sword the Celtic nationality of Ireland." De Róiste implied that Lloyd George could hardly claim to be a "Celt" when "he flouts the most precious characteristics of the Celt—the characteristic of mercy and justice."[44] James O'Grady, MP for Leeds, went further, saying that Lloyd George's attitude toward Ireland made him "a traitor to the race and to the psychology of the race."[45]

Advocates for the revival of the Irish language claimed that Lloyd George's mockery was driving Irish people to take up the language in defiance of the prime minister. Speaking at the Pan-Celtic gathering in Neath in 1919, Agnes O'Farrelly said that the day Lloyd George taunted the Irish for losing their language was "the day he did more for us than crowds of organizers could have done." O'Farrelly recalled meeting one Dublin man who had taken his family to Donegal to learn Irish. When she asked "what reason" he had for going to such lengths, "'Lloyd George!' was his simple reply."[46] A columnist for the *Freeman's Journal*, "H.H.," echoed these sentiments, stating that "Lloyd George's sneers about the Irish language have made thousands of potential Irish speakers." He believed that these learners were motivated by a desire to "slip it across the Welshman." In short, "H.H." declared that Lloyd George was "the greatest propagandist the Gaelic League ever had."[47] The *Nenagh Guardian* urged its readers to take up Irish as a rebuff to Lloyd George, stating that any "student of ordinary intelligence could get a fair knowledge of the Irish language in a year or so, by earnest study, and it is up to the Irish boys and girls now to assert themselves and study their own language or swallow the taunt and insult of the Welsh wizard."[48] Meanwhile, Michael O'Ryan, the chairman of the Clonmel board of guardians, responded to the prime minister's ridicule by saying it was "the duty of the Irish people to teach Lloyd George and the people of England that there was a language in Ireland and that the Irish people were true to it and to the history it brought down to them."[49]

The strongest response to Lloyd George's comments on the Irish language came from none other than Michael Collins. Speaking in Armagh in September 1921, one month before negotiations on the Anglo-Irish treaty began, Collins first spoke in Irish and then repeated his speech in English. Beginning his English translation, Collins told his audience that his opening remarks were in "the language which our vocal organs have been designed to speak; the language which we should all be speaking but do not; the language which we should all understand, but do not." Collins then addressed Lloyd George's boast that more Welsh people spoke Welsh than Irish people spoke Irish:

> Would there have been more if this Welsh language had been placed under a ban for generations? ("No.") Would there have been more if the teachers of their language had been hunted into hiding? Would there have been more if the public educational authority had been entirely hostile to their language? ("No.") Would there have been more if the speakers of their language were killed in thousands and driven out of their own land in millions by arranged famine, as happened in Ireland seventy years ago, and again to a lesser degree fifty years ago? ("No, no.") Would there have been more if, as in this country until July last, the organisation existing for preserving and fostering the National Tongue were held in suppression by armed force, with many of its teachers in jail, with its functions constantly being dispersed by the same force, and, above all with its most ardent spirits dying in battle or being killed by the enemy? ("No, no.")[50]

What Collins had done, in seeking to respond to Lloyd George, was invert the traditional narrative on the Welsh language that had been commonplace within Gaelic League circles. Two decades earlier, Gaelic League organizers regularly told their audiences that the Welsh language had once decayed beyond the worst decline experienced by Irish but that it had been revived. Irish learners were told that the obstacles facing the Welsh language had been far greater than those facing Irish but that the Welsh people had overcome those challenges and spoke their language defiantly. Yet now Collins was insisting that the fact that Irish had been preserved at all, in the face of such hostility, was the true triumph of the Celtic languages, and was implying that the Welsh language would not have survived such trauma. No longer were the Welsh the linguistic heroes of the Gaelic League; now their most famous politician, the most prominent Welsh speaker in the world, was leading the attack on the Irish language.

The exchange between Lloyd George and Irish nationalists over the position of the Irish language came to a head when the Irish delegates visited London to negotiate a permanent solution to the Irish question. Although Lloyd George never repeated some of his more cutting remarks about Irish while interacting in person with the Sinn Féin representatives, he did subtly remind the Irish delegation that the Welsh language thrived in a way Irish did not. When the Irish leaders visited Downing Street, Lloyd George pointed to a biography, written in Welsh, of the renowned Welsh preacher, John Jones Talysarn. He asked his guests "if there were sufficient people in Ireland interested in national literature who would make it worthwhile to publish a similar book in the Irish language. They confessed there were not."[51] At one stage, a discussion on the two languages took place, with the Irish leaders complaining about the restrictions that had been placed on Irish. Lloyd George simply responded that the Welsh people "went through all that long ago."[52] When Éamon de Valera visited London to meet with Lloyd George in July 1921, the prime minister asked him what the Irish word for *republic* was. De Valera was unable to think of one and asked his colleagues in English what reply to give. As the Irish delegates conferred, Lloyd George spoke aloud in Welsh with his secretary, Thomas Jones, who noticed that this produced "discomfiture" for the Irish visitors.[53]

Jones's account of what happened in this exchange doesn't match up exactly with that given in de Valera's official biography. According to this, Lloyd George began by saying that John Bull was a bit strange in that he didn't mind having a Celt as prime minister. He asked why the Irish wouldn't want to come into "the big house of nations," alongside the other Celts. Lloyd George then picked up a letter that de Valera had sent him earlier and drew attention to the word *respublica* in the letter heading. The prime minister said that there was no Welsh word for *republic* and asked what the Irish word was. De Valera replied that it was *saorstát* although he noted that the word *poblacht* had initially been used until certain scholars concluded that *saorstát*, literally meaning "free state," would be a more fitting translation. Lloyd George responded by saying that he didn't envision any difficulties in terms of terminology at any rate.[54]

Which account to believe? It certainly would have been odd were de Valera unable to think of the Irish translation for *republic*. As de Valera's own biography points out, the word *poblacht* had already been used by Irish republicans, and it was even the first word on the heading of Pearse's 1916 proclamation. It is possible that as an adult learner of the language, put on the spot, de Valera simply could not recall the accurate translation. Lloyd George, however, in speaking in Welsh while his guests struggled in English to think of an Irish word, undoubtedly felt he had proved his point about the respective positions of the two languages. According to Thomas Jones's version of events, Lloyd George pressed the matter home, asking de Valera, "Must we not admit that the Celts were never Republicans and have no native word for such an idea?" De Valera's biography says nothing about this particular line of reasoning, although both accounts confirm that in one way or another Lloyd George tried to use Celticness as a justification for keeping Ireland within the United Kingdom. Thomas Jones told Andrew Bonar Law that de Valera had dropped the demand for a "republic" because the prime minister told him that "there was no Irish or Welsh word for it, and therefore it was alien to the spirit of the Celt."[55] History has shown that de Valera hadn't quite given up on the republic idea yet. After he returned to Dublin, de Valera continued to send communications to Lloyd George, usually in Irish, but with an English translation attached.[56] In doing so, he was to a degree reinforcing the point that Lloyd George had made throughout the war, that the Irish language was being used as a symbol to demand independence, but with little practical application for its use.

Nor was this to be the last attempt to use Celticness to influence negotiations between the British state and Sinn Féin nationalists. One of the men tasked with helping prepare Michael Collins for the negotiations that would lead to the Anglo-Irish treaty was Crompton Llewelyn Davies. Although he had a Welsh last name, Llewelyn Davies had been born and raised in London before marrying Moya O'Connor, daughter of James O'Connor, who had been a Home Rule MP. Both husband and wife were sympathetic to the Sinn Féin cause. When a truce was declared in Ireland in 1921, Crompton Llewelyn Davies was charged with preparing Collins for negotiations by creating a document describing the personalities of the British negotiators. Llewelyn Davies, who knew Lloyd George personally, attempted to explain the prime minister's approach to the war in Ireland: "He is careful to keep alternative avenues open: while authorizing the Terror and ready to claim credit if it succeeded, he has kept himself personally free to go off at a tangent and make a magnanimous Peace. No English statesman would have had the imagination or the agility or daring to do this. Above all he has the Celtic gift of imagination to see visions of 'rare and refreshing fruits' for his country and mankind, and power of vivid utterance to impress them upon the more sluggish English imagination."[57] Llewelyn Davies believed that the Celtic characteristics that made Lloyd George a successful politician could also be used against him. He told Collins that the prime minister "is 'proud of Wales': appeal to him as a brother Celt."[58] Whether Collins ever attempted this approach with Lloyd George is unclear, but it shows that just as Lloyd George tried to deploy Celticness as a weapon to outmaneuver de Valera in earlier negotiations, the Irish side believed they could play the Celtic card to their advantage.

A sense of Celtic ethnic identity had grown steadily since the midnineteenth century, promoted by Irish and Welsh nationalists who wished to emphasize their all-encompassing distinctiveness from England. This had led to something of an intellectual rapprochement between Ireland and Wales, with commentators on both sides of the Irish Sea increasingly willing to emphasize their common Celticness in discussing the social, political, and economic issues faced by their respective populations. However, the Irish Revolution served to bring aspects of Irish and Welsh identity together on the public stage as never before, offering a test for how deeply felt this sense of common Celticness was. The years between 1916 and 1922 best demonstrated the plasticity of Celtic identity. Celticness couldn't be ignored, but it was something to be played up or played down according to circumstance.

Thus Irish prisoners in Frongoch, as well as journalists sympathetic to their cause in Ireland, sought to celebrate their shared Celticness with the

Welsh, possibly as a way of making their confinement more bearable. At times, this may have even led them to exaggerate the closeness between the two peoples. Yet even as they marveled at the vitality of the Welsh language, some Irish observers couldn't help feeling that they had a greater sense of national spirit than the Welsh. This ability to embrace or reject Celticness was best demonstrated by the response of Irish-language activists to the jeers of Lloyd George. Where once the story of the Welsh-language revival had offered hope for the Irish language precisely because it told how a Celtic language had been revived by a Celtic people, Gaelic Leaguers flipped their traditional narrative. Instead, they spoke of the miracle of the survival of Irish in the face of crown hostility, in marked contrast to Welsh, promoted at every turn by a government led by the Celtic traitor Lloyd George. These revisions were no less cynical than the efforts of Lloyd George to use the relative strength of the Welsh and Irish languages as a propaganda tool to undermine Sinn Féin's mandate to demand an independent Irish state. This willingness to find a way to use Celticness to gain some kind of political advantage was evident in peace negotiations between Westminster and Sinn Féin representatives, with both sides hoping that a plea to Celtic sentimentality could convince their opponent to shift their political position. Of course, once peace was signed, Irish interest in Wales dropped. Having attained independence, Irish-language activists believed the Irish government would now set about reviving Irish. Ireland was in charge of its own destiny and no longer required inspiration from Wales. Furthermore, with Welsh starting to show some real signs of decline, coupled with the fact that the efforts to stifle Irish independence were led by a son of Wales, there was little appeal in highlighting the two countries' shared Celticness anymore. The Welsh, once heroes in the mind of Irish nationalists, had become the villains.

CHAPTER 9

THE SEARCH FOR A
WELSH SINN FÉIN

For Irish nationalists during the Irish Revolution (1916–23), the premiership of David Lloyd George did not provoke any kind of existential crisis. Either Lloyd George could be dismissed as a Celtic traitor, or his presence in Downing Street could be interpreted as proof of a kind of "Irish exceptionalism" within the United Kingdom—evidence that the Irish people were fundamentally different from the Welsh, English, and Scottish and therefore required an independent state. For Welsh political nationalists, however, the Irish crisis did raise a series of unsettling questions about loyalty, ethnic identity, and Welsh values. The Irish War of Independence marked a significant turning point in the evolution of Welsh political nationalism, when the final failure of the Cymru Fydd movement was confirmed and was replaced by a nascent form of vigorous, self-sufficient nationalism embodied by the rise of Plaid Cymru.

At the core of the dilemma for old-school Cymru Fydd activists was the outbreak of a war with David Lloyd George on one side and Irish nationalists on the other. At the height of the Welsh home rule movement in the 1890s, Lloyd George was the leader and Ireland was the inspiration, and surviving members of Cymru Fydd tended to hold both in high regard. But by 1919 both had changed. Lloyd George was the prime minister largely because of the supporting votes of the Conservative Party, long viewed as the enemy of the Welsh people, while Irish nationalists used violent tactics to advance their radical agenda of complete separation from Britain. The question of which side to support divided Welsh nationalists. Some called for loyalty to their fellow countryman while he sought to combat Irish lawlessness, while others excoriated Lloyd George for condoning reprisal attacks on innocent Irish subjects, which flew in the face of all the principles of Welsh liberalism. A few Welsh nationalists still clung to the belief that a resolution to the Irish question could also see Welsh nationalist aspirations met. But what exactly would this entail? Some former Cymru Fydd members argued that if the government would just practice leniency with the Sinn Féin rebels, then a form of home rule all round could be implemented. But such advocates were living in the past, ignoring the fact that Ireland and Irish nationalism had changed beyond all recognition from the Parnell years. The Irish home rule engine that had pulled its Welsh equivalent with it had been derailed, while the Liberal Party had entered its death throes, with both of these developments effectively killing off Cymru Fydd for good. A younger generation of Welsh nationalists recognized this, and just as Sinn Féin had usurped the Irish Home Rule Party, they hoped a Welsh equivalent could create a more vibrant, active, and militant brand of Welsh nationalism.

Although most Irish nationalists paid little attention to Wales during this time period, Welsh nationalists were preoccupied with developments in Ireland. Welsh nationalism had lost the vibrancy of the 1890s. On the one hand, its most politically astute representative had climbed the ranks of the Liberal Party on his way to becoming prime minister, paying scant attention to Welsh affairs as his own star ascended. On the other, Wales was no longer a bastion of liberalism, with the growth of the Labour Party reflecting a shifting focus from issues of national justice to class justice among the Welsh voters.[1] Although truncated, Welsh nationalism had not disappeared, with the journal *Welsh Outlook* serving as the primary instrument for commentators to analyze the significance of the Irish Revolution for Wales. Despite taking pride in the esteemed position held by Lloyd George, Welsh nationalists were largely sympathetic to the Irish cause. They deplored the violence used by the Irish Republican Army, but they remained adamant that the Irish cause was just and proclaimed that any settlement should include recognition of the Welsh, as well as the Irish, right to self-govern. They also viewed the indifference of the Welsh electorate to the Irish cause as a betrayal of the Nonconformist principles that served as the foundation of Welsh national identity.

Some historians have made a passing comment on the impact of the war in Ireland upon the Welsh national consciousness. In his book *A History of Wales*, John Davies makes only fleeting references to the role of Ireland in shaping Welsh nationalism in the postwar period, acknowledging that Welsh liberals were upset by Lloyd George's policies in Ireland and that one of the founders of Plaid Cymru, Huw Robert Jones, was fascinated by the Irish national struggle.[2] Similarly, Kenneth O. Morgan and David Hywel Davies both acknowledge Welsh liberal discontent with government actions in Ireland, as well as mentioning the influence of Ireland on the formation of Plaid Cymru, but without much analysis of the extent of this Irish influence.[3]

Indeed, one scholar has sought to downplay the role of Irish nationalists in the development of a Welsh nationalist party. J. Graham Jones has challenged the perception that the ideas and policies of Plaid Cymru were based on an Irish model. Jones states that Saunders Lewis, who quickly became the dominant figure in Plaid Cymru, was adamant that his party would deviate from the path followed by de Valera and Sinn Féin in Ireland. He writes that the leaders of Plaid Cymru "generally were determined that the movement should be moderate, constitutional, respectable and law-abiding. The Irish example was disowned."[4] While Jones was correct in highlighting some of the differences between Plaid Cymru and Sinn Féin, I shall show in this chapter that Lewis and other Welsh nationalists derived much of their political thinking from the example of Irish nationalists and that the early policies of Plaid Cymru were taken directly from the ideas of Arthur Griffith and the Sinn Féin movement.

Welsh nationalists had used Ireland as a reference point for exploring the political possibilities of their own nation in the 1880s and 1890s. This continued in the second decade of the twentieth century, even before the eruption of violence in Ireland. In 1914 a new journal, *Welsh Outlook*, was established, with Thomas Jones, the future deputy secretary to Lloyd George's cabinet, as its first editor. Kenneth Morgan has written that *Welsh Outlook* preached "a kind of gradualist devolution while always indicating the gulf that lay between Welsh aspirations and Irish."[5] In truth, the *Outlook* was quite sympathetic to the Irish cause and constantly emphasized that Wales had much to learn from Ireland. The *Outlook*'s issue of March 1916 had a distinct emphasis on Ireland, with an article on George William Russell and the Irish literary revival, as well as an analysis of Irish-language poetry by Thomas Gwynn Jones. Also included in this issue was an article by John Arthur Price about Thomas Davis. Price had been a prominent nationalist writer in the 1890s, and in many ways his article rehashed one he had written in *Cymru Fydd* twenty-five years before.[6] Price wrote about how Thomas Davis had inspired Tom Ellis and the nationalists behind the Cymru Fydd movement decades earlier.[7] Such sentiments found a positive reception among some of the *Outlook*'s readers. One, writing under the name of "G," admitted that his "blood boiled" upon reading of the injustices suffered by the Irish nation, and he added, "I found myself in agreement with the views of Thomas Davis, even when he contemplated the idea of an independent Ireland."[8]

When news of the Easter Rising in Dublin was reported, the Welsh public was shocked. Not surprisingly, there was strong criticism of the Irish rebels. The *Western Mail* declared that the rebellion was "a seven days' madness, a crazy exploit of unscrupulous enemies and their lean-witted tools."[9] Similarly the *Celt and London Welshman* described the event as a "mere fiasco," stating that as "an organized revolt it was of a purely local character, and no person of influence could be found to direct its operations. The whole crowd of agitators were a set of irresponsible fanatics without policy, without ideas and without a spark of practicality."[10] However, what is remarkable about the Welsh reaction to the Irish rebellion is the restraint some showed in criticizing the participants, while blaming the government and Ulster unionists for bringing about the events in Dublin. The *Cambrian News and Merionethshire Standard* noted that "stern measures will have to be taken" in punishing the rebels but rejected the calls for "vengeance," believing this would only add to the distrust between Ireland and Britain. The paper stated that it was the unionists under Edward Carson, rather than Irish nationalists, who should have allied themselves with the Kaiser, as both "stand for the defence of privilege against the flowing tide of liberty and progress."[11] A few months later, the newspaper went further, declaring that "the late rebellion in Ireland would never have been recorded in her annals but for the deplorable lack of courage displayed by the Government with reference to the Irish question during the two years which immediately preceded the outbreak of the war." The reason for this was the failure of the government to tackle unionist resistance to the Home Rule Bill, with the editorial staff stating, "We do not subscribe to the views of those who maintain that under no circumstances can Ireland be granted a measure of self-government unless on a basis agreed upon between Orangemen and Nationalists. That would be contrary to the accepted principles of majority rule."[12] Other Welsh writers had a similarly sympathetic view. One maintained that the rebels had not "acted impetuously" but rather had shown a greater love and loyalty for their homeland than the "English who filled the streets of London with khaki." He was adamant that "Sinn Féin had not ever meant to be a militant movement—it had been Sir Edward Carson who had brought the devil into the circle."[13]

The idea that Edward Carson should be blamed for the Easter Rising was also popular among the newspapers of the laboring classes. The *Llais Llafur* stated that the "real criminal behind the disagreeable incidents in Dublin is . . . Carson. It was he who set the fashion in raising armed forces, and bringing 'rebellion' into the arena of immediate possibilities." The paper maintained that in the wake of the rebellion "we ought to hear no more from the anti-Government press of Carson as a possible substitute for Mr Asquith in the Premiership." While blaming unionist activity in 1914 for the outbreak of violence, its editor, David James Rees, rejected the idea that the uprising had discredited the home rule movement, pointing out that the events in Dublin were the actions of a small minority.[14] Unsurprisingly, the newspaper was sympathetic to the socialist element of the rebellion, and while condemning the actions of James Connolly, *Llais Llafur* viewed the uprising as the inevitable result of the crushing defeat inflicted upon striking Dublin workers in the lockout of 1913. Rees asked, "Who is responsible for the Dublin slum-dwellers, of whose poverty and misery they [the leaders of the rebellion] are in part the expression? British misgovernment and Irish capitalism."[15]

At least one Welsh trade unionist was sufficiently inspired by the efforts of the Irish Citizen Army to join their cause. Arthur Horner was a labor activist in Wales who was impressed by Connolly's goal of creating a socialist republic in Ireland. Refusing to respond to his call-up to fight in the First

World War, Horner wrote that that the Irish Citizen Army "represented to me the only possible struggle—a movement of the working class aimed at economic as well as political freedom."[16] Although Horner was interested in the uprising in terms of his socialist views, he indicates that many of his fellow trade unionists empathized with Ireland on nationalist lines as well, writing, "As a small nationality ourselves, we had watched with sympathy the Irish people's fight for independence long before the war broke out." Given that it was the Conservative Party, the party of the wealthy, who were vocal in their opposition to home rule, Horner noted that among the miners "it is easy to understand how we, who had seen the viciousness of the coal owners, regarded what was happening in Ireland as the real struggle for the rights of small nations in a war-torn world."[17] Facing potential imprisonment for not accepting conscription into the army, Horner fled, writing on the first page of his memoirs, "I had smuggled away to Ireland to fight in Connolly's Citizen Army because I believed that the Irish were the only people waging a war for real freedom."[18] This sentence is slightly misleading, as Horner did not go to Ireland until 1917, when Connolly had already been executed. Horner admits that he did not take part in any battles but recalls how he lived in Ireland for five months under the alias "Jack O'Brien," taking part in Citizen Army drills and signing rebel songs.[19] His story shows that some members of the Welsh working class did see a common cause with the Easter rebellion, in terms of both its socialist and its nationalist aims, but such sympathy was not easily converted to action.

Not all Welsh trade unionists expressed admiration for the nationalist elements of the Dublin rebellion. D. J. Rees, through his editorial in *Llais Llafur*, was scathing in his assessment of nationalists like Pearse, describing them as "an Ishmaelitish sect, their hand against every man, and every man's hand against them. Largely because of this they attracted to their ranks those unbalanced neurotics, misnamed intellectuals, who are the bane of every progressive movement."[20] Other Welsh commentators were not quite as critical of the nationalist revolutionaries. David John Williams, a student at Oxford who would go on to be one of the founding members of Plaid Cymru, wrote an article praising the rebels three days after the rising. Williams wrote, "Give to Ireland a free government free from the English according to centuries of aspirations, and we prophesise for it, in the light of the present awakening, a flourishing period of service to the nations of the world. Trample on it further and Vesuvius will shudder once more." He lamented the servility of the Welsh nation in comparison to Ireland, writing sarcastically that the Welsh "should be meek and servile occasionally, and be prepared to bend the knee to the god of Empire when asked to do so, there is something grand, after all, in fawning to the great, and it always pays for us to be good little children." Leaving no doubt about where his sympathies lay, Williams concluded, "Were we, the Welsh, possessed of a third of the courage and unquenchable flame of the Irish in their fight for freedom . . . we would have the ability to move the world."[21] Williams's views were certainly extreme compared to those of the Welsh public at large, but it was the idealism that a minority of Welsh nationalists attached to the Irish independence movement that was to spur the development of a more militant Welsh nationalism in the twentieth century.

The most prominent nationalist publication, *Welsh Outlook*, did not join Williams in praising the Irish rebels, but it was reluctant to harshly criticize them either. As other newspapers had done, the *Outlook* attributed the blame for the uprising to Edward Carson, declaring, "The appeal to Physical Force as a political remedy was becoming far less frequent until it was revived the other day under the leadership of Sir Edward Carson."[22] Such criticism of Carson may appear surprising given that one reason Welsh writers were hesitant to support Irish home rule in the 1880s was the fear that a Protestant minority would be forced to live in a Catholic state. However, by 1916, British war rhetoric had cemented the link between democracy and nationalism in the minds of the public, and *Welsh Outlook* in particular promoted a sense of national identity based on cultural and political, rather than religious, values. Furthermore, Carson was strongly allied with the Conservative Party, which only encouraged Welsh nationalists with liberal leanings to view him with suspicion. Nevertheless, there was genuine admiration for the Sinn Féin ideals that were mistakenly believed to be the inspiration for the Easter Rising. Robert Silyn Roberts, editor of *Welsh Outlook*, declared that the economic protectionism advocated by Sinn Féin was "far more thorough and logical" than the similar policies supported by the Conservative Party, and despite his own belief in free trade Roberts praised the organizational abilities of Sinn Féin in promoting Irish protectionism. He also counseled against the execution of Roger Casement, who had tried to import German arms to assist the uprising. Roberts wrote that Casement might have been a "fool and a traitor" but that "you don't explain him by calling him names, and when you shoot him you will place him with Wolfe Tone and the men of '98 in the Sinn Fein Valhalla."[23] John Arthur Price reminded *Outlook* readers that the uprising had not been supported by the majority of Irish nationalists. He noted that the majority of Welshmen supported the government's war for small nationalities in Europe and that Britain could show "her real zeal for nationalism" by introducing some measure of home rule in Ireland immediately.[24]

Of course, 1916 was also a historic year in Welsh history, with David Lloyd George becoming prime minister. As a result, when the Irish War of Independence broke out in 1919, the British government's response was directed by the "Welsh Wizard." Lloyd George had once been the champion of Welsh liberalism, but when it came to the war in Ireland many Welsh liberal nationalists proved to be more sympathetic to the efforts of Sinn Féin than the prime minister. The most obvious example in this regard was Edward John, the man who had taken up Lloyd George's former mantle of leading the crusade for Welsh home rule. John was not alone in empathizing with Ireland, however. Thomas Gwynn Jones, a professor of Welsh literature at the University College of Wales in Aberystwyth, was also fascinated with the Irish struggle. Jones had studied Old Irish under John Strachan at the School of Irish Learning in Dublin, where he met Tadhg Ó Donnchadha, an Irish-language poet.[25] The two men became good friends, and perhaps their friendship best embodied the type of Pan-Celtic embrace that men like Fournier and Edward John tried to encourage between the people of Irish and Wales. In their correspondence, Ó Donnchadha wrote in Welsh and Jones replied in Irish. Their respective interests in Ireland and Wales stemmed in part from the fact that both believed that they had some Irish and Welsh ancestry. Jones told Cecile O'Rahilly, another Celtic scholar with a deep interest in both Ireland and Wales, that he had fallen in love with Ireland as a boy when his mother informed him that her father had descendants from Ireland and therefore that he had Irish blood in his veins.[26] Ó Donnchadha claimed that one of his ancestors had married a woman from the Lavallin (Llewelyn) family who had taken part in the Norman invasion and that therefore he carried some Welsh blood in him, from which stemmed his passion for Welsh culture.[27] In 1912, Ó Donnchadha published *Guth ón mBreatain / Llais o Gymru* (A voice from Wales), a collection of Welsh poems translated into Irish.

Indeed, Ó Donnchadha went so far as to write a *rocs-catha* (battle song) that featured himself and Jones as heroes fighting for their native cultures. It read:

> Torna and Fionn Mic Eoghain [Ó Donnchadha's pen name and
>   Jones's adopted Irish name]
> Their proper heritage they will follow
> And beating Dicod Seón
> In hot fires for eternity
>
> The devil will say to them,
> "You resemble neither fish nor fowl,
> Mister Dicod Seón,
> Down forever and carry your soul with you."
>
> What is right and proper
> And not an author of English habit
> And put an end to Dicod Seón
> Weren't the wretched rabble denied?
>
> Up on high you will yet see
> The Gael and the Briton,
> And Dicod Seón seated, burning,
> In a place where nothing will comfort him.[28]

In this poem, Ó Donnchadha identifies the common enemy of the Irish and Welsh people as Dicod Seón, a hybridization of the Irish *seoinín* and the Welsh *Dic Siôn Dafydd*, both insults for Irish and Welsh people, respectively, who were believed to be too English in their habits. His vision of a fiery hell for those who ape English manners speaks volumes about the intensity of his passion for Irish and Welsh culture. Jones, for his part, was enthralled with Ireland. Twice he sought academic positions in Ireland, applying to the position of lecturer in Welsh at the new National University of Ireland in 1909 and for the chair of Celtic studies in University College Cork in 1919. Neither application was successful. Nevertheless, he remained enchanted with Ireland. During the Irish War of Independence, Jones wrote (in Irish) to fellow Welsh nationalist Saunders Lewis, declaring, "I hope poor Ireland will have freedom without delay. There is no country in the world I love like Ireland—it was and will be always in my mind, and day and night I think of it."[29]

Just as Ó Donnchadha tried to introduce Welsh poetry to the Irish reading public, Jones produced three collections of Irish literature as war unfolded in Ireland, namely *Iwerddon* (1919), *Peth nas Lleddir* (1920), and *Awen y Gwyddyl* (1922), to convince Welsh readers of the merits of Irish nationhood. Yet Jones also sought to persuade his readers that they had more in common with Sinn Féin than they might believe. Describing Ireland as "a country I love," Jones tried to convince his audience to support Irish republicans by emphasizing racial kinship and historical analogies.[30] He stated that the leaders of Sinn Féin were descended from Norman, English, and "especially Welsh" backgrounds, in particular referring to the fact that Arthur Griffith, the founder of Sinn Féin, had Welsh ancestry.[31] Jones was concerned that too many people in Wales believed the English narrative of the Irish conflict, asking, "Why are the foreigners' lies accepted?" especially since the English were, according to him, "a people so dishonest and hypocritical."[32] He argued that the Irish republican movement had developed when Irish people sought to return to their language, and he was surprised that many Welsh people who "prattle loudly for keeping Welsh" failed to see their common cause with Ireland and supported the suppression of Sinn Féin.[33] He lamented that so many "kind and honest" people in Wales "cannot forgive the Irish for fighting for their language, and because they are Catholic." The Irish, Jones maintained, did not want "alien tyranny" any more than the Welsh people who had rejected the "treachery of the Blue Books" in the nineteenth century.[34] In short, Jones believed that the Welsh needed to be more supportive of the Irish because both were fighting to preserve their distinct language and culture.

Other Welsh commentators occasionally attempted to generate sympathy for Ireland by making comparisons with Wales. Thomas Huws Davies, editor of *Welsh Outlook*, while deploring the violence being used by nationalists in Ireland, pointed out that "if policemen were used in Wales to break up Eisteddfodau, as policemen are used in Ireland to break up meetings of the Gaelic League, they would probably not be murdered, but they would certainly have an unhappy time."[35] Discussing the suppression of the *Freeman's Journal* in Ireland, the newspaper *Y Cymro* declared, "Put the Welshman in the place of the Irishman, and supposing that this was happening in Wales, his angry spirit can be understood."[36] Yet these comments were not typical of writers who sought to mobilize Welsh support for Ireland. Instead, such commentators, often through the main organ of Welsh nationalism, *Welsh Outlook*, argued that Wales needed to rally to the Irish cause because in Ireland the core values of liberal government were being violated by the British state. John Arthur Price rejected the analogy that Lloyd George had tried to make between the situation in Ireland and the secession of the Confederate states prior to the American Civil War. By threatening to bring "fire and sword" to Ireland, Price argued, Lloyd George was preparing "to govern the country permanently on Prussian principles rather than concede independence." Price lamented Lloyd George's rationale for such an approach, that an Irish republic could not be tolerated because it might pose a future threat to the security of Britain. Price translated this to mean "One nation has the right to hold another nation in slavery for the sake of its own safety from a purely problematical peril," and he worried that this essentially justified any aggressive action by one nation against another.[37]

The two editors of *Welsh Outlook* during the Irish war, Robert Silyn Roberts and then Thomas Huws Davies, consistently made the point that the government of Ireland was similar to that of the ancient régimes ruling Europe in the nineteenth century and as such was in violation of traditional liberal values. Roberts wrote that even the rights of the Magna Carta had not been extended to Ireland and that "the Castle Government in Ireland is in a bad way. It is reaping the reward of its innumerable past iniquities. The condition of the country is horrible, as the condition of every country is horrible when its government defies public opinion. The natural leaders of the land are in prison, literary societies are broken up or suppressed, the spy and the agent provocateur rule and the hideous tyranny is called Law and Order."[38] Roberts and Huws Davies compared Lloyd George's government to that of King Bomba suppressing the rebels of Young Italy and to Metternich's governing of Venitia and Lombardy in the 1840s, and they accused the prime minister of pursuing a "Habsburgian policy" in Ireland by fighting a war on true "Hohenzollern lines."[39] Gladstone, Roberts commented, had criticized such abuses of governmental power, both on the

Continent and in Ireland, and by condoning the repression of Irish democratic expression Lloyd George appeared to have abandoned the core values of the political party that had elevated him to the office.

This abandonment of Gladstonian ideals, some Welsh nationalists believed, had allowed Sinn Féin to supersede the Home Rule Party as the dominant political force in Ireland. An anonymous article in *Welsh Outlook*, entitled "Wales and Ireland," concluded that "the Irish, it is said, want a Republic and complete separation from the Empire. If this be true, it is because the present Government has thrown over the policy of Gladstone and has established in that country a military tyranny." If coercion was abandoned immediately and a parliament was established in Dublin, the writer claimed, demands for a republic would peter out.[40] This idea was supported by *Y Dinesydd Cymreig*, which claimed that Sinn Féin supporters "are good people who have taken the wrong road, and if they only had reason to believe that Great Britain is in earnest . . . we are convinced that those people who are responsible for so many terrible outrages could be transformed into loyal subjects of the Empire."[41] Indeed, outside of Edward John and Thomas Gwynn Jones, most Welsh nationalists wanted to see a solution to the Irish problem that did not create an independent republic. John Arthur Price believed Ireland should be granted home rule but not a republic, stating that "nationalism and democracy can be reconciled on the footing of free and equal union in a democratic alliance between the nations constituting the British Empire."[42] Silyn Roberts rejected the Sinn Féin claim that Ireland could renounce allegiance to the crown, writing, "We are too good Imperialists to adopt President Wilson's dictum that any nation is absolutely free to choose its own form of government."[43] Huws Davies stated that the Irish position was based on the "most extreme theory of self-determination as stated by President Wilson" and denied that Sinn Féin had the right to wage war to attain its goal. Indeed, Huws Davies was adamant that republicanism was not a traditional Irish trait, stating that "it is not the political creed of more than a small minority of Irishmen" and that all the great Irish nationalists "pleaded for the golden link of the crown."[44] In many ways, there was a strong contradiction in the position of lambasting Lloyd George for ignoring the democratic demands of Ireland, yet ultimately denying that the core principle of these demands had any legitimacy. It seems likely that these commentators, strong advocates of Welsh home rule, failed to fully comprehend that Irish nationalism after 1916 had changed and that local political autonomy under the crown, the dream of Welsh nationalists, was no longer palatable to many in Ireland.

Yet while Welsh nationalists did not support the idea of a republic they tended to be more sympathetic to the second core demand of Sinn Féin, namely, a united Ireland. Throughout the Irish War of Independence, David Lloyd George had insisted that some accommodation would have to be made for Ulster if and when a Dublin parliament was established. In his Welsh speeches, the prime minister told his audience that Ulster was like the old Welsh kingdom of Gwynedd and was entitled to some autonomy from the rest of Ireland on the basis of its ancient, independent history.[45] The writers of *Welsh Outlook*, on the other hand, were largely hostile to Ulster's claim for separation from Ireland. When Lloyd George spoke in favor of allowing Ulster to opt out of Irish home rule, John Arthur Price declared that this was "not the speech of a nationalist, it is not even the speech of a Victorian Liberal, or an eighteenth century Whig." Accusing Lloyd George of abandoning his principles and those of his party, Price stated that the prime minister's words "appear to me a plea for an anti-nationalist Jingoism, a disguised plan for the maintenance of the Protestant ascendancy of sectarian Ulster over Ireland."[46] What alarmed many in Wales was that if the logic for allowing Ulster separate treatment were extended to Wales, then the justification for Welsh disestablishment, which had been passed over the heated opposition of Anglican churchmen in the Principality, disappeared. Speaking of Edward Carson's conscientious objections to Ulster being governed from Dublin, Price asked whether Lloyd George "and the Welsh Liberals who support him, had forgotten that the Bishop of St. David's made a similar plea against Disestablishment in Wales?"[47]

It also appears that Welsh nationalists were offended by the idea that the people of Ulster constituted a distinct nation. This is not surprising. Since Wales was the only constituent nation of the United Kingdom not to have had its own parliament or crown at some stage, the idea that an area even smaller than Wales, and without a culture as distinctive as the Principality, could be granted its own national parliament must have been upsetting. The *Welsh Outlook* declared that the belief that northeastern Ulster was a "separate nation" was "entirely mistaken," pointing out that many of the Scottish settlers in Ulster came from parts of Scotland that had been settled by Irish migrants to begin with.[48] Price was even blunter when writing that "to talk of Ulster as a nation, to place her in respect to claims for autonomy or self-determination on a level with Wales, is to do to Wales a gross injustice."[49] An editorial of *Yr Herald Cymraeg*, a newspaper that supported some measure of autonomy for Wales, made the same point. It noted that the population, tax base, and wealth of Wales were all much greater than those of the proposed Northern Irish state and asked, "Why, therefore, must Wales be denied what Ulster has gained?"[50] The manner in which the question of Ulster was discussed in Wales shows how the attitudes to religion and nationality had changed in the Principality. In the 1880s, the likelihood of Irish home rule produced several pamphlets urging the Welsh not to abandon their Protestant brethren in Ulster. Such dialogue was almost nonexistent by 1920, pointing not so much to a decline of religion in Wales as to the death of the belief that religious considerations should outweigh democratic and nationalist principles.

Indeed, when appeals were made to the religious conscience of Wales with regard to Ireland, they did not seek to rally people to the cause of Irish Protestantism but rather demanded that Irish nationalists be supported on the traditional principles of Nonconformist Wales. For some, the continued willingness of Welsh MPs to support Lloyd George's policy of coercion in Ireland, and the failure of the Welsh public to voice their opposition, signaled a decline in the vitality of the Welsh nation. One Welsh writer, speaking of the suppression of the Irish nationalist cause, asked, "Would Nonconformist Wales of fifty years ago have hesitated in raising its voice against the treatment of the conscientious objectors?"[51] Thomas Huws Davies declared that the failure "to adopt a Christian policy in Ireland is shocking the world's conscience and doing unspeakable harm. . . . It is bringing the name of Nonconformity, for which Mr. George cares, and with which he is intimately associated, into shame and disgrace."[52] After the Anglo-Irish treaty, Huws Davies stated, "The Nonconformist Conscience in politics appears to have slumbered heavily in these latter years, if we may judge by its feeble and uncertain protests against such vile atrocities as the official Reprisals in Ireland."[53] The Reverend Morgan Watcyn Williams, who had served alongside Irish soldiers in France, described the Irish as "a finicky people, but a great one." Speaking of the government's policy in Ireland, he asked, "How long is the Christian Church in Wales prepared to stand this kind of thing?" In reference to the prime minister, Williams stated, "Mr. Lloyd George is not Pilate. For him I reserve another name."[54]

For other commentators, Lloyd George's actions in Ireland, and the support for his position among the Welsh population, was a betrayal of its Welsh and Celtic identity. Edward John told Agnes O'Farrelly that "it has been extremely painful to those of us who hail from the Principality to feel that through the apostasy of our most prominent countryman, Wales should be in some measure responsible for the unpardonable courses which the Government have adopted."[55] One of the staunchest critics of the prime minister was the Reverend John "Dyfnallt" Owen. In his column in *Y Darian*, Owen wrote, "The world must be changing when it becomes possible for a man who was nurtured on the bosom of Nonconformity to glorify the Black and Tans."[56] Owen felt that the support for Lloyd George in Wales was a sign that "Wales politically is to be a narrow gateway. She must choose between hero worship and principles." On the same theme, he continued, "All I will say is that Wales counts for nothing—nothing, nothing! Lloyd George is on his pinnacle. What matters Wales any longer! The nation has been bought and sold by him, and he will sell us yet again when the need arises."[57] The Celtic connection between Ireland and Wales did not go unnoticed by those who criticized Lloyd George. An editorial in *Y Genedl Gymreig* wondered how Welsh MPs could vote against a proposal to investigate government reprisals in Ireland, stating, "Wales has been wont to boast of her love for freedom and justice. In her festivals she has been accustomed to assert that she led in the union of the Celtic nations."[58] Similarly, *Y Dinesedd Cymreig* claimed, "We are alarmed that Mr. Lloyd George, of all people, should be found cherishing a spirit which is so diametrically opposed to everything Welsh and Celtic."[59] Kenneth Morris, a Welsh writer living in San Diego, wrote to Edward John to praise him for his criticisms of Lloyd George, which Morris termed "a stand . . . for Celticism as opposed to the vulgar imperialism." Morris noted that the Welsh of San Diego were "Lloyd Georgian imperialists to a man, the name of the Celt means nothing to them."[60] John "Dyfnallt" Owen also criticized Lloyd George's behavior along Celtic lines, writing, "There can be no doubt that the message of Wales as it is represented by Mr. Lloyd George is absolutely identical with the message of the Teuton—mailed fist, sword, force, and materialism. This is the unkindest blow of all to the ideal of the Celt."[61]

Despite these appeals to Nonconformist idealism and Celtic national-ism, many in Wales did not have a guilty conscience about events unfolding in Ireland. Several Welsh newspapers offered unyielding support for Lloyd George and the actions of British forces in the Emerald Isle. An editorial in the *South Wales Daily Post* noted:

> Our Irish Constabulary have been tried by a positively torturing test; shunned, hounded down, amidst their own people, held up to univer-sal odium and execration. Let this at least stand to the credit of their race, that men of it have shown a devotion to duty amidst terrible trials such as it would be hard to parallel—a transcendent loyalty. To censure harshly men for eventual reprisals—though amongst the fore-most responsible have been the British auxiliary body, the "Black and Tans"—is a task that any British man, with a spark of generosity in his soul, will refuse.[62]

Similar ideas were expressed in the organ of the Anglican Church, *Y Llan and Church News*, which declared, "The Government must adopt stern measures at once, and put down with a strong hand and an unyielding de-termination the cowards who by assassination of the innocent and the destruction of property scorn every moral and social law, and those who protect the laws of the realm must be armed."[63] The *Herald* also had scath-ing words for Lloyd George's enemies in Wales, saying that they were "a small class of small men who have been disappointed in not receiving hon-ours or office . . . and they are sometimes helped by a small preacher here and there who thinks he can gain fame by abusing the Prime Minister. . . . Having been miserable failures in the pulpit, they seek to attract public notice by barking at the heels of the Premier and their barks have become so common that we are all sick of them."[64]

In October 1920, Lloyd George gave a speech in Caernarfon and ad-dressed the charge that crown forces had engaged in reprisals for attacks upon the Royal Irish Constabulary. Rather than condemning the reprisals, the prime minister declared, "The police and soldiers do not go burning houses or shooting men down wantonly, without provocation, and there-fore you must, if you are going to examine reprisals, find out how they arose." Lloyd George's refusal to criticize reprisals in Ireland provoked outrage. Agnes O'Farrelly wrote to Edward John to say, "You are I hope properly ashamed (indeed, I know you are) of that thimble-rigging countryman of yours. His last performance at Caernarvon 'Bangs Banagher' as we say here—and Banagher is supposed to bang the devil. In my heart of hearts I always knew Lloyd George hated Ireland. He has at last thrown off the mask."[65] William Llewelyn Williams was a Welsh journalist and a founding member of the Cymru Fydd movement. He criticized Lloyd George's Irish policies in the prime minister's presence at a meeting of the Welsh Liberal Federation at Llandudno in October 1920, although some in the audience reacted angrily and "booed and brayed" Williams from the platform.[66] An editorial in *Y Darian* asked, "Why cannot we see enforced the principles which Mr. Lloyd George himself enunciated to us in the years gone by, instead of making a burnt sacrifice daily of a nation that was once famous and cultured, in order to keep away bogies from our own door?"[67] *Y Genedl Gymreig* compared the actions of crown forces in Ireland to those of German soldiers in Belgium and lamented that Lloyd George, "instead of taking the opportunity to condemn these atrocities, has sought to excuse them? The reputation of Britain in the eyes of the world because of these things is lower than it has been for many generations."[68] Yet others were quick to defend Lloyd George. *Y Cymro* noted that one man who heard Llewelyn Williams's criticism of the prime minister declared, "Well, I prefer to face the future with him than with anyone else I know of."[69] An editorial in *Y Brython* nailed its support firmly on the side of the premier, stating:

> We are for him because we cannot be different. We are for him for reasons that satisfy all the judgment and conscience we possess. And we are for him today because he has stood the test in the past. And we shall continue to be for him until he does something that will make us believe that the Prime Minister has ceased to be David Lloyd George. We believe that in him we have the most suitable person to be at the head of the Government, and that he has no equal even if his enemies succeed in dethroning him.[70]

The divide among the Welsh public manifested itself in a series of bitter by-elections. In December 1920, two by-elections were held in Abertillery and Rhondda West. Two Labour Party candidates, George Baker in Abertillery and William John in Rhondda West, won seats at the expense of representatives of Lloyd George's coalition government. For Edward John this was proof that Wales had rejected Lloyd George's policies in Ireland. In a telegram to the successful William John (no relation), Edward John declared, "Heartiest Congratulations. Wales evidently determined stand shoulder to shoulder with Ireland for complete national freedom at home and real peace abroad. The only possible path to popular comfort and contentment. Celts the world over will rejoice in this welcome Christmas greeting from Wales to Ireland." In the same vein, John also sent a telegram to the editor of the *Freeman's Journal* in Dublin that read, "Congratulate Ireland upon Abertillery and West Rhondda results so emphatically repudiating Carnarvon speech and Coalition policy. They constitute most appropriate Christmas greetings from Wales to Ireland."[71]

Whether these Labour Party victories could really be interpreted as measures of Celtic support for Ireland against Lloyd George is open for debate. If John believed that these elections were evidence of Welsh sympathy for the suffering of Ireland, then he was to be sorely disappointed with the by-election that took place in Cardiganshire in February 1921. Ernest Evans, a close ally of Lloyd George, and William Llewelyn Williams, the man who had publicly criticized the prime minister at Llandudno, contested the seat. The campaign was notable for the electioneering efforts of Margaret Lloyd George on behalf of her husband's ally. The debate on the Irish policy was a central focus of the campaign, with the Cardiganshire Women's Liberal Association passing the following resolution: "That we, women Liberals, protest against the inhuman Government policy of reprisals, and demand that justice should be dealt out to those who have dragged the name of Great Britain in the dust by the maltreatment of our brothers and sisters of the Irish nation."[72] Nevertheless, the voters of Cardiganshire backed the prime minister by giving Ernest Evans a reasonably comfortable victory.[73] Saunders Lewis wrote that the by-election was "disgusting. We expected Mrs Lloyd George to win, but hardly such a majority. Ireland means nothing to these people, but a handshake from Mrs George and a word that you mustn't stab Lloyd George in the back—that has won the women and men."[74]

Despite the verdict of the Cardiganshire voters, voices continued to be raised demanding that Wales acknowledge that Ireland was being governed in a manner contradictory to Nonconformist principles. As more ministers openly opposed the prime minister's Irish policy, John Hinds, MP for Carmarthen and a supporter of Lloyd George, declared, "Wales has been roused from end to end by seeing its principles and religious convictions trodden under foot, and I fear that the Government and the Prime-Minister have not realised that."[75] In April 1921, a group of twenty-seven Welsh professors and lecturers signed a letter of protest against the manner in which the authorities were handling matters in Ireland. The letter stated, "We claim, on behalf of all kindly and Christian men in Wales, to extend to our sister nation whatever comfort she may find in a genuine sympathy." Noting the lack of popular support in Wales for Ireland, the letter declared that those who had fought to establish university education in Wales in the nineteenth century "would have been overwhelmed with shame to think that their children, for whom they had toiled so painfully, should have lost the passion for righteousness and the desire to protest against all cruelty and oppression."[76] This letter produced a strong rebuke from *Y Tyst* in defense of the prime minister. An editorial noted that the letter of protest made "no reference to the horrible atrocities of the Sinn Feiners" and asked, "Should there not be some movement initiated by the teachers and the ministers of Wales to approach the leaders of Sinn Fein, and to make one great effort to induce them to change their standpoint and to accept what is safe and fair and reasonable?"[77]

Other commentators opined that the failure of the Welsh people to mobilize in support of Ireland was a betrayal not just of Nonconformist values but of Welsh nationality itself. One Welshman living in England, writing under the name "Welsh Graduate," believed that "because a Welshman happens to be the head of an administration that is doing its utmost to stamp out a similar movement in Ireland, we are too timid, too servile to speak out our minds." He believed that the Welsh people "have become so lethargic that we are content with the reflected glory of a Welshman sitting in the seats of the mighty at Downing Street. We have forgotten the past—we are unworthy of it."[78] In particular, many nationalists felt that the failure of Welsh MPs to challenge Lloyd George was a disgrace to the Welsh nation. One writer noted that although "Wales owes a heavy debt to Ireland" for Irish support of Welsh disestablishment, Welsh MPs approved of coercion in Ireland because they had made Lloyd George into a "Pope." He asked, "Shall we leave these men who have brought dishonour on Wales in their shame? It would be too cruel."[79] Another commentator, using the pseudonym "Welsh Nationalist," felt that the indifference of the Welsh people to Ireland showed "a general deterioration in our political character." He wrote that in "the old Cymru Fydd times there was in the country a real enthusiasm for enslaved peoples. . . . Wales was sufficiently sensitive to the moral character of the issue involved to stand true to the nationalist ideal against some of its most highly respected representatives and in the face of the most intense religious prejudices."[80]

This was a common theme in many of the criticisms of Welsh MPs and the Welsh public at large, namely that the idealism of Tom Ellis and the Cymru Fydd movement was being abandoned. John Arthur Price wrote that Lloyd George's government of Ireland "must cause deep pain to those who remember how his old friends Tom Ellis and Llewelyn Williams once fought for the cause of Celtic nationalism in Ireland and Wales as a holy cause, one and indivisible."[81] An anonymous writer in *Welsh Outlook* noted that in the time of Tom Ellis Wales "rejected the appeals of intolerance and passion and declared for the liberty of a sister Celtic people, and by this act placed on unassailable foundations her own claims for the recognition of her national rights." The writer continued in this vein, declaring that a "brave return of the Welsh MPs to the principles of Tom Ellis would go far to solve the Irish question."[82] Comparing the failure of Welsh MPs unfavorably to the support given to Ireland by Tom Ellis in the 1880s, Silyn Roberts predicted that "a few years hence Welshmen will speak of the betrayal of Ireland in much the same way as the Welshmen of '86 talked of the doings of Welsh soldiers in Ireland in 1798."[83]

When the war in Ireland ended and a peace settlement was signed, Lloyd George's supporters loudly praised his role in this development. Many felt that the fact that it took a Welshman to resolve the intractable Irish question that had stumped a generation of British statesmen should be a cause of celebration for all of Wales. One Welshman, D. Austin Harries, spoke for many in his letter published in the *Western Mail*:

> In bringing about a satisfactory settlement of the Irish question the Prime Minister has reached the peak of his attainment, and everyone should take his hat off to the genius who has so ably contributed to the happy conclusion of an issue which was fraught with such grave

possibilities. The achievement overshadowed anything in political history, and the Irish people are getting more than Parnell, O'Connell and Redmond demanded. Great statesman as he was, Mr. Gladstone split the Liberal party thirty six years ago in trying to find a solution, and the present achievement of Mr. Lloyd George is, surely, the most brilliant feat of statecraft on record! Well might we be proud of the "little lawyer from Wales."[84]

The *Baner ac Amserau Cymru* expressed similar sentiments when it stated, "This is without doubt the crowning triumph of his remarkable career. Wales may well feel proud of him, and may congratulate herself for having produced one who is now acclaimed as the greatest and most successful statesman in the whole world."[85] The *Herald Cymraeg* declared that Lloyd George was "the greatest political genius of his age" and said the Irish settlement was a sign that the prime minister "is a sincere lover of freedom, otherwise he could not have moved towards restoring peace in Ireland. And not only did he himself move, but he carried others with him, and this was his greatest triumph—that he enrolled Ireland's old-time enemies amongst its heartiest well-wishers."[86]

Some Welsh newspapers used the signing of the Anglo-Irish treaty as a moment to celebrate Welsh identity. The *Weekly Mail*, a Cardiff newspaper, pointed out the important role the Welsh language had played in helping achieve peace. The paper reported, "Mr. J. T. Davies, the Prime Minister's secretary, and Mr. Tom Jones, one of the secretaries of the Cabinet, talked Welsh as fluently as the Prime Minister himself, and not only important conversations took place in Welsh between them at different times, but a running translation into Welsh of important documents was made in order that there could be no possibility of leakage of their contents."[87] The Reverend Thomas Williams "Llynfi" Davies penned a celebratory poem to mark the occasion, also seeking to emphasize that the prime minister was a Welsh speaker. Entitled "Settlor of Ireland in the Welsh Language," the poem sought to celebrate the ancient languages of Ireland and Wales:

Amidst the confusion and long arguments,
And Ireland aflame underneath,
At the top of every language in the land,

Was the old language of the old shore of Wales;
Hurrah for the Welshman on top of the tower,
And Hurrah for the Welsh language to be sure!
She herself and the Irish language! May all wounds heal,
Sisters in adversity ever they have been.[88]

By emphasizing the relationship between the Welsh and Irish languages, Davies was implying that Lloyd George had been a friend, even a savior, to his fellow Celtic nationalists. The *Western Mail* made this claim more explicitly in announcing the initial cease-fire in Ireland, stating, "If the susceptibilities of the affectionate and romantic Celtic race on the other side of the Irish Sea will be soothed and their wrongs adjusted through the efforts of that other Celt now in supreme control of the negotiations what a dramatic topic will be provided for the historian of these tremendous days." They predicted that negotiations would be arduous, however, because "the Celt is an almost impossible person sometimes."[89] These comments perfectly encapsulate the flexibility that could be employed in relation to Celticness. In a single paragraph, the *Western Mail* could celebrate the Celtic connection between Ireland and Wales in praising the achievement of the cease-fire and then hint that negotiations could be slow because of Celtic (read, Irish Celtic) stubbornness.

Among Welsh nationalists who were critical of the prime minister during the conflict, there was a mixed response. An editorial in *Y Genedl Gymreig* celebrated the declaration of peace in Ireland but stated, "Amidst all the joy, Wales cannot help but feel some disappointment. A full blooded Welshman as Prime Minister, what has Wales got from the hand of the government? The attitude of the Prime Minister and the Government towards Wales is one of the weakest points of the coalition. Mr. Lloyd George has done nothing up to now apart from throwing cold water on the wishes of Wales. Under his Government there is no hope of Home Rule or even a secretary for Wales."[90] On the other hand, Thomas Huws Davies, editor of the *Welsh Outlook*, tried to restore the image of Lloyd George as a champion of nationalism after all. He wrote that when Lloyd George began peace negotiations with de Valera, it felt "as though a long plague had been lifted" from the Welsh people. Depicting Lloyd George as the man who would finally bring peace to Ireland, Huws Davies declared that it was a "great opportunity for one of the race who gave Ireland St. Patrick to hand it another blessing."[91] Huws Davies believed that, whatever had happened in Lloyd George's political career, "he must always remain at heart a Nationalist. He may talk proudly, even vainly, of his position as an Imperial Prime Minister, but by nature and tradition he will always remain a Joseph in the court of Pharaoh."[92] Not everyone was quite so eager to embrace the prodigal son of nationalist, liberal Wales. The victory of Reginald Clarry, a member of the Conservative Party, in a by-election in Newport in 1922, encouraged the Conservative Party to pull out of the coalition government, triggering Lloyd George's immediate resignation as prime minister. In the ensuing general election, the "National Liberals," who supported Lloyd George, performed poorly at the polls.[93] Thomas Huws Davies believed the cause of this split in Welsh liberalism was obvious, recording "that nowhere outside Ireland are the Irish reprisals remembered so bitterly as in Cardiganshire."[94]

In the 1880s, Ireland and its home rule campaign had been an important influence in creating the Welsh political nation. At the end of the First World War, the Irish independence struggle served as a barometer of the vitality of Welsh nationalism. Welsh nationalists found that the Principality, by its indifference to the Irish cause, was failing to live up to the standards of the Cymru Fydd era. They believed that the traditions of Welsh liberalism, Welsh Nonconformity, and Welsh nationalism were being forgotten by the Welsh people of the twentieth century and that this did not bode well for the future of the Welsh nation. But like the nationalist writers of *Welsh Outlook*, who in downplaying the Irish demand for a republic failed to understand how Ireland had changed, they failed to appreciate how Wales was changing. They didn't comprehend that it wasn't that the Welsh people had lost interest in political justice but rather that they were now more focused on issues of class rights as opposed to national rights. The mining disputes from 1919 to 1921 had created a more politically active proletariat, resulting in the Labour Party making major gains in formerly Liberal strongholds during the general elections of the 1920s.[95] In short, the Irish War of Independence killed off the old nationalism of Cymru Fydd. It demonstrated to Welsh nationalists that only a small and shrinking minority were interested in a Cardiff parliament governing Wales according to the principles of Gladstonian liberalism, while the role model for this development, Ireland, had adopted a form of statehood that was too extreme for almost everyone in Wales.

Welsh nationalists may have viewed the Irish struggle as a test of Wales' own nationalist principles, but as in the 1880s there was also interest in some quarters in how Irish methods could be used in Wales to achieve some form of self-government. Such interest in the Irish independence movement was not confined to Wales, however. Minority nationalist groups across western Europe took hope and inspiration from the efforts of Sinn Féin to establish an independent Irish state. Father Jules Callewaert, a Flemish nationalist, described members of Sinn Féin in 1922 as "good Catholics and heroes without equal" and said Ireland was a "model of self-sacrifice and ideal Catholicism."[96] Basque separatists, meanwhile, adopted Easter Sunday as *Aberri Eguna*, or "Fatherland Day," chosen to venerate devout Catholicism and the sacrifice of Irish rebels in the 1916 Rising.[97] Catalan nationalists, who had closely followed the progress of the Irish Home Rule Party under Charles Stewart Parnell, initially deplored the Easter Rising. However, disappointed by the failure of the Paris Peace Conference to discuss Catalonia's desire for independence, Catalans became more supportive of Sinn Féin. The death of Terence MacSwiney, the lord mayor of Cork, on hunger strike in 1920 saw funerals held across Catalonia in his honor.[98] While most Catalan nationalists preferred to pursue independence through constitutional means, Francesc Macià formed Estat Català in 1922, a paramilitary group modeled on the IRA. Macià hoped that an armed rebellion could be ignited, believing that even if he failed, his campaign could be a Catalan Easter Rising, instilling a new idealism among Catalans.[99] Macià was arrested and the proposed uprising never took place, but other Catalans continued to look to Ireland for inspiration in the 1930s, including Daniel Cardona, who formed a group called Nosaltres Sols, a Catalan translation of Sinn Féin.

Breton nationalists similarly hoped that they could learn from the example of the Irish independence movement. Louis Napoléon Le Roux, a Breton nationalist, published *La vie de Patrice Pearse* in 1932, writing, "The heroes of Easter Week and particularly P. Pearse became our heroes alongside the Breton heroes of the past: more real since they were our contemporaries."[100] Célestin Lainé was a Breton nationalist who said the Bretons should not "beg crumbs off the French table"[101] but should mobilize as the IRA had done, while another Breton, Olier Mordrel, stated that true Breton nationalists dreamed of making a romantic last stand as Irish rebels had done in 1916.[102] This interest in Ireland manifested itself during the Second World War, when Breton nationalists like Camille Le Mercier d'Erm rephrased the old mantra of Irish nationalists to read "France's difficulty is Brittany's opportunity." Lainé, Mordrel, and other Breton nationalists collaborated with the Nazis in the hope of establishing an independent Brittany, although ultimately their actions did much to discredit Breton culture and identity throughout France.[103]

In Wales, particularly among the writers contributing to *Welsh Outlook*, Ireland was also their source of inspiration for achieving devolution, but it was the old Irish Home Rule Party, rather than Sinn Féin, to which they looked. Indeed, Ireland served as the motor driving the hopes of Welsh home rulers. With little popular demand among the Welsh public for political autonomy, Welsh nationalists continued to hope that the Principality would receive self-government through the granting of home rule for all the nations of the United Kingdom. In particular, they believed that home rule all around was the obvious, and only, solution to the problem of Ulster. John Arthur Price stated in 1917 that a conference on British federalism would be held after the war and that "Welsh Home Rule would emerge from this conference an established fact."[104] David Davies, the Welsh industrialist who financed *Welsh Outlook*, wrote that if Ireland received home rule there was no reason "why the same principles should not be applied to Scotland and Wales, both on the grounds of nationality and also for the more efficient conduct of public affairs."[105] Others insisted that Wales could not hope to have home rule fall into its lap but would have to organize itself politically as Ireland had done. The Reverend W. D. Rowlands said he would "gladly welcome any effort put forward to create a real Welsh party, one which would wield an influence in the House of Commons similar to that wielded by the Irish party."[106] J. E. Powell, a businessman who regularly traveled to Ireland, stated that enormous progress "has been made there in every direction owing to the united and determined action of the Irish Parliamentary Party. I feel sure much more could be secured for Wales if the Welsh Members were imbued with the same spirit."[107] The Reverend Herbert Morgan believed likewise, stating that if nationalists wanted to learn how to make progress "we can very well go to school to Ireland. Their self-denying ordinance in the matter of accepting government posts is calculated to get rid of the time-serving and self-seeking ranter."[108]

Indeed, the idea that the Welsh cause could not be advanced unless nationalists made sacrifices akin to those endured by their Irish counterparts was a common theme in many of the laments about the state of Welsh politics. Edward John commented that "Ireland gets everything because Irish members get nothing. Wales gets nothing because Welsh members get everything from peerages and the Premiership downwards."[109] Another commentator observed that the "leaders of Irish Nationalism live a great deal of their time in gaol, and many of them die on the gallows. In Wales they live in comfort, and die with a considerable amount of property to dispose of under their wills."[110] Yet despite these calls to action, very little was done during the Irish War of Independence to form a Welsh political party. A series of conferences were held in Wales from 1918 to 1922 in the hopes of finding a path to devolution in the Principality. In August 1920, a few Welsh MPs approached Lloyd George about the possibility of the government creating a secretary for Wales, an office that already existed for Ireland and Scotland. Lloyd George politely demurred. The *Baner ac Amersau Cymru* expressed disappointment in Lloyd George's attitude and asked, "Is it not high time that Wales should draft a Home Rule Bill for itself? A measure on these lines has already been drafted and printed by Mr. E. T. John, and we suggest that that contains much matter that would suit excellently in a new measure."[111] The writer "Bera" in *Y Darian* went further, exclaiming, "It is high time we Welshmen should tell the Englishman very plainly that we will no longer be ruled by him—not ask him in fear and trembling will he be kind enough to let us have a Secretary of State, but tell him that as a nation, and a nation with a glorious history before he was heard of, we demand the right to govern ourselves. We can assure him that he need have no anxiety for his own Empire in the event of our being enfranchised."[112]

The announcement that a treaty had been signed between Irish representatives and the British government in December 1921 produced a flurry of activity among Welsh nationalists who felt some measure of autonomy might be extended to Wales also. "Wales' duty is to profit from the example of Ireland," stated *Yr Herald Cymraeg*. "The obvious moral is that we must press forward some definite scheme. Ireland succeeded by making all things serve its own ends, and we must act likewise if we are to have any measure of success."[113] John "Dyfnallt" Owen lamented that Welsh MPs had failed to raise the issue of Wales when the Irish settlement was debated in Westminster. He urged, "The whole encampment must be set ablaze! This is the hour. It is cast in our face that there is no demand in the land for self-government and freedom for Wales. Ireland has saved her soul at the cost of a great sacrifice, and we are about to lose it owing to a carelessness that is rotting our sinews."[114] These views were far from unanimous. One journalist wrote that these calls were put forward by a tiny number of people who opposed the prime minister, noting, "These people in Wales are, as regards bitterness of spirit, though not of equal numbers, comparable to the De Valeras in Ireland. . . . We hope that Snowdon will never be found to give shelter to a clique which will conspire treachery towards a statesman in whom Wales has been so greatly honoured."[115]

In 1922, a Government of Wales Bill, introduced by Sir Robert Thomas, and a Government of Scotland and Wales Bill, introduced by the Scottish MP Murray MacDonald, offered a glimmer of hope, but nothing came of either. Beriah Gwynfe Evans, the former secretary of Cymru Fydd, described this as a "fiasco."[116] In truth, the changing political situation in Ireland did much to deflate the Welsh home rule cause. The presence of a large number of Irish Home Rule MPs in Parliament had been the engine to which Welsh home rulers had hitched their wagon in the past, but with Irish representatives now removed from Westminster, the limping campaign for Welsh self-government was devoid of impetus. As David Davies noted, the "repeated failures to settle the Irish controversy always gave the devolutionists an opportunity of bringing forward their case."[117] By 1922, the Irish home rule cause no longer existed to prop up its Welsh counterpart, and the Irish Free State was not a role model that former Cymru Fydd supporters aspired to. Ireland, it seemed, was no longer nearly as relevant in the Welsh political landscape.

Yet the Sinn Féin movement and the Irish War of Independence did catch the imagination of a new generation of Welsh nationalists, who believed that aspects of Ireland's national struggle could be adopted to the Welsh cause. One of the strongest advocates for a more proactive Welsh nationalism was the *Druid*, a Welsh American newspaper published in Pittsburgh. In the immediate aftermath of the Irish War of Independence, the newspaper cautioned that "Sinn Féinism" was growing in Wales, something to be viewed as a negative development. It noted that among Welsh university students there were many "who openly champion Sinn Feinism, for, as one of them recently declared, 'no true Welshman can fail to sympathize with such a movement, if thereby Welsh rights may be won as were Irish rights by Sinn Fein.'"[118] However, as the prospect of Welsh home rule faded over the course of 1922, the *Druid* began to change tack, suggesting that "Wales must emulate Ireland and assume a more pugnacious attitude if she is to realize her ideals and aspirations."[119] The newspaper repeated one of the standard claims of Welsh nationalism, namely, that Irish national spirit prospered because those serving its cause were willing to make sacrifices. "Irish patriots were imbued with one purpose, and they held to it steadfastly—that Ireland was a nation, and in the attainment of this purpose they rejected every alluring proposal that conflicted with their avowed declaration that all authority, political and judicial, for the government of Ireland was derived from the people. This is a practical object lesson for the constitution-mongers of Wales, who are blinded by gaudy and tinselled imperialistic epaulets and forget that Wales was a nation long before the Saxon invaded the British Isles." The *Druid* dismissed the fact that Ireland was currently embroiled in a civil war, stating that this state of affairs would soon pass, and insisted, "Until Wales manifests the same persistent attitude as Ireland, the Principality will be merely chasing a rainbow in its quest for Home Rule."[120]

The Druid hinted at the possible need for a Welsh Sinn Féin, without ever calling for it directly, because "Sinn Fein is a term that does not appeal to the average Welshman, for the alleged reason that it has fostered many violent acts in Ireland, the land of its inception."[121] Some Welsh nationalists, however, like Reverend Fred Jones of Treorchy, were not shy about explicitly demanding a Welsh form of Sinn Féinism. At a speech to the National Union of Welsh Societies in Bridgend in 1923, Jones pointed out that Sinn Féin had delivered self-rule to Ireland after decades of constitutional politics had failed. He declared, "Wales has been loyal to Great Britain, and the Principality, in proportion to her size and population, did as much, if not more, than any other part of the United Kingdom to save her in the most critical part of her history. And what is the meed of her gratitude? There is not a semblance of it in evidence in her action, for her gratitude is best expressed in her innate desire to crush Wales and her ancient language and make her a part and parcel of England." Jones was adamant that "if Welsh Sinn Feinism will avert this calamity, then every true Welshman should enlist under its banner. If it will save the integrity of Wales as a nation and perpetuate her ancient language, her ideals and aspirations, let Sinn Fein in lieu of a better medium, serve as a means to attain that objective."[122]

Jones was not alone in seeking to find a Welsh equivalent to Sinn Féin. Saunders Lewis would become the principal architect behind the formation of Plaid Genedlaethol Cymru (the National Party of Wales) in 1925.[123] J. Graham Jones has written that Lewis "was anxious to dissociate Plaid Cymru from de Valera and the Sinn Fein movement."[124] In fact, letters from Saunders Lewis to his fiancée, Margaret Gilcriest, during the Irish conflict reveal that he was fascinated by the Irish independence movement and hoped to replicate certain aspects of it in Wales. Lewis had long admired the writers of the Irish literary revival, and in 1920 he began learning the Irish language. Although he initially found the language "very difficult," he was soon exchanging letters entirely in Irish with Thomas Gwynn Jones, and he told his wife of his dream to someday live in the Irish-speaking regions of Ireland.[125] He was horrified by government actions in Ireland, and sarcastically asked, "Isn't Lloyd George the grand Welshman and true Celt? I'm proud to sign myself his countryman—I suppose Cromwell must have been Welsh too."[126]

Lewis was unambiguous about his admiration for Sinn Féin, writing, "Nothing proves to me the rightness of the Sinn Fein cause so much as the fact that every poet and artist in Ireland is devoted to it." After a truce had been announced in Ireland, Lewis declared to Gilcriest, "Ireland must be treated with as a separate nation, and it's the great victory of Sinn Fein. When Dominion government comes, won't you want to live in the free Ireland? I think I'll adopt its nationality."[127] Lewis commented several times about the idea of creating a Welsh Sinn Féin. He told Gilcriest that he had a revolver and "I am keeping it for the Welsh Sinn Fein which is to start in Cardiff this year—next year—sometime—never." Speaking of his efforts to create Welsh-language societies in Cardiff, he wrote, "If you only knew how our Sinn Fein movement is growing in south Wales." Working as a county librarian in Glamorganshire, Lewis boasted that the "library grows, but its chief interest is as a centre of Sinn Fein propaganda for Welsh literature." When interviewed for a teaching position at the University of Wales, Swansea, Lewis recalled, "They examined me for nearly an hour on Sinn Fein in Wales. I was never so flattered in my life." Having been successful in his application, he told Gilcriest that "students who pass through my classes will be soundly inoculated with good Sinn Fein principles!!"[128]

At this stage, Lewis was also an admirer of de Valera. He told his fiancée that "de Valera is a great statesman . . . for he's got principle and courage."[129] That view would change. J. Graham Jones asserts that Lewis did not want Plaid Cymru having anything to do with Sinn Féin; in fact, it is more accurate to say that Lewis did not want Plaid Cymru to have any connection with de Valera. Having met de Valera after the Irish Civil War, Lewis found him to be "drunken, windy and disorganized."[130] But despite disliking de Valera personally, Lewis was to adopt many Sinn Féin ideas, particularly the political philosophy of Arthur Griffith, in devising a program for Plaid Cymru.

But Lewis and Fred Jones were not the only founding members of Plaid Cymru to be interested in Sinn Féin. Huw Robert Jones was a Welsh salesman who was fascinated by the military campaign of Sinn Féin. Lewis described him as the only Welsh nationalist who "would have received a post from Michael Collins."[131] Jones formed the Byddin Ymreolwyr Cymru (Welsh Home Rule Army) in 1924 and appears to have contemplated the possibility of using violence to achieve self-government for Wales. When the Byddin Ymreolwyr Cymru held a demonstration in Caernarfon in November 1924, many in the English media were outraged. The *Druid* newspaper rushed to the defense of the group, writing:

> Ireland remonstrated for years against tyrannical and despotic officials, and only after a warfare that caused much unnecessary bloodshed did truth eventually triumph the removal of the irksome Saxon yoke. Wales, whose loyalty to the British throne has been unflinching, has serious grievances which should have been remedied long ago. . . . Whether Wales' demands shall be achieved through peaceful methods rests with the government, for in the event that Wales is forced to emulate Ireland's drastic tactics, no-one but the government itself will be responsible for the consequences, for right and justice, sooner or later, must prevail.[132]

The Byddin Ymreolwyr Cymru, however, were a minority within a minority in considering the possibility of violence. Unlike some radical nationalists in Breton and Catalan circles, young Welsh nationalists did not want to copy Sinn Féin's military tactics but were interested in Arthur

Griffith's idea of using passive resistance to create an autonomous government that could safeguard the nation's culture and language. Sinn Féin's electoral manifesto of 1918 promised that party candidates would not take their seats at Westminster but rather would form their own parliament in Dublin. They believed that if the Irish people accepted this body as their government, then ultimately the British state would have to accept its legitimacy and Irish autonomy would be achieved. The practicality of this plan was never tested, however. The Irish Republican Army, independently of the Sinn Féin Dáil, began a campaign of violence against British forces in Ireland on the same day as the Dáil's first meeting in January 1919. David John Williams, the Oxford graduate who had written approvingly of the 1916 Rising, crossed over to Ireland in 1919. Meeting with Arthur Griffith and visiting the proscribed Dáil, he was highly impressed by the organization and commitment of the Irish nationalists.[133] On returning to Wales, Williams spoke to one Irishman about the success of the Dáil. The Irishman told him that Wales already had its own de Valera, Collins, and Griffith and that among the young Welsh nationalists "you have the nucleus of a Welsh Cabinet as truly representative of the genius of Wales as the others are of the spirit of Ireland." Williams was flattered by the comparison, and wrote, "Wales, I said to myself, will draw its political inspiration for the future either from Ireland and the Italy of Mazzini or from Bunyan's Pilgrim's Progress."[134] Williams also admired the efforts of the Irish Free State to promote the Irish language, writing that the "Irish government has realized that Ireland without the Irish language is a negation in terms." He called for similar efforts to be made in Wales to promote Welsh.[135]

In 1925, Jones's Byddin Ymreolwyr Cymru merged with Saunders Lewis and Fred Jones's Mudiad Cymreig (Welsh Movement) to form Plaid Cymru. The primary aim of Plaid Cymru was to preserve the Welsh language and encourage its growth in areas where it was not regularly spoken. Despite having once boasted privately about possessing a revolver to use in the name of a Welsh Sinn Féin, Lewis was clear that "there will be no need for war, nor the shedding of blood, and our policy does not lead to that."[136] Reporting on the formation of Plaid Cymru, the *Druid* observed, "The party aims to fight along constitutional lines and will not, for the present, resort to the tactics of the Sinn Fein movement, which many declare justifiable because Ireland had utterly failed to secure freedom and recognition along constitutional lines."[137] However, this newspaper constantly hinted that going beyond political actions might be in the best interests of Wales. When the Powys Eisteddfod Association passed a motion protesting the appointment of a chief constable in Montgomeryshire who could not speak Welsh, the *Druid* retorted, "Such passive action is merely a waste of words and time, and the members of the Eisteddfod Association, if they covet the hope of perpetuating the Welsh language and fostering the ideals and aspirations of Wales, should cross the Irish Sea and take a course from their Irish cousins in the art of meting punishment to base traitors."[138]

By 1925, such ideas were anathema to Saunders Lewis. However, for him, there were two distinct branches of Sinn Féinism. One was the use of violence to achieve political ends, as the IRA had done in Ireland. This Lewis ruled out completely, but he did believe that Plaid Cymru could borrow ideas from Sinn Féin's political philosophy, namely the development of a political party that was self-reliant and completely free of influence from the English political system. He declared that Plaid Cymru insisted "its members break the connection with English parties, and refuse to send representatives to the English parliament."[139] Lewis did not specifically refer to Arthur Griffith's ideas in saying this, but the influence is obvious. Plaid Cymru did not aspire to Irish-style independence, however; Lewis stated, "Let us not ask for independence for Wales, not because it is impractical, but because it is not worth having." This was not to say that some measure of self-government was not important. Lewis maintained that "the government of Wales must be Welsh in spirit and language. That being so, we must have self-government."[140] This concept of using political autonomy to establish a minority indigenous culture as the predominant feature of national life, to make, in Lewis's words, "Welsh Wales a fact," was also clearly modeled on the Sinn Féin example.[141] Ironically, Sinn Féin's pursuit of an "Irish Ireland" can be traced back to Richard Henerby's letter to Eoin MacNeill in 1899, advising MacNeill to copy the term *Welsh Wales* in Ireland to shame people into embracing Gaelic culture.

Despite the strong interest in Sinn Féin among some of Plaid Cymru's founders, the policy of abstention from Westminster was not maintained. In 1930, members of Plaid Cymru advocated contesting parliamentary elections. D. J. Davies, one of the founding members of Plaid Cymru, pointed out that the Sinn Féin boycott of Westminster was accepted by the Irish people only because decades of promoting home rule in Parliament had failed. Lewis opposed changing the policy of Plaid Cymru but eventually relented to the wishes of the majority.[142] Plaid Cymru was to remain an insignificant body in Welsh politics for decades, with Gwynfor Evans the first elected Plaid Cymru MP in 1966. But as a movement, it has steadily grown in national importance in Wales in recent decades, thereby indirectly preserving the last major influence of Irish politics in the Principality.

In conclusion, the Irish Revolution produced a crisis in Welsh nationalism. It forced the remnants of the Cymru Fydd movement to choose between their former leader and the country that had been a considerable source of inspiration for them in the past. While the majority of the Welsh population disapproved strongly of Irish nationalists using violence to achieve their goals, most Welsh nationalists were horrified that Lloyd George could approve gross injustices in his bid to pacify Ireland. As a result, they tended to sympathize with the cause of Irish nationalism, even as they believed that the fullest extent of Sinn Féin demands were too extreme. Yet their support of Irish home rule, as opposed to an Irish republic, only highlighted how out of touch the Cymru Fydd idealists were with the changing reality both at home and across the Irish Sea. The cause of Welsh political nationalism and the possibility of a measure of autonomy for Wales had been built upon the dual pillars of Irish home rule activity and an appeal to the principles of the Liberal Party. By 1925, Irish home rule was dead, the Liberal Party was dying, and Welsh political nationalism had nowhere to turn. Some younger Welsh nationalists recognized this and sought to forge a replacement for the old Cymru Fydd approach. Their role model was Sinn Féin, which had married Irish constitutional politics with the zeal of cultural nationalism to create a vibrant new political movement. This ideology influenced the founders of Plaid Cymru, who identified the Welsh language and culture as the central markers of Welsh nationhood and sought political solutions to ensure their preservation. Paradoxically, however, the very success of Sinn Féin removed Ireland as an influence on the Welsh political landscape. Irish independence meant the end of mainstream, secessionist, constitutional nationalism in British politics for a century. Without Irish MPs in Westminster, the possibility of Welsh political autonomy shifted from unlikely to fantastical. Furthermore, Sinn Féin's triumph gave credence to those who had always maintained that home rule activism would inevitably lead to independence demands and that it was therefore incompatible with loyalty to the British state. Just as the achievement of independence convinced Irish cultural nationalists that they no longer could learn lessons from Wales, Welsh political nationalists increasingly struggled to look across the Irish Sea and see something they wished to emulate. Even those who aspired to develop a form of Welsh Sinn Féinism were primarily interested in Irish means rather than Irish ends, and as the Irish question became a distant memory in Britain, Ireland's political influence on Wales faded.

CONCLUSION

In 1924, Cecile O'Rahilly published *Ireland and Wales: Their Historical and Literary Relations*. O'Rahilly was a scholar of medieval Celtic literature, and the bulk of her book focused on representations of Ireland and Wales in the respective corpuses of old Irish and Welsh manuscripts. She also briefly commented on the increased interest in Irish and Welsh connections that had developed over the course of her lifetime. O'Rahilly attributed this to the growth of mutual study of the two languages. This, she stated, had led to the establishment of a chair of Welsh at University College Dublin and another chair at St. Patrick's College, Maynooth. O'Rahilly was sure that "in due course of time, separate chairs and lectureships will be established in the other colleges of the National University of Ireland." She noted, however, that in the reciprocal study of Irish, Wales was lagging behind, as none of the four constituent colleges of Wales had a chair in Irish.[1] Furthermore, she claimed that, in relation to wider Irish issues, "Wales has shown little sympathy with Ireland in the present century." O'Rahilly did, however, fondly recall the great support shown by Tom Ellis for the cause of Irish home rule in the nineteenth century and the manner in which Irish political agitation had contributed to the Welsh disestablishment campaign.[2] She hoped that her book could help promote further growth in Irish and Welsh relations, writing, "It is a matter of no small importance both to Wales and to Ireland that this modern development of a feeling of kinship should be fostered in both countries. The study of each other's language and literature in both countries alike will help Ireland in the task of conserving her language, [and] will guarantee to Welsh its present proud position among the Celtic languages."[3]

In some ways, the early 1920s represented the highwater mark for collective interest between Irish and Welsh nationalists in each other's respective affairs. Despite O'Rahilly's hopes, Welsh universities never did promote Irish studies among their students, and enthusiasm for the Welsh language waned among Irish students. But the two peoples' interest in each another's affairs did not disappear completely. Once Lloyd George's comments about the Welsh language during the Irish War of Independence were forgotten, Irish politicians occasionally used the Welsh once more as role models for the revival of the Irish language.[4] In 1946, Éamon de Valera wrote a message in Irish and Welsh that appeared in *Y Ddraig Goch*, the journal of Plaid Cymru. He declared that a "strong link binds the people of Wales and Ireland together, not only because they derive from the same Celtic stock but . . . by the passionate desire of the two nations to preserve their cultures."[5] When Welsh protesters opposed the development of a reservoir to supply water to Liverpool in the 1950s, as it would flood the village of Capel Celyn, they wrote to ask Éamon de Valera for his support. De Valera replied that he had the greatest sympathy with their efforts to preserve Capel Celyn.[6] In brief, Irish and Welsh nationalists continued to show interest in each other's respective countries after the Irish War of Independence but, as I have argued above, not with the same eagerness or relevance that they had for the previous half century or so.

Indeed, Ireland's secession from the United Kingdom meant that Irish political developments no longer earned the same attention in Britain, and Ireland's association with independence from, if not outright hostility toward, Britain meant that it was not a positive role model for the majority of Welsh nationalists who sought limited autonomy for their nation. On top of this, the outbreak of the Troubles, which led to bombings and murders in England, only accentuated the connection between Irish nationalism, fanaticism, and extreme violence, making Ireland even more unsuitable as an inspiration to those who wanted a measure of Welsh self-government.

Yet as Ireland has faded from relevance on the Welsh political scene, Welsh political nationalism has grown, culminating in the referendum to establish a Welsh Assembly in 1997. Plaid Cymru has become a major player in Welsh politics, although it has never attained the dominance that the Irish Parliamentary Party once had in Ireland, or that the Scottish National Party currently enjoys in Scotland. Indeed, the small minority of Welsh people who express support for political independence look to Scotland and the SNP, rather than to Ireland, for inspiration. This is hardly surprising. Just as the Irish Home Rule Party was the vibrant nationalist force within the British state at the turn of the twentieth century, this role has been taken up by the Scottish National Party today. Ironically, the success of Irish nationalists in actually attaining independence from the United Kingdom is less relevant to those supporting Welsh independence because almost a century of separation has created the impression that Ireland was always an anomaly in the British state, in a way that Scotland is not.

On the other hand, in debates about the promotion of the Irish language in Ireland, the Welsh example is still used as an example of what can be done to improve the status of Ireland's indigenous tongue. In September 2016, Dan Boyle, a former TD in the Dáil, compared the position of the Irish and Welsh languages, drawing on his experience working in Wales: "I was really impressed with how the Welsh have made their language a living language. From what I could see this has been because of the emphasis on spoken language, as opposed to the defeatist emphasis on grammar in how Irish is taught. . . . Most of the interactions the Welsh have with their language are seen to be positive. . . . It has made me want to acquire some *cúpla focal eile*."[7] Meanwhile, in the weeks before the February 2016 general election in Ireland, the short-lived political party Renua issued its party manifesto. Tucked away at the back of the document was a reference to the party's Irish-language policy:

> With English established as the language of commerce in an increasingly globalized economic environment, our national language is at a crossroads. Either we allow it to increase its slow downward trend towards extinction, or as a nation, we collectively decide to arrest its decline and embrace the most fundamental aspect of our national identity. We believe that the modern revival of the Welsh language provides a roadmap for a revitalization of the Irish language. Ireland can and will rediscover the pride it has for its native tongue and the great cultural and artistic history that goes with it.[8]

The idea that Welsh has been "revived" in recent times and offers a lesson for those seeking to spread the use of the Irish language is regularly put forward by people commenting on online articles about the promotion of Irish. Of course, this provides a historical echo to the rallying cry of the Gaelic League at the turn of the twentieth century, namely that Welsh has been revived and the same can be done for Irish. And, as in the past, this idea of a Welsh revival is largely a figment of the Irish imagination. Certainly the Welsh language has become more visible across Wales in recent decades, with Welsh-medium education becoming increasingly popular in parts of the country that had become predominantly English speaking. However, census figures show a steady decline in the percentage of the Welsh population who could speak Welsh over the course of the twentieth century. A modest increase in these figures was recorded in the 2001 census, up to 20.8 percent from 18.7 percent in 1991, but this dropped back to 19 percent in the 2011 census. Furthermore, in predominantly Welsh-speaking areas the percentage of people who can speak Welsh has continued to fall. In other words, while the number of people who can (but not necessarily do) speak Welsh is being bolstered by a growth in Welsh-medium education, the number of people who use Welsh daily as a community language is falling. Undoubtedly, Irish people who might visit areas like Gwynedd would be astounded with the vitality of the Welsh language compared to that of Irish in Ireland, even in Gaeltacht regions. It may be that Irish visitors to Wales, who spend some time in Welsh-speaking areas and who hear of increasingly positive attitudes toward the Welsh language generally, believe that the former has been created by the latter. In reality, the two are somewhat unrelated. The strength of certain Welsh-speaking areas, likely to be impressive to Irish visitors, is the result of the language declining much more slowly there compared to Irish-speaking areas rather than the result of a Welsh-language revival. The growth of the Welsh-language education system certainly is producing more Welsh speakers in areas that had become primarily English speaking, but it resembles the Gaelscoileanna movement in Ireland in that it is not changing the primary language through which most of its students live and work once they leave school. In short, there is no real Welsh revival that can serve as a role model for how to revive Irish. However, so long as the Welsh language remains stronger as a community language than its Irish equivalent, there are likely going to be Irish people who believe that the Welsh can teach their Celtic cousins about language revival.

What is the future for the relationship between Ireland and Wales? The uncertainty in the wake of the decision of the electorate of the United Kingdom to leave the European Union could lead to significant political changes in the islands of Britain and Ireland. Already, *Irish Times* journalist Fintan O'Toole has suggested the possibility of a new state that unites Ireland, Northern Ireland, and Scotland.[9] This seems highly unlikely. However, one assumes that if Scotland leaves the United Kingdom, and the reunification of Ireland and Northern Ireland takes place, Welsh nationalists will demand independence in part on the basis that this has already been achieved by the other "Celtic" countries. Whether the wider Welsh population would be responsive to such suggestions remains to be seen. Undoubtedly, as dynamic political, social, and economic changes continue to take place in Britain and Ireland, one might imagine a time in the future when Welsh and Irish interests will closely merge once again. If they do, it seems inevitable that the shared Celtic heritage and history of the two populations, both ancient and modern, will once more be deployed as a justification for why the Irish and Welsh should cooperate with, and learn from, their fellow Celts across the Irish Sea.

Indeed, the Celtic connection between the two countries has continued to be celebrated since the 1920s. The Pan-Celtic congress established by Edward John continued even after his death in 1931, allowing scholars and musicians to come together to acknowledge their shared heritage. Pan-Celticism still endures in the twenty-first century through a number of organizations, although these groups do not attract much in the way of publicity. A Pan-Celtic music festival is held every year in Ireland, with performers representing the six Celtic nations competing for the title of best Celtic act. The International Celtic Congress, founded by John, is still in existence, dedicated to holding an annual conference in one of the Celtic countries and giving attendees an opportunity to hear lectures and visit sites connected to Celtic history and culture. The Celtic League is a political Pan-Celtic body that promotes independence for all the Celtic nations and produces a Pan-Celtic magazine, *Carn*. In short, today, much as in the time period covered in this book, the existence of a common Celtic identity across the various Celtic countries is widely acknowledged, but only a few people seek to promote and deepen ties between these nations. Most people in Ireland or Wales would probably agree that their nation is a "Celtic" one. However, evidence that people in either country feel a strong affinity for other Celtic nations is thin. If a common sense of Celtic kinship can be said to exist at all across the populations of Ireland, Wales, and Scotland, it probably extends no more than to general well wishes toward the soccer and rugby teams of the other Celtic nations.

Yet even this shallow, but broad, sense of Celticness could disappear over the twenty-first century. Since the middle of the nineteenth century, Celticness has been synonymous with Irishness, Welshness, or Scottishness. It has been easy to imagine that the people who lived in Ireland, Wales, and Scotland were almost a homogeneous Celtic population, especially if one ignored the history of mass movement into and out of these countries. As noted in the Introduction, the concept of Celtic identity has always implied, though rarely articulated, a sense of racial kinship. In that sense, people saw being Irish and being Celtic, or being Welsh and being Celtic, as one and the same thing.

But the migration of people from outside Europe to the Celtic countries threatens to undermine this link between national identity and a wider sense of Celtic heritage. In blunt terms, being Celtic has implicitly meant being white, and as the populations of Ireland, Wales, and Scotland become more ethnically diverse the relationship between national identity and a broader Celtic identity is likely to become problematic. One can be black and Welsh, but can one be black and Celtic? Undoubtedly, some would deny that Celticness is based on any kind of racial status, and they might argue that a Celtic identity is open to anyone who can speak a Celtic language or participate in Celtic music and Celtic dance. The problem with this, as noted in the Introduction, is that the Celtic languages and Celtic cultural activities are minority interests within their respective countries and, as things currently stand, cannot be the basis for the Celtic identity claimed by the majority of people in the various Celtic nations.

Furthermore, white supremacist groups across the Western world have co-opted Celtic symbols into their iconography in recent decades.[10] They have revived the link between Celticness and racial identity, which had been all but ignored by wider society as a result of the revulsion for "blood nationalism" in the wake of the Second World War. That Celticness would hold considerable appeal for white supremacists is hardly surprising. Ernest Renan and Matthew Arnold helped create the original myth of Celtic purity in the nineteenth century, describing a people whose characteristics were unchanging over vast stretches of time and who resisted the advances of the modern world. It doesn't require a great deal of imagination to see how this story of an "unsullied" Celtic people could be adopted and tweaked to suit the purposes of modern white nationalism. Stormfront.org, one of the largest neo-Nazi websites, uses a Celtic cross as its logo. Indeed, Celtic crosses have replaced swastikas in many of the flags flown by white supremacists in Europe and the United States, with Celtic cross tattoos also increasingly common among them. While neo-Nazi groups appear to have very little popular support in Ireland and Wales, one does not have to search too hard online to discover that they are also using the Celtic cross to represent their brand of identity politics. Should these groups grow, and should their racial sense of Celticness become more widely known, serious questions might be raised about what being Celtic really means.

Since the middle of the nineteenth century, the word *Celtic* has been employed as a convenient synonym for *Irish*, *Welsh*, and/or *Scottish*. But this may become a thing of the past, as immigration into these countries is creating a shift from an ethnic sense of national identity to a civic one. Put simply, the parameters of Irishness, Welshness, and Scottishness can be expanded to include immigrants and other groups. This is because these identities are based on political entities. To be Irish, in the eyes of both the Irish state and the majority of the population, is to hold Irish citizenship, and citizenship is open to anyone, regardless of color or creed. Although Wales and Scotland are not nation-states, they are political entities, and a similar sense of individual "belonging" through civic participation exists. But Celticness is not as flexible in terms of who can self-identify as a Celt. There is no Celtic nation-state, no Celtia, that needs to redefine what it means to be Celtic, and as a result, Celticness retains a sense that it is based on race. In the same way that Celticness became a central part of Welshness and Irishness in the nineteenth century, it is possible that the twenty-first century will witness a disentangling of these identities once more.

NOTES

Abbreviations in Notes

AOB	Art Ó Briain Papers
BMH	Bureau of Military History
CAS	Castletown Papers
DON	Doneraile Papers
JOH	Edward Thomas John Papers
MacC	Fionán MacColuim Papers
McC	McCall Papers
McN	MacNeill Papers
Min-GL	Minute Books of the Executive Council of the Gaelic League
NLI	National Library of Ireland
NLW	National Library of Wales
SPIL	Society for the Preservation of the Irish Language
TGJ	Thomas Gwynn Jones Papers
WS	Witness Statement

Introduction

1. Paul O'Leary, "Accommodation and Resistance," 123.
2. Mac Cana, "Ireland and Wales," 17.
3. Wmffre, "Post-Roman Irish Settlement," 46.
4. Ibid., 61.
5. Thomas Gwynn Jones, "The Celtic Tradition," lecture presented at University College Cork, 1925, in Thomas Gwynn Jones Papers, (hereafter TGJ), National Library of Wales (hereafter NLW), D354.
6. Mac Cana, "Ireland and Wales," 29.
7. O'Rahilly, *Ireland and Wales*, 52–58.
8. Mac Cana, "Ireland and Wales," 30.

9. O'Rahilly, *Ireland and Wales*, 64–69.

10. Etchingham, "Viking Age Gwynedd," 150.

11. Ibid., 160.

12. O'Rahilly, *Ireland and Wales*, 74–78.

13. Mac Cana, "Ireland and Wales," 39–40.

14. Duffy, "1169 Invasion," 98.

15. Ibid., 106–13.

16. Mac Cana, "Ireland and Wales," 43.

17. Ibid., 45.

18. O'Rahilly, *Ireland and Wales*, 82–83.

19. Mac Cana, "Ireland and Wales," 27; Sims-Williams, "Celtomania and Celtoscepticism," 14.

20. O'Rahilly, *Ireland and Wales*, 84–87.

21. Paul O'Leary, *Immigration and Integration*.

22. Newby, *Ireland, Radicalism;* Jackson, *Two Unions;* Ó Catháin, *Irish Republicanism in Scotland.*

23. Coupland, *Welsh and Scottish Nationalism.*

24. Sahlins, *Boundaries.*

25. Kiberd, *Inventing Ireland*, 2.

26. G. Williams, "When Was Wales?," 192–204.

CHAPTER 1.   The Coming of the Celts

1. Leslie et al., "Fine-Scale Genetic Structure," 309–14.

2. Pallab Ghosh, "DNA Study Shows Celts Are Not a Unique Genetic Group," BBC News, March 18, 2015, www.bbc.com/news/science-environment -31905764; *Daily Mail*, March 18, 2015.

3. Pittock, *Celtic Identity*, 111; *Irish Independent*, June 20, 2014.

4. Pittock, *Celtic Identity*, 1.

5. Chapman, *Celts*, 69.

6. James, *Atlantic Celts*, 36–40.

7. Sims-Williams, *Irish Influence*, 4.

8. Buchanan, *History of Scotland*, 80.

9. Ibid., 97.

10. P. Morgan "Abbé Pezron," 288.

11. P. Morgan, "From a Death," 68.

12. Pezron, *Antiquities of Nations*, 233.

13. Nice, *Sacred History*, 10–11.

14. Pezron, *Antiquities of Nations*, 195.

15. James, *Atlantic Celts*, 45.
16. Lhuyd, *Archaeologia Brittanica*, 1.
17. James, *Atlantic Celts*, 45; Lhuyd, *Archaeologia Britannica*, 293.
18. James, *Atlantic Celts*, 46–47.
19. Bradshaw, "English Reformation," 47.
20. Pittock, *Celtic Identity*, 24–36.
21. Nott and Gliddon, *Types of Mankind*, 314–15.
22. Renan, *Poetry*, 4–5.
23. Ibid., 1–2.
24. Ibid., 2.
25. Davis, *Development of Celtic Linguistics*, xi–xiv.
26. Koch, *Celtic Culture*, 4:1070–71.
27. Ibid.
28. Arnold, *Celtic Literature*, 100–102.
29. Ibid., 102.
30. Ibid., 104–5.
31. Ibid., 105.
32. Ibid., 109.
33. James, *Atlantic Celts*, 137.

CHAPTER 2.   A Celtic Paradise

This chapter is a revised and expanded version of my article "A Gallant Little Tírín: The Welsh Influence on Irish Culture Nationalism," which appeared in *Irish Historical Studies* 39, no. 153 (May 2014): 58–75. The material that appeared in this article is reproduced with the kind permission of Robert Armstrong, editor of *Irish Historical Studies*.

1. *Irish Press*, July 10, 1934.
2. Newspaper clipping, n.d., in Douglas Hyde Papers, National Library of Ireland, (hereafter NLI), MS 28,909 (13).
3. Nelson, *Irish Nationalists*, 11.
4. Hutchinson, *Dynamics of Cultural Nationalism*, 36.
5. Deane, introduction to Eagleton, Jameson, and Said, *Nationalism, Colonialism and Literature*, 7.
6. Kibred, *Inventing Ireland*, 1.
7. Greene, "Founding of the Gaelic League," 16.
8. Janet Davies, *Welsh Language*, 36–53.
9. *Anglo-Celt*, February 27, 1909.
10. *Nation*, August 27, 1864.

11. Ibid., October 4, 1844.

12. Ibid., August 27, 1864.

13. Ibid., October 19, 1844.

14. Ibid., August 27, 1864.

15. Ibid., October 23, 1875.

16. Ibid., October 12, 1844.

17. SPIL, Report, December 29, 1876, in NLI, P 9173.

18. SPIL, Annual Report for 1882, 10–15, in Minute Books of the Council of the SPIL, NLI, MS 32,630.

19. Minute Books of the Executive Council of the Gaelic League, November 1, 1893 (hereafter Min-GL), in NLI, MS 19,315.

20. Gaelic League, *The Means and Objectives of the Gaelic League* (Dublin, 1896), in NLI, IR 49,162.

21. Hogan to MacNeill, October 3, 1894, in MacNeill Papers (hereafter McN), NLI, MS 10,881.

22. *Freeman's Journal*, February 1, 1896.

23. "Report of the Gaelic League for Two Years Ending September 30th, 1896," in McN, NLI, MS 10,900.

24. *Anglo-Celt*, October 26, 1907.

25. *Fáinne an Lae*, January 22, 1898.

26. *Southern Star*, October 27, 1900.

27. *Freeman's Journal*, May 15, 1877.

28. *Freeman's Journal*, April 30, 1899.

29. *Connaught Telegraph*, January 5, 1907.

30. Ibid.

31. *An Claidheamh Soluis*, December 30, 1899.

32. *Southern Star*, October 27, 1900.

33. *Tuam Herald*, October 23, 1897.

34. *Southern Star*, October 27, 1900.

35. *An Claidheamh Soluis*, December 30, 1899, 657.

36. M. Williams, *At Anchor in Dublin*, 34.

37. *Nation*, September 8, 1888.

38. *Connaught Telegraph*, April 27, 1907.

39. *Nation*, January 16, 1875.

40. *Southern Star*, March 7, 1908.

41. *Nation*, September 13, 1890.

42. *Fáinne an Lae*, February 12, 1898.

43. Ibid.

44. *Fáinne an Lae*, April 9, 1898.

45. *An Claidheamh Soluis*, July 22, 1899.

46. *Anglo-Celt*, December 29, 1900; *Meath Chronicle*, December 29, 1900.

47. *Nation*, October 2, 1880.

48. SPIL, Report of the SPIL, 1892, in NLI, P 9173.

49. *Kildare Observer*, March 23, 1901.

50. *Fáinne an Lae*, April 15, 1899.

51. *Freeman's Journal*, February 1, 1896.

52. *Freeman's Journal*, August 8, 1899.

53. *Anglo-Celt*, March 28, 1908.

54. *Anglo-Celt*, December 1, 1900.

55. *Westmeath Examiner*, March 2, 1901.

56. *Fáinne an Lae*, July 16, 1898.

57. P. Morgan, *Eighteenth Century Renaissance*.

58. John Davies, *History of Wales*, 306–8; Janet Davies, *Welsh Language*, 31–32.

59. Janet Davies, *Welsh Language*, 36–56.

60. *Nation*, October 23, 1875.

61. *Fáinne an Lae*, July 8, 1899.

62. Ryan, *Lessons*, 31.

63. *Nation*, October 4, 1844.

64. *Freeman's Journal*, March 11, 1872.

65. *Fáinne an Lae*, February 5, 1898.

66. *Freeman's Journal*, March 11, 1872.

67. *Freeman's Journal*, June 18, 1883.

68. *Freeman's Journal*, November 1, 1899.

69. *Freeman's Journal*, February 12, 1898.

70. *Fáinne an Lae*, February 18, 1899.

71. *Fáinne an Lae*, March 11, 1899.

72. *Anglo-Celt*, February 25, 1905.

73. *Connaught Telegraph*, March 11, 1905.

74. *Fáinne an Lae*, December 3, 1898.

75. *Anglo-Celt*, February 27, 1909.

76. *Nation*, August 27, 1864.

77. *Fáinne an Lae*, January 8, 1898.

78. *Fáinne an Lae*, March 12, 1898.

79. *Fáinne an Lae*, June 11, 1898.

80. *Fáinne an Lae*, April 2, 1898.

81. *Nation*, October 19, 1844.

82. SPIL, Report of the SPIL, December 29, 1876, in NLI, P 9173.

83. Ryan, *Lessons*, 31.

84. Barrett, *Proceedings of the Third Oireachtas*, 15.

85. *An Claidheamh Soluis*, October 27, 1900.

86. *Nation*, March 10, 1877.

87. Price, *Languages of Britain*, 102.

88. Philip O'Leary, *Prose Literature*, 1.

89. Ní Chonceanainn and Ó Coigligh, *Tomás Bán*, 26.

90. Min-GL, May 30, 1899, in NLI, MS 9,800.

91. Farmer to MacNeill, March 14, 1897, in McN, NLI, MS 10,881.

92. *Connaught Telegraph*, April 6, 1901.

93. John Davies, *History of Wales*, 362–63, 387.

94. Philip O'Leary, *Prose Literature*, 376–77.

95. *Nation*, September 15, 1866.

96. *Nation*, September 28, 1866.

97. *Freeman's Journal*, September 17, 1884.

98. *Nation*, September 27, 1884.

99. *Nation*, July 6, 1889.

100. *Féis Ceoil Program, 1897*, in NLI, MS 40,226.

101. Circular for Public Meeting on April 4, 1895, in NLI, MS 10,894.

102. *Féis Ceoil Program, 1897, in* NLI, MS 40,226.

103. *Freeman's Journal*, May 18, 1897.

104. *Irish Daily Independent*, June 30, 1897.

105. Undated newspaper article, in NLI, MS 34,915 (1).

106. *New Ireland Review* 8 (1898): 349.

107. Ibid., 357.

108. Ibid., 359–60.

109. Barrett et al., *Full Report*, 7.

110. *Nation*, March 20, 1897.

111. Hyde to Castletown, March 23, 1897, in Lord Castletown Papers (hereafter CAS), NLI, MS 35,306 (6).

112. *Freeman's Journal*, May 11, 1897.

113. *Nation*, May 15, 1897.

114. Barrett, *Full Report*.

115. Barrett, *Proceedings of the Third Oireachtas*.

116. *Fáinne an Lae*, June 4, 1898.

117. Barrett, *Proceedings of the Third Oireachtas*, 43–51.

118. Ibid.

119. Ibid.

120. *Fáinne an Lae*, January 7, 1899.

121. *Nation*, May 15, 1897.

122. Min-GL, January 11, 1899, in NLI, MS 9800.

123. Ibid., August 1, 1899.

124. Feiseanna Programmes, 1904–21, in Mac Coluim Papers, NLI, MS 24,401.

125. R. Jones, "Nonconformity," 251–54.

126. On this difference, see Paul O'Leary, "Accommodation and Resistance," 127.

127. Henebry to MacNeill, April 7, 1899, in McN, NLI, MS 10,881.

128. Moran, *Philosophy of Irish Ireland*.

129. *Nation*, September 15, 1866.

130. *Freeman's Journal*, May 25, 1877.

131. *Freeman's Journal*, June 18, 1883.

132. *Freeman's Journal*, August 30, 1893.

133. *Anglo-Celt*, October 26, 1907.

134. *Freeman's Journal*, December 28, 1908.

135. *Nation*, September 27, 1884.

136. *Southern Star*, March 20, 1897.

137. *Tuam Herald*, October 23, 1897.

138. *Southern Star*, January 5, 1895.

139. Ryan, *Lessons*, 31.

140. Barrett, *Proceedings of the Third Oireachtas*, 44.

141. *Fáinne an Lae*, March 26, 1898.

142. *Nation*, September 27, 1884.

143. *An Claidheamh Soluis*, June 26, 1900.

144. Henebry to MacNeill, January 22, 1898, in McN, NLI, MS 10,881.

145. *Connaught Telegraph*, July 9, 1904.

146. *Freeman's Journal*, April 4, 1896.

147. *Fáinne an Lae*, May 28, 1898.

148. *Anglo-Celt*, October 26, 1907.

149. *Anglo-Celt*, February 25, 1905.

150. *Connaught Telegraph*, April 27, 1907.

151. *Kildare Observer*, March 23, 1901.

152. *An Claidheamh Soluis*, December 30, 1899.

153. Feis Ceoil Program, 1899, in NLI, MS 40,226.

154. *New Ireland Review* 9 (March–August 1898): 43–48.

155. *Irish Independent*, August 4, 1906.

156. *An Claidheamh Soluis*, November 5, 1904.

157. John Davies, *History of Wales*, 455–56.

158. "Report of the Gaelic League for Two Years Ending September 30th, 1896," 19, in McN, NLI, MS 10,900.

159. *Freeman's Journal*, April 4, 1896.

160. Barrett, *Proceedings of the Third Oireachtas*, 50.

161. *Freeman's Journal*, April 14, 1900.

162. *Fáinne an Lae*, November 25, 1899.

163. *Fáinne an Lae*, July 14, 1900.

164. *Freeman's Journal*, January 5, 1909.

165. *Irish Independent*, May 3, 1910.

166. *Freeman's Journal*, January 14, 1909.

167. *Freeman's Journal*, January 21, 1909.

168. *Freeman's Journal*, January 22, 1909.

169. J. Ellis, "Prince and the Dragon," 272–94.

CHAPTER 3.   Celts, Catholics, Criminals

1. *North Wales Chronicle*, December 8, 1877.

2. Glazer and Moynihan, introduction to *Ethnicity, Theory and Experience*, 21.

3. Harrison, *Hubert Harrison Reader*, 137–39.

4. Hill, *Marcus Garvey*, 1:xxxii–lxxii.

5. Crosbie, *Irish Imperial Networks*, 251.

6. Howell, "Less Obtrusive and Exacting," 65.

7. Paul O'Leary, *Immigration and Integration*, 1.

8. O'Rahilly, "Antipathy of Irish and Welsh"; Paul O'Leary, *Immigration and Integration*, 17.

9. Paul O'Leary, *Immigration and Integration*, 164.

10. *Baner ac Amserau Cymru*, July 18, 1860.

11. *Y Goleuad*, September 25, 1880.

12. "WFT," *Red Dragon* 6 (1884): 248.

13. Ibid.

14. *Red Dragon* 4 (1883): 539.

15. *Cymru Fydd* 1, no. 1 (1888): 54.

16. *Baner ac Amserau Cymru*, September 23, 1882.

17. *Y Goleuad*, September 25, 1880.

18. *Western Mail*, April 26, 1893.

19. *Y Goleuad*, March 12, 1881.

20. G. Williams, *When Was Wales?*, 126.

21. *Y Goleuad*, September 25, 1880.

22. *Baner ac Amserau Cymru*, August 6, 1879.

23. *Y Goleuad*, October 2, 1875.

24. *Western Mail*, May 23, 1890.

25. K. Morgan, *Rebirth of a Nation*, 3.

26. Ibid., 40.

27. Ibid., 26.

28. Cragoe, "Conscience or Coercion?," 156.

29. K. Morgan, *Rebirth of a Nation*, 28–30.

30. *Baner ac Amserau Cymru*, January 5, 1870.

31. Bell, *Disestablishment in Ireland*, 226.

32. A. C. Humphreys-Owen in O. Morgan et al., "New Round Table," 415.

33. *Cymru Fydd* 2, no. 7 (July 1889): 380.

34. R. Morgan, *Disestablishment of the Church*, 44.

35. *Liverpool Mercury*, June 18, 1894.

36. *Cymru Fydd* 1, no. 5 (1888): 272–73.

37. John Davies, "Wales and Ireland," 8.

38. G. Williams, *When Was Wales*, 213.

39. K. Morgan, *Wales in British Politics*, 84–87.

40. John Davies, "Wales and Ireland," 7.

41. T. E. Ellis, *Speeches and Addresses*, 108.

42. "A Celt," *Cymru Fydd Gymru Rydd*, 2.

43. *Cymru Fydd* 3, no. 10 (1890): 639.

44. *Cymru Fydd* 1, no. 8 (1888): 501.

45. *Y Goleuad*, July 1, 1882.

46. *North Wales Chronicle*, February 4, 1888.

47. *Western Mail*, January 18, 1888.

48. *Western Mail*, February 18, 1888.

49. *North Wales Chronicle*, February 20, 1888.

50. *Red Dragon* 11 (1887): 224.

51. K. Morgan, *Wales in British Politics*, 70.

52. *Morning Post*, September 9, 1886.

53. *North Wales Chronicle*, February 20, 1888.

54. *Western Mail*, February 20, 1886.

55. *Baner ac Amserau Cymru*, September 29, 1875.

56. *Cymru Fydd*, 3, no. 10 (1890): 625.

57. *Western Mail*, December 23, 1890.

58. *Western Mail*, February 11, 1890.

59. *Red Dragon* 1 (1882): 454.

60. Ibid.

61. K. Morgan, *Wales in British Politics*, 74–75.

62. *Y Genedl Gymreig*, November 2, 1887.

63. *Cymru Fydd* 1, no. 1 (1888): 33.

64. *Baner ac Amserau Cymru*, November 16, 1892.

65. *Cymru Fydd* 1, no. 12 (1888): 402.

66. *Cymru Fydd* 2, no. 1 (1889): 19.

67. *Western Mail*, December 21, 1885.

68. *Western Mail*, June 18, 1886.

69. *North Wales Chronicle*, May 22, 1886.

70. K. Morgan, "Liberal Unionists in Wales," 163–71.

71. H. Evans, *Y Berw Gwyddelig*, 3.

72. Ibid.

73. Ibid., 5.

74. Ibid., 6.

75. Ibid., 43.

76. Ibid., 56.

77. N. Evans and Sullivan, "*Yn Llawn o Dân Cymreig*," 569–70.

78. *Cymru Fydd* 1, no. 1 (1888): 20.

79. Ibid., 35.

80. The contents of the *Oswestry Advertizer* article are reported in *Cambrian* 22, no. 10 (1892): 290.

81. *Cymru Fydd* 2, no. 2 (1889): 90.

82. *Y Genedl Gymreig*, January 11, 1893.

83. *Cymru Fydd* 2, no. 7 (July 1889): 381.

84. The contents of the *Oswestry Advertizer* article are reported in *Cymru Fydd* 3, no. 8 (1890): 495.

85. K. Morgan, *Rebirth of a Nation*, 32.

86. G. Williams, *When Was Wales?*, 230.

87. *Red Dragon* 3 (1883): 273.

88. *Cymru Fydd* 1, no. 5 (1888): 345.

89. *Baner ac Amserau Cymru*, July 20, 1887.

90. Ibid.

91. Ibid.

92. K. Morgan, *Wales in British Politics*, 104–6, 159–65.

93. K. Morgan, *Rebirth of a Nation*, 164.

94. *Cymru Fydd* 1, no. 10 (1888): 612.

95. *Wrexham Advertizer*, February 11, 1888.

96. *Baner ac Amserau Cymru*, August 22, 1894.

97. *Cambrian* 14, no. 11 (1894): 325.

98. T. E. Ellis, *Speeches and Addresses*, 189–92.

99. *Wrexham Advertizer*, November 16, 1888.

100. *Baner ac Amserau Cymru*, July 24, 1886.

101. *Western Mail*, November 21, 1895.

102. *Western Mail*, October 1, 1886.

103. Jones in O. Morgan et al., "New Round Table," 400–402.

104. *Y Genedl Gymreig*, February 11, 1891.

105. "A Celt," 64.

106. *Y Genedl Gymreig*, January 1, 1890.

107. *Cymru Fydd* 1, no. 5 (1888): 348.

108. *Cymru Fydd* 3, no. 8 (1890): 495.

109. The contents of the *Oswestry Advertizer* article are reported in *Cambrian* 12, no. 10 (1891): 290.

110. *Cymru Fydd* 3, no. 12 (1890): 757.

111. *North Wales Chronicle*, January 28, 1888.

112. *Western Mail*, August 19, 1886.

113. *Wrexham Advertizer*, January 14, 1888.

114. *Cambrian* 12, no. 10 (1891): 364.

115. *Western Mail*, August 15, 1894.

116. *Cymru Fydd* 3, no. 3 (1890): 177.

117. *Western Mail*, December 23, 1890.

118. *Western Mail*, August 30, 1890.

119. *North Wales Chronicle*, August 6, 1887.

120. *Baner ac Amserau Cymru*, December 22, 1886.

121. *Cymru Fydd* 1, no. 7 (1888): 392.

122. *Y Genedl Gymreig*, October 9, 1894.

123. *Cymru Fydd* 1, no. 1 (1888): 22–27.

124. John Davies, *History of Wales*, 391–92.

125. *Cornhill Magazine* 36 (1877): 663.

126. Ibid., 664–65.

127. Ibid., 666.

128. *North Wales Chronicle*, December 8, 1877.

129. *Red Dragon* 4 (1883): 347.

130. *Cymru Fydd* 3, no. 10 (1890): 625.

131. *Wrexham Advertizer*, February 18, 1888.

132. *Y Genedl Gymreig*, February 11, 1891.

133. *Baner ac Amserau Cymru*, November 6, 1895.

134. *Cymru Fydd* 1, no. 1 (1888): 19.

135. *Baner ac Amserau Cymru*, August 31, 1892.

136. *Red Dragon* 4 (1883): 348.

137. "A Celt," 2.

138. *North Wales Chronicle*, May 7, 1881.

139. Beriah Gwynfe Evans in O. Morgan et al., "New Round Table," 404–5.

140. *Cymru Fydd* 1, no. 5 (1888): 346.

141. *Western Mail*, November 16, 1880.

142. *Y Goleuad*, October 25, 1884.

143. *Cymru Fydd* 3, no. 7 (1890): 412.

144. *Red Dragon* 4 (1883): 348.

145. *Cymru Fydd* 1, no. 1 (1888): 29.

146. Jones in O. Morgan et al., "New Round Table," 403.

CHAPTER 4.   Gathering the Clans

1. Snyder, *Macro-nationalisms*, 4.

2. Ibid., 18.

3. Kohn, *Pan-Slavism*, 3–10.

4. Ibid., 33–34.

5. Chickering, *We Men*, 49.

6. Ibid., 78.

7. Jackisch, *Pan-German League*, 1–3.

8. Snyder, *Macro-nationalisms*, 95.

9. Ibid., 96–98.

10. Horsman, *Race and Manifest Destiny*.

11. P. Ellis, *Celtic Dawn*, 60–65.

12. De Gaulle, *Celts*, 54.

13. SPIL, circular, June 17, 1882, in Doneraile Papers (hereafter DON), NLI, MS 34,178 (1).

14. Ryan, *Irish Literary Society*, 39.

15. "Rules, Constitution, and Objects of the Pan-Celtic Society," March 1888, in McCall Papers (hereafter McC), in NLI, MS 13,855 (2).

16. Ibid.

17. McCarthy, *Book of Irish Ballads*, 23.

18. "Rules, Constitution, and Objects."

19. Newspaper extract, June 1888, in NLI, MS 7971.

20. "Rules, Constitution, and Objects."

21. "Biographies of the Pan-Celtic Society," in McC, NLI, MS 13,855 (2).

22. Newspaper extract, June 7, 1889, in NLI, MS 7971.

23. "Rules, Constitution and Objects."

24. Ryan, *Irish Literary Society*, 39.

25. "Biographies of the Pan-Celtic Society."

26. Newspaper extract, February 7, 1890, in NLI, MS 7971.

27. "Biographies of the Pan-Celtic Society."

28. Ryan, *Irish Literary Society*, 49.

29. *Fáinne an Lae*, June 28, 1898.

30. P. Ellis, *Celtic Dawn*, 74; McGuire and Quinn, *Dictionary of Irish Biography*, 3:1078–80.

31. Fournier to Castletown, June 16, 1900, in CAS, NLI, MS 35,305 (4).

32. Fournier to Castletown, April 16, 1908, in CAS, NLI, MS 35,307 (7); Fournier to Castletown, June 17, 1898, in CAS, NLI, MS 35,305 (1).

33. P. Ellis, *Celtic Dawn*, 73–74.

34. *Fáinne an Lae*, July 29, 1899.

35. Nagai, "'Tis Optophone Which Ontophanes," 61.

36. Fournier to Castletown, July 13, 1898, in CAS, NLI, MS 35,305 (1).

37. *Celtia* 1, no. 1 (1901): 3.

38. *Celtia* 1, no. 5 (1901): 66.

39. *Celtia* 1, no. 10 (1901): 150

40. *Celtia* 1, no. 1 (1901): 3.

41. Ibid., 2.

42. Ibid., 15.

43. Ibid., 1.

44. Ibid., 14.

45. *Scotia: The Journal of the St. Andrew Society* 1 (1907): 325–28.

46. *Celtia* 1, no. 9 (1901): 133.

47. Castletown, "The Future," n.d., in CAS, NLI, MS 13,747 (2).

48. Castletown, notes for a speech entitled "Our Celtic Inheritance," n.d., in CAS, NLI, MS 13,747 (3).

49. Ibid.

50. Castletown, "Future."

51. Castletown, "In the Air," n.d., in CAS, NLI, MS 13,747 (3).

52. Castletown, "Future."

53. Fournier to Castletown, October 19, 1900, in DON, NLI, MS 34,178 (1).

54. Fournier to Castletown, October 26, 1900, in CAS, NLI, MS 35,305 (4).

55. *Fáinne an Lae*, January 6, 1900.

56. *An Claidheamh Soluis*, May 27, 1899.

57. *Celtia* 1, no. 1 (1901): 14.

58. Fournier to Castletown, July 13, 1898, in CAS, NLI, MS 35, 305 (1).

59. *Celtia* 1, no. 1 (1901): 3.

60. Snyder, *Macro-nationalisms*, 17–34; Loffler, "Agweddau ar yr Undeb Pan-Geltiadd," 43–59.

61. Fournier to Castletown, July 13, 1898, in CAS, NLI, MS 35, 305 (1).

62. Ibid.

63. Pan-Celtic Association, circular, February 7, 1899, in CAS, NLI, MS 35,305 (3).

64. Stokes to Castletown, n.d., in CAS, NLI, MS 35, 305 (3).

CHAPTER 5.   Protestants Playing Pagans

This chapter is a revised and expanded version of my article "Protestants Playing Pagans? Irish Nationalism and the Rejection of Pan-Celticism," which appeared in *Authority and Wisdom in the New Ireland: Studies in Literature and Culture*, ed. Carmen Zamorano Llena and Billy Grey, Reimagining Ireland 73 (Bern: Peter Lang, 2016). The material that appeared in this article is reproduced with the kind permission of Peter Lang.

1. Fournier to Castletown, December 27, 1923, in CAS, NLI, MS 35,305 (6).

2. Uí Chollatáin, *An Claidheamh Soluis*, 46.

3. Min-GL, September 6, 1898, in NLI, MS 9779.

4. "Biographies of the Pan-Celtic Society," in McC, NLI, MS 13,855 (2).

5. McGuire and Quinn, *Dictionary of Irish Biography*, 1:664.

6. Min-GL, November 9, 1898, in NLI.

7. Ibid., November 16, 1898.

8. Ibid., January 18, 1899.

9. Ibid., March 21, 1899.

10. Ibid., April 18, 1899.

11. *Fáinne an Lae*, May 6, 1899.

12. *Freeman's Journal*, April 25, 1899.

13. *An Claidheamh Soluis*, May 27, 1899.

14. Min-GL, June 20, 1899, in NLI.

15. Ibid., July 11, 1899.

16. Ibid., January 16, 1900.

17. P. Ellis, *Celtic Dawn*, 76.

18. *Fáinne an Lae*, July 29, 1899.

19. Ibid.

20. *An Claidheamh Soluis*, August 12, 1899.

21. Ibid.

22. Quoted in P. Ellis, *Celtic Dawn*, 76.

23. Pearse to Fournier, August 17, 1899, in CAS, NLI, MS 35,305 (3).

24. Boyd to MacNeill, in McN, NLI, MS 10,880.

25. Min-GL, August 15, 1899, in NLI.

26. Fournier to MacNeill, August 17, 1899, in McN, NLI, MS 10,883.

27. Pearse to Fournier, August 17, 1899, in CAS, NLI, MS 35,305 (3).

28. Min-GL, August 29, 1899, in NLI.

29. Fournier to Castletown, July 13, 1898, in CAS, NLI, MS 35,305 (1).

30. *Fáinne an Lae*, September 9, 1899.

31. Ibid.

32. Min-GL, October 10, 1899, in NLI.

33. Charles MacNeill to Castletown, October 28, 1899, in CAS, NLI, MS 35,306 (6).

34. Memo of Eibheúr Tierney, September 30, 1956, in McN, NLI, MS 10,879.

35. Ibid.; O'Leary to MacNeill, October 29, 1899, in McN, NLI, MS 10,879.

36. *Fáinne an Lae*, January 27, 1900.

37. *Freeman's Journal*, January 8, 1900.

38. *Fáinne an Lae*, February 10, 1900.

39. Fournier to Castletown, December 29, 1899, in CAS, NLI, MS 35,305 (1).

40. Fournier to Castletown, July 20, 1900, in CAS, NLI, MS 35,305 (4).

41. *Freeman's Journal*, January 20, 1900.

42. *Fáinne an Lae*, January 12, 1900.

43. *Freeman's Journal*, January 15, 1900.

44. *Freeman's Journal*, January 17, 1900.

45. Ibid.

46. *Freeman's Journal*, January 19, 1900.

47. Ibid.

48. *Freeman's Journal*, January 25, 1900.

49. The contents of the *Gael* article are reported in *Fáinne an Lae*, May 19, 1900.

50. Fournier to Castletown, July 20, 1900, in CAS, NLI, MS 35,305 (4).

51. Memo on Celtic Association, n.d., in CAS, NLI, MS 35,305 (4).

52. Prospectus for *Celtia*, in CAS, NLI, MS 35,305 (4).

53. *Celtia* 1, no. 7 (1901): 98.

54. *Celtia* 1, no. 6 (1901): 81.

55. *Celtia* 1, no. 7 (1901): 97.

56. *Fáinne an Lae*, January 6, 1900.

57. *Celtia* 1, no. 9 (1901): 131.

58. Pan-Celtic Congress, *Official Programme*.

59. *Celtia* 1, no. 9 (1901): 130.

60. Ibid.

61. Ibid., 138.

62. Ibid.

63. Pan-Celtic Congress, *Official Programme*.

64. Pearse to Doyle, August 31, 1901; Pearse, *Letters*, 45–46.

65. Fournier to Castletown, October 15, 1904, in DON, NLI, MS 34,178 (1); Fournier to Castletown, October 24, 1907, in DON, NLI, MS 34,178 (6).

66. Logue to Castletown, July 25, 1901, in CAS, NLI, MS 35,305 (5).

67. *Celtia* 1, no. 8 (1901): 113.

68. Fournier to Castletown, June 3, 1901, in CAS, NLI, MS 35,305 (5).

69. Hogan to MacNeill, August 3, 1899, in McN, NLI, MS 10,881.

70. *Freeman's Journal*, April 25, 1899.

71. "Objects and Means of the Gaelic League," October 1896, in NLI, Ir 49162. Rule 8 of the Gaelic League Constitution for all branches stated, "The League shall be strictly non-political and non-sectarian."

72. Henebry to MacNeill, January 11, 1899, in McN, NLI, MS 10,881.

73. Henebry to MacNeill, February 18, 1899, in McN, NLI, MS 10,881.

74. Lloyd to MacNeill, n.d., in McN, NLI, MS 10,878 (2).

75. Rolleston to MacNeill, August 16, 1901, in McN, NLI, MS 10,883.

76. Young to Castletown, August 22, 1907, in DON, MS 34, 178 (3).

77. Rolleston to MacNeill, August 16, 1901, in McN, NLI, MS 10,883.

78. Hyde to MacNeill, n.d., ca. 1901, in McN, NLI, MS 10,874 (1).

79. Ibid.

80. McCracken, *Forgotten Protest*.

81. Anonymous letter to MacNeill, n.d., ca. 1899, in McN, NLI, MS 10,881.

82. Boyd to Castletown, July 1, 1899, in CAS, NLI, MS 35,304 (1).

83. Dennehy to Castletown, July 23, 1903, in CAS, NLI, MS 35,304 (2).

84. Fournier to Castletown, October 26, 1900, in CAS, NLI, MS 35,305 (4).

85. Fournier to Castletown, August 3, 1900, in CAS, NLI, MS 35,305 (4).

86. Ibid.

87. Notes on a speech entitled "The Celtic Awakening," n.d., in DON, NLI, MS 13,747 (3).

88. Ibid.

89. This sentiment appears in the private notes and essays in Castletown's papers. In one essay, he wrote about his ancestor Barnabie Fitzpatrick. The work was titled "A Man of His Time, A Memoir of One Barnabie Fitzpatrick, a Celt, 'They went out to battle, but they always fell.'" In CAS, NLI, MS 13,747 (3).

90. Lord Castletown, speech to the Gaelic Society of London, n.d., ca. 1897, in CAS, NLI, MS 13,747 (3).

91. *Celtia* 1, no. 2 (1901): 20.

92. Lord Castletown, notes for "Our Celtic Inheritance," in CAS, NLI, MS 35,307 (10).

93. One member of the League, W. H. Brayden, said that Castletown had been in South Africa "performing as a yeoman." *Cambrian* 21 (1901): 436–38.

94. Min-GL, December 8, 1897. The committee received a letter from Fournier "asking that the committee of the Gaelic League meet him to consider the advisability of establishing a bardic chair, or Gorsedd, for Irish music."

95. *An Claidheamh Soluis*, August 12, 1899.

96. MacNeill, memo, n.d., ca. 1898, in McN, NLI, MS 10,883.

97. Hogan to MacNeill, August 3, 1899, in McN, NLI, MS 10,881.

98. Ibid.

99. *An Claidheamh Soluis*, May 27, 1899.

100. *An Claidheamh Soluis*, August 12, 1899.

101. *An Claidheamh Soluis*, May 27, 1899.

102. The phrase inspired the name of the Sinn Féin Party, established in 1905 by Arthur Griffith.

103. Pan-Celtic congress, *Official Programme*.

104. *Celtia* 1, no. 9 (1901): 142.

105. *Celtia* 1, no. 12 (1901): 194; Pan-Celtic congress, *Official Programme*; Lord Castletown, *Ego*, 215.

106. Nagai, "'Tis Optophone Which Ontophanes," 64–71.

107. *Fáinne an Lae*, July 13, 1899.

108. *Fáinne an Lae*, January 27, 1900.

109. *Fáinne an Lae*, November 4, 1899.

110. Nagai, "'Tis Optophone Which Ontophanes," 58.

111. Loffler, "Agweddau ar yr Undeb Pan-Geltiadd," 58.

112. *Celtia* 1, no. 9 (1901): 140–42.

113. Ibid.

114. *Celtia* 1, no. 7 (1901): 109.

115. Ibid., 112.

116. Fournier to Castletown, July 1, 1899, in CAS, NLI, MS 35,305 (3).

117. *An Claidheamh Soluis*, May 27, 1899.

118. *An Claidheamh Soluis*, August 12, 1899.

119. Hogan to MacNeill, August 3, 1899, in McN, NLI, MS 10,881.

120. Fournier to Castletown, June 3, 1901, in CAS, NLI, MS 35,305 (5).

121. *Cambrian* 21 (1901): 436.

122. Ibid., 437–38.

123. Ibid.

124. Foster, *Modern Ireland*, 448.

125. Hutchinson, *Dynamics of Cultural Nationalism*, 168–80. Hutchinson points in particular to the efforts of Arthur Griffith and D. P. Moran to link the cause of developing native Irish industry to the Irish-language cause; McMahon, *Grand Opportunity*, 140–53. McMahon highlights how many rank-and-file members of the Gaelic League were dedicated to bringing economic and industrial growth to Ireland.

126. *Cambrian* 21 (1901): 436.

127. Ryan, *Lessons*, 32.

128. Young to Castletown, August 22, 1907, in DON, MS 35,178 (4); Young notes that the industrial section of the *oireachtas*, which filled two rooms, "was capital, or did good trade."

129. Program for *Féise Uibh Ráthaigh*, June 28–29, 1908, in Fionán Mac-Coluim Papers (hereafter MacC), NLI, MS 24,401.

130. Syllabus for *Feis Tuadh-Mumhan 1905*, June 30–July 2, 1905, Limerick, in MacC, NLI, MS 24,401.

131. Program for *Féise Uibh Ráthaigh*, in MacC, NLI, MS 24,401.

132. Ibid.

133. Program for *Feis Naoimh Chuilim Chille*, June 29, 1909, in MacC, NLI, MS 24,401.

134. Program for *Féis Mór Lios-Tuathail*, July 12, 1908, in MacC, NLI, MS 24,401.

135. Program for Mitchelstown *feis*, 1908, in MacC, NLI, MS 24,401.

136. Nagai has argued that Fournier, who was a scientist, "saw Celtic revivalism as a modernist project which attempted to reconcile technological and linguistic futures with the Celtic vision" ("'Tis Optophone Which Ontophanes," 59). Perhaps he did, but I have not come across any of Fournier's writings that explicitly linked Pan-Celticism with modernity. Even if Nagai is correct, many members of the Gaelic League viewed Fournier's Pan-Celticism as the antithesis of the modern Ireland they wished to forge.

137. *An Claidheamh Soluis*, May 27, 1899.

138. D. Williams, "Another Lost Cause?," 97.

CHAPTER 6.   Dancing to a Different Tune

1. Fournier to Lord Castletown, July 13, 1898, in CAS, NLI, MS 35,305 (1).

2. Betts, *A Oedd Heddwch*, 67.

3. Ibid.

4. Loffler, "Agweddau ar yr Undeb Pan-Geltiaid," 43–59; Loffler, *Book of Mad Celts*.

5. Loffler, "Agweddau ar yr Undeb Pan-Geltiaid," 56.

6. Price, "Celtic Languages," 7–8.

7. Loffler, "Agweddau ar yr Undeb Pan-Geltiaid," 45.

8. *North Wales Express*, July 28, 1899.

9. Loffler, "Agweddau ar yr Undeb Pan-Geltiaid," 45.

10. *Rhyl Journal*, September 3, 1904.

11. Fournier to Castletown, July 13, 1898, in CAS, NLI, MS 35,305 (1).

12. Pan-Celtic Association circular, February 7, 1899, in CAS, NLI, MS 35,305 (1).

13. *Weekly Mail,* February 11, 1899.

14. Fournier to Castletown, March 2, 1898, in CAS, NLI, MS 35,305 (1).

15. *Llangollen Advertizer, Denbighshire, Merionethshire, and North Wales Journal,* March 17, 1899.

16. *Western Mail,* May 19, 1899.

17. *Western Mail,* May 22, 1899.

18. *Western Mail,* June 7, 1899.

19. *Western Mail,* May 23, 1899.

20. *Western Mail,* July 17, 1899.

21. *South Wales Echo,* July 19, 1899.

22. *Cardiff Times,* July 15, 1899.

23. *Western Mail,* July 19, 1899. A binioù is a form of Breton bagpipes.

24. Whether anyone noticed that Castletown's medieval Irish sounded like Italian is unknown.

25. *Cardiff Times,* July 22, 1899

26. *Western Mail,* July 19, 1899.

27. *Cardiff Times,* July 22, 1899.

28. Ibid.; *Wrexham Advertizer and North Wales News,* July 22, 1899.

29. *Western Mail,* July 19, 1899.

30. *Cardiff Times,* July 22, 1899.

31. *Western Mail,* July 19, 1899.

32. Ibid.

33. Ibid.

34. Ibid.

35. *North Wales Chronicle,* July 22, 1899.

36. *Western Mail,* July 19, 1899.

37. *Baner ac Amserau Cymru,* July 26, 1899.

38. *Western Mail,* July 18, 1899.

39. H. Edwards, "Welsh Language," 345.

40. *Cardiff Evening Express,* July 18, 1899.

41. *Western Mail,* July 18, 1899.

42. Ibid.

43. *Cardiff Times,* July 22, 1899.

44. *Baner ac Amserau Cymru,* July 26, 1899.

45. *Y Celt,* July 22, 1899.

46. *Tarian y Gweithiwr,* July 27, 1899.

47. Fournier to Castletown, July 25, 1899, in CAS, NLI, MS 35, 305 (1).

48. *Western Mail,* July 22, 1899.

49. *Western Mail,* July 21, 1899; *Baner ac Amserau Cymru,* July 26, 1899.

50. *North Wales Observer and Express,* September 30, 1904.

51. *Y Cymro,* October 6, 1904.

52. *Liverpool Mercury,* July 21, 1899.

53. *Western Mail,* July 21, 1899.

54. *Tarian y Gweithiwr,* July 27, 1899.

55. *Baner ac Amsersau Cymru,* July 26, 1899.

56. *Sheffield Independent,* July 24, 1899.

57. *Liverpool Mercury,* July 21, 1899; *Western Mail,* July 21, 1899.

58. *Western Mail,* July 21, 1899.

59. *Tarian y Gweithiwr,* July 27, 1899.

60. *Western Mail,* July 21, 1899.

61. *Sheffield Independent,* July 24, 1899.

62. *Liverpool Mercury,* July 21, 1899.

63. *Western Mail,* July 21, 1899.

64. *Sheffield Independent,* July 24, 1899.

65. *Western Mail,* July 21, 1899.

66. Ibid.

67. Ibid.

68. Ibid.

69. *Western Mail,* July 22, 1899.

70. Ibid.

71. *Western Mail,* July 24, 1899.

72. *Baner ac Amserau Cymru,* July 26, 1899.

73. *Gwyliedydd,* July 26, 1899.

74. *Western Mail,* July 22, 1899.

75. Ibid.

76. *Baner ac Amserau Cymru,* July 26, 1899.

77. *Western Mail,* July 22, 1899.

78. *Tarian y Gweithiwr,* August 3, 1899.

79. *London Kelt,* July 29, 1899.

80. *South Wales Echo,* July 24, 1899.

81. *Fáinne an Lae,* July 29, 1899.

82. *Western Mail,* July 22, 1899.

83. *Aberdeen Journal,* July 27, 1899.

84. *Western Mail,* July 28, 1899.

85. *Cambrian* 11, no. 10 (1890): 438.

86. *Western Mail,* July 22, 1899.

87. *Western Mail,* July 24, 1899.

88. *Y Cymro,* July 27, 1899.

89. *Western Mail,* July 24, 1899.

90. *Cambrian* 11, no. 10 (1890): 436–38.

91. Content of the *United Irishman* article is reported in *Manchester Courier,* August 26, 1901.

92. *Cambrian News and Merionethshire Standard,* August 30, 1901.

93. *North Wales Express,* August 23, 1901.

94. *Weekly Mail,* August 24, 1901.

95. *Cardiff Times,* August 24, 1901.

96. *Y Celt,* August 30, 1901.

97. *Weekly Mail,* August 24, 1901.

98. *Brython Cymreig,* August 30, 1901.

99. *South Wales Echo,* August 21, 1901.

100. *South Wales Echo,* August 22, 1901.

101. *South Wales Echo,* August 26, 1901.

102. *North Wales Express,* September 6, 1901.

103. *Weekly Mail,* September 3, 1903.

104. *Celtic Review* 1, no. 2 (1904): 189.

105. *Weekly Mail,* September 3, 1903.

106. *London Kelt,* September 3, 1904.

107. *Celtic Review* 1, no. 2 (1904): 189–90.

108. *North Wales Express,* September 2, 1904.

109. *Sheffield Daily Telegraph,* August 31, 1904.

110. *North Wales Express,* September 2, 1904.

111. Ibid.

112. *Sheffield Daily Telegraph,* September 1, 1904.

113. *Y Celt,* September 9, 1904.

114. *Cardiff Times,* September 10, 1904.

115. *Celtia* 4, no. 4 (1904): 67.

116. *Western Mail,* September 5, 1904.

117. *Celtia* 4, no. 6 (1904): 108.

118. *Western Mail,* September 7, 1904.

119. *South Wales Echo,* September 5, 1904.

120. *South Wales Echo,* September 1, 1904.

121. *South Wales Echo,* August 31, 1904.

122. Ibid.

123. Ibid.

124. *North Wales Observer and Express,* September 27, 1907.

125. *North Wales Observer and Express,* September 2, 1904.

126. Loffler, *Book of Mad Celts,* 64.

127. *North Wales Observer and Express,* September 2, 1904.

128. *North Wales Observer and Express*, September 9, 1904.

129. *London Kelt*, September 10, 1904.

130. *North Wales Observer and Express*, September 9, 1904.

131. *Celtia* 4, no. 6 (1904): 92.

132. *Celtia* 4, no. 1 (January 1904): 3.

133. *Celtia* 4, no. 5 (Summer 1904): 87.

134. Jones to Castletown, October 15, 1904, in DON, MS 34,178 (1).

135. Fournier to Castletown, October 24, 1907, in DON, MS 34,178 (6).

136. *Rhyl Journal*, September 10, 1904.

137. *North Wales Observer and Express*, September 16, 1904.

138. *North Wales Express*, September 2, 1904.

139. Fournier to Castletown, October 17, 1904, in DON, MS 34,178 (1).

140. *Western Mail*, September 7, 1904.

141. *Y Celt*, September 9, 1904.

142. *North Wales Observer and Express*, September 9, 1904.

143. *Y Celt*, September 9, 1904.

144. *Celtia* 4, no. 6 (1904): 106. Fournier implied here that the protestor who was struck with the umbrella was Welsh. However, Samuel Coupe Fox, in his "Man about Town" column, said the man had been a "non-Welsh Celt." *South Wales Echo*, September 5, 1904.

145. *Aberystwyth Observer*, September 8, 1904.

146. Boyd to Castletown, in CAS, NLI, MS 35,304 (1).

147. *Rhyl Journal*, September 10, 1904.

148. *Y Celt*, September 9, 1904.

149. *Western Mail*, September 7, 1904.

150. *North Wales Observer and Express*, September 9, 1904.

151. Gibson to Castletown, October 6, 1904, in DON, NLI, MS 34,178 (1).

152. Ibid.

153. Castletown to William Gibson, n.d., in DON, NLI, MS 34.178 (1).

154. Fournier to Castletown, June 30, 1907, in DON, NLI, MS 35, 178 (4).

155. Fournier to Castletown, September 4, 1907, in DON, NLI, MS 35, 178 (6).

156. *North Wales Observer and Express*, September 27, 1904.

157. *Cardiff Times*, September 10, 1904.

158. *Weekly Mail*, September 3, 1904.

159. *Western Mail*, September 7, 1904.

160. *Western Mail*, July 19, 1899.

161. Ibid.

162. Ibid.

163. *Western Mail*, June 1, 1899.

164. *Western Mail*, July 19, 1899.

165. *Western Mail*, July 24, 1899.

166. *Western Mail*, July 20, 1899.

167. Ibid.

168. *Western Mail*, July 21, 1899.

169. *Western Mail*, July 19, 1899.

170. *Western Mail*, July 10, 1899.

171. *Western Mail*, May 20, 1899.

172. *London Kelt*, September 10, 1904.

173. *Western Mail*, July 19, 1899.

174. *North Wales Express*, July 28, 1899.

175. *Baner ac Amserau Cymru*, July 26, 1899.

176. *North Wales Express*, July 21, 1899.

CHAPTER 7.   Bringing the Moon and Mars Together

1. *Western Mail*, May 9, 1914.

2. K. Morgan, *Rebirth of a Nation*, 119.

3. John Davies, *History of Wales*, 467.

4. John, speech, April 1912, in Edward Thomas John Papers (hereafter JOH), NLW, ETJ 5272.

5. Ibid.

6. Ibid.

7. John, speech, September 16, 1913, in JOH, NLW, ETJ 5289.

8. John to Hughes, October 3ʼ 1912, in JOH, NLW, ETJ 619.

9. Arnold to John, May 1, 1914, in JOH, NLW, ETJ 1202.

10. Watkins to John, May 24, 1916, in JOH, NLW, ETJ 1599.

11. Phillips to John, July 21, 1912, in JOH, NLW, ETJ 480.

12. John to Phillips, July 25, 1912, in JOH, NLW, ETJ 489.

13. Phillips to John, July 26, 1912, in JOH, NLW, ETJ 491.

14. John, "Home Rule for Wales—Address to 'Young Wales,'" 1912, in JOH, NLW, ETJ 5377.

15. John, speech, April 4, 1911, in JOH, NLW, ETJ 5257.

16. John, speech, in JOH, NLW, ETJ 5289.

17. Pan-Celtic circular, 1917, in JOH, NLW, ETJ 5556.

18. Celtic Congress Constitution, adopted October 18, 1919, in JOH, NLW, ETJ 5558.

19. Raithde to Rhys Phillips, March 28, 1917, in JOH, NLW, ETJ 1672.

20. *Welsh Outlook* 8, no. 8 (1921): 172.

21. Cooke to John, June 12, 1920, in JOH, NLW, ETJ 2580.

22. John, speech, May 24, 1920, in JOH, NLW, ETJ 5354.

23. Ibid.

24. *Western Mail*, July 2, 1921.

25. Raithde to Rhys Phillips, March 28, 1917, in JOH, NLW, ETJ 1672.

26. Collins to John, August 26, 1918, in JOH, NLW, ETJ 1974.

27. Erskine to Jones, n.d., in TGJ, NLW, G3905.

28. John to Phillips, March 8, 1917, in JOH, NLW, ETJ 1666.

29. Liam Ó Briain to John, September 9, 1919, in JOH, NLW, ETJ 2295.

30. Bergin to John, June 19, 1919, in JOH, NLW, ETJ 2200.

31. Erskine to John, August 26, 1918, in JOH, NLW, ETJ 1975.

32. Erskine to John, September 12, 1918, in JOH, NLW, ETJ 1985.

33. Henderson to Art Ó Briain, September 11, 1919, in Art Ó Briain Papers (hereafter AOB), NLI, MS 8433/28.

34. Erskine to John, January 3, 1919, in JOH, NLW, ETJ 2060.

35. Phillips to John, September 18, 1919, in JOH, NLW, ETJ 2318.

36. John to Phillips, September 25, 1919, in JOH, NLW, ETJ 2328.

37. Celtic congress, circulating letter, 1920, in JOH, NLW, ETJ 2490.

38. John to Phillips, April 5, 1920, in JOH, NLW, ETJ 2494.

39. John to Erskine, August 29, 1919, in JOH, NLW, ETJ 2263.

40. Ibid.

41. John to Erskine, August 29, 1919, in JOH, NLW, ETJ 2264.

42. *Welsh Outlook* 7, no. 8 (August 1920): 196.

43. Ibid.

44. Erskine to John, January 3, 1919, in JOH, NLW, ETJ 2060.

45. *Welsh Outlook* 7, no. 9 (1920): 224.

46. *Welsh Outlook* 7, no. 8 (August 1920): 196.

47. John to Farrelly, June 14, 1919, in JOH, NLW, ETJ 2194.

48. John to Macbean, August 16, 1919, in JOH, NLW, ETJ 2240.

49. John to O'Farrelly, August 16, 1919, in JOH, NLW ETJ 2243.

50. O'Farrelly to John, September 3, 1919, in JOH, NLW, ETJ 2285.

51. Art Ó Briain to John, September 3, 1919, in JOH, NLW, ETJ 2284.

52. John to Art Ó Briain, September 11, 1919, in JOH, NLW, ETJ 2299.

53. Art Ó Briain to John, September 12, 1919, in JOH, NLW, ETJ 2303.

54. John to Art Ó Briain, September 22, 1919, in JOH, NLW, ETJ 2315.

55. Art Ó Briain to John, September 22, 1919, in JOH, NLW, ETJ 2322.

56. Gillies to Art Ó Briain, September 20, 1919, in AOB, NLI, MS 8433/28.

57. Letter from Henderson, forwarded to Art Ó Briain by unknown author, September 15, 1919, in AOB, NLI, MS 8433/28.

58. Erskine to Art Ó Briain, September 20, 1919, in AOB, NLI, MS 8433/28.

59. Liam Ó Briain to John, September 9, 1919, in JOH, NLW, ETJ 2295.

60. Liam Ó Briain to Art Ó Briain, September 13, 1919, in AOB, NLI, MS 8433/28.

61. Erskine to Art Ó Briain, September 20, 1919, in AOB, NLI, MS 8433/28.

62. John to O'Farrelly, December 23, 1920, in JOH, NLW, ETJ 2776.

63. John to Evans, June 12, 1920, in JOH, NLW, ETJ 2581.

64. Phillips to John, July 10, 1920, in JOH, NLW, ETJ 2616.

65. Erskine to Jones, July 25, 1920, in TGJ, NLW, G3911.

66. John to Macbean, August 18, 1920, in JOH, NLW, ETJ 2651; *Welsh Outlook* 7, no. 8 (August 1920): 196–97.

67. *Welsh Outlook* 7, no. 8 (August 1920): 196.

68. Ibid., 196–97.

69. Ibid.

70. *Welsh Outlook* 7, no. 9 (September 1920): 224.

71. Erskine to Art Ó Briain, September 20, 1919, in AOB, NLI, MS 8433/28.

72. *Welsh Outlook* 7, no. 9 (September 1920): 224.

73. Ibid., 245.

74. Ibid. In a private letter to O'Farrelly, John confirmed that he wished to see MacNeill in Edinburgh but admitted, "I was never very confident that he would be a persona grata to the Members of the Edinburgh Committee." John to O'Farrelly, August 25, 1920, in JOH, NLW, ETJ 2669.

75. Ibid.

76. *Welsh Outlook* 7, no. 11 (November 1920): 273–74.

77. Ibid.

78. Ibid.

79. Phillips to John, August 15, 1920, in JOH, NLW, ETJ 2645.

80. John to O'Farrelly, August 25, 1920, in JOH, NLW, ETJ 2669.

81. John to Macbean, August 18, 1920, in JOH, NLW, ETJ 2651.

82. John to Phillips, August 18, 1920, in JOH, NLW, ETJ 2652.

83. Macbean to John, August 19, 1920, in JOH, NLW, ETJ 2653.

84. John to Macbean, August 21, 1920, in JOH, NLW, ETJ 2658.

85. John to Erskine, July 17, 1918, in JOH, NLW, ETJ 1944.

86. Speech by John at Neath, August 2, 1918, in JOH, NLW, ETJ 5350.

87. John to Erskine, January 2, 1919, in JOH, NLW, ETJ 2056.

88. John to Howard, January 2, 1919, in JOH, NLW, ETJ 2057.

89. John to Evans, April 14, 1920, in JOH, NLW, ETJ 2510.

90. John to various Cardiff newspapers, February 12, 1919, in JOH, NLW, ETJ 2082.

91. John to Atkins, October 30, 1919, in JOH, NLW, ETJ 2387.

92. John to Price, August 17, 1919, in JOH, NLW, ETJ 2247.

93. John to Bruce, April 22, 1920, in JOH, NLW, ETJ 2517.

94. John to Hyde, June 1, 1921, in JOH, NLW, ETJ 2858.

95. Hyde to John, June 3, 1921, in JOH, NLW, ETJ 2865.

96. John to Hyde, June 4, 1921, in JOH, NLW, ETJ 2867.

97. John to Hyde, June 27, 1921, in JOH, NLW, ETJ 2900.

98. Gruffydd to John, May 25, 1921, in JOH, NLW, ETJ 2847.

99. John to Gruffydd, June 3, 1921, in JOH, NLW, ETJ 2864.

100. John, speech, July 7, 1921, in JOH, NLW, ETJ 5355.

101. Motion of Celtic Congress in Douglas, in JOH, NLW, ETJ 5560.

102. John to de Valera, December 8, 1921, in JOH, NLW, ETJ 3022.

103. John to Lloyd George, December 8, 1921, in JOH, NLW, ETJ 3023.

104. Lewis to John, March 7, 1922, in JOH, NLW, ETJ 3095.

105. Ibid.

106. Forestier-Walker to John, February 22, 1922, in JOH, NLW, ETJ 3085.

107. John to Phillips, May 22,1922, in JOH, NLW, ETJ 3299.

108. John to Evans, October 5, 1922, in JOH, NLW, ETJ 3671.

109. John to Davies, October 4, 1923, in JOH, NLW, ETJ 3996.

110. John to MacDonald, November 21, 1923, in JOH, NLW, ETJ 4044.

111. *South Wales News*, December 7, 1923.

112. Lloyd to Evans, September 22, 1924, in JOH, NLW, ETJ 4219.

113. *Welsh Outlook* 6, no. 3 (March 1919): 58.

114. John to Hyde, January 4, 1921, in JOH, NLW, ETJ 2790.

115. John to O'Farrelly, January 4, 1922, in JOH, NLW ETJ 3043.

116. John to O'Farrelly, July 30, 1923, in JOH, NLW, ETJ 3968.

117. John, speech, September 6, 1924, in JOH, NLW, ETJ 5361.

118. Jaffrennou to Phillips, April 22, 1921, in JOH, NLW, ETJ 2826.

119. Hyde to John, May 29, 1921, in JOH, NLW, ETJ 2852.

120. Phillips to John, December 7, 1921, in JOH, NLW, ETJ 3021.

121. O'Farrelly to John, January 22, 1922, in JOH NLW, ETJ 3058.

122. John to O'Farrelly, July 17, 1922, in JOH, NLW, ETJ 3449.

123. O'Farrelly to John, May 14, 1923, in JOH, NLW, ETJ 3910.

124. Phillips to John, July 16, 1923, in JOH, NLW, ETJ 3960.

125. O'Farrelly to John, n.d., in JOH, NLW, ETJ 3964.

126. John to O'Farrelly, July 30, 1923, in JOH, NLW, ETJ 3968

127. O'Farrelly to John, January 27, 1925, in JOH, NLW, ETJ 4313.

128. O'Farrelly to John, April 7, 1925, in JOH, NLW, ETJ 4358.

129. John, speech, June 30, 1925, in JOH, NLW, ETJ 4358.

130. John, speech, July 18, 1927, in JOH, NLW, ETJ 5365.

CHAPTER 8.   Celtic Heroes and Celtic Villains

1. *Cambrian News and Merionethshire Standard*, September 25, 1914.

2. Witness Statement (hereafter WS) 1753: Liam Tobin, 14, Bureau of Military History (hereafter BMH) (1913–1921) Collection at Military Archives, Dublin.

3. Parry, "Black Hand," 142.

4. Brennan-Whitmore, *With the Irish*, 25.

5. Ibid.

6. WS 1497: Joseph McCarthy, 82, BMH.

7. WS 755: Sean Prendergast, 184, BMH.

8. Ibid., 184–85.

9. Parry, "Black Hand," 140.

10. WS 755: Seamus Prendergast, 185, BMH.

11. WS 406: Frank Hardiman, 21, BMH.

12. *Irish Independent*, August 7, 1916.

13. WS 800: Michael O'Flanagan, 45, BMH.

14. Parry, "Black Hand," 148.

15. *Irish Independent*, August 7, 1916.

16. *Freeman's Journal*, December 25, 1916.

17. WS 660: Thomas Leahy, 30, BMH.

18. WS 406: Frank Hardiman, 21, BMH.

19. WS 1497: Joseph McCarthy, 82, BMH.

20. Ebenezer, *Fron-goch Camp*, 90–91.

21. O'Connor, *With Michael Collins*, 91.

22. Taylor, *Michael Collins*, 75.

23. O'Mahony, *Frongoch*, 74.

24. O'Connor, *With Michael Collins*, 91.

25. Ebenezer, *Fron-goch Camp*, 138.

26. WS 955: Patrick Mullooly, 13–14, BMH.

27. WS 600: Donnacha O hAnnagáin, 23, BMH.

28. WS 714: Thomas Hynes, 10, BMH.

29. WS 1718: Mícheál Ó Droighnáin, 3, BMH.

30. WS 1770: Kevin O'Shiel, 70, BMH.

31. Ibid., 232–34.

32. *Limerick Leader*, July 11, 1918.

33. *Irish Independent*, October 11, 1920.

34. *Irish Independent*, March 31, 1920.

35. *Irish Independent*, August 27, 1921; *Anglo-Celt*, September 3, 1921.

36. *Anglo-Celt*, September 3, 1921.

37. *Irish Independent*, January 5, 1919.

38. *Irish Independent*, September 19, 1921.

39. Ibid.

40. *Irish Independent*, July 15, 1918.

41. *Irish Independent*, May 24, 1924.

42. Ibid.

43. *Irish Independent*, March 2, 1921.

44. *Freeman's Journal*, September 3, 1920.

45. *Limerick Leader*, August 29, 1920.

46. *Irish Independent*, June 17, 1919.

47. The contents of the *Freeman's Journal* article are reported in *Meath Chronicle*, February 4, 1921.

48. *Nenagh Guardian*, January 10, 1919.

49. *Limerick Leader*, July 11, 1918.

50. *Freeman's Journal*, September 4, 1921; *Anglo-Celt*, September 10, 1921.

51. *Irish Independent*, August 24, 1922.

52. Thomas Jones, *Whitehall Diary*, 122.

53. Ibid., 89.

54. Ó Neill and Ó Fiannachta, *De Valera*, 225.

55. Ibid., 90.

56. Ibid., 95.

57. Letters of Moya Llewelyn Davies to P. S. Hegarty, in NLI, MS 41,780.

58. Ibid.

CHAPTER 9.   The Search for a Welsh Sinn Féin

1. K. Morgan, *Rebirth of a Nation*, 142–55.

2. John Davies, *History of Wales*, 527, 547.

3. K. Morgan, *Rebirth of a Nation*, 206; D. Davies, *Welsh Nationalist Party*, 21–25.

4. J. Morgan, "Forming Plaid Cymru," 183–84.

5. K. Morgan, *Rebirth of a Nation*, 132.

6. *Cymru Fydd* 3, no. 10 (1890): 625.

7. *Welsh Outlook* 3, no. 3 (1916): 89.

8. *Welsh Outlook* 3, no. 4 (1916): 111.

9. *Western Mail*, May 2, 1916.

10. *Celt and London Welshman*, May 6, 1916; Ebenezer, *Fron-goch Camp*, 35.

11. *Cambrian News and Merionethshire Standard*, May 5, 1916.

12. *Cambrian News and Merionethshire Standard*, October 27, 1916.

13. Ebenezer, *Fron-goch Camp*, 37.

14. *Llais Llafur*, April 29, 1916.

15. *Llais Llafur*, May 5, 1916.

16. Horner, *Incorrigible Rebel*, 25.

17. Ibid., 26.

18. Ibid., 9.

19. Ibid., 25–31.

20. *Llais Llafur*, May 16, 1916.

21. Quoted in Ebenezer, *Fron-goch Camp*, 45–46.

22. *Welsh Outlook*, 1, no. 5 (1916): 140.

23. Ibid.

24. *Welsh Outlook* 1, no. 10 (1916): 311.

25. Ó Donnchadha to Jones, in TGJ, NLW, G4226B.

26. Jones to O'Rahilly, November 12, 1920, in TGJ, NLW, G6692.

27. Ó Donnchadha to Jones, December 19, 1914, in TGJ, NLW, G4208.

28. Ó Donnchadha to Jones, March 28, 1912, in TGJ, NLW, G4195.

29. Jones to Lewis, May 2, 1921, in TGJ, NLW, G3648.

30. Thomas G. Jones, *Iwerddon*, 49.

31. Ibid., 31–32.

32. Ibid., 5–7.

33. Ibid., 4.

34. Ibid., 5.

35. *Welsh Outlook* 7, no. 5 (1920): 109.

36. *Y Cymro*, December 24, 1919.

37. *Welsh Outlook* 7, no. 2 (1920): 30.

38. *Welsh Outlook* 7, no. 5 (1920): 109.

39. Ibid.; *Welsh Outlook* 7, no. 10 (1920): 223; *Welsh Outlook* 8, no. 6 (1921): 125.

40. *Welsh Outlook* 6, no. 5 (1919): 118.

41. The contents of the *Y Dinesydd Cymreig* article are reported in *Western Mail*, August 3, 1920.

42. *Welsh Outlook* 7, no. 2 (February 1920): 31.

43. *Welsh Outlook* 7, no. 10 (October 1920): 233.

44. *Welsh Outlook* 9, no. 1 (January 1922): 4.

45. John Davies, "Wales, Ireland and Lloyd George."

46. *Welsh Outlook* 7, no. 2 (1920): 30.

47. Ibid.

48. Ibid.

49. *Welsh Outlook* 5, no. 9 (1918): 274.

50. The contents of the *Yr Herald Cymreig* article are reported in *Western Mail,* January 21, 1921.

51. *Welsh Outlook* 7, no. 1 (1920): 6.

52. *Welsh Outlook* 8, no. 6 (1921): 125.

53. *Welsh Outlook* 12, no. 8 (1925): 200.

54. *Welsh Outlook* 8, no. 7 (1921): 152.

55. John to O'Farrelly, December 23, in JOH, NLW, ETJ 2776.

56. The contents of the *Y Darian* article are reported in *Western Mail,* May 3, 1921.

57. *Western Mail,* October 25, 1920.

58. The contents of the *Genedl Gymreig* article are reported in *Western Mail,* November 2, 1920.

59. The contents of the *Dinesedd Cymreig* article are reported in *Western Mail,* December 14, 1920.

60. Morris to John, June 23, 1921, in JOH, NLW, ETJ 2890.

61. *Western Mail,* October 25, 1920.

62. *South Wales Daily Post,* October 2, 1920.

63. The contents of the *Y Llan and Church News* article are reported in *Western Mail,* December 7, 1920.

64. The contents of the *Herald* article are reported in *Western Mail,* December 29, 1920.

65. O'Farrelly to John, October 12, 1920, in JOH, NLW, ETJ 2711.

66. *Welsh Outlook* 11, no. 12 (1924): 319.

67. The contents of the *Y Darian* article are reported in *Western Mail,* October 19, 1920.

68. The contents of the *Genedl Gymreig* article are reported in *Western Mail,* October 26, 1920.

69. The contents of the *Y Cymro* article are reported in *Western Mail,* October 19, 1920.

70. The contents of the *Y Brython* article are reported in *Western Mail,* October 19, 1920.

71. Telegrams sent John on December 21, 1920, in JOH, NLW, ETJ 2773.

72. *Welsh Outlook* 8, no. 1 (1921): 93.

73. K. Morgan, *Rebirth of a Nation,* 189–90.

74. Lewis to Gilcriest, February 20, 1921, in Lewis, *Letters to Margaret Gilcriest,* 441.

75. *Freeman's Journal,* March 16, 1921.

76. *Irish Independent,* April 7, 1921; *Freeman's Journal,* April 6, 1921.

77. The contents of the *Y Tyst* article are reported in *Western Mail,* May 3, 1921.

78. *Welsh Outlook* 7, no. 10 (1920): 274.

79. *Welsh Outlook* 6, no. 9 (1919): 226.

80. *Welsh Outlook* 5, no. 12 (1918): 348.

81. *Welsh Outlook* 7, no. 2 (1920): 32.

82. *Welsh Outlook* 6, no. 5 (1919): 118.

83. *Welsh Outlook* 7, no. 9 (1920): 208.

84. *Western Mail,* December 9, 1921.

85. The contents of the *Baner ac Amserau Cymru* article are reported in *Western Mail,* December 13, 1921.

86. The contents of the *Herald Cymreig* article are reported in *Western Mail,* December 20, 1921.

87. *Weekly Mail,* December 10, 1921.

88. *Western Mail,* December 10, 1921.

89. *Western Mail,* July 11, 1921.

90. *Y Genedl,* December 13, 1921.

91. *Welsh Outlook* 8, no. 8 (1921): 171.

92. *Welsh Outlook* 8, no. 9 (1921): 195.

93. K. Morgan, *Rebirth of a Nation,* 190–92.

94. *Welsh Outlook* 10, no. 5 (1923): 115.

95. K. Morgan, *Rebirth of a Nation,* 190–92.

96. Leach, "Repaying a Debt," 268.

97. Ibid.

98. Balcells, "Catalanism," 87–94.

99. Ibid., 96.

100. Leach, "Repaying a Debt," 268; Leach, "*Bezen Perrot.*"

101. Leach, "*Bezen Perrot,*" 5.

102. Leach, "Repaying a Debt," 268.

103. Ibid.

104. *Welsh Outlook* 4, no. 7 (1917): 247.

105. *Welsh Outlook* 5, no. 7 (1918): 214.

106. *Welsh Outlook* 5, no. 2 (1918): 47.

107. *Welsh Outlook* 5, no. 3 (1918): 81.

108. Ibid., 87.

109. *Welsh Outlook* 5, no. 2 (1918): 55.

110. *Welsh Outlook* 9, no. 2 (1922): 31–32.

111. The contents of the *Baner ac Amersau Cymru* article are reported in *Western Mail,* August 24, 1920.

112. The contents of the *Y Darian* article are reported in *Western Mail*, August 24, 1920.

113. The contents of the *Y Herald Cymreig* article are reported in *Western Mail*, December 20, 1921.

114. *Western Mail*, December 27, 1921.

115. *Western Mail*, December 20, 1921.

116. K. Morgan, *Rebirth of a Nation*, 204; D. Davies, *Welsh Nationalist Party*, 20–22.

117. *Welsh Outlook* 5, no. 3, 1918, 77; D. Davies, *Welsh Nationalist Party*, 22.

118. *Druid*, April 1, 1922

119. *Druid*, August 15, 1922.

120. Ibid.

121. Ibid., June 15, 1923.

122. Ibid.

123. D. Davies, *Welsh Nationalist Party*, 43.

124. J. Morgan, "Forming Plaid Cymru," 184.

125. Lewis to Margaret Gilcriest, September 26, 1920, November 11, 1920, and May 7, 1921, in Lewis, *Letters to Margaret Gilcriest*, 419, 427, 451.

126. Lewis to Margaret Gilcriest, January 21, 1921, in Lewis, *Letters to Margaret Gilcriest*, 437.

127. Lewis to Margaret Gilcriest, February 14, 1921, and July 17, 1921, in Lewis, *Letters to Margaret Gilcriest*, 440 and 460.

128. Lewis to Margaret Gilcriest, October 17, 1921, October 31, 1921, May 5, 1922, and n.d., 1922, in Lewis, *Letters to Margaret Gilcriest*, 472, 474, 487, and 496.

129. Lewis to Margaret Gilcriest, July 17, 1921, in Lewis, *Letters to Margaret Gilcriest*, 460.

130. D. Davies, *Welsh Nationalist Party*, 203. Lewis was to modify his position on de Valera again once he became Irish prime minister, or taoiseach. In 1938 Lewis described de Valera as "one of the most important statesmen in Europe."

131. Ibid., 39.

132. *Druid*, December 1, 1924.

133. Ibid., 24.

134. *Welsh Outlook* 9, no. 3 (1922): 70.

135. *Welsh Outlook* 12, no. 5 (1925): 129.

136. D. Davies, *Welsh Nationalist Party*, 44.

137. *Druid*, August 15, 1925.

138. *Druid*, November 1, 1925.

139. Lewis, *Egwyddorion Cenedlaetholdeb*, 15. Lewis delivered this lecture at the Plaid Cymru Summer School in 1926.

140. Ibid., 9–15.

141. D. Davies, *Welsh Nationalist Party*, 41.

142. Ibid., 41–42.

Conclusion

1. O'Rahilly, *Ireland and Wales*, vi.

2. Ibid., 89–91.

3. Ibid., vi–vii.

4. *Irish Press*, July 10, 1934.

5. P. Ellis, *Celtic Dawn*, 88.

6. Parry, "Black Hand," 148.

7. Dan Boyle, "Speaking in Tongues," September 22, 2016, www.broad sheet.ie/2016/09/22/speaking-in-tongues/.

8. "Renua Ireland Party Manifesto: Rewarding Work, Rewarding Trust," January 4, 2016, no longer online but quoted in "The Renua Election Manifesto, Light on the Taxes, Lighter on the Irish," *An Sionnach Fionn* (blog), January 5, 2016, https://ansionnachfionn.com/2016/01/05/the-renua-election-manifesto -light-on-the-taxes-lighter-on-the-irish/.

9. *Irish Times*, July 26, 2016.

10. Pittock, *Celtic Identity*, 5.

BIBLIOGRAPHY

PRIMARY SOURCES

Bureau of Military History Collection, 1913–21

National Library of Ireland

Art Ó Briain Papers
Bibliography of Irish Philology and Manuscript Literature: Publications: 1913–
    41
Doneraile Papers
Douglas Hyde Papers
Eoin MacNeill Papers
Fionán Mac Coluim Papers
Lord Castletown Papers
Minute Books of the Council of the Society for the Preservation of the Irish
    Language
Minute Books of the Executive Council of the Gaelic League
Minute Books of the *Oireachtas*
Patrick McCall Papers
Records of the Feis Ceoil Association

National Library of Wales

Edward Thomas John Papers
Thomas Gwynn Jones Papers

Irish Newspapers and Journals

An Claidheamh Soluis
Anglo-Celt

Celtia
Connaught Telegraph
Fáinne an Lae
Freeman's Journal
Irish Daily Independent
Irish Independent
Irish Press
Kildare Observer
Limerick Leader
Meath Chronicle
Nation
Nenagh Guardian
New Ireland Review
Southern Star Tuam Herald
Westmeath Examiner

Welsh Newspapers and Journals

Aberystwyth Observer
Baner ac Amserau Cymru
Brython Cymreig
Cambrian
Cambrian News and Merionethshire Standard
Cardiff Evening Express
Cardiff Times
Celt and London Welshman
Cymru Fydd
Druid
Gwyliedydd
Liverpool Mercury
Llais Llafur
Llangollen Advertizer, Denbighshire, Merionethshire, and North Wales Journal
London Kelt
Morning Post
North Wales Chronicle
North Wales Express
Red Dragon
Rhyl Journal
South Wales Daily Post
South Wales Echo
Tarian y Gweithiwr

Weekly Mail
Welsh Outlook
Western Mail
Wrexham Advertizer
Y Celt
Y Cymro
Y Genedl Gymreig
Y Goleuad

OTHER PRINTED PRIMARY SOURCE MATERIAL

A Celt. *Cymru Fydd, Gymru Rydd, or The National Movement of Wales.* Carnarvon: Welsh National Press, 1895.

Arnold, Matthew. *Culture and Anarchy: An Essay in Political and Social Criticism.* 1869. Reprint, London: Macmillan, 1938.

Barrett, S. J., ed. *Full Report of the Proceedings of the Oireachtas, or, Irish Literary Festival, Held in the Round Room, Rotunda, Dublin, on May 17th, 1897.* Dublin: Gaelic League, 1897.

————, ed. *Proceedings of the Third Oireachtas, held in Dublin on Wednesday, 7th June, 1899.* Dublin: Gaelic League, 1899.

Brennan-Whitmore, W. J. *With the Irish in Frongoch.* Dublin: Talbot Press, 1917.

Buchanan, George. *The History of Scotland from the Earliest Period to the Present Time.* Vol. 1. Glasgow: Blackie and Son, 1749.

De Gaulle, Charles. *The Celts of the Nineteenth Century: An Appeal to the Living Representatives of the Celtic Race, Translated from the Original French with Notes by J. Davenport Mason.* London: J. Russell Smith, 1865.

Ellis, T. E. *Speeches and Addresses by the Late T. E. Ellis.* Wrexham: Hughes and Son, 1912.

Ellis, Thomas Iorwerth. *Life of Thomas Edward Ellis.* 2 vols. Liverpool: Cofiant, 1944 and 1948.

Evans, Henry Tobit. *Y berw Gwyddelig: Gipolwg ar gyflwr presenol yr Iwerddon yn nrych hanesyddiaeth, ac yn ngoleuni yr hyn welwyd ac a glywyd yn ystod ymweliad diweddar a'r wlad.* Wales: Cyhoeddedig Gan Gymdeithas Y Wasg Undebol, 1889.

Harrison, Hubert. *A Hubert Harrison Reader.* Edited by Jeffrey Perry. Middletown, CT: Wesleyan University Press, 2001.

John, Edward T., and Ruaraidh Erskine, eds. *Enter the Celt.* Perth: Milne, Tannahill and Methven, 1918.

Jones, D. Lloyd. *Gofleuni ar gyflwr yr Iwerddon.* London: Cassell, 1889.

Jones, Thomas. *Whitehall Diary*. Vol. 3. Edited by Keith Middlemas. London: Oxford University Press, 1971.

Jones, Thomas Gwynn. *Iwerddon*. Aberdar: Pugh and Rowlands, 1919.

Lewis, Saunders. *Egwyddorion Cenedlaetholdeb / Principles of Nationalism*. Translated by Bruce Griffiths. [Caerffili]: n.p., [1975].

———. *Letters to Margaret Gilcriest*. Edited by Mair Saunders-Jones, Ned Thomas, and Harri Pritchard. Cardiff: University of Wales Press, 1993.

Lhuyd, Edward. *Archaeologia Britannica: An Account of the Languages, Histories and Customs of Great Britain, from Travels through Wales, Cornwall, Bas-Bretagne, Ireland and Scotland*. Oxford: Bateman, 1707.

Lord Castletown. *Ego: Random Records of Sport, Service, and Travel in Many Lands*. London, 1923.

McCarthy, Denis Florence. *The Book of Irish Ballads*. Dublin: James Duffy, 1846.

Morgan, R. H. *Disestablishment of the Church in Wales*. Wrexham: Hughes and Son, 1888.

Nott, Josiah Clark, and George Robins Gliddon. *Types of Mankind or, Ethnological Researches, Based upon the Ancient Monuments, Paintings, Sculptures, and Crania of Races, and upon Their Natural, Geographical, Philological and Biblical History*. 2nd ed. Philadelphia: Lippincott, Grambo, 1854.

O'Connor, Batt. *With Michael Collins in the Fight for Irish Independence*. London: P. Davies, 1929.

O'Rahilly, Cecile. *Ireland and Wales: Their Historical and Literary Relations*. London: Longman, 1924.

Pan-Celtic Congress. *Official Programme of the Pan-Celtic Congress: Dublin, August 20, 21, 22 & 23, 1901*. Dublin: N.p., 1901.

Pearse, P. H. *The Letters of P. H. Pearse*. Edited by Seamus Ó Buachalla. Buckinghamshire: Colin Smythe, 1980.

Pezron, Paul-Yves. *The Antiquities of Nations; More Particularly of the Celtae or Gauls, taken to be Originally the Same People as our Ancient Britains, Containing a Great Variety of Historical, Chronological and Etymological Discoveries, Many of Them Unknown both to the Greeks or Romans. Englished by Mr. Jones*. London: R. Janeway, 1706.

Renan, Ernest. *Poetry of the Celtic Races and Other Essays by Ernest Renan*. London: W. Scott, 1896.

Rhys, John, and David Brynmor-Jones. *The Welsh People: Chapters on Their Origin, History, Laws, Language, Literature and Characteristics*. New York: Macmillan, 1900.

Ryan, William Patrick. *The Irish Literary Society: Its History, Pioneers, and Possibilities*. London: W. P. Ryan, 1894.

———. *Lessons from Modern Language Movements: What Native Speech Has Achieved for Nationality*. Dublin: Gaelic League, 1900.

Skene, William. *The Four Ancient Books of Wales*. Vol. 1. Edinburgh: Edmonston and Douglas, 1868.

SECONDARY SOURCES

Balcells, Albert. "Catalanism and National Emancipation Movements in the Rest of Europe between 1885 and 1939." *Catalan Historical Review* 6 (2013): 85–104.

Bell, P. M. H. *Disestablishment in Ireland and Wales*. London: SPCK, 1969.

Betts, Clive. *A Oedd Heddwch?* Cardiff: Gwasg ap Dafydd, 1978.

Bew, Paul. *Ideology and the Irish Question: Ulster Unionism and Irish Nationalism, 1912–1916*. Oxford: Clarendon Press; New York: Oxford University Press, 1994.

Biagini, Eugenio. *British Democracy and Irish Nationalism, 1876–1906*. Cambridge: Cambridge University Press, 2007.

Boyce, David George. *Nationalism in Ireland*. London: Routledge, 1995.

Bradshaw, Brendan. "The English Reformation and Identity Formation in Wales and Ireland." In *British Consciousness and Identity: The Making of Britain, 1533–1707*, edited by Brendan Bradshaw and Peter Roberts, 43–111. Cambridge University Press, 1998.

Burness, Catriona. *Strange Associations: The Irish Question and the Making of Scottish Unionism, 1886–1918*. East Linton: Tuckwell Press, 2003.

Cameron, E. A. "Communication or Separation? Reactions to Irish Land Agitation and Legislation in the Highlands of Scotland, c. 1870–1910." *English Historical Review* 120, no. 487 (2005): 633–66.

Chapman, Malcolm. *The Celts: The Construction of the Modern Myth*. New York: St. Martin's Press, 1992.

Chickering, Roger. *We Men Who Feel Most German: A Cultural Study of the Pan-German League, 1886–1914*. Boston: Allen and Unwin, 1984.

Connolly, Claire, and Katie Gramich. "Introduction." *Irish Studies Review* 17, no. 4 (February 2009): 1–4.

Coupland, Reginald. *Welsh and Scottish Nationalism: A Study*. London: Collins Press, 1954.

Cragoe, Matthew. "Conscience or Coercion? Clerical Influence at the General Election of 1868 in Wales." *Past and Present* 149, no. 1 (1995): 194–204.

Crosbie, Barry. *Irish Imperial Networks: Migration, Social Communication and Exchange in Nineteenth Century India*. Cambridge: Cambridge University Press, 2011.

Davies, David Hywel. *The Welsh Nationalist Party, 1925–1945: A Call to Nationhood*. Cardiff: University of Wales Press, 1983.

Davies, Janet. *The Welsh Language*. Cardiff: University of Wales Press, 1993.

Davies, John. *A History of Wales*. London: Penguin, 1993.

———. "Wales and Ireland." *Planet* 95 (October–November 1992): 7–16.

———. "Wales, Ireland and Lloyd George." *Planet* 67 (February–March 1988): 20–28.

Davis, Daniel. *The Development of Celtic Linguistics, 1850–1900*. Vol. 1. Routledge: London, 2001.

Dean, Seamus. Introduction to *Nationalism, Colonialism and Literature*, edited by Terry Eagleton, Fredric Jameson, and Edward Said. Minneapolis: University of Minnesota Press, 1990.

De Barra, Caoimhín. "A Gallant Little Tírín: The Welsh Influence on Irish Culture Nationalism." *Irish Historical Studies* 39, no. 153 (May 2014): 58–75.

———. "Protestants Playing Pagans? Irish Nationalism and the Rejection of Pan-Celticism." In *Authority and Wisdom in the New Ireland: Studies in Literature and Culture*, edited by Carmen Zamorano Llena and Billy Grey, Reimagining Ireland 73, 203–22. Bern: Peter Lang, 2016.

Duffy, Seán. "The 1169 Invasion as a Turning Point in Irish-Welsh Relations." In *Britain and Ireland, 900–1300: Insular Responses to Medieval European Change*, edited by Brendan Smith, 98–113. Cambridge: Cambridge University Press, 2006

Dunleavy, Janet, and Gareth Dunleavy. *Douglas Hyde: A Maker of Modern Ireland*. Berkeley: University of California Press, 1991.

Durkacz, Victor E. *The Decline of the Celtic Languages*. Edinburgh: John MacDonald, 1983.

Ebenezer, Lyn. *Fron-goch and the Birth of the IRA*. Llanrwst, Wales: Gwasg Carreg Gwalch, 2012.

Edwards, Hwyel Teifi. "The Welsh Language in the Eisteddfod." In *The Welsh Language and its Social Domains, 1801–1911*, edited by Geraint H. Jenkins, 293–316. Cardiff: University of Wales Press, 2000.

Edwards, Owen Dudley. "Ireland and Nationalism in Scotland and Wales." In *The Celtic Consciousness*, edited by Robert O'Driscoll, 445–58. New York: George Braziller, 1981.

Edwards, Owen Dudley, Gwynfor Evans, Ioan Rhys, and Hugh MacDiarmid. *Celtic Nationalism*. London: Routledge and Kegan Paul, 1968.

Edwards, Ruth Dudley. *Patrick Pearse: The Triumph of Failure*. Dublin: Irish Academic Press, 2006.

Ellis, John S. *Investiture: Royal Ceremony and National Identity in Wales, 1911–1969*. Chicago: University of Chicago Press, 2008.

———. "The Prince and the Dragon: Welsh National Identity and the 1911 Investiture of the Prince of Wales." *Welsh History Review / Cylchgrawn Hanes Cymru* 18 (1996): 272–94.

———. "Reconciling the Celt: British National Identity, Empire and the 1911 Investiture of the Prince of Wales." *Journal of British Studies* 37, no. 4 (1998): 391–418.

Ellis, Peter Berresford. *The Celtic Dawn: A History of Pan Celticism*. London: Constable, 1993.

Etchingham, Colmán. "Viking Age Gwynedd and Ireland: Political Relations." In *Ireland and Wales in the Middle Ages*, edited by Karen Jankulak and Jonathan M. Wooding, 149–67. Dublin: Four Courts Press, 2007.

Evans, Neil, and Kate Sullivan. "'*Yn Llawn o* Dân *Cymreig*' (Full of Welsh Fire): The Language of Politics in Wales, 1880–1914." In *The Welsh Language and Its Social Domains, 1801–1911*, edited by Geraint H. Jenkins, 561–85. Cardiff: University of Wales Press, 2000.

Ford, Alan. "James Usher and the Creation of an Irish Protestant Identity." In *British Consciousness and Identity: The Making of Britain, 1533–1707*, edited by Brendan Bradshaw and Peter Roberts, 185–212. Cambridge: Cambridge University Press, 1998.

Foster, R. F. *The Irish Story: Telling Tales and Making It Up in Ireland*. London: Allen Lane, 2001.

———. *Modern Ireland, 1600–1972*. London: Allen Lane; New York: Viking/ Penguin, 1988.

Garvin, Tom. "Priests and Patriots: Irish Separatism and Fear of the Modern, 1890–1914." *Irish Historical Studies* 25, no. 97 (1986): 67–81.

Glazer, Nathan, and Daniel Moynihan. Introduction to *Ethnicity, Theory and Experience*, edited by Nathan Glazer and Daniel P. Moynihan, 1–26. Cambridge, MA: Harvard University Press, 1975.

Greenberg, William. *The Flags of the Forgotten: Nationalism on the Celtic Fringe*. Brighton: Clifton Books, 1969.

Greene, David. "The Founding of the Gaelic League." In *The Gaelic League Idea*, edited by Séan Ó Tuama, 9–19. Dublin: Mercier, 1992.

Grote, Georg. *Torn between Politics and Culture: The Gaelic League, 1893–1993*. New York: Waxmann, 1994.

Hechter, Michael. *Internal Colonialism: The Celtic Fringe in British National Development, 1536–1966*. Berkeley: University of California Press, 1975.

Hill, Robert A., ed. *The Marcus Garvey and Universal Negro Improvement Association Papers*. Berkeley: University of California Press, 1983.

Horner, Arthur. *Incorrigible Rebel*. London: MacGibbon and Gee, 1960.

Horsman, Reginald. *Race and Manifest Destiny: The Origins of American Racial Anglo-Saxonism*. 1981. Reprint, Cambridge, MA: Harvard University Press, 2006.

Howell, David. "A 'Less Obtrusive and Exacting Nationality': Welsh Ethnic Mobilisation in Rural Communities, 1850–1920." In *Roots of Rural Ethnic Mobilisation: Comparative Studies on Governments and Non-dominant Ethnic*

Groups in Europe, 1850–1940, edited by David Howell, 51–98. Aldershot: Dartmouth, 1993.

Hutchinson, John. *The Dynamics of Cultural Nationalism: The Gaelic Revival and the Creation of the Irish Nation State*. London: Allen and Unwin, 1987.

Jackisch, Barry A. *The Pan-German League and Radical Nationalist Politics in Interwar Germany, 1918–39*. Burlington, VT: Ashgate, 2012.

Jackson, Alvin. *The Two Unions: Ireland, Scotland and the Survival of the United Kingdom, 1707–2007*. Oxford: Oxford University Press, 2011.

James, Simon. *Atlantic Celts: Ancient People or Modern Invention*. Madison: University of Wisconsin Press, 1999.

Jenkins, Geraint H. *The Welsh Language and Its Social Domains: A Social History of the Welsh Language*. Cardiff: University of Wales Press, 2000.

Jenkins, Geraint H., and J. B. Smith, eds. *Politics and Society in Wales, 1840–1922*. Cardiff: University of Wales Press, 1988.

Jenkins, Philip. *A History of Modern Wales, 1536–1990*. London: Longman, 1992.

Jones, Aled, and Bill Jones. "The Welsh World and the British Empire, c. 1851–1939." *Journal of Imperial and Commonwealth History* 2, no. 31 (May 2003): 57–81.

Jones, J. Graham. "Michael Davitt, David Lloyd George and T. E. Ellis: The Welsh Experience, 1886." *Welsh History Review* 18 (1996–97): 450–82.

Jones, Robert Tudur. "Nonconformity and the Welsh Language in the Nineteenth Century." In *The Welsh Language and Its Social Domains, 1801–1911*, edited by Geraint H. Jenkins, 239–63. Cardiff: University of Wales Press, 2000.

Kenny, Kevin, ed. *Ireland and the British Empire*. The Oxford History of the British Empire Companion Series. Oxford: Oxford University Press, 2004.

Kiberd, Declan. *Inventing Ireland*. London: Jonathan Cape, 1995.

Koch, John T., ed. *Celtic Culture: A Historical Encylopedia*. Vol. 4. Santa Barbara, CA: ABC-CLIO, 2005.

Kohn, Hans. *Pan-Slavism: Its History and Ideology*. 2nd ed. New York: Vintage Books, 1960.

Leach, Daniel. "*Bezen Perrot:* The Breton Nationalist Unit of the SS, 1943–1945." *e-Keltoi* 4 (May 2012): 1–38.

———. "Repaying a Debt of Gratitude: Foreign Minority Nationalists and the Fiftieth Anniversary of the Easter Rising in 1966." *Eire-Ireland* 43, nos. 3–4 (Fall–Winter 2008): 267–89.

Leslie, Stephen, et al. "The Fine-Scale Genetic Structure of the British Population." *Nature* 519 (March 19, 2015): 309–314.

Loffler, Marion. "Agweddau ar yr Undeb Pan-Geltiadd, 1898–1914" [Aspects of the Pan-Celtic Union, 1898–1914]. *Y Traethodydd* 155 (2000).

————. *A Book of Mad Celts: John Wickens and the Celtic Congress of Caernarfon 1904*. Llandysul: Gomer Press, 2000.

MacAonghusa, Prionsias. *Ar son na Gaeilge: Conradh na Gaeilge, 1893–1993*. Dublin: Conradh na Gaeilge, 1993.

————. *Ros Muc agus Cogadh na Saoirse*. Dublin: Conradh na Gaeilge, 1992.

Mac Cana, Prionsias. "Ireland and Wales in the Middle Ages: An Overview." In *Ireland and Wales in the Middle Ages*, edited by Karen Jankulak and Jonathan M. Wooding, 17–45. Dublin: Four Courts Press, 2007.

Masterman, Neville. *The Forerunner: The Dilemmas of Tom Ellis, 1859–1899*. Llandybie: C. Davies, 1972.

Mathews, P. J. *Revival: The Abbey Theatre, Sinn Féin, the Gaelic League and the Co-operative Movement*. Cork: Cork University Press, 2003.

McCracken, Donal. *Forgotten Protest: Ireland and the Anglo-Boer War*. Belfast: Ulster Historical Foundation, 2003.

McGuire, James, and James Quinn, eds. *Dictionary of Irish Biography under the Auspices of the Royal Irish Academy*. Vols. 1–3. Cambridge: Cambridge University Press, 2009.

McMahon, Timothy. *Grand Opportunity: The Gaelic Revival and Irish Society, 1893–1910*. Syracuse, NY: Syracuse University Press, 2008.

Moran, D. P. *The Philosophy of Irish Ireland: D. P. Moran*. Edited by Patrick Maume. Dublin: University College Dublin Press, 2006.

Morgan, J. Graham. "Forming Plaid Cymru: Searching for a Policy, 1926 to 1930." *National Library of Wales Journal* 23, no. 2 (Winter 1983): 427–61.

Morgan, Kenneth O. "The Liberal Unionists in Wales." *National Library of Wales Journal* 16, no. 2 (Winter 1969): 163–71.

————. *Rebirth of a Nation: Wales, 1880–1980*. New York: Oxford University Press, 1981.

————. *Wales in British Politics, 1868–1922*. Cardiff: University of Wales Press, 1980.

Morgan, Osborne, et al. "New Round Table: Home Rule for Wales." *Westminster Review* 133 (1890): 394–416.

Morgan, Prys. "The Abbe Pezron and the Celts." *Transactions of the Honourable Society of Cymmrodorion* 1965 (1965): 286–95.

————. *The Eighteenth Century Renaissance*. Swansea: Christopher Davies, 1981.

————. "From a Death to a View: The Hunt for the Welsh Past in the Romantic Period." In *The Invention of Tradition*, edited by Eric Hobsbawm and Terence Ranger, 43–100. Cambridge: Cambridge University Press, 1983.

Nagai, Kaori. "'Tis Optophone Which Ontophanes: Race, the Modern, and Irish Revivalism." In *Modernism and Race*, edited by Len Platt, 58–76. Cambridge: Cambridge University Press, 2011.

Nelson, Bruce. *Irish Nationalists and the Making of the Irish Race*. Princeton, NJ: Princeton University Press, 2012.

Newby, Andrew. *Ireland, Radicalism, and the Scottish Highlands, 1870–1912*. Scottish Historical Review Monograph 15. Edinburgh: Edinburgh University Press, 2007.

———. "Michael Davitt, Celtic Nationalism and Land in the British Isles, 1879–1890," *SFKS-Tiedote: Suomen Keltogisen Seuran Jäsentiedote* 5 (2000): 8–14.

Nic Congáil, Riona. *Úna Ní Fhaircheallaigh agus an Fhís Útóipeach Ghaelach*. Dublin: Arlen House, 2010.

Nice, Jason. *Sacred History and National Identity: Comparisons between Early Modern Wales and Brittany*. London: Routledge, 2016.

Ní Chonceanainn, Finnín, and Ciarán Ó Cóigligh. *Tomás Bán*. Galway: Clódóirí Lurgan Teo, 1996.

Ní Mhuiríosa, Mairín. *Reamhchonraitheoiri: Notai ar chuid de na daoine a bhi gniomhach i ngluaiseacht na Gaeilge idir 1876 agus 1893*. Dublin: Clodhanna, 1978.

O'Brien, Maria. "Thomas William Rolleston: The Forgotten Man." In *The Irish Revival Reappraised*, edited by Betsey Taylor FitzSimon and James H. Murphy, 154–66. Dublin: Four Courts Press, 2004.

Ó Catháin, Máirtín Séan. *Irish Republicanism in Scotland, 1858–1916: Fenians in Exile*. Dublin: Irish Academic Press, 2007.

Ó Duibhín, Ciarán. "Aoidhmín Mac Gréagóir: A Little Known Gaelic Scholar." *Scottish Language*, nos. 14–15 (1995–96): 31–41.

Ó Fearaíl, Padraig. *The Story of Conradh Na Gaeilge: A History of the Gaelic League*. Dublin: Clódhanna Teo, 1975.

Ó Glaisne, Risteard. *Gaeilge i gColáiste na Tríonóide, 1592–1992*. Dublin: Trinity College University Press, 1992.

O'Leary, Paul. "Accommodation and Resistance: A Comparison of Cultural Identities in Ireland and Wales, c.1880–1914." In *Kingdoms United? Great Britain and Ireland since 1500: Integration and Diversity*, edited by S. J. Connolly, 123–34. Dublin: Four Courts Press, 1999.

———. *Immigration and Integration: The Irish in Wales, 1798–1922*. Cardiff: University of Wales Press, 2000.

———, ed. *Irish Migrants in Modern Wales*. Liverpool: Liverpool University Press, 2003.

———. "Public Intellectuals, Language Revival, and Cultural Nationalism in Ireland and Wales: A Comparison of Douglas Hyde and Saunders Lewis." *Irish Studies Review* 17, no. 1 (February 2009): 5–18.

———. "Religion, Nationality and Politics: Disestablishment in Wales and Ireland." In *Contrasts and Comparisons: Studies in Irish and Welsh Church History*, edited by John R. Guy and W. D. Neely, 89–112. Llandysul: Gomer Press, 1999.

O'Leary, Phillip. "'Children of the Same Mother': Gaelic Relations with the Other Celtic Revival Movements, 1882–1916." *Proceedings of the Harvard Celtic Colloquium* 6 (1986): 101–30.

———. *The Prose Literature of the Gaelic Revival, 1881–1921: Ideology and Innovation*. University Park: Pennsylvania State University Press, 1994.

O'Mahony, Sean. *Frongoch: University of Revolution*. Dublin: FDR Teoranta, 1987.

Ó Neill, Tomás, and Pádraig Ó Fiannachta. *De Valera*. Dublin: Cló Morainn, 1968.

Ó Tuama, Seán, ed. *The Gaelic League Idea*. Dublin: Mercier Press, 1993.

Parry, Jon. "'The Black Hand': 1916 and Irish Republican Prisoners in North Wales." In *Irish Migrants in North Wales*, edited by Paul O'Leary, 139–55. Liverpool: Liverpool University Press, 2004.

Paseta, Senia. *Before the Revolution: Nationalism, Social Change and Ireland's Catholic Elite, 1879–1922*. Cork: Cork University Press, 1999.

Piggott, Stuart. *Celts, Saxons and the Early Antiquaries*. Edinburgh: Edinburgh University Press, 1967.

Pittock, Murray. *Celtic Identity and the British Image*. Manchester: Manchester University Press, 1999.

Pocock, J. G. A. "British History: A Plea for a New Subject." *Journal of Modern History* 27, no. 4 (December 1975): 601–21.

Price, Glanville. "The Celtic Languages." In *The Celtic Connection*, edited by Glanville Price, 1–9. Gerrards Cross: Colin Smythe, 1992.

———. *The Languages of Britain*. London: Edward Arnold, 1984.

Robbins, Keith. *Nineteenth Century Britain: Integration and Diversity*. Oxford: Clarendon Press, 1988.

Sahlins, Peter. *Boundaries: The Making of France and Spain in the Pyrenees*. Berkeley: University of California Press, 1989.

Sheehy, Jeanne. *The Rediscovery of Ireland's Past: The Celtic Revival, 1830–1930*. London: Thames and Hudson, c1980.

Sims-Williams, Patrick. "Celtomania and Celtoscepticism." *Cambrian Medieval Celtic Studies* 36 (1998): 1–35.

———. *Irish Influence on Welsh Medieval Literature*. Oxford: Oxford University Press, 2010.

Snyder, Louis. *Macro-nationalisms: A History of the Pan-movements*. Westport, CT: Greenwood Press, 1984.

Taylor, Rex. *Michael Collins*. Ireland: Hutchinson, 1958.

Uí Chollatáin, Regina. *An Claidheamh Soluis agus Fáinne an Lae, 1899–1932: Anailís ar phríomhnuachtán Gaeilge ré na hAthbheochana*. Dublin: Cois Life Teoranta, 2004.

Williams, Daniel. "Another Lost Cause? Pan-Celticism, Race and Language." *Irish Studies Review* 17, no. 1 (February 2009): 89–101.

Williams, Gwyn A. "When Was Wales?" In *Nationalism in Europe: From 1815–Present*, edited by Stuart Woolf, 192–204. London: Routledge, 1996.

———. *When Was Wales? A History of the Welsh*. London: Penguin Books, 1991.

Williams, J. Gwynn. *The University of Wales, 1893–1939*. Cardiff: University of Wales Press, 1997.

Williams, Meirion Llewelyn. *At Anchor in Dublin*. Dublin: Genealogical Society of Ireland, 2012.

Wmffre, Iwan. "Post-Roman Irish Settlement in Wales: New Insights from a Recent Study of Cardiganshire Place-Names." In *Ireland and Wales in the Middle Ages*, edited by Karen Jankulak and Jonathan M. Wooding, 46–61. Dublin: Four Courts Press, 2007.

INDEX

Caoimhín De Barra is assistant professor of Irish studies at Drew University.